The Postmodern Saints of France

The Postmodern Saints of France

Refiguring 'the holy' in contemporary French philosophy

Edited by
Colby Dickinson

t & t clark

Bloomsbury T&T Clark

An imprint of Bloomsbury Publishing Plc

50 Bedford Square	175 Fifth Avenue
London	New York
WC1B 3DP	NY 10010
UK	USA

www.bloomsbury.com

First published 2013

British Library Cataloguing-in-Publication Data
A catalogue record for this book is available from the British Library.

ISBN: HB: 978-0-567-29653-5
PB: 978-0-567-17058-3
ePDF: 978-0-567-48334-8
epub: 978-0-567-43248-3

Library of Congress Cataloging-in-Publication Data
Dickinson, Colby
The Postmodern Saints of France/Colby Dickinson p.cm
Includes bibliographic references and index.
ISBN 978-0-567-29653-5 (hardcover) – ISBN 978-0-567-17058-3 (pbk.)
2012045678

Typeset by Newgen Imaging Systems Pvt Ltd, Chennai, India
Printed and bound in Great Britain

CONTENTS

NOTES ON CONTRIBUTORS

Elisabeth Bayley is a doctoral student at the Katholieke Universiteit Leuven in Leuven, Belgium. Her doctoral work focuses on the writings of Willa Cather and how they intersect with concepts of lying. She has published essays on John Steinbeck and Willa Cather.

Charlie Blake has taught Philosophy, Literature and Film at the Universities of Oxford, Cambridge, Oxford Brookes, Hertfordshire, Manchester Metropolitan, Northampton and Liverpool Hope University, where he was Principal Lecturer in Critical and Cultural Theory and Chair of the Department of Media, Film and Communications. He is an executive editor of *Angelaki: Journal of the Theoretical Humanities* and, among other publications, has recently co-edited and written for the collections: *Shadows of Cruelty: Sadism, Masochism and the Philosophical Muse* (two volumes) and *Beyond Human: From Animality to Transhumanism*. He is currently working on the spiritual aspects of pornotheology, on immanence and extinction, on spectralism and electronic music, and is co-editing a collection with Nadine Boljkovac on *Deleuze and Affect*.

Ward Blanton is Reader in Biblical Cultures and European Thought at the University of Kent. He is the author of *Displacing Christian Origins: Philosophy, Secularity, and the New Testament* (University of Chicago Press, 2007), *A Materialism for the Masses: Paul the Apostle and Other Partisans of Undying Life* (Columbia University Press, 2013), and editor with Hent de Vries of *Paul and the Philosophers* (Fordham University Press, 2013).

Clayton Crockett is Associate Professor and Director of Religious Studies at the University of Central Arkansas. He is the author of five books, most recently *Deleuze Beyond Badiou: Ontology, Multiplicity and Event* (Columbia University Press, 2013). He is a co-editor, along with Slavoj Žižek, Creston Davis and Jeffrey W. Robbins, of the book series 'Insurrections: Critical Studies in Religion, Politics, and Culture' for Columbia University Press.

Phillip E. Davis is a doctoral student at the Catholic University of Leuven in Belgium. His dissertation is entitled *Towards a Christian Open Narrative of Love: An Exploration of the Theological Implications of its Openness*.

Colby Dickinson is Assistant Professor of Theology at Loyola University, Chicago. He is the author of *Agamben and Theology* (London: T&T Clark, 2011), *Between the Canon and the Messiah: The Structure of Faith in Contemporary Continental Thought* (London: Continuum, 2013), as well as a number of articles on the intersection of theology and contemporary continental theory.

W. Chris Hackett is Research Fellow/Lecturer in Philosophy, and member of the Centre for Philosophy and Phenomenology of Religion, Faculty of Theology and Philosophy, Australian Catholic University (Melbourne). He is the translator of Emmanuel Falque's *God, the Flesh and the Other: From Irenaeus to Duns Scotus* (Northwestern, forthcoming).

Kevin Hart teaches at the University of Virginia and at the Australian Catholic University. He is the author of, among others, *The Trespass of the Sign: Deconstruction, Theology and Philosophy* (1990) and *The Dark Gaze: Maurice Blanchot and the Sacred* (2004).

Meghan Helsel is a graduate student in the Department of Political Science at Johns Hopkins University. She is currently a visiting student at the University of Mannheim, Germany, and spent two years as a Pensionnaire Etrangère at the Ecole Normale Supérieure, Rue d'Ulm, in Paris, France.

Robyn Horner is Associate Professor and Associate Dean (Learning and Teaching) in the Faculty of Theology and Philosophy at Australian Catholic University. Her publications include *Rethinking God as Gift: Marion, Derrida, and the Limits of Phenomenology* (Fordham University Press, 2001) and *Jean-Luc Marion: A Theo-logical Introduction* (Ashgate, 2005), as well as numerous book chapters and journal articles engaging the thought of Jean-Luc Marion, Emmanuel Lévinas and Jacques Derrida.

Phyllis H. Kaminski is Professor in the Department of Religious Studies at Saint Mary's College, Notre Dame, Indiana. She has been studying Irigaray's texts for the past two decades. Among her prior publications are 'What the Daughter Knows: Re-thinking Women's Religious Experience with and against Luce Irigaray' in *Encountering Transcendence*, Lieven Boeve, Hans Geybels and Stijn Van de Bossche, eds (Leuven, Belgium: Peeters Press, 2005), and 'Seeking Transcendence in the Modern World' in *Catholicism Contending with Modernity*, Darrell Jodock, ed. (Cambridge: Cambridge University Press, 2000).

Grant Kaplan is Associate Professor in the Department of Theological Studies at Saint Louis University. His primary interest is in fundamental theology, in particular the doctrine of revelation. He is currently working on a monograph, tentatively titled, *René Girard and Fundamental Theology* (est. 2014).

Todd S. Mei is Lecturer in Philosophy at the University of Dundee. His main area of research is hermeneutics and political economy. He is author of *Heidegger, Work, and Being* (Continuum, 2009) and co-editor of *From Ricoeur to Action* (Continuum, 2012).

Michael Purcell is Senior Lecturer in Systematic Theology in the University of Edinburgh, Scotland. Having been educated in Leuven (Belgium) and Edinburgh (Scotland), he pursues interests in the crossroad between phenomenology and theology, both in a French theological vein.

Joseph Rivera is a PhD candidate in philosophical theology at the University of Edinburgh Divinity School. He is the translator of Didier Franck's *Flesh and Body: On the Phenomenology of Husserl* (Continuum, 2013). He has published articles on Husserl, Henry, Marion and St Augustine.

Anthony Paul Smith is Assistant Professor in the Religion Department, La Salle University (Philadelphia, USA) and Fellow at the Institute of Nature and Culture, DePaul University (Chicago, USA). He is the co-editor with Daniel Whistler of *After the Postsecular and the Postmodern: New Essays in Continental Philosophy of Religion* (Cambridge Scholars Publishing, 2010) and with John Mullarkey of *Laruelle and Non-Philosophy* (Edinburgh University Press, 2012). He is the translator of François Laruelle's *Future Christ: A Lesson in Heresy* (Continuum, 2010), co-translator with Drew S. Burk of Laruelle's *Struggle and Utopia at the End Times of Philosophy* (Univocal Publishing, 2012), and co-translator with Nicola Rubzcak of Laruelle's *Principles of Non-Philosophy* (Continuum, forthcoming, 2013). He has published numerous articles on the philosophy of religion, environmental theory and the non-philosophy of François Laruelle.

Beth Sutherland studies medieval hagiography as a doctoral student in the University of Virginia's English Department. Her work explores the 'criminal ethic' of sainthood, focusing on the essentially transgressive nature of *imitatio Christi* and its implications for a more liberating soteriology. Other interests include cultic devotion in the contemporary South and the relationship of narrative to moral philosophy.

Petra Elaine Turner is a doctoral student studying Philosophical Theology at the University of Virginia. She specializes in both phenomenology and systematic theology, and is particularly interested in the ways in which God's revelation is received and the manner in which human beings respond to it. She is presently working on her dissertation, which examines the theological epistemologies of Augustine and Karl Barth in light of a phenomenological methodology drawn from Jean-Luc Marion's work.

ACKNOWLEDGMENTS

This volume was first conceived as a panel for the Catholic Theological Society of America's annual conference in San Jose, California in June of 2011. My sincerest thanks go out to those who helped that panel become a reality, including Phyllis Kaminski and Petra Elaine Turner, who presented their work alongside my own paper, but also John Thiel, Christopher Ruddy, Grant Kaplan, Vincent Pizzuto, James Nickoloff, Lieven Boeve and Anthony Godzieba, who eagerly embraced the subject and welcomed it at the conference that year.

At the time, there were enough people interested in being a part of the panel, I felt, to merit an entire volume of essays. I am very grateful to those who were willing to take part in the project, as well as those who offered guidance and advice throughout the process, including Ken Surin, Kevin Hart, Tom Beaudoin, Kari-Shane Davis, William Hackett, John Caputo, Philip Goodchild, Nick Mansfield, Ellen Armour, Jeff Bloechl, Steven Shakespeare, Neal DeRoo and Joshua Delpech-Ramey. Special thanks are due especially to Charlie Blake and Robyn Horner for their enthusiasm for the project and willingness to contribute to it when two earlier essayists were forced by circumstance to withdraw.

I would also like to thank the K.U. Leuven Research Fund – and, I must add, the fantastic Belgian higher educational system in general – for its financial support when this project was conceived. Accordingly, there were many colleagues and friends who took part in support of this research, either directly or indirectly, and whom I wish to thank explicitly, including Lieven Boeve, Frederiek Depoortere, Joeri Schrijvers, Phil Davis, Kristien Justaert, Tom Jacobs, Joke Lambelin, Anneleen Decoene, Pieter De Witte, John Friday and *all* the wonderful members of the research group 'Theology in a Postmodern Context' within the Faculty of Theology and Religious Studies at the Katholieke Universiteit Leuven in Belgium. I am truly grateful to have shared in so many heartening and thoughtful conversations during my time there.

Thanks are explicitly singled out for Thomas Kraft for first embracing the vision of this project as an edited volume, and seeing that it initially came to be as a book. I hope your career change suits you well these days! Many thanks as well to Anna Turton, also at T&T Clark/Bloomsbury, for following through on its vision and for answering a host of inquiries.

An early and somewhat surprising inquiry on the content of the essays collected here, as well as a sustained enthusiasm for the project, on the part of Beth Sutherland led to late entry into the project as well as her writing the introduction to it – a fact I am very pleased (and grateful!) to note. As the completion of this volume caught me in the middle of a move overseas, I was incredibly heartened to read such fitting introductory words to a volume that has come to occupy many of my thoughts over the past couple of years, and I eagerly adopted it in lieu of my own thoughts on the topic. Thanks, Beth, for being able to step back, see the larger picture and provide such a wonderful take on the subject at hand.

Finally, I wish to thank Elisabeth and Rowan, again and again, for their support in getting all of my thoughts and feelings together for this, no matter on what part of the globe or at what time such activity takes place. Especially at this time in our lives.

I wish also to gratefully acknowledge that Kevin Hart's essay contains an excerpt from T. S. Eliot's *Four Quartets* © Estate of T. S. Eliot and reprinted by permission of Faber and Faber Ltd. (UK); Copyright 1936 by Houghton Mifflin Harcourt Publishing Company (US); Copyright © renewed 1964 by T. S. Eliot. Copyright 1940, 1941, 1942 by T. S. Eliot; Copyright © renewed 1968, 1969, 1970 by Esme Valerie Eliot. Reprinted by permission of Houghton Mifflin Harcourt Publishing Company. All rights reserved.

Introduction

Beth Sutherland

You also hurt me very much one day by using the word false when you meant nonorthodox.

SIMONE WEIL, *In a Letter to her Father*[1]

In 1942, Simone Weil wrote a letter to a priest. The epistle catalogues the scruples keeping her from full communion with the Catholic Church. Her objections cut through the Church's history, infrastructure and literature like a scalpel. Yet this eloquent articulation of doubt – this shout of protest – reveals a deep, underlying faith. A faith constitutive of the doubt. It takes intimate knowledge of a thing to worry it in just the right way. She claimed the Church had failed to realize its heavenly mission, becoming a mere shade of Christ's body. This zeal prompted Weil to voice criticisms similar to those traditionally heard from atheists. Like them, she adopted a counter-institutional idiom, positioning herself outside the Church. At the letter's start, she says,

> [. . .] the bonds which attach me to the Catholic faith become ever stronger and stronger, ever more deeply rooted in the heart and intelligence. But at the same time the thoughts which separate me from the Church also gain in force and clarity. [. . .] I do not see how I can avoid the conclusion that my vocation is to be a Christian outside the Church. The possibility of there being such a vocation would imply that the Church is not Catholic in fact as it is in name, and that it must one day become so, if it is destined to fulfill its mission.[2]

Even in her retreat from institutional religion, the Church compelled Weil, driving her into extremes of compassion. She remained outside of the Church until her death, which, due to an intensely ascetic lifestyle, volunteer hard labour and poor health, came at the age of 34. Weil viewed self-exile as the only mode of sanctity available to her. Her devotional life both paralleled and clashed with that of the 'official' church militant. She perched at a crossroads, or perhaps at a cross.

The history of Christian sanctity is one of paradox. From the virgin martyrs' callous abandonment of kin and culture; to the Franciscan rebellion against monastic life; to Martin's desecration of pagan shrines; to Joan's battle cry; to Nicholas's legendary assault of Arius; to Thomas More's simultaneous adherence to conscience and burning of reformers; to Marina's transvestism; to the self-starvation of Eucharistic devotees; to the 'little way' of St Thérèse; to the cynocephalic bark of Christopher – interpreters of Christianity have negotiated and renegotiated the meaning of *sanctus*. They imagine the project of sainthood in countless, often conflicting, ways. Few intellectual movements have demonstrated as keen an awareness of this – the fraught nature of Christian sainthood – as the philosophers and theologians working in France from the mid to late twentieth century. Whether ethicists (Levinas), historians (Foucault), post-structuralists (Derrida), aesthetic heresiarchs (Bataille), radical activists (Weil), mythographers (Girard), novelists (Blanchot), criminals (Genet), or phenomenologists explicitly engaged with the 'theological turn' (Henry, Marion, Lacoste), these thinkers laboured under a hagiological zeitgeist that coloured their ideas. Some of them continue to do so. The essays in this volume explore the concept of sainthood as deployed by the French postmodernists who understand it variously as a hermeneutic, a metaphor, a style, a literary genre, a model for emulation, an aesthetic spectacle, a subversive practice, a practice *to be* subverted, a historical relic, an ethical pedagogy, a theological problem and an anthropological constant.

That this hagiographical infusion of Continental philosophy occurs definitively in France, with all the force of a 'movement', is no coincidence. The French have never let secular concerns get in the way of their cult heroes: they *will* have their saints. Nor are they overly fastidious about sacred/profane dichotomies. Even France's greatest atheists have never been so gauche as to forego the tremendous aesthetic yield offered by the structure and semiotics of religion. And why should they? – when the sacred itself proves equally unwilling to remain bounded. French saints are compromised, glorious and loosely defined from the beginning. The land of Count Roland, Louis IX, Bernard of Clairvaux and the martial orders, France has mingled sanctity with power politics since Late Antiquity. The Frankish queen St Clotilde (c. 475–545), like the visionary Joan a millennium later, launched her country into a war motivated partially by revenge. French sanctity dallies with the erotic as well. Legend has it that Mary Magdalene retired to Provence to lead a life of penance. The apostle's vow of asceticism did not prevent her from using the skill set acquired as a sex worker to help a royal couple conceive.

Throughout all of Europe, the canonizing process proves as complex as the evolving conceptions of sanctity, and the two intertwine. Cultic devotion began as a primarily lay movement. For a long time, scholars imagined the process of identifying and revering these folk heroes belonged chiefly to the peasant class, as a sort of grassroots movement. The field-forming work of Peter Brown, however, drew attention to the cultic initiative taken by Roman aristocrats, who often obtained and enshrined martyred bodies.[3] In an acclaimed work of journalistic investigation, Kenneth Woodward elucidates the politics and bureaucracy of contemporary saint-making. He briefly summarizes the history of canonization, explaining that church authorities assumed increasing control over these cults because they recognized the necessity of domesticating an alternate source of spiritual authority, and because practitioners had begun to cult individuals willy-nilly. The encroachment was gradual, and the papacy only obtained official control over canonization in 1234. The decentralized quality of early cultic devotion resulted in the reverencing of many individuals never declared saints by the institutional Church.[4] The sixth-century Gallic hymnist Venantius Fortunatus, for example, was cherished as a saint but never canonized. Even after the institutional Church began to claim control over sainthood, most Frankish cults retained their local flavours for several centuries.[5]

Perhaps more than any other French *vita*, 'Saint' Guinefort's story demonstrates the expansive and playful nature of medieval French devotion. Having fought a serpent to protect his infant ward, Guinefort was covered in blood when the child's father came home. The cradle had flipped in the tumult, hiding the child beneath it. Assuming Guinefort had slain his son, the man killed him. Upon discovery of the serpent's carcass and the unharmed baby, the father realized his mistake and buried Guinefort next to a well. The grave attracted numerous devotees, who brought infant children there for healing. Not having approved the cult itself, the Church ordered Guinefort's bones exhumed and burned (a standard punishment for heresy). Why did the Church react so strongly? No doubt because Guinefort was a dog. In a time when most children did not survive their first year, the people welcomed a champion of infants – even one who, according to 'orthodox' theology, could not have possessed a soul.

This idiosyncratic, improvisational attitude towards saints continued into the New World. At turns under French, Spanish and US governance, New Orleans remains one of the most Catholic spaces in North America. The importation of slaves from both West Africa and Haiti (especially after the revolution), as well as the existence of a free black class, resulted in a Creole Catholicism that interacted with Vodun (Voodoo) in interesting ways. Many of the Voodoo spirits (loa) came to be identified with various Catholic saints. This imbued traditional saints with a double-valence. Papa Legba (guardian of the crossroads) continues to be associated with St Peter (gatekeeper of heaven). This syncretic, utilitarian approach to sainthood also resulted in the culting of several 'Voodoo saints', heroic figures appealed to by practitioners of a uniquely Creole Voodoo-Catholicism (or Catholic

Voodoo). St Expedite, patron of urgent cases, and St Marron, patron of runaway slaves and maroon communities, provide two such examples.

Just as French religion has celebrated heroes with heterodox baggage, so has French secularity, if such a thing can be said to exist, been implicated in the religious since its earliest days. Though many have considered courtly romance a fairly secular genre, for example, this designation breaks down time and again – often due to hagiographical imagery. We might think of Chrétien's Lancelot, who suffers numerous humiliations out of devotion to Guinevere and even puts some of her hair under his shirt, next to his breast, invoking the idea of an ascetic's hairshirt. Or better yet: Galahad, who all but undergoes canonization in the *Queste del Saint Graal*, essentially a Eucharistic parable. Later, Michel De Montaigne's *On Prayer* becomes a model of traditionalism when placed alongside the startlingly relativistic *On the Cannibals*, an essay thought to signal the Early Modern advent of secularism. In his *Meditations*, Descartes will require a logically necessary moment of atheism in order to evoke the Cogito and bolster his ontological proof of God's existence.

Religion even intrudes upon explicitly profane realms. The infinite penetration in the Marquis de Sade's economy of suffering and sacrifice, ecstasy and torture, often occur in sacred spaces. Justine, Sade's most famous sexual martyr, suffers mostly at the hands of monks and could be the virgin martyr Justina of Padua reincarnate. Christianity provides more than Gothic ambience for eighteenth-century pornography, though. It determines the possible modes of relationality, articulating the shattering, material realities of eros while drawing attention to the fleshy consummation of the Real Presence: '[. . .] they light candles, they place the image of our Saviour squarely upon the little girl's back and upon her buttocks they dare consummate the most redoubtable of our mysteries'.[6] Incarnation is carnal knowledge. Sade's theatre of perversions dramatizes the violence and failure of secularization, inasmuch as it cannot exit its dialectic with religion and is, perhaps, a product of that back-and-forth. (Indeed, Augustine used the word *saeculum* to describe an 'age' in-between the Resurrection and Second Coming. Later, the term came to denote a kind of priest who worked in town parishes, as opposed to leading a monastic life.) Sade's work also illustrates secularization's success: it imagines religion in new and radical ways, often ways explicitly resisted. In so doing, it both scandalizes and opens up the sacred. At turns a servant and political prisoner of the Revolution, Sade illustrates with both his life and work how Enlightenment France was itself a kind of Dark Ages.[7]

In *Christianity: The First Three Thousand Years*, Diarmaid MacCulloch describes a 'secular form of sainting' which took place in Revolutionary France, where the longing for 'cultural heroes of a self-consciously renewed and secularized society' reigned.[8] The first saints of this 'new' France? Voltaire and Rousseau, subsequently enshrined in the Parisian Panthéon, formerly the Catholic Church of Ste-Geneviève. As Sade's extreme materialism suggests, the desacralized world of post-revolutionary France had attempted to remove the signifying force of the Church. Life became a permanently immanent sphere. This denial of the transcendent both liberated and lowered the human, not necessarily into a world of sin, which still bore a trace of the transcendent – but into a world where we are all utterly exposed as the creatures we are. As Baudelaire once remarked, 'Life swarms with innocent monsters'.[9] He suggested that losing one's soul (a thing without use-value, an end in itself) might even feel as slight as dropping a business card in the street.[10] And such is the daily life many experience.

In a post-Kantian world, where subjectivity vanishes into singularity and no thing-in-itself can be known – where we are all Deleuzian assemblages taking things in by means of an ever-contingent perspectivalism – perhaps it makes sense to look not inward, not upward, but *outward* for metaphysical value. The saint offers up her body (or life, or *vita*) as a locus of concentration, an ad hoc centrepoint for the focusing of communal energies – a makeshift altar in the desert. The saint is our Other, and we are hers. Her care for humanity guarantees its value; her faith reflects some kind of absolute, if only provisionally. Edith Wyschogrod's work of moral philosophy, *Saints and Postmodernism*, has helped legitimate recourse to holy lives as templates for meaningful existence in a world of deconstructed truth-systems.[11] The volume of essays gathered in *Saints: Faith Without Borders*, edited by Françoise Meltzer and Jaś Elsner, considers the saint's universality – including pieces on the multiculturalism, political potential and cultural adaptability of the holy exemplar.[12]

Others have focused on the centrality of the sacred as an organizing principle in high French theory. As the title suggests, *Derrida and Negative Theology* contains essays that consider the proximity of Derridean post-structuralism to Christian apophasis, a tradition reaching back to the *Mystical Theology* of Pseudo-Dionysius.[13] (Derrida himself rejected the notion that he was doing negative theology, and Martin Hägglund's *Radical Atheism: Derrida and the Time of Life* expands this protestation.)[14] Peter Tracey Connor's *Georges Bataille and the Mysticism of Sin*[15] and Amy Hollywood's *Sensible Ecstasy: Mysticism, Sexual Difference, and the Demands of History* address the recurrent mysticism *topos* within this context.[16] Alexander Irwin takes up a more political tack in *Saints of the Impossible: Bataille, Weil, and the Politics of the Sacred*. He claims that Weil and Bataille consciously *performed* their lives of extreme activism and self-marginalization, inspired by the logic of saintly exemplarity.[17] This volume contributes to the tide of attention paid to the role of the sacred in French postmodern thought. More specifically, it scrutinizes through the lens of sainthood. Why the saints? Why put these often (though not always!) avowedly non-religious voices in dialogue with a chorus of *hagioi*? What is the justification and what might such a conversation yield?

One concrete, historical reason for such a project is that many of the French postmodernists received explicit training in the field of medieval studies. They possessed an intimate familiarity with the culture producing the (Western European) hagiographical genre, enabling them to riff on it effectively. For the most part, this commonality in the educational backgrounds of so many French thinkers remained understudied until Bruce Holsinger's poly-biographical *The Premodern Condition: Medievalism and the Making of Theory*. The work draws attention to the medieval/medievalist roots of postmodern French thought, as indicated by the title's cooption of Lyotard's *The Postmodern Condition*. Even those who did not make an overt study of the Middle Ages found themselves in constant dialogue with contemporary Catholic thinkers (see Jean Danielou's extended conversation with Bataille) and relied on medieval texts and *topoi*. Bataille's anti-aesthetic work with *Tel Quel* and, especially, his understanding of 'general' versus 'restricted' economies were the products of a mind trained in paleography at the École Nationale des Chartes then applied to numismatics and archival work at the Bibliothèque Nationale. Throughout the course of his education and first career, Bataille acquired an expertise in 'chivalric literature, Gothic architecture, scholasticism, feudalism', paleography, Old French, 'medieval numismatics, codicology, editorial practice, and romantic philology'.[18] Holsinger presents similar case studies of several French philosophers, making the bold claim that:

> So wide-ranging and energetic was the French avant garde's preoccupation with medieval formations during this decade that it merits recognition as one of the most significant epiphenomena accompanying the emergence and consolidation of so-called French theory as a meta-discourse of posthumanistic inquiry. This epiphenomenon – let us call it *theoretic medievalism* – embraces a spectrum of approaches and attitudes toward the Western Middle Ages shaping postwar French critical discourse in its myriad forms: from the straightforward appropriation of medieval philosophical texts and an enthusiastic affiliation with modern medievalist scholarship to a range of abnegations, elisions, and denials of the premodernities at the heart of the modern [. . .] a brilliantly defamiliarizing amalgamation of medievalisms that together constitute the domain of the avant-garde premodern.[19]

The book insists that any productive reading of French postwar philosophy necessitates some engagement with the Middle Ages, which often amounts to engagement with the sacred. It is no coincidence that Bataille offers a cathedral as his central image of excess. Or that Lacan studied under premodernist philosophers like Jean Baruzi, relied on the courtly love tradition to make psychoanalytic points and alludes to Bernard of Clairvaux in the opening to *The Ethics of Psychoanalysis*. Erin Labbie treats Lacan's premodern influences at length in *Lacan's Medievalism*.[20] Additionally, Bourdieu appropriates Panofsky's work on Gothic architecture and scholasticism, and Foucault's *History of Sexuality* uses the medieval confessional to describe the relationship between speech and sex. Barthes' interest in biblical exegesis informs his critical work and provides a structuring principle for *S/Z*.[21] For a collection of essays devoted to the medieval intellectual structures that continue to inform modern and postmodern philosophy, see *The Legitimacy of the Middle Ages: On the Unwritten History of Theory*, edited by Andrew Cole and D. Vance Smith.[22] Brad Gregory's *The Unintended Reformation: How a Religious Revolution Secularized Society* handles similar themes by means of a longue durée historical perspective.[23] In light of this 'theoretic medievalism', it should come as no surprise to discover a horde of holy helpers animating French philosophy. If postmodernism's secret palimpsest is comprised of saints' *legenda*, then a targeted examination of this cultic repurposing is both logical and urgent.

Personal biographies aside, intellectual history itself compels us to note French philosophy's reliance on the sacred. Critical theory has its foundations in religious praxis – down to the etymological level. Andrea Nightingale explores this genealogy in *Spectacles of Truth in Classical Greek Philosophy: Theoria and its Cultural Context*. The Greek word 'theoria' originally referred to a kind of religious tourism, wherein an individual would leave his polis (as either a government hiree or a private citizen) in order to witness and participate in the religious mysteries of another polis. If acting as an official delegate, the individual would report his impressions to the government and recommend the rite be adopted or not. Nightingale's central thesis is that Plato uses this religio-cultural practice as a metaphor to illustrate the philosopher's search for truth. He interiorizes this experience of travel, spectacle and return with the cave parable. Western philosophy's foundational paradigm owes its texture to a religious practice.[24] Additionally, Greco-Roman philosophy conceived of the search for the 'good life' in a less intellectualized way than does contemporary philosophy. The philosopher experiences 'conversion' and retreats from the world, living ascetically – like the saints who would point back to the 'noble pagans', especially Aristotle, as models of virtue. Even Epicurus reportedly lived in this manner. So compatible with Christian ethics was much pagan philosophy, that the first Christian theologians, like Origen Adamantius, thought of themselves as Christian *philosophers*, seeking after the *hagia sophia* of God. A religious idiom gives birth to Western philosophy, which would perhaps explain why thinkers from Anselm to Descartes to Kant to Weil feel the need to contend with, for example, the ontological proof. This volume shows that, while religion as such might have retreated to a sub-category of analytic philosophy, it continues to colour the Continental idiom.

In addition to the historical reasons for such a volume, more abstract, structural justifications for performing a hagiographical exegesis of postmodern thought also present themselves. Too often the word 'saint' inspires a saccharine sentimentality, conjuring images of baby-faced figures on prayer cards or beatifically frozen ghosts. Such idealization risks downplaying the saint's troubling role as *skandalon*, in the Pauline/Girardian sense. The one quality common to all saints is their project of *imitatio Christi*.[25] Certainly, this entailed performing acts of mercy and leading as perfect a life as possible (a goal reinterpreted by each generation). But Christ's *vita* also tells a story of descent into criminality, incredulous crowds, political execution, and, in the earliest manuscripts of *Mark*, a seeming grave robbery. In *The Aesthetics of Antichrist: From Christian Drama to Christopher Marlowe*, John Parker meditates on the revelatory nature of Antichrist, whose presence signals the imminent coming of the true Christ. Paradoxically, hell's avatar accomplishes his mission by *resembling* Christ – by aesthetic similitude, not, as one might expect, by radical difference.[26] The disturbing quality of Jesus's life (as well as evil's ability to approximate it) meant that the imitation of Christ was anything but a straightforward practice. Following Christ, even metaphorically, necessitated transformation into something socially scandalous. The martyrs – Christianity's first saints – were rebels in the political sense, criminalized for their failure to demonstrate loyalty to Rome by paying homage to its gods. As with Thomas à Becket and the Early Modern 'renaissance' of martyrdom, religious and political concerns bind themselves to one another inextricably. In fact, the consistency of this heroic subversion – such as the virgin martyrs' rejection of parental, erotic and political authorities – problematized their exemplary function, forcing late medieval devotees to creatively adapt the lessons of these *vitae* to more domestic, institutionally Christian lives. Catherine Sanok tackles this issue in *Her Life Historical: Exemplarity and Female Saints' Lives in Late Medieval England*.[27]

We should not forget that at its founding moment, the dominant culture viewed Christianity as transgressive, criminal and perverse. Popular imagination accused Christians of enacting all the most dramatic social taboos: cannibalism, infanticide, free love and atheism. With its Eucharistic praxis, devotion to an infant god born to die, a-filial communism, privileging of merciful grace over discerning justice, and rejection of the pagan pantheon in favour of an executed criminal, Christianity more than justified these accusations: it realized them in the profoundest sense, transvaluing them into 'truer truths'. These 'slanders' pointed to a deeper, miraculous level of meaning, but were also revelatory in an immanent sense, as purely surface observations. They may not have been entirely true, but they were not false.

This tradition of criminality continues past Christianity's legalization with the Edict of Milan (313). Aside from the transgressive modes of sanctity previously listed (such as the cross-dressing ploy enabling St Marina to enter a monastery with her father), there exists the conversion narrative, enabling murderers and prostitutes to attain a spiritual authority rendered even more dramatic for their previous lives. In a sense, past sins stay with them, constantly proving the present miracle of grace. Paul, Mary Magdalene and the good thief crucified beside Jesus afford the most famous examples, but later examples of sinners-turned-pious (such as St Augustine) abound. Iscariotic devotion constitutes a more direct example of criminality qua criminality considered as a mode of sanctity. In the short story 'Three Versions of Judas', Borges suggests that Judas's soul-sacrifice was more profound than the bodily sacrifice of crucifixion.[28] Many of the Voodoo saints (such as St Marron and St Blackhawk, the Native American freedom fighter) possess a distinctly Robin Hood quality. Similarly, Mexican drug cartels have canonized their own pantheon of 'narco saints', headed by the bandit Jesús Malverde. The striking thing about this alternate devotion is that it looks – in both form and content – a great deal like 'official', orthodox Catholicism. Which is exactly the point. Exciting as holy highwaymen are, we need not turn to overt vigilantism or outlawry to see unregulated sanctity in action. For the best example of a sociopath, one positioning himself literally above the law and to whom people came for extra-legal solutions, we have but to crane our necks for a glimpse of St Simeon Stylites.[29]

Transgression inheres in postmodern thought as an almost ethical imperative. Rather than view this as a phenomenon separate from the use of hagiographical themes, we should consider the two coidentifiable. In *Our Lady of the Flowers* Jean Genet recounts the *vita* of a transvestite and her sufferings.[30] Like his narrator, Genet himself spent time in prison for a number of different offenses. And like so many hagiographers (Jerome, for example), Genet undergoes a kind of literary canonization with Sartre's *Saint Genet: Actor and Martyr*.[31] Perhaps a writer worthy of the task will take it upon herself to canonize Sartre next. Similarly, Michel Foucault resisted police during the student protests of the late 1960s, endured bigotry for his queer lifestyle, helped found an organization through which prisoners might have a voice and focused on penal history in *Discipline and Punish*. At the same time, he supported the Islamist revolution in Iran, opposed aspects of the gay rights movement and considered himself a serious Nietzschean. Despite (or perhaps *because of*) this moral complexity, David Halperin has authored the theorist's *vita* with *Saint Foucault: Towards a Gay Hagiography*.[32] Simone Weil's Marxism, pacifism, labour striking and eventual anarchism won her a fair share of condemnation as well. And Bataille's valorization of the anal scandalized the contemporary avant-garde, resulting in his denunciation by leading Surrealist André Breton. Acéphale, the secret society he helped found, came close to practising human sacrifice, yet Bataille had considered joining the priesthood at one point. Postmodern thinkers, like saints, say the 'hard things'. The Frankfurt School appended 'critical' to 'theory' in order to differentiate it from the tidy, closed system-building they thought European philosophy had become. Both saints and theorists serve as intellectual, cultural and spiritual watchdogs – from Bataille's avowed heterodoxy to Weil's counter-institutional catholicity.

Whether engaged in a hermeneutics of suspicion, recollection, or – as D. Z. Phillips has offered as a third option – contemplation, the theorist acts as an intercessory figure, mediating between the nature of reality and a literate public.[33] Just as Hermes bore messages from pagan deities to humanity, interpreting the language of the gods for mortal ears, so do theorists create and deploy a language meant to 'translate' reality into concepts, or tools with which to deconstruct concepts. Christianity conceives of the saintly mission in similar terms. Extending Christ's mediation as members of his body, the saints occupy the space between God and humanity, passing prayers upward and consolation/advice/wonders downward. (Incidentally, the process of moving relics from one location to another is called 'translation'.) By em-bodying interpretation itself, both saints and theorists offer up the hope of understanding. As Lyotard says in his posthumously published prose-poem about Augustine's *Confessions*, 'if we saw and heard the dazzling clamor of your wisdom without any filter, if we received it all at once, it would contort our faces, would unfix the orbit of our eyes, would turn us into a white-hot firebrand, subsiding quickly into ashes'.[34] Ultimately, the very processes of interpretation – the necessity of a hermeneutic language – only re-emphasize the infinite inaccessibility of truth, if, indeed, 'truth' exists at all. By freeing philosophy of its systemizing, explicative impulses, postmodern theory introduces an element of mystery back into the equation, cutting aporias into its structure to let out some of certainty's harsh light, quieting its fluorescent buzz until only the dark silence of apophasis remains. The enigmatic spectacle of hagiodrama inspires as many questions as answers, its eccentric actors gesturing wildly at an inscrutable deity. Similarly, French postmodernism has offered us more than answers: it has given us new and better questions. Perhaps what philosophy has actually undergone is a theological re-turn: the disciplines have been about each other's business since ancient times.

Notes

1 Simone Weil, *Waiting for God* (trans. Emma Craufurd, New York: Harper & Row, 1992), p. 96.
2 Simone Weil, *Letter to a Priest* (trans. A. F. Wills, London: Routledge, 2002), p. 3.
3 Peter Brown, *The Cult of the Saints: Its Rise and Function in Latin Christianity* (Chicago: University of Chicago Press, 1981), p. 32.
4 Kenneth L. Woodward, *Making Saints: How the Catholic Church Determines who Becomes a Saint, Who Doesn't, and Why* (New York: Simon & Schuster, 1990).
5 Thomas Head, *Hagiography and the Cult of Saints, The Diocese of Orleans, 800–1200* (Cambridge: Cambridge University Press, 1990). Woodward's book offers an accessible introduction to the evolution of the cult of the saints, focusing on the contemporary Catholic Church. For a more academic overview of the cult's development throughout the Middle Ages, students of hagiography should see Thomas Head's magisterial *Medieval Hagiography: An Anthology*. Both volumes emphasize the fluidity of cultic devotion.
6 Marquis De Sade, *Justine, Philosophy in the Bedroom, & Other Writings* (trans. Richard Seaver and Austryn Wainhouse, New York: Grove Press, 1965), p. 613.
7 Max Horkheimer and Theodor W. Adorno, *Dialectic of Enlightenment: Philosophical Fragments* (trans. Edmund Jephcott, Stanford: Stanford University Press, 2002).

8 Diarmaid MacCulloch, *Christianity: The First Three Thousand Years* (New York: Viking Press, 2009), p. 800.

9 Charles Baudelaire, *Paris Spleen* (trans. Louise Varèse, New York: New Directions, 1970), p. 98.

10 Ibid., p. 61.

11 Edith Wyschogrod, *Saints and Postmodernism: Revisioning Moral Philosophy* (Chicago: University of Chicago Press, 1990).

12 Françoise Meltzer and Jaś Elsner, eds, *Saints: Faith Without Borders* (Chicago: University of Chicago Press, 2011).

13 Harold Coward and Toby Foshay, eds, *Derrida and Negative Theology* (Albany, NY: State University of New York Press, 1992).

14 Martin Hägglund, *Radical Atheism: Derrida and the Time of Life* (Stanford: Stanford University Press, 2008).

15 Peter Tracey Connor, *Georges Bataille and the Mysticism of Sin* (Baltimore: Johns Hopkins University Press, 2000).

16 Amy Hollywood, *Sensible Ecstasy: Mysticism, Sexual Difference, and the Demands of History* (Chicago: University of Chicago Press, 2002).

17 Alexander Irwin, *Saints of the Impossible: Bataille, Weil, and the Politics of the Sacred* (Minneapolis: University of Minnesota Press, 2002).

18 Bruce Holsinger, *The Premodern Condition: Medievalism and the Making of Theory* (Chicago: University of Chicago Press, 2005), p. 2.

19 Ibid., p. 4.

20 Erin Felicia Labbie, *Lacan's Medievalism* (Minneapolis: University of Minnesota Press, 2006).

21 Holsinger, *Premodern Condition*, p. 158.

22 Andrew Cole and D. Vance Smith, eds, *The Legitimacy of the Middle Ages: On the UnwrittenHistory of Theory* (Durham: Duke University Press, 2010).

23 Brad Gregory, *The Unintended Reformation: How a Religious Revolution Secularized Society* (Cambridge, MA: The Belknap Press of Harvard University Press, 2012).

24 Andrea Wilson Nightingale, *Spectacles of Truth in Classical Greek Philosophy: Theoria in its Cultural Context* (Cambridge: Cambridge University Press, 2004).

25 Candida R. Moss, *The Other Christs: Imitating Jesus in Ancient Christian Ideologies of Martyrdom* (Oxford: Oxford University Press, 2010).

26 John Parker, *The Aesthetics of Antichrist: From Christian Drama to Christopher Marlowe* (Ithaca: Cornell University Press, 2007).

27 Catherine Sanok, *Her Life Historical: Exemplarity and Female Saints' Lives in Late Medieval England* (Philadelphia: University of Pennsylvania Press, 2007).

28 Jorge Luis Borges, *Labyrinths: Selected Stories & Other Writings* (ed. Donald A. Yates and James E. Irby, New York: New Directions, 1964), p. 97.

29 Peter Brown, 'The Rise and Function of the Holy Man in Late Antiquity', *The Journal of Roman Studies* 61 (1971), p. 88.

30 Jean Genet, *Our Lady of the Flowers* (trans. Bernard Frechtman, New York: Grove Press, 1964).

31 Jean-Paul Sartre, *Saint Genet: Actor and Martyr* (trans. Bernard Frechtman, New York: George Braziller, 1963).

32 David M. Halperin, *Saint Foucault: Towards a Gay Hagiography* (New York: Oxford University Press, 1995).
33 D. Z. Phillips, *Religion and the Hermeneutics of Contemplation* (Cambridge: Cambridge University Press, 2001).
34 Jean-François Lyotard, *The Confession of Saint Augustine* (trans. Richard Beardsworth, Stanford: Stanford University Press, 2000), pp. 40–41.

1

Jean Genet versus *Saint Genet*: Searching for Redemption among the 'Unredeemable'

Colby Dickinson

My detractors would never rise up against a Saint Camus. Why do
they protest against Saint Genet? [. . .] I was a bastard child,
I had no right to the social order. What was left to me if I wanted an
exceptional destiny? If I wanted to make the most of my freedom,
my possibilities or, as you say, my gifts, since I wasn't yet aware of
having any gift as a writer, assuming I do? What was left for me was
nothing other than wanting to be a saint, that is, a negation of man.[1]

Such was the position, as Hadrien Laroche has put it, of one who was
determined to 'wage war on himself', though it was a peculiar type of
warfare to be sure.[2] What is one to make of such an embracing of the abject
of society, an identification of oneself with the 'excrement' of culture that is
bold enough not simply to empathize with an 'unfortunate' lot, but to live
and act as one of them, to become the very labels that others often callously
foist upon the discarded members of our social order? Could this be in some
way a most radicalized form of saintly living?

Though his various writings often put him at odds with the prevailing
moral norms of society, put simply, Jean Genet tried, through his novels,

plays, occasional essays and late memoirs, to create a form of subjectivity for the marginalized persons he was often identified with: those prisoners, criminals, prostitutes and homosexuals who were (and still are) often thrust to the limits of what we consider 'proper' society to be. Each resonance with such facile categorizations that Genet accepted was something of a scandal to the French literary culture of the mid-twentieth century, though his work rose quickly to fame after the publication of Jean-Paul Sartre's lengthy study of his first (and *only*) five novels: *Saint Genet*. In this work, Sartre attempted to highlight the cosmological theo-drama of Genet's world, his virtual recreation of our universe into 'another moral order' founded on the 'consecration of evil'[3] – that is, a form of perverse and paradoxical sanctity founded on the betrayal of the morality around which we typically solidify our social existence. For Sartre, Genet's renunciation of saintliness and his embrace of wickedness (evil) was a 'cheap trick' to attain martyrdom (and consequently some new form of 'sanctity'), therefore proving that any possible truer form of saintliness does not really exist for Genet as such.[4] Hence, he sought to *expose* Genet, to champion but also provide a 'corrective' appropriation to his work, a move which could likewise be said to have 'sanitized' or 'castrated' Genet in some sense.[5]

Taking Genet's entire body of writing into account, however, which Sartre was unable to do at the time – and which perhaps gave rise hence to his almost exclusive focus on Genet's 'consecration of evil' – seemingly grants a dramatic alteration to this common perception.[6] A more just account of Genet's worldview – one that could be said to *listen* to Sartre's focus on the concept of evil in Genet's work, but also that tries to *go beyond* its singularizing trajectory – is something only possible after the 1986 publication of his final memoirs recounting his time of political activism, spent mainly among the Black Panthers and certain Palestinian revolutionary groups. This work, *Prisoner of Love*, is one still needing to be more fully understood against the backdrop of his earlier work, for in it one finds the culmination of his 'saintly' principles, as well as his own declarations of a sort of canonization. These are embodied principles, moreover, that become more than simply ideals: they are the cornerstone for a new form of subjectivity that Genet distils from its hagiographical origins.

In general, however, and as it remains as the guiding principle behind his writings, Genet sought to upend the moral order imparted to a Judeo-Christian Europe, though, it should also be said, he was determined at the same time to preserve something of this very same heritage within his own core, albeit in an inverted form – hence the *saintly* gestures he found so appealing. For the man who once wrote that 'Dehumanizing myself is my own most fundamental tendency',[7] betrayal now becomes a virtue on the path towards sainthood, an immersion in 'evil' (or being beyond the dichotomous good and evil) the target rather than a rebellion against society, a profanation of all things considered holy as the only possible route to the sacred, though each of his inversions might also be said to be rarely understood for what he ultimately saw them to be (and such is my contention against Sartre's reading). Indeed, things appear quite differently when we focus in closer for further examination. For example, we witness his acts of profanation extended to all manner of things that had once enchanted him, a critical deconstruction of himself without mercy.[8] His various attempts to immerse himself in evil were often in reality an embracing of the moral codes of marginalized persons (e.g. women, homosexuals, ethnic minorities, Palestinians). And, from there, betrayal became a betrayal of one's own inner solitude (or peace), something that puts the self at risk through a genuine encounter with the other. Such, in the latter case, is what in fact motivated his movement *towards* forms of political solidarity, and what appeared to work actively against his solitary, artistic existence.[9]

The link between subject and saint appears to us bathed in this dark light, as the saint becomes for Genet the person who *creates* new forms of subjectivity, always singular, always in contrast with the homogenous tendencies of society, and one finds this in his every gesture, written or otherwise. In this fashion, one may renounce society's propensity towards sameness, though this is an act that does not renounce the individual person standing before us, as we will see. The link between the saint and the establishment of one's subjectivity therefore indicates how we might (re)inform the very coordinates of an inter-subjectivity formulated on the basis of a principle of *substitution*, the one for the other, through love – a principle that Genet stumbled upon during a ride on public transport one day in Istanbul. Through such an understanding, Genet comes, even against his will, to embrace the margins of social living in a very hands-on manner, devoid of the distance normally ascribed to the saint. As he put it with characteristic bravado: 'I distrust the saintliness of Vincent de Paul. He should have been willing to commit the galley slave's crime instead of merely taking his place in irons'.[10] Any act of substitution, as will gradually become clearer to us, must not proceed falsely as a distant form of empathetic gesturing, but must be genuinely and wholly undergone, an immersion into the excremental nature of reality, even if, paradoxically, this means that one must 'become God' to oneself in order to experience a more profound depth to reality.

In what follows, I want to address two fundamental aspects of Genet's form of saintliness as expressed in his work, and as they depict a fuller expression of what saintly being might be: *solitude* and *substitution*.

The solitude of the saint

Genet's novels have been described as 'masturbatory' – such was Sartre's portrayal – and there is certainly more than a fair share of truth in this statement. His solitary existence seemed to promote nothing less than a circular routing of pleasure and imagery in relation to the self. 'Pleasure of the solitary, gesture of solitude that makes you sufficient unto yourself, possessing intimately others who serve your pleasure without their suspecting it, a pleasure that gives to your most casual gestures, even when you are up and about, that air of supreme indifference toward everyone [. . .]'.[11] It is this reading of his inner life of solitude and its grand schemes of creation that propel him to write and to interlace himself with a pantheon of underworld gods. It is also what presumably drove his fiction to be highly autobiographical and to draw in the various characters that haunted his periphery. In this vein, he relished his ability to weave a rich literary tapestry composed of those around him. It was the very force of his artistic creativity and its intermingling with a deeply fascinated religious imagination. It is only as such that he was once able to proclaim: 'It was a good thing that I raised egoistic masturbation to the dignity of a cult!'[12] Solitude was in short, for Genet, our 'secret glory' and the only means towards achieving an internal peace, as it is a withdrawal from society, a renunciation of all that the world values.[13]

Solitude, of course, is nothing new to the history of the saints. It has often been a treasure long sought after, and has even been perceived more recently as something that needs to be cultivated in the midst of an active and worldly lifestyle. Genet certainly confirms such an understanding. At an early point in his life he in fact recognizes the problematic associated with trying to sever solitude from saintliness, a connection he could never fully dismiss: 'I run the risk of going astray by confounding saintliness with solitude. But am I not, by this sentence, running the risk of restoring to saintliness the Christian meaning which I want to remove from it?'[14] And this is the difficulty he would encounter again and again: he desired to *subvert* saintliness while yet *preserving* its traditional adherence to the practice of solitude. Nonetheless, he would continue to try to make sense of this merger between an inverted saintliness and a somewhat more traditional and personal solitude that would inform his sense of self.[15]

For a period during the mid-1950s, Genet cultivated a friendship with the artist Alberto Giacometti who proved to be something of an inspiration to Genet, an especially significant one as Genet found himself at this point in his life at a literary crossroads, having ceased the writing of novels and embarked on a more theatrical career. What Giacometti's statues transmitted to Genet, what he in fact saw in the beauty of an 'eternal' art form, is the fact of our solitude 'being exactly equivalent to any other'. *This* in fact became the source of art's incorruptibility to him, what appears as eternal through the elimination of all accidental qualities, *even if* the art is made by human hands. As Sartre relayed in a subsequent conversation with Genet: Giacometti wishes to fade behind the work, as if he were no longer there – the base evocation of one's death so that one's art might truly live, that it might live even in the face of the death of our world. 'He would be even happier if the bronze had appeared of its own accord', as Genet put it.[16]

The totem, the fetish, the idol that rises from the ground and is given to humanity from a divinity beyond – this is the invocation of a form of paganism, or rather those animistic impulses in Genet's cosmology which counter the Christian-atheist cultural legacy.[17]

Just as he had lived among various peoples with whom he did not share a language, Genet perpetually encounters the foreign word that begins to strip him of his Judeo-Christian morality, leaving him naked, shorn even of the grotesque struggle that he had previously been waging against certain Western moral orders.[18] This is the experience of a solitude as *revolutionary* as it is saintly.[19] Hence, for him, 'Solitude [. . .] does not signify an unhappy state, but rather secret royalty, profound incommunicability yet a more or less obscure knowledge of an invulnerable singularity'.[20] This is what Genet sees when he rides on a bus and only glimpses the faces and gestures that have not the time to appear *for him* – they are presented to him, rather, in their nude form. These are the faces that jump out at Genet and bear a presence, like those dislodged faces in Giacometti's sketches. The presence that protrudes *from* each person in effect creates a reality *for* each person, a 'truly terrible' reality when grasped by the one who genuinely sees it.[21] It is terrible because it yields a creative force beyond what any 'good society' could tolerate – it is the very force that threatens to undo our social bonds, and therefore has more than a passing resonance with some of our most basic religious impulses. It is also, if we follow Genet closely, what allows us to make peace with the world, with those others who surround us.

> This visible world is what it is, and our action upon it cannot make it radically different. Hence our nostalgic dreams of a universe in which man, instead of acting so furiously upon visible appearance, would attempt to rid himself of it – not only to refuse any action upon it, but to strip himself bare enough to discover that secret site within ourselves that would capacitate an entirely different human enterprise. More specifically, an altogether different moral enterprise.[22]

This is what lurks behind every face we see; it is its inherent beauty that at once terrifies and provokes the undoing of our world.

The face, as such, is capable of transcending history, of not giving itself over to the other, but of maintaining its singularity as a form of solitude that is 'our surest glory', and which remains central to us when our 'traditional' (Judeo-Christian) mores have been stripped of their previous meaning.[23] And it is *this* glory which is conveyed through a thing's solitude (its 'inaccessibility'), which *is* its beauty. Such an insight is what prompts Genet to declare elsewhere that 'I am for every man who is alone'.[24] Solitude, he contends, is what unites the saint and the criminal as '[t]here is no visible agreement between society and the saint'.[25] A *recognition* of this fact is a recognition of a thing's beauty beyond any sense of goodness, such as Genet had himself experienced upon seeing a 'dreadful little old man' who was 'filthy and obviously nasty'.[26] It was his confrontation with this 'extremely ugly' man that led Genet towards an epiphany of sorts: 'Our eyes met, as they say, and whether this was a momentary or prolonged sensation I no longer know, but I suddenly had the painful – yes, painful – conviction that any man was "worth" exactly [. . .] as much as any other. "Anyone," I said to myself, "can be loved beyond his ugliness, his foolishness, his nastiness"'.[27] Giacometti's art, from Genet's point of view, expresses the defect of a thing until the defect itself shines through, until the hidden aspect refuses to be hidden any longer, shows itself, and in fact *becomes* the thing's very beauty. It is a beauty that must then be recognized for what it is, not unjustly harnessed to some insipid notion of goodness, something he was often forced to call 'evil', though such a label often distorts the reality of what he sought to present in his fictionalized worlds. Going beyond Sartre's reading in this regard, what Genet was after, it would seem, was something more profound than the simplistic contrast of good and evil; what he sought was the origin of the subject and our potential to create it as such ourselves, a deep and persistent truth that moved beyond being simply a literary endeavour. Hence he can proclaim that '[. . .] there was no question of any goodness proceeding from me, but of a recognition', the beginning point of a recognizable subjectivity.[28]

For someone who grew up an orphan in a small French village, the desire to *be* someone, someone great even, was what propelled Genet to attempt to stand above those around him, while at the same time always being called back to the reality of his roots, of his abandonment and interminable exilic life. In this, he was entirely alone, and yet always pining for the entrance of a sublime other worthy of his every attention. This is something Sartre had noticed already in another form, how '[t]he metamorphosis that threatens him unceasingly is the constituent revelation that occurred one day through the mediation of others and that can recur at any moment'.[29] Genet's most fervent problematic, it would seem, was how to translate himself from his inner saintly solitude – the source and fountain of his creative subjectivity – to the world outside him, to the ordinary and otherwise 'ugly' people he continuously saw before him – what one might call *the* problematic of civilization itself. Whatever one makes of it, it was certainly the source of his bold literary career. Sartre had maintained that Genet was only attracted to the 'eternal' forms of persons, not their contingent character (e.g. the pimp, the prostitute, the sailor, etc), a fact which his biography tells us often caused him to be rather terse or hostile to those who had considered themselves to be his friend at some point in time: 'The truth is that Genet never *encounters* anybody. He never sees a contingent, a particular creature moving toward him out of the night or from the back of a bar, a creature who would have to be observed, studied, comprehended [. . .]'.[30]

Yet, perhaps the later Genet would have reason to call Sartre's caricature into question. If he was initially given over only to eternal forms, preoccupied with those divinities he saw around him that possibly shared a secret alliance with our traditional forms of transcendence, then his last writings saw this vision utterly transformed. In a staged debate with a member of the *fedayeen* who was among the Palestinian revolutionaries with whom Genet was staying in solidarity with their struggle and who strove to establish God as a necessary, eternal and uncreated being, for example, Genet appears to contradict such a search for eternal forms. Rather, he ponders 'What if God could be given and taken away? What if he were not unmoving?'[31] Perhaps, we might say, the contingent characters that Genet had once avoided had somehow become part of his quest to embody a form of betrayal that is *yet the vital translation (presentation) to another of the vulnerable self that Genet had always tried to conceal.*[32]

Translation is certainly an act of betrayal to the original language being conveyed. It is a turning away from what one knows and towards what is foreign. Yet, as he remarked on occasion in his last memoir, translation was a *necessary betrayal* of what lies inside us.[33] We all must speak outward, from out of our solitude to an-*other* that we encounter. In terms of the saint, to translate oneself *out of* an inner solitude (or peace) *is* to betray one's saintliness – it is the ultimate betrayal of an image that may in fact lead to a form of 'saintliness' beyond our capacity to be disenchanted with it. Hence, we witness the powerful summary of solitude he gives depicted in terms of a holy interior house to be compared only with St Elizabeth, Queen of Hungary's single nun cell given her by God and which only she could see around her as she walked. Hence also, the prominence he gives to the Virgin Mary's house, that was itself carried up to heaven.[34] Genet was able to reject real property (he lived most of his life in hotels and with only a suitcase of possessions) because he had had an interior home within that he had been given, one that he had yet to constantly 'deconstruct'.[35] It was this interior home that he had trouble translating to others as it seemed a betrayal of his saintliness, the only betrayal that he was yet *un*comfortable with and mainly unwilling to let go of. Despite this reticence, however, his last memoir ends with the attempted presentation of such an inner gift that appeared to have birthed a miracle from within: Genet took the risk to betray his own inner solitude through his participation in the collective struggles of revolutionary groups, that which could be symbolized best, he tells us, by the miracles he had *avoided* his entire life. Now, rather, after sacrificing his own desire to be a saint, he writes: 'On 26 June 1970, on the first step of the escalator at Kuwait airport, I rose up in the air without moving so much as my foot'.[36] Another 'cheap trick' in his pantheon of deceptions? Or the recognition of a 'saintly' subjectivity beyond the confines of our cultural and religious heritages?

Substitution

According to his biographer Edmund White, for Genet, 'Love is the form of captivity that permits us at one and the same time to see the universality *and* the particularity of a person. Love reconciles Genet's feeling that everyone is of equal value and that each person is priceless'.[37] Though the many 'loves' of his life are kept at a distance from his fictional creations in an effort to preserve the depth of his regard for them, Genet does produce a stunning conclusion to his oeuvre through the recurring image of *substitution*, or, using an example from one significant context, a (mother and son) relationship into which he entered. Indeed, this most meaningful image from his last book, *Prisoner of Love*, comes across to us as fundamentally an act of substitution that Genet underwent again and again, though here while staying at the home of a youthful Palestinian fighter whose mother brought him tea in the middle of the night: 'For one night and for the duration of one simple but oft-repeated act, a man older than she was herself became the mother's son. For "before she was made, I was"'.[38] Bounding from this scriptural reference to the Christ-god, he continues, 'His mother was bound to be so diaphanous as to be almost invisible. But was it necessary *for me* to see more in her than the ruins of a life? Hadn't their love, hers and her son's, and my love for them, told me all there was to tell about myself?'[39] In other words, was not this act of substitution all there was to tell about the self or subject that Genet – or anyone else for that matter – could become?

It was through just such a substitution, the one for the other, that Genet recognized the movement of love among persons – the betrayal of an inner solitude that was yet necessary in order to translate oneself *into* another, the supreme insight that revolutionized his perception of himself, and, more importantly, of those around him. There is no doubt that such an understanding lies at the heart of the Christian narrative in particular (and its subsequent saints), embodied most concretely in Jesus' suffering on the cross for the sake of humanity. Such a resonance with the God who was mistaken for a criminal moves underneath Genet's symbolic universe, and is as commented upon by him as it was also indirectly emulated. It was his unique (and perhaps *not so unique*) insight into the saintly life that would (and still *does*) challenge our perceptions of 'holy living'. In stark contrast to the moral norms of his age (and ours as well), Genet took such a comprehension of the substitutability of our selves to an entirely different level than mainstream, Western religious culture could (or can) stomach.

For Genet, however, there appeared to be no other way to construct the human beings that we are. The very reality of our lives seemed to cry out that such a justice to the reality of our symbolically constructed selves be heard:

> [. . .] that symbolic image, where one figure as soon as it came to mind inevitably summoned up the other, always hovered over its counterpart, the image still of human proportions. I'd seen Hamza and his mother for too short a time – real, chronometric time – to be sure it was always their

true faces I remembered during the fourteen years I thought about them. But I did remember truly, I think, my feelings when I met them – Hamza and his mother, with her gun. Each was the armour of the other, who otherwise would have been too weak, too human.[40]

'Too weak, too human', when on their own and without each other, without the substitution that would establish each of us as subjects split from within by this other who is yet capable of becoming each of us. The vulnerable image haunts Genet for 14 years. It claims Genet as the crux of a solution to a problem he had been aching to resolve his entire life, and to which his entire written work had been dedicated: the resolution of his solitude amidst a backdrop of 'evil', his desire for saintliness amidst the criminals and marginalized of this world, and, quite simply, his searing ability to commune with the beloved other (who remained a stranger) before him. If his writings took on a dramatized cosmo-theological nature, as Sartre suggested, this new realization of one's substitutability was what humanity was really seeking after, what it had wrapped fast inside every religious urging:

What archetypal image was it that painters and sculptors really followed for so long, when, apparently inspired by the Gospels, they took the grief of motherhood as their subject? And above all why was it the image of that group that haunted me for fourteen years as persistently as an enigma? And lastly, why did I undertake a journey, not to find out the meaning of the enigma, but to see if it existed, and if so in what terms?[41]

In short, one might reason, he had been searching for a love that could puncture his solitude, a love once lost now needing to be regained, or perhaps simply the copy of an original that had never existed in the first place but which he somehow knew himself to have always needed. He had been searching for a love for which he would substitute himself, would risk the betrayal of his inner solitude, the secret source of his inner art – a risk to which his periods of artistic dryness in the face of budding relationships testify. What he discovered, no less, was not merely an ability to fall deeply in love with one person – the beloved – but *each* particular, contingent other before him, the ultimate act of substitution. This is how we are to read those otherwise strange remarks on Genet's search for the 'declared enemy': 'No friends. Especially no friends: an enemy declared but not divided':

[. . .] the delicious disarmed enemy whose balance is off, whose profile is vague, whose face is unacceptable, the enemy knocked down by the slightest puff of air, the already humiliated slave, throwing himself out of a window when the sign is given, the enemy who has been beaten: blind, deaf, mute. No arms, no legs, no belly, no heart, no sex, no head: in sum, a complete enemy [. . .].[42]

The completely marginalized and incapacitated, someone paradoxically who ceases to be the enemy, who rather comes to 'live in my stead', as he puts it.[43] And the radical gesture stops there. Here is the enemy *that substitutes for the self* and that is yet no friend because *the enemy is now the beloved, the other become the self that I am.*

What Genet conditions is a powerful presentation of a saintly becoming, a command issued to us from the depths of our core, from the otherness both within and without. Such a notion dictates that we risk the betrayal of our inner world, of our inner peace. We must move out towards the contingent other with the love that arises within us as a revolutionary creative force, so that, in the end, our betrayal of an inner solitude becomes the 'sacrifice' (here using Genet's word for it) necessary to achieve a love that accords a sense of pricelessness and yet equality to each individual. This is to substitute oneself *for* another, but also to recognize that this substitution has already occurred, *is already* at work within us. We simply drift in-between oneself *and* another, between the self *and* the enemy, between an inner solitude *and* its translated betrayal – the very essence of literature or the creative, poetic and singular act that can be a form of saintliness if formed within a person's everyday life. It is here that we are capable of dwelling, of finding our being, or, as Genet finally had the resolve to put it, 'The reality lay in involvement, fertile in hate and love; in people's daily lives; in silence, like translucency, punctuated by words and phrases'.[44]

Notes

1   Jean Genet, 'Interview with Madeline Gobeil', *The Declared Enemy: Texts and Interviews* (ed. Albert Dichy, trans. Jeff Fort, Stanford: Stanford University Press, 2004), p. 10.

2   Hadrien Laroche, *The Last Genet: A Writer in Revolt* (trans. David Homel, Vancouver: Arsenal Pulp Press, 2010), p. 289.

3   Rivca Gordon and Haim Gordon, 'Sartre on Genet's Consecration of Evil: A Rejection of Fanaticism', *American Catholic Philosophical Quarterly* 67:2 (1993), pp. 185–200.

4   Jean-Paul Sartre, *Saint Genet: Actor and Martyr* (trans. Bernard Frechtman, New York: Pantheon, 1963), pp. 337–38.

5   Genet himself indicated that Sartre's work has indeed 'castrated' him. Note also how a reviewer of Sartre's book in 1963 in the popular periodical *The Christian Century*, for example, extended his gratitude to Sartre for helping us to defend ourselves against Genet's 'evil' impulses. Tom F. Driver, 'The Spiritual Diabolism of Jean Genet', *The Christian Century* (20 November 1963), pp. 1433–35.

6   There have been few studies in English devoted to the work of Genet in any form. Beyond Laroche's book just cited, as well as Sartre's early tome, the major point of reference has become Edmund White's momentous *Genet: A Biography* (New York: Vintage, 1993). Another notable intervention in the

world of Genet scholarship would be Jacques Derrida's *Glas* (trans. John P. Leavey and Richard Rand, Lincoln, NE: University of Nebraska Press, 1990). As it relates to the topic at hand, mention should also be given to Loren Ringer's *Saint Genet Decanonized: The Ludic Body in* Querelle (Amsterdam: Rodopi, 2001).

7　Jean Genet, *Our Lady of the Flowers* (trans. Bernard Frechtman, New York: Grove Press, 1963), p. 92.

8　Cf. White, *Genet*, p. 484.

9　Ibid., p. 624.

10　Jean Genet, *The Thief's Journal* (trans. Bernard Frechtman, New York: Grove Press, 1964), p. 213.

11　Genet, *Our Lady*, p. 139.

12　Ibid.

13　Ibid., p. 294.

14　Genet, *Thief's Journal*, p. 215.

15　There is some sense in his later writings that solitude is not the 'highest virtue', though this remains theoretically unresolved in the early stages of his literary career. See ibid., p. 215.

16　Jean Genet, 'The Studio of Alberto Giacometti', *The Selected Writings of Jean Genet* (ed. Edmund White, Hopewell, NJ: Ecco Press, 1993), p. 321.

17　Jean Genet, *Prisoner of Love* (trans. Barbara Bray, Hanover, NH: Wesleyan University Press, 1989), p. 35. This is also a conclusion drawn by Stathis Gourgouris in his superb essay on Genet's many convergent themes, 'A Lucid Drunkenness (Genet's Poetics of Revolution)', *South Atlantic Quarterly* 97:2 (1998), pp. 413–56.

18　Genet, *Prisoner*, p. 44.

19　See the revolutionary themes in Gourgouris, 'A Lucid Drunkenness', as well as in the essay of Michael Hardt, 'Prison Time', *Yale French Studies* 91 'Genet: In the Language of the Enemy' (1997), pp. 64–79.

20　Genet, 'Studio', p. 317.

21　Ibid., p. 319.

22　Ibid., p. 310.

23　Ibid., p. 314.

24　Genet, 'Interview', p. 5.

25　Ibid., p. 10.

26　Genet, 'Studio', p. 316.

27　Ibid.

28　Ibid.

29　Sartre, *Saint Genet*, p. 4.

30　Ibid., p. 312.

31　Genet, *Prisoner*, p. 229.

32　Cf. Paul Ricoeur, *On Translation* (trans. Eileen Brennan, London: Routledge, 2006).

33　Genet, *Prisoner*, p. 59.

34　Ibid., pp. 319–20.

35　Ibid., p. 319.

36　Ibid., p. 320.

37　Edmund White, 'Introduction', *Prisoner of Love*, pp. xvii–xviii.

38　Genet, *Prisoner*, p. 167.

39 Ibid., p. 204.
40 Ibid., p. 176.
41 Ibid.
42 Jean Genet, 'J.G. Seeks . . . ', *Declared Enemy*, p. 1.
43 Ibid.
44 Genet, *Prisoner*, p. 3.

2

To Accept in Order to Create: Albert Camus

Elisabeth Bayley

Introduction

David Sherman describes Albert Camus' work in the following way: '[. . .] Camus was working at the margins of philosophy, attempting to rehabilitate the interests of flesh-and-blood human beings, which had been all but driven from philosophy by virtue of its overweening proclivity for systematic reason'.[1] Flesh-and-blood was of course what Camus was interested in. He did not attempt to create a type of philosophical system or to determine all the parts that would belong to one. Instead, he worked outside of any systematic framework, even those that many philosophers[2] of his time had worked within.

Camus produced a great deal of literature and drama, mastered the form of the essay and penned a large corpus of journalism in his all-too-short life. Through this large body of work he continually pointed towards what became the major thematic of his writings: the absurd position of human beings in this world. It was from this unique angle that he explored the various ways in which humans might live, even in a serious manner, with the absurdity before us as a constant reality. In this essay I will look at the ways in which Camus sought to accept humanity's absurd positioning in the world, the significance of the absence of transcendence, how he perceived time and how he thought these points of view called for an individual act of rebellion. Branching off from these foundational concepts in his writings,

I will explore how he used the act of creation itself – or *art* – as *the* important act that constantly grounds a person in their absurd situation. As such, I will likewise explore how this insight actually serves as a calling forth of the self into a continuous reality of life lived solely in the present moment. Through these notions of creation, limitation and the lack of transcendence in our world, I will locate Camus' arguments made against murder, that is, claims based on particular notions of solidarity.

One's acceptance of the absurdity of life is certainly not a traditional path towards saintliness, nor would any traditional saint be known for their renunciation of seeking transcendence or the divine. Camus' work calls the individual to a different conception of personal integrity that challenges our notions of 'being saintly'. What he offers us, in fact, is a notion of personhood that is grounded in one's own humanity and an acceptance of the fundamental state of our existence. In the end, then, through the work of Camus, it is possible to find aspects of saintliness that exist in the self when there is a realization of the present moment that is only made more real through solidarity with others and rebellion against the absurd. After all, it is good to recall, even Jesus was human.

The absurd and the non-transcendent

Camus' work *pivots* around the notion of the absurd. He described the absurd as a state wherein one feels like one lives '[. . .] in a universe suddenly divested of illusions and lights, man feels an alien, a stranger. His exile is without remedy since he is deprived of the memory of a lost home or the hope of a promised land. This divorce between man and his life, the actor and his setting, is properly the feeling of absurdity'.[3] For Camus, one's natural state of absurdity is based upon the feeling of being deprived of a home one constantly longs for, of being perpetually divided from the reality of dwelling in this place. Acceptance of this estrangement between the self and the surrounding world travels along the lines of what Fernando Pessoa once described as: 'The only way to be in agreement with life is to disagree with ourselves. Absurdity is divine'.[4]

A disagreement with one's own self consists in a conscious rejection of this split between a desire for, and yet the inaccessibility of a home. It is through such an act of disagreement, or the lack of acceptance for this state, that Camus sought to explore how one could yet live despite such a scission at the core of our experience of the self. He wrote: 'It is a matter of living in the state of the absurd. I know on what it is founded, this mind and this world straining against each other without being able to embrace each other. I ask for the rule of life of that state and what I am offered neglects its basis, negates one of the terms of the painful opposition, demands of me a resignation'.[5] It is one's natural inclination to seek refuge from this absurd reality because it is too painful to have to face. As a result, people often desire an alternative to having to live with this reality. Often, the alternative to such a situation in life is sought through those fabricated notions of a transcendent being or supposed experiences of transcendence itself. Despite such attempts, however, Camus wrote about the need to reject this temptation as, after all, he argued, seeking transcendence proves to be an absurd action in and of itself.[6] Instead of seeking after transcendence or a transcendent being, Camus believed it was necessary to *accept* one's absurd reality, no matter the insurmountable difficulties which such an acceptance would seem to entail.

One interpretation of his novel *The Plague*, for example, is that Camus used the existence of the plague itself to represent the state of all of humanity, thus showing how everyone is 'plagued' by one's absurd position in relation to the world. Within the conversations that take place throughout the book, he examined what this state means to different individuals. In particular, he looked at the way God might be addressed or understood within those circumstances that present us with the sheer force of absurdity. In *The Plague*, one of the main characters is a doctor named Rieux, someone who helps the people of the city in dealing with the plague that has come upon them. Rieux speaks about the need not to look for God, but to struggle against the reality of death. As he says to his friend Tarrou, '[. . .] since the order of the world is shaped by death, mightn't it be better for God if we refuse to believe in Him and struggle with all our might against death, without raising our eyes toward the heaven where He sits in silence?'[7] Rieux is in point of fact asking whether it is not better to deal with what we have before us here on earth, the material reality of which leads inevitably *to* death, than to seek God. Camus lays out his exploration of this situation throughout this section in his novel and likewise provokes the reader to question what benefit can be found in seeking the transcendent when we have the physical reality of death before us. This is a powerful question returned to again and again in the most powerful novels.

One can think here of Alice Walker's *The Color Purple*, where, in the midst of so many scenes that try to deal with the nature of oppression and racial tensions, Sophia says to Celie: 'You ought to bash Mr. _____ head open, she say. Think bout heaven later'.[8] The reason such stark contrasts are so startling is because the power of the here and now, the material reality of our lives and our deaths, is in radical opposition to our conceptualizations of the transcendent. Overcoming oppression, historically speaking, has often in fact meant defying the normativity of the latter through an increased (political) focus on those powers that circulate within the former.

In the story before us, Camus continues to question where one's absurd positioning in this world puts a person if he or she does not believe in the transcendent as such. What such formulations prompt us to speculate upon, of course, is, if there is no God, then is there anything 'saint-like' that is possible to achieve within a person's life? And this would appear to be where an inverted notion of sainthood perhaps becomes available to us in Camus' thoughts as presented in *The Plague*:

'It comes to this,' Tarrou said almost casually; 'what interests me is learning how to become a saint.'

'But you don't believe in God' [replied Rieux].

'Exactly! Can one be a saint without God? – that's the problem, in fact the only problem I'm up against today' [replied Tarrou].[9]

Through these characters' words and actions, Camus begins to question whether there is a more authentic possibility of becoming a 'saint' beyond our traditional, religious notions of it, one in fact which is possible even when one does not believe in God. In other words, the essential matter becomes how one lives a saintly existence without yet believing in a transcendent being. Here it is possible to see how, through his idea of living within the present moment, there is an exploration of a radically new understanding of the reality of immanence, one which calls forth a saintly perspective of humanity in a way alternative to the more traditional notions of sainthood found in our historical concepts of transcendence.

This present moment and limitations

Further along in *The Plague*, Camus addresses how trying to avoid or escape one's absurd position (e.g. through seeking a transcendent explanation or meaning behind something) is an exhausting habit. In another conversation between the characters Tarrou and Rieux, Tarrou states:

Yes, Rieux, it's a wearying business, being plague-stricken. But it's still more wearying to refuse to be it. That's why everybody in the world today looks so tired; everyone is more or less sick of plague. But that is also why some of us, those who want to get the plague out of their systems, feel such desperate weariness, a weariness from which nothing remains to set us free except death.[10]

Through trying to deny one's position within the absurdity around us, one is constantly stricken with a sense of exhaustion from trying to escape it. And this is precisely why, for Camus, an acceptance of absurdity and yet one's willingness to live in this reality despite it, is an act of true integrity. For him, as he puts it elsewhere, 'The danger, on the contrary, lies in the subtle instant that precedes the leap. Being able to remain on that dizzying crest – that is integrity and the rest is subterfuge'.[11] As is clear from so much of his writing, Camus believed it was best for individuals to stop trying to escape or deny their absurd position in the world, because it is only by accepting it that one might live a life with some degree of integrity. He realized, however, that this was no easy thing to accept.

Acceptance of the absurd status of our being-in-the-world, moreover, results in what Camus described as a different conception of time. He understood that if there was no stretching forth of one's desire to transcend –

a reaching *towards* transcendence – then an individual might actually become aware of – or find themselves *wholly within* – the present moment. Time, for Camus, thus takes on a different meaning when one is completely present to it, versus always having to seek a future moment or an ulterior reality outside of one's life and reality. As he tried to demonstrate in one of his most powerful essays, 'The Myth of Sisyphus', itself a long meditation on one's choice to either embrace life or end it:

> But for a proud heart there can be no compromise. There is God or time, that cross or this sword. This world has a higher meaning that transcends its worries, or nothing is true but those worries. One must live with time and die with it, or else elude it for a greater life. [. . .] If I choose action, don't think that contemplation is like an unknown country to me. But it cannot give me everything, and, deprived of the eternal, I want to ally myself with time. I do not want to put down to my account either nostalgia or bitterness, and I merely want to see clearly.[12]

As it is, this quote focuses on the way one *can* live wholly within the present moment: by choosing to either transcend it through the varied, created notions of God that humanity has held high over the course of history or accept the world as all that there is. Living in the present moment and being aware of that moment as the only one present to us is to cultivate the capacity, some might argue, to truly be alive. It is the definition of one's being-alive in the first place. After all, 'The present, and the succession of presents before a constantly conscious soul, is the ideal of the absurd man'.[13]

To live in this place of the present moment is not a new concept. It has been looked at by many religions, in the past as in the present, as the *true* way to exist and *the* way towards a certain sense of freedom. For, as the Buddha once put it: 'There is only one time when it is essential to awaken. That time is now'. The only time one really has *is* the present (there is no time like it!), and thus Camus' argument is very simple, yet incredibly difficult to achieve. It shares in a certain religious sensibility even as it denies it. Even so, Camus pointed out that there is no separation to be made between a person and time. For the individual who accepts the absurd reality of their life, this link between their life and time is an ever-present reality: 'The absurd man is he who is not apart from time'.[14]

What is a consequence of becoming aware of time and living in the present moment? It could be said that a result of this new mindfulness is an awareness of one's limitations.[15] These are limitations, as such, that are bound in the human condition, as well as within one's reason,[16] and these are what Camus discovered to be essential in order for one to be true to one's own condition: '[. . .] we simply lack the pride of the man who is faithful to his limitations – that is, the clairvoyant love of his human condition'.[17] What does it mean when one is 'faithful to his limitations'? It means that one is able to accept how they are limited in the present moment – for example, through their limited reasoning or by their limited physical capabilities. The present moment, in return, likewise then creates certain aspects of such limitations due to the present moment itself being constricted both *within* and *by* time. When one is able to accept this position, then one is being 'faithful' to the true status of the self. These limitations are not something that need be distinguished or fled from, but something that is a part of every human reality. When it is accepted, the context of a human genuinely living in the absurd is an acceptable one. With the acceptance of one's human limitations, one can in fact end up being more connected to the reality of one's limited position. This awakening to one's limitations can in turn provide space for a more cooperative way to live with one's self, instead of striving again and again against the self by seeking to transcend it and all of its limitations.

Ethically, we are to rebel and create

'With rebellion, awareness is born.'[18] Camus is well known for his arguments made on behalf of rebellion and how, he argued, it provokes a rise in one's awareness.[19] To be aware of our state in life is a true gift. Yet, what exactly is the awareness that Camus was speaking of? Of course it was based on a notion of absurdity such as has already been shown. Despite this, however, he was not insensitive to the fact that his argument for the absurd can lead down the path of indifference. As he described the challenge of facing this temptation towards indifference, '[. . .] if all experiences are indifferent, that of duty is as legitimate as any other. One can be virtuous through a whim'.[20] It was through taking up such a position himself that he was able to argue how, even in the midst of indifference,[21] we are able to see that duty is as 'legitimate' as any other experience. It is this duty to the self that he described as being the most important reason to rebel. Once again, the crucial question arises, for how, then, is the rebel to behave when there is no transcendent being or ideological absolute against which guidelines for behaviour might be propped up?[22]

As one rebels against one's absurd position, the main purpose of this rebellion is to defend what one is. For Camus, he saw it as such: 'But one envies what one does not have, while the rebel's aim is to defend what he is. He does not merely claim some good that he does not possess or of which he was deprived. His aim is to claim recognition for something which he has and which has already been recognized in him, in almost every case, as more important than anything of which he could be envious'.[23] It is through this defense of *who* and *what* one is, that Camus, once again, located the place where one can live with a sense of integrity. In this defense, there is no attempt to conquer but rather to *impose* oneself.[24] Within such an imposition, a truth comes to light through the life and reasoning of others.[25]

For his part, Camus argued that the most effective way to revolt against one's absurd position in life is to *create*. Camus indeed focused heavily on the need to create art, because it is such a task that continuously asks of us to be present to our absurd reality. It is as such that it gives us a greater awareness:

> Elsewhere I have brought out the fact that human will had no other purpose than to maintain awareness. But that could not do without discipline. Of all the schools of patience and lucidity, creation is the most effective. It is also the staggering evidence of man's sole dignity: the dogged revolt against his condition, perseverance in an effort considered sterile. It calls for a daily effort, self-mastery, a precise estimate of the limits of truth, measure, and strength. It constitutes an *ascesis*. All that 'for nothing,' in order to repeat and mark time. But perhaps the great work of art has less importance in itself than in the ordeal it demands of a man and the opportunity it provides him of overcoming his phantoms and approaching a little closer to his naked reality.[26]

It is through one's creations in fact that one is able to understand the symbols before them, symbols moreover which, in themselves, contain the absurd. As some recent commentators on his work have put it: 'Camus's aesthetics make it clear that it is the philosophical novelist who creates "new" symbols. Yet, artists are not free to create arbitrarily. In order for symbols to achieve social significance they must be in solidarity with the pathos of the common man'.[27] This creation and constant recreation of symbols must coincide with a somewhat common or recognizable understanding of the symbols that are part of the 'pathos of the common man', thus making art an act of solidarity with others. The purpose of art is to unify people through the depictions of those symbols that come to define our shared notions of absurdity. Hence, Camus could also argue, from another angle, that the creation of art is also *not* a significant act, because it coincides with everyday existence and depicts the everyday reality of the absurd. He wrote:

> Creating is living doubly [. . .] it has no more significance than the continual and imperceptible creation in which the actor, the conqueror, and all absurd men indulge every day of their lives. All try their hands at miming, at repeating, and at re-creating the reality that is theirs. We always end up by having the appearance of our truths. All existence for a man turned away from the eternal is but a vast mime under the mask of the absurd. Creation is the great mime.[28]

Because of this, creation is not about solving anything per se, but about describing the indifference to which art itself is a victim.[29] Thus, art and the creation of art plays a vital role in the acceptance and living in of the absurd and furthermore, assists one in becoming aware of and living in the present moment and one's limitations.

Solidarity

Camus was very aware of the potential for a moral arbitrariness to arise from his thoughts on the absurd. Camus addressed this line of reasoning directly and asked accordingly, 'Is it possible to find a rule of conduct outside the realm of religion and its absolute values? That is the question raised by rebellion'.[30] After all, what is there to stop a person from killing another person, let alone oneself, if everything indeed is arbitrary? Camus was greatly intrigued by this question and thus provided an in-depth exploration of murder (and likewise, capital punishment) in his novel *The Stranger*. In the novel, Camus depicts a man who has become indifferent to his absurd position and thus his life – that ends by the guillotine – ends in 'peace': '[. . .] for the first time, in that night alive with signs and stars, I opened myself to the gentle indifference of the world. Finding it so much like myself – so like a brother, really – I felt that I had been happy and that I was happy again'.[31] Camus used the main character, Meursault, to depict what an extreme indifference to the absurd situation looks like. However, Camus' answer against this indifferent acceptance was that, through the act of rebellion, one might be able to better understand a moral perspective on murder. The rebel not only accepts his or her absurd position, but moreover, as noted above, rebels against it by acting contrary to what its own absurd conclusion of total meaninglessness might suggest.

It is through the act of rebellion that a person is able to see how there are certain identifiable judgements in the world. As Stephen Eric Bronner has summed up this idea, 'Rebellion is, for Camus, a product of human nature. It is the practical expression of outrage at injustice by anyone who has experienced the transgression of a certain limit by a master'.[32] This is the same argument that Camus made in his later work, *The Rebel*:

> Rebellion cannot exist without the feeling that, somewhere and somehow, one is right. It is in this way that the rebel slave says yes and no simultaneously. He affirms that there are limits and also that he suspects – and wishes to preserve – the existence of certain things on this side of the borderline. He demonstrates, with obstinacy, that there is something in him which 'is worth while . . .' and which must be taken into consideration.[33]

It is through this recognition of the simultaneous 'yes and no' that the consciousness of the rebel is awakened, there is then a demand[34] realized by the rebel that speaks of one's own value or of something that is 'worth while'. This foundation of value is highlighted in Sherman's point:

'Camus's argument is essentially very simple: if I do not kill myself, it must be because I accept that my own life is a necessary good; if I accept this for myself, then I must accept it for all others as well, so that if I reject suicide I also reject murder'.[35] It is through this acceptance of one's own life as good and through this realization that there is a realization that other people's lives are likewise good, that there is a solidarity that can be recognized as existing between humans. 'When he rebels, a man identifies himself with other men and so surpasses himself, and from this point of view human solidarity is metaphysical'.[36] If we are to locate something of the transcendent in Camus' writing, it would be here, at the level wherein one is able to find something 'greater' than themselves in the solidarity experienced with those around them.

The solidarity that arises out of one's rebellion against the absurdity of life was the foundation upon which Camus argued against the acceptability of murder. After all, if we are in solidarity with our neighbour against meaninglessness, then there must be some meaning in our solidarity.[37] Colin Davis, for example, writes that Camus, '[. . .] wishes to, but can never quite, expunge the fundamental insight that before all ethics is the simple desire to kill, to acquire being by annihilating what endangers my full possession of the world'.[38] Davis goes on to argue that because of this desire to kill that lies before all ethics, Camus' argument that solidarity from revolt results in a desire not to kill, is flawed. From this line of reasoning, Davis asks, 'Faced with the Other, why shouldn't I just destroy it to preserve my own being?'[39] Are we then to assume that Camus merely 'cover[ed] over' the desire to kill that lies within each person, *or* did he attempt to point to some alternative notion of ethics that in fact incorporates Davis' question?

In order to tease out some of the ethical implications that follow from such reasonings, Tal Sessler interprets Camus' work alongside the work of Emmanuel Levinas. Sessler writes: 'The revolt constitutes the Camusian ontological version of the Levinasian notion of "Otherwise than Being/Beyond Essence". It is the means through which man discovers his essence as a being that is linked to other subjects. The revolt establishes this mode of inter-subjective consciousness and is exemplified by solidarity'.[40] In his argument, Sessler points out how Camus' thesis is one that promotes an 'inter-subjective consciousness' and thus argues along the same lines of the Levinasian understanding of how we can be said to dwell in a state 'Otherwise than Being'. This solidarity with the Other was where, Sessler argues, Camus found a reason to not murder. Against Davis' argument, Sessler believes that Camus' reason for not murdering is an awareness of the Other through our shared solidarity in revolt. Sessler's argument in this respect certainly goes along with a point mentioned earlier, that Camus located a specific consciousness within the solidarity of rebellion.

According to Sessler, it seems that Camus did address the question of one's desire to kill insofar as it goes beyond the realm of ethics, and he did so through a positing of an inter-subjective reality *of* the other who is encountered in one's solidarity with them. Further, I would argue, Camus also addressed the topic of murder by incorporating the notions of time and limitation into his work. If one is living with a greater awareness of time and their limitations, then one knows that every action performed is done within one's own limitations and thus the judgement of taking another person's life, if it were through the death penalty or through murder,[41] is done with a limited reasoning in a particular moment of time (where the next moment might not be filled with the same desire to murder as was the moment immediately preceding it). The notion of being present to a moment within time allows one to become present to one's own existence *within* that moment of time. This is also what creates the potential for one to become aware of the Other's presence within that same moment. Hence, the awareness of one's own limitations and the other within a moment of time – instead of what Davis had argued was a reason to murder another – might also be interpreted as a reason not to murder. Further, Davis' question as to why one should not just destroy the other in order to 'preserve' one's own being, could be looked at from a Girardian[42] notion of mimesis, for example: if one wants to destroy another, and truly believes that this destruction will preserve the self, then one must perceive the other as being in the way of one's own preservation, or having something which the self does not have. If one is aware of one's limitations, and at the same time one's desire for self-preservation (based on a perception of the self as something *to be* preserved and the other as *threatening* such an attempt at preservation), the result then is an understanding of how destroying the other offers only a limited perspective based on certain false conceptions of self-preservation. Out of this argument it is possible to subsequently trace Camus' thoughts and note, once again, how both art and the creation of art, functions in his thinking. After all, it is through the awareness of one's limitations and, furthermore, constrictions within the present moment of time, that one is asked to create in order to depict symbolic realities in the world. Furthermore, this is to create relationships with others from out of a perspective of being in solidarity with the Other.

Conclusion

The founder of the Catholic Worker Movement Dorothy Day, once remarked, 'Don't call me a saint. I don't want to be dismissed so easily'. In many ways, Camus would seem to fit alongside just such a perspective. Through his refusal to seek a transcendent being and his devotion to an acceptance of the absurdity within life, Camus not only did not categorize himself along the lines of a saint, he, in fact, would have found the notion itself to be more or less *absurd*.

However, Camus also asks individuals to be willing to take the more difficult road: one of an acceptance of the state of absurdity. Along this road, individuals are asked to live *in* the moment, accept their limitations, rebel against the absurd and create, all in order to continuously be active in life and to attempt to look at and interpret the symbols around them. This, in and of itself, is a difficult decision to make. If one chooses to walk down this path then it can provide the individual with an affirmation of oneself that is connected with a responsible action to the self and to others. If one feels 'called' to this lifestyle, then there are plenty of challenges that lie ahead in one's life, but there is also a certain 'saintly' aspect to be found in this decision to live in the present moment.

There is a great struggle in deciding to live out the Camusian perspective and that is why, for the most part, this state is rejected rather than accepted. However, as Camus himself put it: 'Conquerors know that action is in itself useless. There is but one useful action, that of remaking man and the earth. I shall never remake men. But one must do "as if". For the path of struggle leads me to the flesh. Even humiliated, the flesh is my only certainty. I can live only on it. The creature is my native land. This is why I have chosen this absurd and ineffectual effort. This is why I am on the side of the struggle'.[43] To be sure, Camus did not align himself with the traditional portraiture of 'the saint'. His determination to accept the hard path of rebellion against the absurdity of life, however, brought him to a clearer understanding of the limitations of oneself and the importance of the present moment in time, truly important aspects of reality that lay at the heart of every human being – including the saints among us. Through such an understanding, Camus was able to pinpoint the importance of how one must live in rebellion as well as the necessity for creation within a determined way of living. To create and remake 'man on earth', in the here and now, is truly an artistic venture, and likewise, something of a saintly calling.

Notes

1   David Sherman, *Camus* (Oxford: Wiley-Blackwell, 2009), p. 2.
2   In an interview with Jeanine Delpech, on 15 November 1945, Camus stated: 'No, I am not an existentialist. [. . .] the only book of ideas that I have published, *The Myth of Sisyphus*, was directed against the so-called existentialist philosophers'. Albert Camus, *Lyrical and Critical Essays* (ed. Philip Thody, trans. Ellen Conroy Kennedy, New York: Vintage, 1970), p. 345. Further, Todd Olivier notes the difference in thought between Camus and Sartre: 'Camus and Sartre both wanted a new, more humane social order, but Sartre remained a violent revolutionary in theory, while Camus was a man in revolt who rejected revolutionary excess, whether Jacobin or Communist in origin'. Todd Olivier, *Albert Camus: A Life* (trans. Benjamin Ivry, New York: Knopf, 1997), p. 310.
3   Further, Camus describes the absurd as: '[. . .] in a universe suddenly divested of illusions and lights, man feels an alien, a stranger. His exile is without

remedy since he is deprived of the memory of a lost home or the hope of a promised land. This divorce between man and his life, the actor and his setting, is properly the feeling of absurdity. All healthy men having thought of their own suicide, it can be seen, without further explanation, that there is a direct connection between this feeling and the longing for death'. Albert Camus, *The Myth of Sisyphus and Other Essays* (trans. Justin O'Brien, New York: Vintage, 1991), p. 6, and 'The absurd is essentially a divorce. It lies in neither of the elements compared; it is born of their confrontation. In this particular case and on the plane of intelligence, I can therefore say that the Absurd is not in man (if such a metaphor could have a meaning) nor in the world, but in their presence together. For the moment it is the only bond uniting them' (p. 30).

4 Fernando Pessoa, *The Book of Disquiet* (London: Penguin, 2002), p. 27.

5 Camus, *Myth of Sisyphus*, p. 41.

6 This idea was interestingly depicted in his work *The Stranger*, where Camus describes the character of Maman as an example of living in the absurd: 'While not an atheist, Maman had never in her life given a thought to religion'. Albert Camus, *The Stranger* (trans. Matthew Ward, New York: Vintage, 1988), p. 6.

7 Albert Camus, *The Plague* (trans. Stuart Gilbert, New York: Vintage, 1972), p. 121.

8 Alice Walker, *The Color Purple* (Toronto: Women's Press, 1983), p. 39.

9 Camus, *Plague*, p. 237.

10 Ibid., p. 236.

11 Camus, *Myth of Sisyphus*, p. 50.

12 Ibid., p. 86.

13 Ibid., p. 64.

14 Ibid., p. 72.

15 'What, in fact, is the absurd man? He who, without negating it, does nothing for the eternal. Not that nostalgia is foreign to him. But he prefers his courage and his reasoning. The first teaches him to live *without appeal* and to get along with what he has; the second informs him of his limits. Assured of his temporally limited freedom, of his revolt devoid of future, and of his mortal consciousness, he lives out his adventure within the span of his lifetime'. Ibid., p. 66.

16 'In this ravaged world in which the impossibility of knowledge is established [. . .]'. Ibid., p. 25.

17 Camus, *Lyrical*, p. 152.

18 Albert Camus, *The Rebel: An Essay on Man in Revolt* (trans. Anthony Bower, New York: Vintage, 1991), p. 15.

19 Camus wrote: 'Rebellion, though apparently negative, since it creates nothing, is profoundly positive in that it reveals the part of man which must always be defended'. Ibid., p. 19. Camus also noted that: 'Accepting the absurdity of everything around us is one step, a necessary experience: it should not become a dead end. It arouses a revolt that can become fruitful. An analysis of the idea of revolt could help us to discover ideas capable of restoring a relative meaning to existence, although a meaning that would always be in danger'. Camus, *Lyrical*, p. 346.

20 Camus, *Myth of Sisyphus*, p. 67.

21 Camus pointed out that: 'All I can do is reply on my own behalf, realizing that what I say is relative. Accepting the absurdity of everything around us is one step, a necessary experience: it should not become a dead end. It arouses a revolt that can become fruitful. An analysis of the idea of revolt could help us to discover ideas capable of restoring a relative meaning to existence, although a meaning that would always be in danger'. Camus, *Lyrical*, p. 346.

22 Camus questioned, 'Is it possible to find a rule of conduct outside the realm of religion and its absolute values? That is the question raised by rebellion'. Camus, *Rebel*, p. 21.

23 Ibid., p. 17.

24 Regarding integrity, Camus wrote: 'He is fighting for the integrity of one part of his being. He does not try, primarily, to conquer, but simply to impose'. Ibid., p. 18.

25 Camus further explores this idea by writing: 'The only truth that might seem instructive to him is not formal: it comes to life and unfolds in men. The absurd mind cannot so much expect ethical rules at the end of its reasoning as, rather, illustrations and the breath of human lives'. Camus, *Myth of Sisyphus*, p. 68.

26 Ibid., p. 115.

27 Cecil L. Eubanks and Peter A. Petrakis, 'Reconstructing the World: Albert Camus andthe Symbolization of Experience', *The Journal of Politics* 61:2 (1999), pp. 293–312, p. 304.

28 Camus, *Myth of Sisyphus*, p. 94.

29 'For the absurd man it [creation] is not a matter of explaining and solving, but of experiencing and describing. Everything begins with lucid indifference'. Ibid., p. 94.

30 Camus, *Rebel*, p. 21.

31 Camus, *Stranger*, pp. 122–23.

32 Stephen Eric Bronner, *Camus: Portrait of a Moralist* (Chicago: University of Chicago Press, 1999), pp. 81–82.

33 Camus, *Rebel*, p. 13.

34 Regarding the demand of the awakened conscious of the rebel, Camus pointed out that: 'Despair, like the absurd, has opinions and desires about everything in general and nothing in particular. Silence expresses this attitude very well. But from the moment that the rebel finds his voice – even though he says nothing but "no" – he begins to desire and to judge. The rebel, in the etymological sense, does a complete turnabout'. Ibid., p. 14.

35 Sherman, *Camus*, p. 111.

36 Camus, *Rebel*, p. 17.

37 In his earlier work, such as *The Myth of Sisyphus*, Camus looks at the relevance of suicide. In his later work, he delves more heavily into the function of murder. Davis sums up Camus' argument as follows: 'Camus's argument is essentially very simple: if I do not kill myself, it must be because I accept that my own life is a necessary good; if I accept this for myself, then I must accept it for all others as well, so that if I reject suicide I also reject murder'. Colin Davis, 'Violence and Ethics in Camus', *The Cambridge Companion to Camus* (ed. Edward J. Hughes, Cambridge: Cambridge University Press, 2007), p. 111. David Sherman shows how the turn from the focus of suicide to murder, occurred in Camus' work: 'Camus believes that with [his] turn from the theoretical to the practical, the question of the Absurd turns into a question of

rebellion, and concomitantly, the question of suicide turns into a question of murder'. Sherman, *Camus*, p. 140.

38   Ibid., p. 116.

39   Ibid.

40   Tal Sessler, *Levinas and Camus: Humanism for the Twenty-first Century* (London: Continuum, 2008), p. 60.

41   'Yes, everything is simple. It's men who complicate things. Don't let them say about the man condemned to death: "He is going to pay his debt to society," but: "They're going to chop his head off." It may seem like nothing. But it does make a little difference. There are some people who prefer to look their destiny straight in the eye'. Camus, *Lyrical*, p. 39.

42   'Girard's anthropology focuses first on *desire* and its consequences. He calls it "mimetic desire" or "mimesis". It's desire that comes into being through imitation of others. These others we imitate Girard calls "models," models of desire. He has also used the word "mediators," because they are "go-betweens," acting as agents between the individual imitating them and the world'. James G. Williams, 'Forward' to René Girard, *I See Satan Fall Like Lightning* (New York: Orbis, 2001), p. ix. In Girard's own words, 'In mimetic desire (see Mimesis) the tendency is for the relationship between subject and model to become one of conflictual, potentially destructive rivalry'. René Girard, *The Girard Reader* (New York: Crossroad Herder, 1996), p. 290.

43   Camus, *Myth of Sisyphus*, p. 87. Camus further looks at this idea in his work *Resistance, Rebellion, and Death* (trans. Justin O'Brien, New York: Vintage, 1974), p. 141.

3

Levinas: Of God: Who Comes to Mind?

Michael Purcell

I said to the almond tree, 'Sister, speak to me of God'. And the almond tree blossomed.

N. KAZANTZAKIS, *Report to Greco*

The notion of 'blossoming' is reminiscent of Heidegger's approach to phenomenology. A phenomenon is that which shows itself, and '*which shows itself in itself*'.[1] Heidegger uses the notion of 'blossoming' to exemplify *physis* which 'says what emerges from itself (for example, the emergence, the blossoming, of a rose), the unfolding that opens itself up, the coming-into-appearance in such unfolding, and holding itself and persisting in appearance – in short, the emerging-abiding sway'.[2] Levinas uses the same notion when speaking of God revealing himself *kath'auto*, or 'according to itself'.[3] However, the relationship with God as God is in God's self is never direct, but is only by way of an other person and enacted in ethical relations. One question to be addressed is the status of this other person, and the notion of Incarnation. The question is a re-phrasing of Levinas' title *Of God Who Comes to Mind* as *Of God: Who Comes to Mind?*

Levinas and holiness

Of God: Who comes to mind? Levinas' work, *De Dieu qui vient à l'idée* (*Of God Who Comes to Mind*)[4] gathers together various texts relating to Immanence, God and Being. The question which is being enquired of here is *Of God? Who Comes to Mind?* (De Dieu? Qui vient à l'idée?) How does God – how can God – become a phenomenon in this world? How does the Holy One appear in the world?

In the sanctoral cycle of the Christian liturgy, there is yet to be a memorial day dedicated to Levinas. Among which group of the holy would we classify him? Among the teachers and doctors of the church? Among those who suffer martyrdom? Among those who spend their lives in the service of the poor and the stranger, the widow and orphan? Among those who have a concern for the education of the youth? Or, among those who (seemingly) withdraw from the world and are caught up in mystical encounter? Somehow or other, the *communio sanctorum* has some relation to the divine, however that is to be conceived or enacted. Levinas is an unlikely candidate for canonization. How can one canonize an atheist? Or might one think holiness otherwise, if holiness might indeed be thought?

Levinas' metaphysical atheism

The atheism of which Levinas writes is not to be confused with the foolishness of the fool who 'has said in his heart "There is no God"'.[5] Rather, what Levinas is contesting is the notion of a theism which would attempt to comprehend and conceptualize God. This metaphysical atheism is an a-theism. Further, Levinas wants to ask where God makes his dwelling among men and women. Where and how is God to be found in this world in which we dwell as pilgrims and strangers? The relation of the atheist to the absolute is a welcoming of the absolute which is 'purified of the violence of the sacred'.[6] Peperzaak points to the God whom Levinas refuses, when he writes that 'the keystone of all systems by Western philosophy has always been a being that simultaneously was origin, support, end, and horizon of the existing universe'. God was autarch and self-sufficient, and although not to be equated with Being, nonetheless God as such was clothed in ontological garb. 'This God is not the God of Levinas'.[7]

In *Totality and Infinity*, Levinas addresses the question of metaphysical and human transcendence. The absolute, or the holy one, who in his infinity is absolutely separate or distanced (i.e. holy) dwells in the heights, and so the human cannot directly attain the divine. The only access to God, as Levinas will constantly stress, is by way of the human. However, for Levinas, the other person also occupies a dimension of height, and that height is ethical before ever it is geometrical. The space that we inhabit is an ethical space. Only in relation to the ethical space we inhabit can we order things in relation to self and other, and so gain access to the God who is inaccessible in God's self.

Now, it is this very notion of separation which makes possible and sustains the metaphysical relation with the absolute, for it is in separation that there is the possibility of transcendence towards the other, while yet assuring the absolution of the self and the other from the relation. Separation, Levinas argues in *Totality and Infinity*, is the first movement of transcendence. Separation, further, is also the condition of discourse: one speaks across the gap that separates the one from the other. Implicated in the distance between the human and God is metaphysical atheism. 'Only an atheist being can relate himself to the other and already *absolve himself* from this relation'.[8] What is being excluded is any notion of participation of the one in the other, and any notion of a mythical religion. A religion without myths is an adult relation and marks the 'dawn of humanity'. Indeed, '[a]theism conditions a veritable relationship with a true God *kath'auto*',[9] that is, with God as he truly is in himself. However, one must not distinguish the relation with God *kath'auto* from the relationship with the other person (*autrui*)[10] too readily or quickly. The true relation with God is enacted in the ethical relation with the other person, who is the sole point of access to God. Access to God as God is in God's self cannot be 'accomplished in the ignorance of men and things'.[11] The relation with the divine departs from a human face and social relations through enigmatic solicitation and appeal.

Now, ethical height meets its counterpart in ontological destitution. In other words, in his or her appeal to me, the other person occupies a position of ethical appeal and injunction and so is ethically above me; yet, this ethical appeal often is most strikingly (in the literal sense of being struck by a blow) articulated from an other person's situation of poverty and destitution and so looks up from the dust and appeals to me. The ethical injunction of doing no harm or *Tu ne me tueras point* which comes forth from on high is encountered in the very poverty and destitution of the poor, the widow, the outcast and the orphan. Ethically, this translates into the principles of beneficence and benevolence or the contraries of non-maleficence and non-malevolence. First, do no harm (*Primum, non nocere*). Violence is always an ethical transgression, without exception. Of course, ethical injunctions do not *necessarily* translate into ontological commitments: I can still kill you.

Ethical metaphysics as responsibility for the other person

But let us go further:

> The atheism of the metaphysician means, positively, that our relation with the Metaphysical is an ethical behaviour and not theology, not a thematisation, be it a knowledge by analogy, of the attributes of God. God rises to his supreme and ultimate presence as correlative to the justice rendered unto men.[12]

Again,

> God is drawn out of objectivity, presence and being. He is neither an
> object nor an interlocutor. His absolute remoteness, his transcendence,
> turns into my responsibility – non-erotic par-excellence – for the other.
> And this analysis implies that God is not simply the 'first other,' the 'other
> par excellence,' or the 'absolute other,' but other than the other [*autre
> q'autrui*], other otherwise, other with an alterity prior to the alterity
> of the other, prior to the ethical bond with an other and different from
> every neighbour, transcendent to the point of absence, to the point of
> possible confusion with the stirring of the *there is*. In this confusion the
> substitution for the neighbour gains dis-interestedness, that is, in nobility,
> and the transcendence of the Infinite arises in glory.[13]

By referring to the 'there is' (*il y a*), Levinas is pointing to the fact that
God, whose name is unutterable, is anonymous, and is accessible only in
justice rendered to the incarnate other; ethics becomes a spiritual optics. 'The
Other (*autrui*) is the very locus of metaphysical truth, and is indispensable
to any relation with God'.[14] However, this incarnate other person 'is not
the incarnation of God'.[15] God yet remains God, transcendent to the point
of absence, but the other person, in his or her very approach to me, is the
locus of God's revelation. In the face of the other person, the trace of God is
inscribed as an immemorial and irrecuperable past, but inscribed, as it were,
with invisible ink that can only be read in the ethical relation with the other
person. In this relationship with the other person, the self or ego is excluded
from determining the ethical scope of the relation; rather the self is obedient
in the face of the other and becomes determined by the other as responsible
for the other. The self is put on the spot, like a rabbit reduced to passivity
when caught by the headlights of an oncoming car. Insofar as the ethical
relation is the way towards God, the ethical relation is a religious relation.
'Everything that cannot be reduced to an interhuman relation represents not
the superior form but the forever primitive form of religion'.[16] For Levinas,
then, the religious relation is reducible to ethics, but reducible to a relation
with an irreducible other person who sustains the relation while yet giving
access to God.

Now, in this logic of relations which defies logic, God is like an excluded
third. It is the other person, the one, for example, who elects to sit beside me
in an empty train compartment, who places me in the awkward predicament
of having to decide whether to speak in welcome, or to continue to occupy
my own place in the sun and look out of the window or become even more
immersed in my newspaper. By occupying my physical space, this space
becomes an ethical space of response and responsibility, and in the simple
gesture of acknowledging the other person, and doing justice to his or her
presence, God enters into the relation between the one and the other as a
distant excluded third.

But this other person is no avatar of God, for God, inhabiting an immemorial past, cannot be a present. God has always passed away, not as in a Nietzschean death of God philosophy, but rather as remote from being and its attributes, and accessible only in mature ethical relations which are the mark of the human and the mark of adult religion. God cannot be recuperated other than in the human. 'That responsibility and justice exists is due to "him" but the unnameable can neither present himself in time nor be represented as a Presence in an other, supernatural, or heavenly world outside the real one. As always already passed away, God is an abyss, not a ground (*archē*), a foundation, a support, or a substance but "he" who left a trace in *an*archical responsibility'.[17] Levinas himself notes that God is (im)precisely the condition of possibility of ethical interaction as the *excluded third* in the relationship between oneself and an other person. The alterity of the other person is sustained by the trace of illeity inscribed in the face, the authorial inscription of which is always anonymous and nameless.

In short, God is accessible in the justice I render to my neighbour because in the opening of illeity I find the trace of God. God, as pre-originary, God as excluded third, is the very condition of the possibility of the beyond. However, in transcendence (which has no 'theological presuppositions'),[18] 'the distinction between transcendence towards the other man and transcendence towards God must not be made too quickly'.[19] The other person (*autrui*) 'is indispensable for my relation with God',[20] for there can be no knowledge of, or access to, God outwith the social relation, whose trace both remains and is effaced in the face of the other person.

An infinite conversation

Separation is the first movement of transcendence. Separation allows the 'banal fact of conversation' or discourse, which is 'the marvel of marvels'.[21] Discourse, which the distance between the one and the other makes possible, is also the possibility of a non-allergic and non-violent relation with the other person. Discourse itself involves interruption. One pauses before the other person and before responding. Indeed only before the person is there the possibility of my uttering a word of welcome and response. This pausing in the face of the other person has both a physical and a phenomenological aspect: in conversation, which is not a dual monologue, one must always of necessity pause for breath, which is the possibility of the intervention of the other into the self-same. The consistency and separate existence of the self is overturned by the very need to breathe. Having to inhale is the very interruption of my monologue and the possibility of traversing the gap between myself and the other person who, while part of the conversation, remains infinitely separate. Phenomenologically, what is inhaled is a 'who'. Thus, conversation is also infinite for the other person is not reducible to the dialogue, but is constantly absolving himself or herself from the dialogical relation which he or she nonetheless makes possible and sustains.

Speech is both a unifying and absolving encounter that defies formal logic. While each dialogue presupposes a general language in which words and concepts are expressed or indicated, within each dialogue or conversation with the other person, translation is always approximate. I cannot translate either what the other person has said or the very saying of the other person into my own framework of comprehension. In the very fact of being other, the other person is incomprehensible. The dialogical relation between me and the other person is an asymmetric *entre-nous*, in which I am more recipient, receptive and obedient, than in control. Speech 'accomplishes a relation between terms that break up the unity of a genus' and in which 'the terms, as interlocutors absolve themselves from the relation, or remain absolute within the relation'. It may be that language is 'the very power to break the continuity of being or of history' and may be eschatological in intent. Conversation speaks of what is yet-to-come.[22] Levinas acknowledges that the whole of *Totality and Infinity* 'aims to show a relation with the other not only cutting across the logic of contradiction, where the other of A is the non-A, the negation of A, but also across dialectical logic, where the same dialectically participates and is reconciled with the other in the Unity of the system'.[23]

The grammar of assent (declining the other)

There are two senses in which one can decline the other person: one can refuse the other person in an act which is essentially and ultimately violent, or one can decline the other in the sense of grammatically declining a noun. If the other person occupies the space of ethical height in his or her very destitution, the self must not only ascend to the other but assent to the other person and receive, like the Torah, the law *from* the other. In a remarkable few sentences in *Ethics and Spirit*, Levinas declines or refuses the subject of modernity and declines the subject ethically. The nominative self, understood as origin, agency, freedom, and reason, is displaced. Instead, to speak and to know the other person involves self-disclosure. The other person is greeted (*salué*). He or she not only becomes the subject (nominative) but is also invoked. 'To put it in grammatical terms, the Other (*autrui*) does not appear in the nominative, but in the vocative'.[24] Then, in a cascade of declension, one becomes *for* the other person in responsibility, *to* the other person in transcendence, and ultimately one is rendered as both accusative and accused *by* the other person. The emergence of subjectivity is *of* and *from* the other. In short, 'a *self* [*moi*] can exist which is not *myself* [*moi-même*]'.[25] Human autonomy rests restlessly on the supreme heteronomy of the other person, and ultimately on God who is absolutely Other than the other person. Levinas refers to Aquinas on causality, but one should pause here, for, like Levinas, Aquinas' leap from argument to origin does not achieve God.

Rather, 'and this all people call God'.[26] In his five ways, Aquinas manages to keep God out of the equation, yet always on the fringes or just beyond, there is something like an excluded third who nonetheless sustains the argument and conversation.

The religious relation

Now, the ethical relation is a religious relation. The ethical relation in its very exceptionality does not compromise the sovereignty of the *I* but rather institutes and invests in it. The other person is not '*a new edition of myself*', but, from the paradoxical confusion of ethical height and destitution, is the place and time at which contact with God is made possible. 'The moral relation [. . .] reunites both self-consciousness and the consciousness of God. Ethics is not the corollary of the vision of God, it is that very vision. Ethics is an optic [. . .].'[27] Divine ethics is not given in the indicative but in the imperative, like a commandment. 'To know God is to know what must be done'.[28] Moses, as the archetypal bearer of the Law, who, like Abraham setting out for an unknown Land, offered to the people of Israel at Sinai what was not his own but what had been given by an other, and what was given was inscribed as Law (Torah). God revealed himself at Sinai in a series of commands rather than as presence. It is no accident that the Torah refers to God initially, and then, without pause, moves on to human relations. Theology and ethics are co-implicated, and ethics is the beginning and the culmination of theology. 'God never came down from Sinai, Moses never ascended to heaven. But God folded back the heavens like a cover, covered Sinai with it, and so found himself on earth without having even left heaven. Here is the desacralisation of the Sacred'.[29] The way to God is not other than the way of the human, through the cultivation and acquisition of the *habitus* or habit of *doing the good* through the rigour of daily ritual and practice. 'The way that leads to God therefore *ipso facto* – and not in addition – to man; and the way that leads to man draws us back to ritual discipline and self-regulation. It lies in its daily regularity'.[30] Levinas illustrates this with three Talmudic opinions which condense the whole of the Torah:

- Ben Zoma: 'I have found a verse that contains the whole Torah: "Listen Israel, the Lord is our God, the Lord is One"'.
- Ben Namus: 'I have found a verse that contains the whole of the Torah: "You will love your neighbour as yourself"'.
- Ben Pazi: 'I have found a verse that contains the whole of the Torah: "You will sacrifice a lamb in the morning and another at dusk"'.[31]

And the Rabbi said, 'the law is according to Ben Pazi'. Levinas comments that the second opinion indicates how the first is true, and third indicates the practical condition of the second.

Levinas as theologian

Levinas mistrusts both theoretical and mystical approaches to God. Yet, in 'The Awakening of I', he recognizes the human quality and attitude of holiness or sanctity. 'Holiness is [. . .] the supreme perfection, and I am not saying that all humans are saints! [. . .] The holiness which cedes one's place to the other becomes possible in humanity. And there is something divine in this appearance of the human capable of thinking of another before thinking of oneself'.[32] I become holy by recognizing the holiness of the other person, in whose face the Holy One is traced. Jacques Derrida in *The Work of Mourning* recalls a conversation with Levinas on the Rue Michel Ange: 'You know, one often speaks of ethics to describe what I do, but what really interests me in the end is not ethics, not ethics alone, but the holy, the holiness of the holy'.[33] So, Levinas is not a dogmatician or a systematician or a mystic, but is one immersed in the human world which is ethical.

Is Levinas a theologian? Well, fundamentally, yes. In the 'Preface' to the second edition of *Of God Who Comes to Mind*, Levinas comments:

> We have often been reproached for ignoring theology; and we do not contest the necessity of a recovery, at least, the necessity of choosing an opportunity for a recovery of these themes. We think, however, that theological recuperation comes after the glimpse of holiness, which is primary.[34]

There is 'an original ethical event which would also be first theology',[35] and which is revealed in the awakening to responsibility *for* the other person. In short, theology is both ethical in intent and origin, and is inspired by the ability to receive a revelation from and of the other person. All theology is first and foremost fundamental and practical theology, and it begins as an ethical enterprise.

An avatar of Incarnation?

For Levinas, the possibility of an Incarnation is problematical. For Christianity, Incarnation is crucial for theology. Incarnation leads to a cross, and then on to resurrection. Faith casts an analeptic glance to its origins. Like thought, which is always now, yet discovers a history which cannot be recuperated, faith is a faith in an other person who inhabits an antecedent past, forever immemorial. One cannot think the other person. But one can have faith in an other person. One receives the other person as gift and grace and promise. Nonetheless, the thought that a God might become human is intriguing, both foolish and scandalous thinking for both Jew and Greek. Incarnation implicates an avatar. Could a God ever reach down from the heavens and not only touch what is human but become fully

enfleshed as human and yet remain a God? How might a God fully reveal
God's self other than in or as the incarnate human, and without becoming
an avatar?

This is a problem that exercised the early Christian community which, for
its part, could not conceive of a God-Man (*Un Dieu-homme*). To counter
second-century Docetic and Gnostic tendencies that claimed that Christ
'was no more than a simple "appearance" (*dokēsis*) of a human body', early
Christian reflection had to consider the appearing of the infinite *in* the finite, or
the more in the less. Incarnation was a scandal. Thus, for Docetism, salvation
and redemption concerned the soul, not the body.[36] Thus, one finds in the
post-resurrection Johannine community's account of the appearance of the
risen Jesus an emphasis on the reality of the flesh of Christ. Thomas, who
doubts, is invited to place his fingers in the fleshly wounds of the risen Christ.[37]
The disciples on the shore eat with the Jesus who appears to them.[38] For
Irenaeus and Tertullian, the reality of Incarnation is the central issue concerning
salvation: 'the flesh is the hinge of salvation' (*caro cardo autem salutis*).[39]

At first, this would seem to have a resonance with the notion of incarnate
existence and its accompanying responsibility for the other person, while yet
avoiding the notion of a divine avatar who, like a sacrificial lamb displaces
that personal and unique responsibility by which personal subjectivity is
specifically defined. But it gets even more complicated: does the notion
of a God-Man in the fleshy commingling of the divine and the human
not run the risk of the heresy of Adoptionism in which Jesus is more or
less the equivalent of the 'local lad who did good'. Lafont suggests that
Adoptionism is more 'a (permanent) temptation of theology than a heresy'
in which it is difficult to reconcile how God 'while remaining God' might
introduce a creature 'within the mystery of divine generation'.[40] 'Christ [. . .]
remains a creature who has been adopted and chosen' with all its Trinitarian
implications (the voice of the Father, the descent of the Spirit in the form of
a dove and the person of Jesus immersed in the Jordan).[41] The Council of
Ephesus (431), in order to counter Nestorius, affirmed Mary as Theotokos
rather than as only Christotokos, and the coming together of the divine and
the human in Incarnation. The theological history of the possibility of a
God-Man has been a history of heresy, and a struggle for orthodoxy. In such
a struggle of mind and imagination, how far can we go with Levinas and
his fundamentally theological and phenomenological insights? In short, Of
God? Who Comes to Mind?

The possibility of a God-Man
(*un Dieu-Homme*)?

Levinas, in *Entre Nous*, considers the possibility of a God-Man (*Un
Dieu-Homme*) in terms of an ethics of responsibility, which takes its

point of departure from the human. God, whose name is unutterable in itself, is only signified and accessible in the ethical relation. Access to the divine is always by way of the human. Even though revelation may have a divine origin, 'the first word of revelation' is human,[42] though this only comes as an afterthought, and involves a careful phenomenological and fundamentally theological reduction.[43] The phenomenological challenge, which theology cannot ignore, is that 'philosophy is a bringing to light' (*phaneisthai*), a blossoming of *physis* in which what gives itself gives itself as itself and from itself (*kath'auto*) but this makes the appearance or the Incarnation of a God-Man – 'the mystery of mysteries' – both paradoxical and scandalous, an affront to the transcendence of the divine. Levinas comments,

> The problem of the Man-God [*Le Dieu-Homme*] includes the idea of self-inflicted humiliation on the part of the Supreme Being, of a descent of the Creator to the level of the Creature; that is to say, an absorption of the most active activity into the most passive passivity.

However,

> The problem includes, as if brought about by this passivity pushed to its ultimate degree in the Passion, the idea of expiation for others, that is, of a substitution. The identical par excellence, the noninterchangeable, the unique par excellence, would be substitution itself.[44]

The cross, and the notion of God subjecting himself and being subjected to a cross, is a further aspect of the scandal of Incarnation. How can the impassable God experience crucifixion and death? Yet, the passion and the ability of Jesus to die 'for-the-other', which reinforces the inversion of activity and passivity, as Levinas suggests, is a human possibility.

To link passion and passivity rather than to stress action and activity is to redefine subjectivity as a unique and irreplaceable responsibility. This, of course, is a constant theme in Levinas, linked as it is to notions of expiation and substitution. One is no long *pour soi* but *pour l'autre*, where the other (*autre*) is always an other person (*autrui*). Whereas for Heidegger, death was Dasein's unique defining moment, for no one can take my place in death or substitute himself or herself for me, Levinas transfigures the uniqueness of the self in terms of substitution, expiation and responsibility. To substitute myself 'for-the-other-person', even to the point of death, is my unique responsibility which I cannot vicariously surrender to anyone else. Responsibility 'for-the-other' translates the nominative I into an accusative and accused me. Expiation therefore involves substituting oneself for the other, even to the point of being wounded and dying for the other in the flesh, and is 'indispensable to the comprehension of subjectivity'.[45] But might this also point to, in a way difficult to discern, the possibility of divine condescension and the humility of the divine in Incarnation? Levinas writes,

> I think that the humility of God, up to a certain point, allows for conceiving the relationship with transcendence in terms other than those of naïveté or pantheism; and that the idea of substitution – in a certain modality – is indispensable to the comprehension of subjectivity.[46]

The notion of condescension, or the humiliation, of the divine in the human further re-casts humanity as humility, which is a 'way of being'. But, unlike the divine who chose to be humble, I do not choose to be humble. I alone am both humbled and humiliated when faced with the depth of the plight of the other and the ethical demand that this imposes upon me from an ethical height. The order of my universe is shaken and disturbed. I cannot send a scapegoat into the desert and visit on it my guilt and my responsibility.[47] 'Humility and poverty are a bearing within being – an ontological (or meontological) mode – and not a social condition. To present oneself in this poverty of the exile is to interrupt the coherence of the universe'.[48]

Yet, the scandal of Incarnation persists.
　　Can the God who humbles himself to 'dwell with the contrite and the humble' (Isaiah 57:17), the God 'of the stranger, the widow, and the orphan', the God manifesting Himself in the world through His covenant with that which is excluded from the world – can He, in his excessiveness, become a present in the time of the world?[49]

For Levinas, God in himself cannot be a present in the time of the world for He is always immemorial, a perpetual past which can neither be presented or represented, for there is 'the original anteriority or the original ultimacy of God in relation to a world which cannot accommodate Him'. This does not mean that God is absent from the world. Rather, there is an incarnate proximity of God in 'the countenance of my fellowmen',[50] and this involves an adult religion. 'God is real and concrete not through incarnation but through Law'.[51]
　　How does one make sense of this? This might no longer be Levinas.
　　For Levinas, ethics becomes the source of access to God. An Incarnation, in the Christian sense of the 'word made flesh' or a 'God-Man' would be a vicarious displacement of responsibility, and a refusal of adult religiosity. Though the other person is the 'the locus of metaphysical truth, and is indispensable for my relation with God',[52] the other person 'does not play the role of mediator' nor is the other person 'the incarnation of God'. The face of the other person, in its summons to responsibility, is 'disincarnate' and yet this is the 'height in which God is revealed'.[53] 'Human autonomy rests on a supreme heteronomy'.[54] The ethical structure of human existence with its notions of passivity and responsibility is the condition of any theology.

A disincarnate other person?

Now, if God *kath'auto* cannot appear in human form in an incarnate avatar, Levinas notes that the other person is also disincarnate in that the other person reveals himself or herself in a face which, if it is to be an absolute ethical summons to responsibility, goes beyond space and time, although appearing in space and time. In 'Ethics and Infinity'[55] Levinas points out that one is only in a truly ethical relation with the other person when physical features are not recognized. The face is not physiognomical but ethical. One can understand why Levinas speaks of the other person as disincarnate. In 'Meaning and Sense', Levinas remarks that '[s]ignification is situated before Culture and Aesthetics; it is situated in Ethics, presupposition of all Culture and signification [. . . and . . .] it is extremely important to stress the anteriority of sense with regard to cultural signs'.[56] Meaning is both a-cultural and a-historical because ethical significance of this other (any other and all others) – who is constitutive of my subjectivity – is prior to any cultural or historical form in which he or she might be clothed. 'The face is abstract' but with an abstraction that moves 'from the particular to the general'. 'The face presents itself in its nakedness'.[57] The face is not hidden behind some concealing form by which it would become significant and find its place in a world of significance. Rather, the face signifies from and by itself rather than through any form. The face of the other person signifies *kath'auto*. Its meaning and identity are its own.

Thus, the ethical relation must transcend all relations of gender, age, race, culture, religion and politics. To classify or categorize the other person runs the risk of the inclusion and exclusion which accompanies totalitarian politics and risks the danger and tragedy of the Holocaust. Genocide remains a reality. Thus is found the exclusion of the stranger, the migrant, the refugee, the homeless and the dispossessed. The national and international erection and strengthening of borders to maintain the security of the same by the exclusion of the other is evidence of this: as one wall fell in Berlin in 1989, other physical, social, cultural and religious walls and fences were being constructed on the basis of excluding the poor, the widow, the stranger and the orphan. Yet, the significance of the other person cannot be reduced to a factor in some cultural, religious, social or economic equation. Rather, the stranger, as the one who knocks at the door or who is fenced in or kept out, is divested of any cultural or historical form, and who, in his or her very nakedness, institutes as from on high an ethical command from his or her very destitution. Levinas is not dismissing the value of culture and history, but rather reminding us that, by clothing the other person in a particular cultural and historical form, the singular identity of the other person is often obscured or masked – so much so that often we cannot, both literally and figuratively, see beyond the veil – and this is the form by which a person is judged. The central insight of *Totality and Infinity* is the intolerance of the same towards difference.

The philosophy and politics of modernity has been characterized by the absorption and assimilation of otherness into the politics of identity and the same, which amounts to a 'neutralization of alterity', or an allergic reaction to alterity. What Levinas intends is a non-allergic relation *with* alterity, which is realized in responsibility for the other person, no matter who that other person might be. The justice that I render to the other person, the justice of which God is the counterpart, is blind. God arises in the blossoming of the justice I render to my neighbour. And 'who is my neighbour?'

Well, 'a man was going down from Jerusalem to Jericho......'.[58]

Canonizing Levinas

Where, then, does one situate Levinas in the *communio sanctorum*? A faithful Jew, a philosopher, a Talmudic scholar: he teaches that ethics is the basis of all human relations and informs all thought, whether theological or otherwise. Is Levinas a theologian? Theology is not his interest, yet, fundamentally, he points to the fount and origin of theology – the holiness of the other person in whom the holiness on the Holy One is glimpsed and whose kingdom is realized here and now in works of justice towards the other person. While Derrida says *A-Dieu* to Levinas, one might also pay fitting tribute in the words of the psalmist:

The just will flourish like the palm tree
And grow like a Lebanon cedar.
Planted in the house of the Lord
They will flourish in the courts of our God.[59]

Notes

1 Martin Heidegger, *Being and Time* (London: Harper & Row, 1962), p. 51.
2 Martin Heidegger, *Introduction to Metaphysics* (New Haven, CT: Yale University Press, 2000), p. 15.
3 Emmanuel Levinas, *Totality and Infinity* (The Hague: Martinus Nijhoff, 1979), p. 77.
4 Emmanuel Levinas, *De Dieu qui vient à l'idée* (Paris: Vrin, 1986); *Of God Who Comes to Mind* (Stanford: Stanford University Press, 1998).
5 Psalm 14.1.
6 Levinas, *Totality*, p. 77.
7 Adriaan Peperzaak, *To the Other: An Introduction to the Philosophy of Emmanuel Levinas* (West Lafayette, IN: Purdue University Press, 1993), p. 35.
8 Levinas, *Totality*, p. 77.
9 Ibid.
10 Levinas distinguishes *autre* and *autrui*. I have chosen to translate *autrui* as 'other person'.
11 Levinas, *Totality*, p. 78.

12   Ibid.
13   Emmanuel Levinas, *Collected Philosophical Papers* (The Hague: Martinus Nijhoff, 1987), pp. 165–66.
14   Levinas, *Totality*, p. 78.
15   Ibid., p. 79.
16   Ibid.
17   Peperzaak, *To the Other*, p. 36.
18   Emmanuel Levinas, *Entre Nous: On Thinking-of-the-Other* (New York: Columbia University Press, 1998), p. 88.
19   Levinas, *Entre Nous*, p. 87.
20   Levinas, *Totality*, p. 78.
21   Emmanuel Levinas, *Difficult Freedom* (London: Athlone Press, 1990), p. 7.
22   Levinas, *Totality*, p. 195.
23   Ibid., p. 150.
24   Levinas, *Difficult Freedom*, p. 7.
25   Ibid., p. 9.
26   Thomas Aquinas, *Summa Theologiae* 1a, q2, ad3.
27   Levinas, *Difficult Freedom*, p. 17.
28   Ibid.
29   Ibid., p. 18.
30   Ibid.
31   Ibid., p. 19.
32   Emmaneul Levinas, 'The Awakening of the I', *Is It Righteous to Be?* (Stanford: Stanford University Press, 2001), p. 183.
33   Jacques Derrida, *The Work of Mourning* (Chicago: University of Chicago Press, 2001), p. 202.
34   Levinas, *Of God*, p. ix.
35   Levinas, *Righteous*, p. 182.
36   R. Braun, 'Docetism', *Encyclopaedia of Christian Theology, I* (ed. Jean-Yves Lacoste, London: Routledge, 2005), pp. 444–45.
37   John 20.27.
38   John 21.9–14.
39   See Irenaeus, *Adversus Haereses*, 8; Tertullian, *De Carne Resurrectionis*, 6–10.
40   G. Lafont, 'Adoptionism' in Lacoste, *Encyclopaedia of Christian Theology, I*, pp. 13–14.
41   Mark 1.10–11.
42   Levinas, *Entre Nous*, p. 56.
43   Michael Purcell, 'The Prevenience and Phenomenality of Grace, or, The Anteriority of the Posterior', *The Exorbitant* (ed. Kevin Hart, New York: Fordham University Press, 2009).
44   Levinas, *Entre Nous*, pp. 53–54. The English translator of *Entre Nous* mis-translates *Un Diew-Homme* as a Man-God.
45   Ibid., p. 54.
46   Ibid.
47   Leviticus 16.7–10.
48   Levinas, *Entre Nous*, p. 55.
49   Ibid., p. 57.
50   Ibid., pp. 57–58.
51   Levinas, *Difficult Freedom*, p. 145.

52 Levinas, *Totality*, p. 78.
53 Ibid., p. 79.
54 Levinas, *Difficult Freedom*, p. 17.
55 Emmanuel Levinas, *Ethics and Infinity* (Pittsburgh: Duquesne University Press, 1985).
56 Emmanuel Levinas, *Humanism of the Other* (Chicago: University of Chicago Press, 2003), p. 36.
57 Ibid., p. 35.
58 Luke 10.25–37.
59 Psalm 92.

4

St Maurice de la Passion du Dehors

Kevin Hart

In 'The Dry Salvages' T. S. Eliot observes in a conversational passage, that 'to apprehend / The point of intersection of the timeless / With time, is an occupation for the saint – / No occupation either, but something given / And taken, in a lifetime's death in love, / Ardour and selflessness and self-surrender'.[1] He contrasts sanctity with how things stand for the rest of us who experience at best only 'the unattended moment in and out of time, / The distraction fit, lost in a shaft of sunlight, / The wild thyme unseen, or the winter lightning / Or the waterfall, or music heard so deeply / That it is not heard at all, but you are the music / While the music lasts'. All these relatively modest experiences are 'only hints and guesses', he says, while the rest of one's religious life is taken up with 'prayer, observance, discipline, thought and action'. What is this 'hint half-guessed, the gift half-understood'? It is 'Incarnation': a perfectly orthodox answer. The Eliot of *Four Quartets* is Anglo-Catholic, and so believes in the saints as those who have been finally redeemed through Christ's atoning sacrifice. To be sure, throughout the *Quartets* he conducts a theology of religions, in which Buddhism and Hinduism are harmonized subordinately to Christianity. The 'distraction fit, lost in a shaft of sunlight' alludes to the incident in the rose-garden of Burnt Norton where an empty pool is suddenly 'filled with water out of sunlight' and 'the lotos rose, quietly, quietly'.[2] Yet over the course from 'Burnt Norton' to 'Little Gidding' the image of the lotos finally yields to that of the rose, including the mystical rose of Dante's *Paradiso*, and the *Quartets* concludes with the resounding Christian hope of a time when 'the fire and the rose are one', when purgation will end and the paradise of the saints shall be complete.[3]

Eliot's lines allow us to grasp as quickly as possible not only some salient aspects of the theology of the saints but also a good deal about how ordinary Christians think of them and of ourselves in relation to them. Odd though it may seem at first, it is against this background that I want to think about Maurice Blanchot, a French author whose writings, both narrative fiction and literary criticism, have deep philosophical resonances. Are there aspects of his thought and life that can come into focus for us under the lens of sanctity as Eliot conceives it? An atheist of an extreme and highly sophisticated kind, someone who rejects the One as well as God, Blanchot cannot be called a saint in the Catholic or Orthodox sense of the word, and I have no wish to dredge his biography in order to make a case for him as a secular saint by documenting a number of acts one might consider 'heroic in virtue'.[4] Close throughout his life to Emmanuel Levinas, Blanchot would have paused before his friend's claim, 'All that one demands of oneself, is demanded of a saint, but what one may demand of the Other is always less'.[5] The pause would bespeak both admiration and disagreement, for Blanchot would wish to recognize the moral power of the asymmetry at issue here, the curvature of the space of communication upwards to the other person, while also establishing a distance from any 'theological context' that it introduces.[6]

For Levinas, one crosses the trace of God when one reaches out to the other person – the orphan, the stranger, the widow – and for him this event is neither theological nor contextual. It is not theological, at least not in the sense of proposing or defending dogma, because he advocates an ethics that cuts across the phenomenality of revelation and never makes existential claims about God of the kind that are familiar in natural theology.[7] What interests Levinas is the 'coming to mind' of God: the deity has concrete phenomenological meaning only in an encounter with another person. Nor is the trace of God contextual, for the face of the other person signifies *kath'auto*, simply by itself, without any mediation by concepts or culture. Yet Blanchot retains both words because, on his understanding, Levinas is committed to the view that the structure of ethics – the order 'of being-for-the-other or of holiness [*sainteté*]' – involves a reference to the deity, even if this deity does not appear as the Creator, and so ethical action always presumes a minimal context: the other person and God.[8] In *The Infinite Conversation* (1969) Blanchot reflects by way of several dialogues on Levinas' *Totality and Infinity* (1961) and argues that we must pass from ethics to community, from asymmetry to double dissymmetry, for 'if it is true that *autrui* is never for me a self, for *him* the same is true of me'.[9] Not that one must therefore conclude that communication occurs on a Euclidean plane. One's speech with other people must take place as though on a Riemannian surface, 'an essentially dissymmetrical field governed by discontinuity'.[10] In this adjustment to Levinas' moral philosophy Blanchot erases any theological context in which it is articulated – 'Let us leave aside God' [*Laissons Dieu de côte*], he says earlier in *The Infinite Conversation* – while keeping the word 'mystery' to denote the relation between myself and the other person.[11]

So Levinas has a theory of ethics grounded in sanctity, and his conception of holiness cuts its figure against the sacred, which, for him, is to be ascertained by way of enchantment, participation and sorcery.[12] Sanctity presumes that the saint has undergone a process of desacralization.[13] Far from being won over by Blanchot's commentary on *Totality and Infinity*, Levinas develops his thought in *Otherwise than Being* (1974), a book that, he says, 'can be viewed entirely as theology'.[14] It is not a dogmatic theology, however, and it has no theodicy; it speaks of God only in a highly restricted sense as that which indicates one's obligation to the other person. In Saying, opening oneself without reserve to the other person, one finds oneself in the trace of God; and this Saying inevitably becomes a Said, becomes entangled in the language of ontology and can therefore be treated as a theme. Yet this is not the end of the story: Levinas insists on unsaying this Said, and consequently no traversing the trace of God can be translated into firm knowledge about the being of the deity. We may therefore speak of Levinas as bringing sanctity to thought outside dogmatic theology. Of course, we may question his insistence on sanctity as the ground of ethics, his claim about the face signifying *kath' auto*, or express reservations about moral saints, or wish to find an element in his thought that acknowledges the 'human, all too human' dimension of moral life, but all these things may be set aside here.[15] Our interest is in how Levinas helps us to think more clearly about Blanchot. Nonetheless, it is worth considering what Levinas, thinker of modern sainthood, has to say about Blanchot whom he knew since their years together as students at the University of Strasbourg.

In an interview with François Poiré conducted in 1986 Levinas says of his friend, 'I must mention especially that he saved my wife during the war while I was in captivity; he also experienced 1968 in an extraordinary manner. He always chose the least expected, most noble and difficult path. This moral elevation [*élévation morale*], this fundamentally aristocratic nature of thinking, is what counts the most and edifies'.[16] A moment or two later, he adds a recollection of Blanchot as an undergraduate, 'For me he stood for the very epitome of French excellence; not so much on account of his ideas, but on account of a certain possibility of saying things which it is very difficult to imitate, appearing like a force from on high. Yes, it is always in terms of height [*en termes de hauteur*] that I speak of him'.[17] Here we find moral and intellectual excellence attributed to Blanchot, leavened by a joke about their respective heights (Levinas was quite short, his friend rather tall) and a restatement of Levinas' view that the other person always speaks from on high. Levinas will not attribute sanctity to Blanchot because, for him, and counter to all common and theological thinking on the matter, one can do that only to oneself. A *Book of Saints* edited by Levinas would be very slim indeed. At least one other person, Blanchot's sometime lover Denise Rollin, will speak differently and, with great affection, call Blanchot an 'idiot' in Dostoievski's sense of Prince Mychkin being a 'holy fool', though these two words are to be understood not by way of Russian Orthodoxy but in the space of an atheism that opens after the death of God.[18] Blanchot the man is characterized by extraordinary humility, simplicity and generosity, Rollin testifies.

As already indicated, I do not wish to pursue a biographical approach to sanctity with respect to Blanchot. Nor do I wish to use the category of sainthood ironically (as Marx and Engels do in *The German Ideology* (1846) when they write of Max Stirner as 'Saint Max', and as Hélène Cixous does when proposing Jacques Derrida as 'a young Jewish saint') or to come up with a new sense of sainthood, as Sartre does when he calls the novelist and playwright Jean Genet 'Saint Genet'.[19] Once the young Genet becomes habituated to theft, Sartre argues, 'there begins the systematic turning of the positive into the negative and the negative into the positive which, later, carried to an extreme, will lead Genet to "saintliness"'.[20] Only one trait of Sartre's portrait of Genet as a saint will be retained here. I have in mind what Sartre sees as Genet's 'moment of awakening': at the age of ten he is told that he is a thief and, if he continues in his wickedness, he is led to apprehend that he will 'end on the gallows'.[21] From that moment, he is '*already dead*',[22] Sartre concludes, adding much later, 'The Saint, too, is a dead man; though he is in this world he is no longer of it. He does not produce, he does not consume; he began by offering up his wealth to God, but that is not enough. It is the entire world that he wants to offer; to offer, that is, to destroy in a magnificent potlatch'.[23] The saint as already dead to the world: this is what I wish to retain from Sartre, though without the reference to destruction.

Eliot proposes two distinguishing traits of sanctity. The first is the apprehension of 'The point of intersection of the timeless / With time', and the second is that such contemplative insight is embedded in 'a lifetime's death in love, / Ardour and selflessness and self-surrender'. I wish to argue that Blanchot ceaselessly seeks a point where time and the timeless intersect, although in a completely different sense from the one that Eliot has in mind, and that this experience – or, more strictly, this experience without experience – is co-ordinate with the *kenosis* that Eliot believes to be the context in which contemplative insight may be given and taken. To my mind, Blanchot can be regarded as generating a model of a counter-saint: an atheistic analogue to what the Church thinks when it calls some exceptional persons of faith 'saints'. Karl Rahner observes of the blessed that, 'They are the initiators and the creative models of the holiness which happens to be right for, and is the task of, their particular age. They create a new style; they prove that a certain form of life and activity is a really genuine possibility; they show experimentally that one can be a Christian even in "this" way; they make such a type of person believable as a Christian type. Their significance begins therefore not merely after they have died'.[24] So there are different ways of being exemplary Christians, varying modes of holiness that appear in distinct historical periods and cultures. Blanchot, too, created a 'new style' of being an exemplary atheist, one that is a phased correlate of being a Christian saint; it is marked along the divided border of his life and his work by conversion, encounters with the sacred, *askesis*, reclusion, radical openness towards others, and private revelation ('The point of intersection of the timeless / With time'); and this perhaps begins to account for the remarkable reverence with which he has been regarded, both personally and as an author.[25]

*

I begin where narratives of the saints often begin, with an account of conversion. Blanchot represents himself, indirectly, as an infant convert to atheism. I quote the central text of *The Writing of the Disaster* (1980):

♦ (A primal scene?) *You who live later, close to a heart that beats no more, suppose, suppose this: the child – is he seven years old, or eight perhaps? – standing by the window, drawing the curtain and, through the pane, looking. What he sees: the garden, the wintry trees, the wall of a house. Though he sees, no doubt in a child's way, his play space, he grows weary and slowly looks up toward the ordinary sky, with clouds, grey light – pallid daylight without depth.*

What happens then: the sky, the same *sky, suddenly open, absolutely black and absolutely empty, revealing* [révélant] *(as though the pane had broken) such an absence that all has since always and forevermore been lost therein – so lost that therein is affirmed and dissolved the vertiginous knowledge that nothing is what there is, and first of all nothing beyond* [que rien est ce qu'il y a, et d'abord rien au-delà]. *The unexpected aspect of this scene (its interminable feature) is the feeling of happiness that straightway submerges the child, the ravaging joy to which he can bear witness only by tears, an endless flood of tears. He is thought to suffer a childish sorrow; attempts are made to console him. He says nothing. He will live henceforth in the secret. He will weep no more.*[26]

This piercing *récit* is a twofold counterpart of Christian conversion and private revelation. The dark vision leads the boy to the firm belief that 'nothing is what there is, and first of all nothing beyond'. It is an anti-type of the events of St Paul on the road to Damascus and St Augustine in the garden in Milan. More finely, we also remember stories such as Jonathan Edwards' narrative of Phebe Bartlet's childhood conversion, and also testimonies of private revelation such as given by St Catherine of Siena and St Simon Stock.[27] What is the meaning of the event that Blanchot no sooner introduces by the Freudian expression 'primal scene' than he takes it back with a question mark?[28]

It has a double significance. Not only does the boy's experience at the window constitute a denial of divine transcendence but also it affirms that the truth of being is 'nothing'. Yet the expression of the vision encodes a philosophical interpretation of what has been seen, for this 'nothing' is given as the 'there is' [*il y a*], which Levinas describes as the impersonal rustling of being even in the heart of non-being. 'But this nothing is not that of pure nothingness', he says in *Existence and Existents* (1947). 'There is no longer *this* or *that*; there is not "something". But this universal absence is in its turn a presence, an absolutely unavoidable presence. It is not the dialectical counterpart of absence, and we do not grasp it through a thought. It is immediately there. There is no discourse. Nothing responds to us, but this silence; the voice of this silence is understood and frightens like the silence of those infinite spaces Pascal speaks of'.[29] And yet Blanchot's testimony of a private revelation is importantly not a conversion to the *il y a* as described by his friend, even though Levinas points us to the first version of *Thomas l'obscur* (1941) as offering an admirable description of it.[30] The *il y a* is horrific, and one escapes it only through turning towards the other person. Rather, in '(A Primal Scene?)', the child becomes attuned to what Blanchot will later call the Outside, the neutral, or 'the *other* night'. His response is not horror or panic but *'the feeling of happiness'* and *'ravaging joy to which he can bear witness only by tears'*. As we shall see, there are times when Blanchot thinks of the *il y a* and the Outside as very close, if not identical, but this is not one of them.[31]

The approach of the Outside brings joy, it seems, because it is salvation from immortality or eternity and, more locally, from the burdens of religious observance and perhaps religious fears. It is also a salvation from the weight of selfhood, a turn from 'I' to 'he', which does not merely enable literature to be written but denotes a more profound change, one that allows the writer to 'surrender to the interminable' and to lose 'the power to say "I"'.[32] Of course, '(A Primal Scene?)' is given in the third person partly because the adult is no longer the child and partly because the approach of the Outside calls the 'I', master of possibility, into question. Nonetheless, Blanchot takes care to suggest in his work that the narrative is autobiographical: the 'Self', he writes in *The Step Not Beyond* (1973), was 'as if fissured, since the day when the sky opened upon its void'.[33] Not that the approach of the Outside always brings happiness: when Blanchot evokes it in *The Space of Literature* (1955), for example, there is nothing to celebrate. 'Art – as images, as words, and as rhythm – indicates the menacing proximity of a vague and vacant outside, a neutral existence, nil and limitless; art points into a sordid absence, a suffocating condensation where being ceaselessly perpetuates itself as nothingness'.[34] In the same work, Blanchot asks, 'Why is art so intimately allied with the sacred?'[35] His answer is that the two, disclosure and concealment, are one when viewed transcendentally. Art is concerned with what appears, while the sacred is the principle of manifestation and therefore always anterior to it.[36] The sacred is neither subject nor object but neutral.[37] Positive theistic religions, Blanchot implies, mistake the Outside for evidence of divinity; and yet it would be a mistake to deny the sacred, since art needs 'the profound *reserve*' of the sacred.[38] As he says, 'the Sacred must be speech'.[39] Besides, the writer is always involved in an act of self-sacrifice: at the extreme moment of composition, his or her 'I' is renounced, leaving only the anonymity of the third person.[40]

Elsewhere in Blanchot's writings, the Outside is regarded affirmatively, as 'entirely *other*', an irruptive state to come to which art points us and that, in a quite different register, to which communism also gestures. 'It is undoubtedly the task of our age to move toward an affirmation that is entirely *other*', Blanchot writes. 'It is to this task that communism recalls us with a rigor that it itself often shirks, and it is also to this task that "artistic experience" recalls us in the realm that is proper to it. A remarkable coincidence'.[41] When reading Robert Musil's *The Man without Qualities* (1943) Blanchot finds 'the most beautiful incestuous passion of modern literature', the erotic relation between Ulrich and Agathe, to signify 'the *other* state'.[42] It is not the last instance in which we find an appeal to otherness. In *The Space of Literature* Blanchot evokes the Outside by way of the figure of 'the *other* night', and in doing so makes the Outside more concrete than is usual for him:

> In the night, everything has disappeared. This is the first night. Here absence approaches – silence, repose, night. Here death blots out Alexander's picture; here the sleeper does not know he sleeps, and he who dies goes to meet real dying. Here language completes and fulfills itself in the silent profundity which vouches for it as its meaning.
>
> But when everything has disappeared in the night 'everything has disappeared' appears. This is the *other* night. Night is this apparition: 'everything has disappeared'. It is what we sense when dreams replace sleep, when the dead pass into the deep of the night, when night's deep appears in those who have disappeared. Apparitions, phantoms, and dreams are an allusion to this empty night.[43]

Here 'other' does not suggest, at the risk of losing intelligibility, a wholly different conceptual scheme from the one we use now, and perhaps all that Blanchot has in mind when he speaks of the 'entirely *other*' is something currently unimaginable and, even when we can discern its outline, regulative rather than constitutive.[44] In any case, there is no sense in the passage just quoted of a different way of writing or living that presses upon us; rather, Blanchot evokes the *il y a* in terms very similar to those that Levinas uses in *Existence and Existents*. It needs to be underlined that this experience of 'the *other* night' is a phenomenological description of an absence that nonetheless impinges on consciousness, not a recounting of a special revelation. Perhaps only once the Outside has been revealed to the young Blanchot can he discern it later. 'Now I see', he may say in parody of 'Amazing Grace'.

What is striking about the approach of the Outside is that it stalls time: not through the experience of happiness or joy, as recounted in '(A Primal Scene?)', but through suffering. I interrupt Blanchot towards the end of a long meditation centred on poetry and the sacred:

> Suffering is suffering when one can no longer suffer it, and when, because of this non-power, one cannot cease suffering it. A singular situation. Time is as though arrested, merged with its interval. There, the present is without end, separated from every other present by an inexhaustible and empty infinite, the very infinite of suffering, and thus dispossessed of any future: a present without end and yet impossible as a present. The present of suffering is the abyss of the present, indefinitely hollowed out and in this hollowing indefinitely distended, radically alien to the possibility that one might be present to it through the mastery of presence. What has happened? Suffering has simply lost its hold on time, and has made us lose time. Would we then be freed in this state from any temporal perspective and redeemed, saved [rachetés, sauvés] from time as it passes? Not at all: we are delivered over to another time – to time as other, as absence and neutrality; precisely to a time that can no longer redeem us [ne peut plus nous racheter], that constitutes no recourse. A time without event, without project, without possibility; not that pure immobile instant, the spark of the mystics, but an unstable . in which we are arrested and incapable of permanence, a time neither abiding nor granting the simplicity of a dwelling place.[45]

Suffering is a prompt to a reduction from the possible to the impossible, one that leads us to undergo 'the passion of the outside' in which one is exposed to 'the incessant', an endless stalling of time that is 'ungraspable' but that 'one cannot let go of'.[46] Here we 'apprehend / The point of intersection of the timeless / With time' but the timeless is beneath time, as it were, rather than above it: not the eternity of redemption but the Outside that exiles us from any secure habitation, beginning with the security of the 'I'.

*

There is a sense in which Blanchot, counter-saint of the Outside, might be seen almost to have become a martyr. I have in mind a crucial scene in *The Instant of my Death* (1994). Fifty years before the book is published, the young Blanchot, it seems, is in his family home, the Château in Quaine, Saône-et-Loire, when suddenly there is a knock at the door. He is called outside by a Nazi lieutenant, and summarily put before a firing squad, presumably for his part in the *maquis*. 'Outside, outside [*Dehors, dehors*]', the lieutenant howls, and once again we are to witness a 'passion of the outside'.[47] The passage is related in the first person about a young man, presumably the narrator's younger self:

> I know – do I know it – that the one at whom the Germans were already aiming, awaiting but the final order, experienced then a feeling of extraordinary lightness, a sort of beatitude (nothing happy, however) – sovereign elation? The encounter of death with death?
>
> In his place, I will not try to analyze. He was perhaps suddenly invincible. Dead – immortal. Perhaps ecstasy. Rather the feeling of compassion for suffering humanity, the happiness of not being immortal or eternal.[48]

As Jacques Derrida rightly says in *Demeure* (1998), his commentary on *The Instant of My Death*, this is a scene of martyrdom, the Passion of Christ, but it is 'mimicked, repeated, and displaced'.[49] Indeed, it is repeated even within the narrative. For if the young man is a witness to the French Resistance and all it stands for, the older man who narrates the story is a witness to what the younger man undergoes: 'a sort of beatitude', 'Perhaps ecstasy'. In being taken outside by the Nazi lieutenant and faced with immanent death, he is also approached by the Outside. When he was a boy, living in the same Château, he experienced happiness and joy at the revelation that '*nothing is what there is*'. Now the event is more nuanced: first, the feeling of lightness is 'nothing happy' and then another feeling, 'the happiness of not being immortal or eternal'.

Two possible explanations of what gives rise to the 'feeling of extraordinary lightness' are tentatively offered: 'sovereign elation?' and 'The encounter of death with death?' The first possibility rejoins the revelation given to the child; he experiences great joy, which enables him to lord it over the coming event. The second possibility is even more surprising, for how can death encounter death? We know that death, in the form of a bullet, is about to hit the young man, but what other modality of death can it possibly meet that is already in him? Blanchot has told us time and again. Here are two instances, each from *The Writing of the Disaster*:

> ♦ Dying means: you are dead already, in an immemorial past, of a death which was not yours, which you have thus neither known nor lived, but under the threat of which you believe you are called upon to live; you await it henceforth in the future, constructing a future to make it possible at last – possible as something that will take place and will belong to the realm of experience.[50]
>
> ♦ 'I' die before being born.[51]

There is no 'I', Blanchot thinks, at least no self-identical 'substantial ego' or 'metaphysical subject' that persists through time, for two reasons, one roughly Nietzschean and the other precisely Levinasian.[52] First, the *cogito* or *psyche* has always and already been a multiplicity of 'who's' – 'the "I" was already no more than a Who?, a whole crowd of Who's', says the narrator of *The Last Man* (1957) – and so has never had any unity in the first place.[53] Second, Blanchot follows the Levinas of *Otherwise than Being*: 'The responsibility with which I am charged is not mine and causes me not to be I'.[54] When another person calls on me it is not by virtue of my uniqueness but rather because I am on the spot. And yet the 'I' that bears a name and acts in the world – the legal, political or psychological subject – must still await its demise as an empirical self. So one's demise will be, in Blanchot's terms, 'the encounter of death with death'.

To be already dead, even if this means no more than a rejection of various philosophical and religious ideas of selfhood, especially those that point to immortality, means for the narrator of *The Instant of my Death* that one may now feel 'compassion for suffering humanity'. Of course, the story goes on: the young man is allowed to move away and hide in a forest because the soldiers are Russian, not German, members of the Vlasov army, the 'Russian Liberation Army' led by Andrei Vlasov, that sought to oppose the Communist régime in the Soviet Union. When he emerges, he sees burning farms, bloated horses and learns that three young farmers have been 'slaughtered', presumably in retaliation for his escape[55]:

> No doubt what then began for the young man was the torment of injustice. No more ecstasy; the feeling that he was only living because, even in the eyes of the Russians, he belonged to a noble class.[56]

'Compassion for suffering humanity' combined with 'the torment of injustice': the young man begins, 'a lifetime's death in love, / Ardour and selflessness and self-surrender'. Not that he will put it in quite those terms: 'writing', 'community' and 'friendship' will be his watchwords.

*

'Maurice Blanchot, novelist and critic, was born in 1907. His life is entirely devoted to literature and to the silence that is appropriate to it'. So reads the biographical note on some of his books; it is one of the things that made his reclusion well known to his readers for several decades. Yet only if we look over the full range of his writings can we see how clearly we are invited to see Blanchot as a child convert, receiver of a special revelation, one who gives his life to the 'sacred word', writes ceaselessly of an *askesis*, what he calls 'losing the power to say "I"', and who involves himself, as an 'invisible partner', for causes of justice. He was no saint, but one effect of his texts on us, by way of their veiled autobiography and oblique testimonies, has been to give us an idea of what an atheistic displacement and mimicking of sanctity might be.

Notes

1   T. S. Eliot, *Four Quartets* (London: Faber and Faber, 1959), p. 44.
2   Ibid., p. 14, my emphasis.
3   Ibid., p. 59.
4   I allude to one of the stages of canonization specified in the apostolic constitution *Divinus perfectionis magister* (1983), promulgated by John-Paul II.
5   Johan F. Goud, '"What One Asks of Oneself, One Asks of a Saint": A Dialogue with Emmanuel Levinas, 1980–81', *Levinas Studies* 3 (2008), p. 23.
6   See Maurice Blanchot, 'Knowledge of the Unknown', *The Infinite Conversation* (trans. Susan Hanson, Minneapolis: University of Minnesota Press, 1993), p. 56. Blanchot admits that Levinas would not accept the expression 'theological context' but nonetheless retains it. See *Infinite Conversation*, p. 441.
7   See Emmanuel Levinas, 'Foreword', *Of God Who Comes to Mind* (trans. Bettina Bergo, Stanford: Stanford University Press, 1998), p. xi. In an interview Levinas observes, 'God is not in heaven. He is in men's sacrifice, in the mercy men show for one another. Heaven is empty but men's mercy is filled with God'. Michaël de Saint Cheron, *Conversations with Emmanuel Levinas, 1983–1994* (trans. Gary D. Mole, Pittsburgh: Duquesne University Press, 2010), p. 16. Also see Emmanuel Levinas, 'Violence of the Face', *Alterity and Transcendence* (trans. Michael B. Smith, London: The Athlone Press, 1999), p. 180.
8   Levinas, 'Preface to the Second Edition', *Of God*, p. ix. For Levinas, the I and the Other constitute the basis of ethics, even though a third person is always pressing on the scene, calling for justice in addition to ethics. Apart from living on a desert island with another person – a scene that Levinas evokes – the context involves, the self, the other person and the trace of God, understood as a sense of obligation to the other person.
9   Blanchot, 'The Relation of the Third Kind: *Man without Horizon*', *Infinite Conversation*, p. 70.
10 Ibid., p. 77.
11 Ibid., p. 72.
12 See Goud, 'What One Asks', p. 23.
13 See Emmanuel Levinas, 'Desacralization and Disenchantment', *Nine Talmudic Readings* (trans. and intro. Annette Aronowicz, Bloomington: Indiana University Press, 1990), pp. 141, 159.
14 Goud, 'What One Asks', p. 6. Blanchot's *The Writing of the Disaster* is partly a response to *Otherwise than Being*, though he does not engage with the theological dimension of the book.
15 See Susan Wolf, 'Moral Saints', *The Journal of Philosophy* 79: 8 (1982), pp. 419–39.
16 Emmanuel Levinas, 'Interview with François Poiré', *Is It Righteous to Be? Interviews with Emmanuel Levinas* (ed. Jill Robbins, Stanford: Stanford University Press, 2001), p. 29. Also see Levinas, 'Judaism and Revolution', *Nine Talmudic Readings*, p. 115.
17 Ibid., p. 30.

18 See Christophe Bident, *Maurice Blanchot: Partenaire Invisible* (Seyssel: Champ Vallon, 1998), pp. 276–78.

19 See Hélène Cixous, *Portrait of Jacques Derrida as a Young Jewish Saint* (trans. Beverley Bie Brahic, New York: Columbia University Press, 2004).

20 Jean-Paul Sartre, *Saint Genet: Actor and Martyr* (trans. Bernard Frechtman, New York: George Braziller, 1963), p. 14.

21 Ibid., p. 20.

22 Ibid.

23 Ibid., p. 201.

24 Karl Rahner, 'The Church of the Saints', *Theological Investigations*, III: *Theology of the Spiritual Life* (trans. Karl-H. and Boniface Kruger, London: Darton, Longman and Todd, 1967), p. 100. Frances Young develops a similar idea by way of a musical metaphor – Scripture as score played by various virtuosi – in her *Virtuoso Theology* (Cleveland: Pilgrim Press, 1993), esp. p. 25.

25 It should be noted that Blanchot has also been criticized roundly for his early political writings. See Jeffrey Mehlman, *Legacies of Anti-Semitism in France* (Minneapolis: University of Minnesota Press, 1983).

26 Maurice Blanchot, *The Writing of the Disaster* (trans. Ann Smock, Lincoln: University of Nebraska Press, 1986), p. 72.

27 See Jonathan Edwards, *A Narrative of Many Surprising Conversions in Northampton and Vicinity* (1736; Worcester: Moses W. Grout, 1832), pp. 66–74.

28 On this topic see my *The Dark Gaze: Maurice Blanchot and the Sacred* (Chicago: Chicago University Press, 2004), ch. 2.

29 Emmanuel Levinas, *Existence and Existents* (rev. edn, trans. Alphonso Lingis, Dordrecht: Kluwer, 1988), p. 58.

30 Ibid., p. 63n. 1.

31 See, for example, Blanchot, 'Everyday Speech', *Infinite Conversation*, p. 245, where the everyday is regarded by way of the *il y a*; and also see *The One Who was Standing Apart from Me* (trans. Lydia Davis, Barrytown: Station Hill Press, 1993), p. 50, where the approach of the Outside brings pain.

32 Maurice Blanchot, *The Space of Literature* (trans. and intro. Ann Smock, Lincoln: University of Nebraska Press, 1982), p. 26.

33 Maurice Blanchot, *The Step Not Beyond* (trans. and intro. Lycette Nelson, Albany: State University of New York Press, 1992), p. 2.

34 Ibid., pp. 242–43.

35 Blanchot, *Space of Literature*, p. 233.

36 See Maurice Blanchot, 'The "Sacred" Speech of Hölderlin', *The Work of Fire* (trans. Charlotte Mandell, Stanford: Stanford University Press, 1995), pp. 119, 122.

37 See Maurice Blanchot, 'The Detour towards Simplicity', *Friendship* (trans. Elizabeth Rottenberg, Stanford: Stanford University Press, 1997), p. 193.

38 See Blanchot, *Step Not Beyond*, p. 73, *Space of Literature*, p. 233.

39 Blanchot, 'The Great Refusal', *Infinite Conversation*, p. 40.

40 See, for example, Maurice Blanchot, *Faux Pas* (trans. Charlotte Mandell, Stanford: Stanford University Press, 2001), p. 5.

41 Blanchot, 'On One Approach to Communism', *Friendship*, p. 97.

42 Maurice Blanchot, 'Musil', *The Book to Come* (Stanford: Stanford University Press, 2003), p. 142.

43 Blanchot, *Space of Literature*, p. 163.

44 On this point, see Maurice Blanchot, 'The Beast of Lascaux', trans. Leslie Hill, *The Oxford Literary Review* 22 (2000), p. 12.
45 Blachot, 'The Great Refusal', p. 44. Also see *Writing of the Disaster*, p. 15.
46 Blachot, 'The Great Refusal', p. 45.
47 Maurice Blanchot, 'The Instant of My Death', *The Instant of My Death* bound with Jacques Derrida, *Demeure: Fiction and Testimony* (trans. Elizabeth Rottenberg, Stanford: Stanford University Press, 2000), p. 3.
48 Ibid., p. 5.
49 Ibid., p. 63.
50 Blanchot, *Writing of the Disaster*, p. 65.
51 Ibid., p. 101.
52 See Friedrich Nietzsche, *The Will to Power* (trans. Walter Kaufmann and R. J. Hollingdale, New York: Random House, 1968), pp. 267–72.
53 See Maurice Blanchot, *The Last Man* (trans. Lydia Davis, New York: Columbia University Press, 1987), p. 11. Also see Blanchot, 'Who?', *Who Comes After the Subject?* (ed. Eduardo Cadava et al., London: Routledge, 1991), pp. 58–60.
54 Blanchot, *Last Man*, p. 18.
55 Ibid., p. 7.
56 Ibid.

5

Of Michel Foucault
(Who May Yet Become St Paul)

Ward Blanton

*What do we fear most? Repetition or difference? The return of
a barbarism that is remote and prehistoric or the advent of a
barbarism that is technological and post-human?
Enigma originates at the precise moment when past and future are
both collapsed into an ambiguous, supremely problematic present.
It is this type of experience that underpins and informs* Enigmas,
*an experience brought about neither by a return of the repressed
nor by future shock, but by the enigma of their coincidence and the
emergence of a condition in which the ancient past and imaginable
future are not merely similar – they can be confused. This is what is
meant by 'Egyptian effect' – something rather different from a vague
interest in ancient Egyptian culture.*

MARIO PERNIOLA, *Enigmas: The Egyptian Moment in Society and Art*[1]

We inhabit a moment when the exceptional and destabilizing significance of
the 'return' of Paul in philosophy and critical theory continues to radiate,
precisely from or to where it remains to be seen. What is clear is that this
ongoing radiation effects a conjuration, through the interstices of our
disciplinary archives, of a saintly energetics whose wild, anarchic or divinely
monstrous capacities are threatening to transform the very institutions
within which we, as it were, house religion, philosophy and cultural criticism

respectively. Consider, just for a start, that the 'return' of Paul in continental philosophy at once constitutes a massive contest between conservative and revolutionary gestures towards 'metapolitics' (or the stable essence of European political spirit); a contestation of Christian institutions and populist ideologies of Christianity; a contestation of a Derridean politics and a Levinasian ethics; a contestation of the triumphalism and anti-Jewish modern narratives of 'Christian origins'; a contestation between the necessity and impossibility of revolutionary newness; and polemics about the best models of the subject of dialectical materialism.[2] It seems that we are all Paulinists now, not because we all admire or identify with the figure but because this has become the name under which are now being negotiated so many of the major intellectual movements of our time. As things slip over onto a Paulinist stage, it strikes me that the intense negotiation of more recent critical theory with the Foucaultian legacy has, surprisingly perhaps, not yet worked itself out to the same degree as a similar mode of reworking the Pauline legacy. This is itself a significant fact, and without saying too much here, it seems safe to say that this has something to do with the way an historicist Foucaultian trajectory was not so quickly caught up into the (admittedly brilliant but) essentially hyper-Lutheran 'Christian origins' stories of Alain Badiou and Slavoj Žižek, with their grace/law (or being/event) stories.[3]

Nevertheless there remains a more Foucaultian mode of attention to the Pauline 'signature', those instances of an effect which is neither merely historical nor merely conceptual but some quasi-transcendental apparatus putting both into operation.[4] Julia Reinhard Lupton has begun to speak in important ways of the 'Paul effect', that odd way in which, from the aesthetics of Shakespeare to the legal theories of Carl Schmitt and the psychoanalysis of Jacques Lacan, there is a peculiar and often unpredictable restaging of this or that moment of transition, this or that conceptual distinction or this or that political event as a kind of repetition of a Pauline moment.[5] The seriality of these moments of restaging or repetition, not to mention their political and cultural forcefulness, itself demands some attention, some (psychoanalytic) analysis.

Here I want to think about Foucault – who has yet to himself 'become' St Paul (as have, apparently, Jacob Taubes, Slavoj Žižek and Alain Badiou, among others) – by allowing Foucault's missed encounter with Paul at the end of the third volume of *The History of Sexuality* to stand in for ongoing philosophical disputes and a kind of new psychoanalytic attention to the immanent force of Enjoyment, what Kiarina Kordela aptly names the problem of 'secular causality'.[6] Here Perniola's ruminations on enigmas do not at all seem beside the point, formulating well the way it seems that our time continues to operate as out of joint, as if we, too, are marked by a kind of enigmatic or displaced time of the contemporary. Perniola, a keen disciple of Deleuzean or radically Stoic immanence, suggests that the most important issue would not simply be whether these contemporary issues are ventriloquizing Paul or whether the ancient Paul is ventriloquizing contemporary issues. Rather, the truth lies elsewhere, in another kind of event whereby all are equally displaced, all become equally untimely, because all are becoming equally something new in a saintly scrambling of our institutions. Or, in Deleuzean terms, we are participating in a singular event, an event without established model, participating in an enigma which will, nevertheless, end up defining us. And so we live, rolling the dice on a Foucault who (see below) may yet become St Paul, and a Paul who may yet become St Foucault.

To democractize sainthood, affirm the paradoxes of an immanent enjoyment!

As will become clear, the crux of the enigmatic or ambiguously comparative moment between Foucault and Paul turns on the outworking of a radically immanent or hyper-modern mode of understanding contemporary sovereignty – which Foucault glosses in his late work as the problem of 'biopolitics' – in relation to the question of an ancient Paulinism imagined by the later Foucault's interest in spiritual exercise and risky political speech or *parrhēsia*.[7] A useful way to approach this issue is by way of what becomes for me a story of a missed encounter between Foucault and Paul at the end of Foucault's third volume of the *History of Sexuality*.[8] There, if you will recall, Foucault wonders aloud about an influential late-nineteenth- and early-twentieth-century debate within biblical and philosophical studies, namely, whether or not one finds important insight in the comparison of Paul with a philosophical contemporary like Epictetus. Interestingly, at that point in his text, Foucault urges his readers to acknowledge that 'we can hardly let the matter remain there' where the nineteenth-century interpreters left it. But in important respects that I want to emphasize, this is precisely what Foucault seems to do inasmuch as Foucault himself never really challenges some of the fundamental organizing axioms of the earlier debate between, especially, Adolf Bonhoffer and Theodore Zahn, both important scholars in the late-nineteenth-century German University.

In this conclusion, a sort of loose appendix to his history of sexuality, Foucault remains surprisingly within a very traditional historical story, even – I want to argue – a classic Christian story of exceptionalism, a stock story of 'Christian origins' whereby the differences imagined to separate Judaism (on the one hand) and philosophy (on the other) from Christianity are all brought to bear on the imagined identity of Paul. The apostle, imagined founding patriarch of Christianity, is in this tradition read as embodying the stable differences between discursive types, thus guaranteeing the 'Christian origins' story.

As I argue at length in *A Materialism for the Masses*, one of my fundamental problems with Nietzsche – no doubt in certain respects one of the astute theorists of religion and culture in the modern period – is the *way* he imagines Christianity to have participated in a Western construction of a dualistic or two-tiered reality. Nietzsche, as you will remember, imagines that Christianity, as a 'Platonism for the masses', was mediated to cultural memory above all as a dogma and desire of salvation in another world.[9] But I have to confess that, increasingly, I think a more fundamental mode of this construction of a two-tiered or idealist conception of the universe occurs in the Platonizing *modes of historical narration* whereby Christian origins were subtracted from the flux and process of history in order to remain in it, but as a break or 'ideal' origin.

And while he excoriates Paul as the founder of Christianity, neither Nietzsche nor Foucault breaks with the fundamental gestures of the old Christian origins stories. In that respect, this is one occasion when I think Foucault's Nietzscheanism does him no favours. For example, I have never heard anyone discuss in any detail the significance of the fact that here Foucault's eventual distinction – through the figure of Paul – between 'religion' or 'Christianity' (Foucault uses both terms) and the 'Greco-Roman moralists' essentially repeats the position of that avowedly anti-modernist and Christian exceptionalist biblical scholar that Foucault mentions, namely, Theodore Zahn. Enigmas anyone? This constellation is really an odd turn of events which deserves some thought. Zahn, as you may know, was that German luminary who became the absolute darling of a dominant form of English biblical scholarship which was, like Zahn, desperate to distance itself and its audiences from a German tradition of critique, criticism and historiographical reconstruction in relation to biblical texts. In this respect, Zahn played a crucial role in the genealogy of modern biblical scholarship in relation to the modern study of religion more generally. English scholars like the equally famous J. B. Lightfoot were particularly keen to distance themselves from the *kinds of comparative research and aggressively interpretive modelling* demanded by the new history-of-religions school. Remember, for example, that the scholars in this movement were, among other things, actively theorizing or modelling 'spirit' in terms of non-personal migrations of mentalities, finding (like Freud) real inspiration in the emergence of new theories of crowd psychology.[10] Similarly, in keeping with new anthropological and philosophical reflection on so-called primitive religion as a kind of non-modern relation of transitivity or as a kind of ungrounded phenomenal relation *between* bodies and ideas, some scholars also in the history-of-religions school were trying to formulate material theories of charismatic aura as a form of ideational 'fluid' (some of this shows up in Gunkel's influential work on spirit, for example).[11]

Needless to say, such new directions in the study of religion were enough to evoke an uncharitable reaction within the common sense of a pious English gentleman like Lightfoot. And, with a little help from Zahn – whom he often presented as the German biblical scholar who could inoculate England against German biblical scholarship – Lightfoot and English biblical scholarship more generally were very effective in their inoculatory campaign, as it were, against the migration of this mentality. Effectively, the English biblical scholars secured for themselves another century of largely canonical or merely biblical *repetitions* of early Christian narrations of Christian origins – from the New Testament book of Acts to the *Ecclesiastical Histories* of Eusebius. Repetition of these stories won out over the (ultimately political) awkwardness of comparative and interpretive modelling, and even now it is sometimes difficult to combat a kind of cloistered exceptionalism which British biblical scholarship affords us as an academic formation which is clearly a direct product of these earlier political and cultural negotiations.

So, again, it strikes us as exceedingly odd that Foucault would in a sense *save* Paul (or the Greco-Roman moralists) from a comparative or analogical explication more in keeping with the history of religions school and its interest in Hellenistic philosophy, effectively securing *the distinction* between these two objects of enquiry within our disciplinary enterprises and the cultural archive these enterprises underwrite. With Foucault as much as Zahn, the move effectively enunciates the uniqueness or exceptionalism of both 'religion' and of 'Christian moral systems' in relation to what Foucault called the 'Greco-Roman moralists'. Zahn and Foucault even use almost the same language in their respective suggestions that, while code elements are similar, scholars should 'not be misled by the analogy' between Paul and philosophical contemporaries like Epictetus.[12]

Of course, when we leave received comparative and narratological paradigms unchallenged, we effectively fail to challenge many of the other discursive tendencies these paradigms underwrite, and I want to mention a few of these challenges which Foucault's siding with Zahn, as it were, fails to mount.

Recall that at the end of Foucault's third volume in the unfinished *History of Sexuality*, the genealogist was reflecting on a vexing 'problematic' or driving question: how shall we understand early Christianity (his terms) in relation to the philosophers and moralists of the Greco-Roman period?[13] Foucault highlights the importance of the question in light of his own narration of the way, compared with older Greek philosophical discussions of pleasure and sexuality, the 'first two centuries of our era' were marked by a strengthening of the demand for austerity.[14] Physicians recommended abstinence, preferring 'virginity over the use of pleasure', and philosophers of the period 'condemn any sexual relation' outside monogamous marriage. In relation to this shift in moral exigency within discourses about sexuality, Foucault poses a critical, which is to say politically charged, question. Should one see in this phenomenological shift in bodily comportment a proleptic 'sketch of a moral future'? More specifically, he wonders:

Must one suppose that certain thinkers in the Greco-Roman world already had a presentiment of this model of sexual austerity which, in Christian societies, will be given a legal framework and an institutionalized support?[15]

As Foucault here indicates very clearly, his genealogical distinction between forms of sexual existence was significant in part because of a long history of Western self-definition which invested heavily in the naming and ritual or discursive maintenance of the *differences* between the various figures on Foucault's genealogical stage, perhaps particularly in relation to the question of philosophy or worldview and sexual roles (a story which no doubt needs further reflection in itself!). Consider the cast of discrete characters on Foucault's stage, just for a start: Classical Greek thought, Hellenistic culture, early Christianity and the age of developed Christian systems of moral governance.

The construction and maintenance of the differences between such delimitable characters, of course, is invested to the same degree that the difference likewise stands in to organize other discursive spaces elsewhere, and, here too, I want to argue, Foucault's cast of characters also stand in for *other* moments and distinctions relevant to his larger genealogical projects. Just consider some of the ways Foucault's larger genealogical interventions are echoed here in the question of where to situate the ancient figure of Paul. For example, remember the remarkably significant gestures of the earlier Foucault who, alongside Louis Althusser and Gilles Deleuze, staked his career, as it were, on the immanentization of our thinking of power relations? In a famous dictum, he asserts:

> We must cease once for all to describe the effects of power in negative terms: it 'excludes', it 'represses', it 'censors', it 'abstracts', it 'masks', it 'conceals'. In fact, power produces; it produces reality.[16]

Which is to say that power exists only immanently, in its effects, rather than from a transcendent outside, a constellation Kordela (as we noted) refers to as 'secular causality'. Of course, this move away from talking about power by way of outside agents was also at the heart of Foucault's well-known diagnoses of the early modern shift in hegemonic power away from a transcendent sovereignty which appears in the form of a localized sovereign who makes threats, demands or promises from outside the sphere of the governed, who become the inside. As he describes it in remarkable prose in *Discipline and Punish*, with this paradigm shift or shift in operations, the locus of power enacts an exodus from the figure of the external sovereign in order to dwell amidst more diffuse and multiple spaces of manageable life itself. Again, power appears only in produced or effected modes, as it were without a why, as an index of an ontology constituted by what Simon Critchley referred to as a 'transcendental contingency'.[17] In Heideggerian terms that I think were important to Foucault's work at this point, this is the historical moment when an ontology of subject–object relations began to blur into an ontology of the standing reserve, 'things' becoming indistinguishable from their place of installation or their capacity to function as apparatuses of accessibility within more diffuse networks of information.[18]

Note also that this move to immanent or network power also constitutes the heart of Foucault's description of the eighteenth-century rise of discourses of political economy, the modern clinic or psychiatric techniques of the self in the nineteenth century, all of which Foucault began to synthesize in terms of the paradoxical governance of life itself, by and in the name of itself. There are more specifics to add in each case, but we should not miss the way a central problem (indeed a central Heideggerian, Althusserian and Deleuzian problem) of *immanence* radiates throughout everything. With the self-feeding labyrinth of life governing the living we hit upon the really compelling problem of the technique, technology or the exercise as the apparatus which makes available for measurement, management or representation a life which is, as it were, otherwise unapproachable in its immanence. This is the odd paradox, folding, or exception of immanence which follows his analyses at every turn.

We could note here also the way Giorgio Agamben articulates the basic Foucaultian problem by way of early-nineteenth-century theological conversations whereby God was encounterable only *in* the form of 'positive religion', specified, singularized *modes* of religion's enactment in a cultural setup.[19] Agamben's expansion of Foucault's or Deleuze's similar diagnosis of the problem of 'the apparatus' is very important, inasmuch as it highlights an issue about transcendence and immanence which everywhere haunts Foucault's discussions of the state, the subject, selfhood and power: there is no entity without technique or technology whereby this entity appears *as* or *to* such gestures or performative enactments. All of which is only to say, fatefully, that there is no selfhood without or apart from, spiritual exercise. Immanence names this labyrinthine or groundless recursivity as the real drama of the epoch of the biopolitical.

If bells are not already ringing here about the problem of immanence as a form also of the classic problem of Paul and the law, then let me push our detour into the larger projects of Foucault one step further, gathering a sense of the significance of a *moment of becoming* wherein Paul and Foucault morph into each other. Remember that this discursive shift from transcendent, or exterior, to immanent forms of governance were directly, and by Foucault himself, sometimes described in terms of stereotypical distinctions between 'Hebraic' and 'Christian' forms of pastoral power.[20] In the former, Foucault suggests, pastoral surveillance and governance of the individual was itself subservient to political forms of *law*. Christian modes of pastoral power were, by contrast, a result of a denigration of exterior or, as it were, heteronymous law, a move which necessarily leads to increased attention to more immanent forms of life as the generative mechanisms which must be put under surveillance and managed. The shift from Hebraic to Christian forms of pastoral power, in other words, was being discursively organized in Foucault's work by way of traditional Pauline tropes of 'law' versus 'spirit', these tropes in turn being understood (again, very traditionally) as referring to a history of religion or, more specifically, a history of *two different* religions.[21] Moreover, this archival tale is obviously affording Foucault an echo of a shift in *modern power relations* whereby exterior, repressive modes of power are increasingly supplanted by immanent, productivist solicitations of subjectivation.

Yes, it is true that according to his sometimes stated views on the difference between idealizing or universalizing or monumentalizing history versus the Nietzschean and Deleuzean attention to flux, multiplicity and the minimal difference or Epicurean *clinamen*, this comparative game is not the *kind of thing* Foucault is supposed to be doing. Nevertheless, Foucault *does* get caught up in these games, these recursivities within the discursive flux, our apologies to some of his formulations about genealogy and history notwithstanding! Gilles Deleuze registered his surprise at this aspect of the late Foucault in his interviews with Claire Parnet, but the real truth is – as I have here sketched briefly – that the game of comparative analogy between epoch or macro-level structures occurs earlier in Foucault's work as well.

This should be enough to demonstrate why I feel a little like Foucault missed his *kairos* (as Benjamin and Taubes put it), his chance opportunity to *intervene* in an important way which could reshape the received conversations. At this point in Foucault's *oeuvre*, Paulinism seems like it could name at once an historical shift from one to another religious form, even as it indicates a shift in modern power from a repressive to a biopolitical model. It was, we might say, a chance for Foucault to *enact* or embrace an 'Egyptian moment' of enigmatic intervention, but instead nothing really seems to happen except that Foucault repeats very traditional (non-) comparative and historiographical coordinates.

What is lost is the opportunity to think differently about both 'religion' and 'Christianity' (not to mention 'Hebraic' modes of ethics) in terms of that twin obsession of immanence, namely, singularity. The missed (transformative) encounter with Paul constitutes a different way of configuring what Foucault named, in good Heideggerian manner, the coming to the end or limit of a 'classical' Western mode of thinking. Along with his late explorations of *parrhēsia* (or bold and risky speech) and Greco-Roman spiritual exercises as counter-classical modes of thinking about life, and good life, as enacted or practiced singularities, Foucault could have forced Paulinism, and with it traditional 'Christian origins' stories, into the sphere of singularity and groundless spiritual exercise. To do so, however, Foucault would have had to, as it were, *become* Paul. As it was, he left Paul on the *other side* of a delineation of culture into foundational and non-foundational or purely relational terms. In doing so, interestingly, Foucault repeated not only the story of Nietzsche (with Paul on the other side of the immanence of life as the guiltiest purveyor of a 'Platonism for the masses'), but also the story of a modern conservative churchman like Theodore Zahn.

Consider the significance of this missed encounter by recalling the way in which in *The Order of Things* Foucault named the emergence of a logic of singularity (which is to say difference and multiplicity) as the essential distinguishing mark separating his nineteenth-century 'modernity', with its emergent bio-power, and the 'prehistory' which was non-modern, representational thought constituted by a stable ground or 'outside'. In other words, Foucault's analyses of a shift in modern power relations (transcendence becoming immanence) also functioned at the level of a distinction between what he calls 'classical' and 'modern' forms of ethics. In ways that evoke once more the old 'problem of the law', and even a question of two dispensations or testaments. He writes in *The Order of Things* that the West has known, basically, 'two ethical forms':

> The old one (in the form of Stoicism or Epicureanism) was articulated upon the order of the world, and by discovering the law of that order it could deduce from it the principle of a code of wisdom or a conception of the city; even the political thought of the eighteenth century still belongs to this general form. The modern one, on the other hand, formulates no morality, since any imperative is lodged within thought and its movement towards the apprehension of the unthought; it is reflection, the act of consciousness, the elucidation of what is silent, language restored to what is mute, the illumination of the element of darkness that cuts man off from himself, the reanimation of the inert – it is all this and this alone that constituted the content and form of the ethical. Modern thought has never, in fact, been able to propose a morality.

There is no need to get lost in his language. The odd paradox of immanent thought, of an imperative residing *in* rather than *outside* the thought is simply the difficulty of trying to think immanent causality. Moreover, the difficulty of the turns of phrase begins to articulate what matter of spiritual practice Foucault thinks we should take up in our efforts to think the imperative of being, being in its stupid being there, as being *its own form of imperative*. Modernity cannot formulate a 'law' or a 'morality' or a representable 'code' of conduct because, Foucault explains further, for modernity 'thought [. . .] is itself an action – a perilous act'. Foucault sees in modernity something like a Heideggerian displacement of the economy of representation (where words are charted onto things) onto a more opaquely self-grounding economy of language, production and life in which there is no *model* to re-present in thinking.[22] Instead, we might say (echoing Foucault's discussion of Deleuze), there are only *singular* exemplars which – for this reason – all the more opaquely or violently constitute the ground of their own operations. When he concludes the section by saying that, therefore, 'modern thought is advancing towards that region where man's Other must become the Same as himself', he is not suggesting the usual handwringing about an appropriation of the other by the same. Rather, the point is that the existence of the same, as a singularity, would bear its own burden of alterity, would carry around with it its *own* shadow. Thought or existence within this setup would always bear the cut of finitude, forever indicating the absence of stable models by always ever and only conjuring the singular other, my 'ownmost' other as Heidegger could have put it.

Notice that, in this respect, Foucault's reading of Paul in the section we are considering leaves Paul on the other side of, precisely, the real issue of immanence he is himself, he tells us repeatedly, trying to formulate, namely, the question of what would it be to formulate an ethic of singularity, an ethic wherein the self has neither identity nor model for what it is, save in its risky techniques of self-making, its spiritual exercises.

To see the Nietzschean story playing out, just follow Foucault's argument. First, he asserts, there certainly *were* distinct lines of demarcation separating, first, Greco-Roman moralism from classical philosophical reflections about sexuality and, second, Greco-Roman moralism from more developed institutional Christianity. In the first case, Foucault summarizes, the transformation in talk about self-governance was marked by a heightened anxiety about the body in the Greco-Roman period, something that led to an intensification of attention to the body itself as the privileged site by which to comprehend sexuality. There was also in the Greco-Roman period the emergence of a tendency to universalize the 'form' of sexual embrace, thereby playing down the more local and contingent role of 'status' in classical theorization of erotic liaison. This universalization or formalization of the pleasurable encounter emerged hand in hand with intensified *practices of reflective internalization* within the emerging subject of sexuality. As Foucault says with usual material, phenomenological verve: 'Problematization and apprehension go hand in hand; inquiry is joined to vigilance.'[23] When sexual encounter becomes a generic form of relationship, individuals, he suggests brilliantly, increasingly become their own overseers, with the vigilant and conscious self appearing in order to maintain or guarantee adherence to the universal rule. These distinctions organize Foucault's summary of the difference between classical and Greco-Roman ethics of the body.

Second, however, Foucault is here particularly interested to point out as well that what he glosses as 'Christianity' represented yet another qualitative shift along a longer trajectory of internalization and universalization. In this additional discursive transformation, the excessive nature of sexual desire and the potential dangers such excesses bring with them become, yet again, increasingly universalized and therefore detached from the contingent local specifics of encounter. With this transformation, 'sexual activity is linked to evil' not only by its possible 'form and effects, but in itself and substantially'. The analysis of the discursive logics is intriguing. Even more than with their Greco-Roman moralist contemporaries, therefore, in Christianity the mode of sexual individuation begins to appear *only by way of transgression of the universalized norm*, a phenomenological stance that itself, we should notice, demands new ideas of the Fall or (transgressive) finitude. Constituting a qualitatively different category from the Greco-Roman moralists, Christianity thus affords a 'mode of subjection in the form of obedience to a general law', a law we should add immediately which – Foucault will suggest – likewise organizes the modern notion of a subject of sexual desire occluded by a repressive law, whether of divine law, the law of the father or the law of the symbolic order. This subject of sexual desire seems to me to be the real stakes of the section – that *topos* which will unite Foucault's discussions here to his later discussions of confession and his earlier descriptions of psychoanalysis as distinct only in ornamental terms from earlier Christian confessionals.

This splitting into unassailable and stable law and necessarily guilty finitude is another name for what Nietzsche so ingeniously labelled a Platonism for the masses.

What does this mean? Paul, at the end of the third volume of *The History of Sexuality*, is an echo chamber of genealogical types and tropes and distinctions. Foucault as it were catalogues the representable causes of the echoes, but not their effect. He transcribes basically a traditional story and without articulating surprising or subversive forms of the echoes' resonance, without reworking the stock and standard categories of the usual story of Christian origins. Put differently, Foucault here *refuses participation* in what Perniola called the Egyptian moment. But that is only to say that he refuses himself, ultimately, a moment of real becoming – a moment which would scramble the relation between original and copy, but which also potentially transforms the specific modes of organization or representation by which we tend to stabilize, which is to say to *still*, these echoes. Why *not* force Paul to give evidence of his activities as irredeemably a part of the world Foucault really *did* believe in, namely, a world of risky, exposed singularities?

Conclusion: A note on Paul who could yet become St Foucault

I conclude with a postscript of a moment that has always piqued my interest. The young Albert Schweitzer, destined to become a central figure within New Testament studies, has taken up a post running a Christian seminary. The moment is poignant. He is training ministers for the denominations which will eventually refuse to support his going to Africa as a humanitarian physician until he promises not to tell the Africans any of his ideas about the New Testament. (Schweitzer would several years later describe his exit from the European academy to work in Africa as an act of judgement against the state of European civilization, which he saw confirmed in the outbreak of the First World War. As you can imagine, the militant Schweitzer allowed these denominations to support his travels and then he ignored them once he got there.) He writes at this precarious moment to his girlfriend, making a sort of confession to her, acknowledging that he feels badly let down . . . strangely . . . let down by Nietzsche. Schweitzer explains the dynamic by suggesting that it was only Nietzsche who 'could have become Saint Paul' but didn't.

I have always been intrigued by this strange love letter, this peculiar confession, but I think I now feel I know what it means, certainly in light of my own work. Nietzsche castigated Paul as the founding father of a 'Platonism for the masses', and he disavowed Paul as having foisted onto the world a dualistic lie which played the Judas in relation to immanence and becoming. But Nietzsche never tried to read Paul, even Paul's dualism (let's say), *as a form of what cannot be transcended or escaped, that from which we will never be sheltered, namely, the finitude of flux and becoming Nietzsche associated with immanence.* In Schweitzer's terms, Nietzsche abused and critiqued Paul, but he did not go all the way, namely (if oddly), by himself becoming Paul, and this in the form of understanding Paul in terms of the way that Nietzsche really believed the world worked.

Foucault, as I have suggested, also leaves the figure of Paul, as a potential figure for *our thought*, for our thinking about how we think the world really works, isolated, sequestered, sheltered and saved. In that sense he repeats Zahn, though not for pious reasons. Perhaps *this* is the great distinction we usually name 'theoretical', that separates Foucault from more recent thoughts of immanence in the work of Alain Badiou or Slavoj Žižek. Foucault, for whatever reasons, here leaves the inherited coordinates that in some sense constitute the significance of the name Paul unscathed, safe, isolated. He is rejected in good Nietzschean fashion, but not rewired *as* an indication of the immanence of thought which explodes the safe framing of traditional metaphysics, above all the safety of a traditional 'Platonism for the masses'. And, as I am suggesting, in their moving beyond Foucault on this score we find that they have rather *become* Paul in a way Foucault never did.

Here is my gamble: Paul has returned along the line of *paradoxes* endemic to a radical thinking of immanence. This phenomenon invites further reflection on ancient or future Pauls whereby a properly materialist or immanent spirituality is revealed to us, as if right on cue. This revelation I think we will see as we continue to become aware of those new handbooks of new materialist spiritualities, so many how-to books about how to experience the enchantment of a new materialism, that we see emerging ever quicker now from philosophers, psychoanalysts and cultural theorists like Jane Bennet, Peter Sloterdijk, William Connolly, Elizabeth Grosz, Manuel Delanda, Eric Santner, Hent de Vries or Jonathan Goldberg (just to name a few). My ongoing work will stay with the theme of singularity and philosophy as practice, but shift the attention on Paul and the philosophers towards the ancient texts and contexts of Paul more directly. I am particularly intrigued to see what we can say about those odd Pauline becomings (becoming crucified, becoming dead, becoming Christ, some of the central images he attaches to central collective rituals in the community). And I am particularly keen to locate Paul within a period of the inflation, as it were, of value-inverting or para-doxical spiritual exercises that we find also among groups like the Stoics.

How shall we understand more generally the proliferation and particular nuance during this period of philosophical self-training in dispossessing experiences of 'stuckness'? Or, turned around, why were these groups becoming so ingenious at that strangely ironic folding of imposed forms of radical passivity and dispossession into forms of collective agency, what Peter Sloterdijk sometimes calls collective or social 'bubbles' of self-protection or co-immunity?[24] Remember how heavily some of these therapies of the soul borrow from the stage and *topoi* of gladiatorial spectacles, these instances of dispossession becoming, precisely, the extremes whereby singular forms of life teach themselves how to live, learn to live, to practice at living a life that appears only under the impress of forms of death.

Here I imagine that Paul is both comparable to other Hellenistic philosophical schools but also – as they *all were already* – in an intriguing form of agonism or 'outbidding' in relation to the spiritual exercises on offer from the other teachers. When we compare Paul and the philosophers not as a set of comparable ideas so much as a comparable and interrelated economy of practices and salesmanship for therapies of the soul, then important new readings of Paul become clear entirely in keeping with the late Foucault's fascination with risky experimentations of individual/ collective being that he associated with Hellenistic discourses of *parrhēsia* and self-as-*technē*. Above all, Paul was not simply *also* presenting spiritual practices that promise the capacity to invert the value of everyday values. He was presenting himself *as* someone who does so, trying to anchor himself into a larger economy of discourse and hierarchy of speakers by presenting himself as doing what, in that economy, one does: offering effective countercultural therapies for the soul.

Paul does so, for example, in a letter like the famous epistle to the Romans, by promising that *his parrhēsia* or bold philosophical discourse (note his forms of self-introduction in the first two chapters) *actually produces* a community of sages who overcome the problem of desire by way of a pneumatic empowering of the mental life (*nous*, cf. chs 6–8), leading to what he summarizes as a *logikē latreia* (or 'reasoned worship') in Romans 12, a way of repeating his emphasis on mind and its relation to life and action. That central therapies are all oriented around the trope of how the community itself becomes a messianic figure of living death, one otherwise effectively repressed by Roman colonial functionaries in Jerusalem, also highlights my interest in historical tales like this one for larger genealogies of the category of Foucaultian biopolitics. Inasmuch as Hellenistic sages of all stripes were peddling paradoxical intertwinings of subjectivity and death or radical expropriation, and this as a mode of inventing little bubbles of communal life, it seems we already have an exploration of spiritual exercises as forms of the negotiation of ancient biopolitical paradoxes. Foucault did not himself *become* Paul (with all the implications of such a possibility) – but he opened the way for others to do so, and precisely by way of radicalizing his own thinking of biopolitical immanence and power.

Notes

1   Mario Perniola, *Enigmas: The Egyptian Moment in Society and Art* (trans. Christopher Woodall, London: Verso, 1995), pp. vii–viii.

2   Important steps have been taken in the work of Sophie Fuggle and Valerie Nicolet Anderson, whose forthcoming books will no doubt reshape discussions in several related disciplines. See, for example, their special issue of the *Journal of Cultural and Religious Theory* on Foucault and Paul 11/1 (2010), www.jcrt. org. They describe there some of the important earlier moves in the work of Halvor Moxnes or Elizabeth Castelli. For a longer discussion, see my lengthy introduction to Ward Blanton and Hent de Vries, eds, *Paul and the Philosophers* (New York: Fordham University Press, 2012). The full story on the way Alain Badiou's encounter with Paul is inextricable from a neo-conservative effort to preserve the ethnic and financially hierarchical essence of Europe by way of a 'metapolitics' remains to be told, though see Alain Badiou, *The Incident at Antioch* (New York: Columbia University Press, 2012); cf. the discussion of metapolitics in Bruno Bosteels. In addition to the well-known works on Paul by Jacob Taubes, Alain Badiou and Giorgio Agamben, note also more recent work by Slavoj Žižek and John Milbank, *The Monstrosity of Christ: Paradox or Dialectic?* (Boston: MIT Press, 2010); Stanislas Breton, *A Radical Philosophy of Saint Paul* (New York: Columbia University Press, 2011); Pier Paolo Pasolini, *Saint Paul* (London: Verso, 2012); and Simon Critchley, *Faith of the Faithless: Experiments in Political Theology* (London: Verso, 2011).

3   I develop important sharings and contestations of a German Lutheran historico-philosophical tradition in Ward Blanton, *Displacing Christian Origins: Philosophy, Secularity, and the New Testament* (Chicago: University of Chicago Press, 2007). Working with Nietzsche and Freud, I develop a further argument on the implicit Platonism carried by an aged historiographical discourse about 'Christian origins' in Ward Blanton, *A Materialism for the Masses: Paul the Apostle and Other Partisans of Undying Life* (New York: Columbia University Press, 2013).

4   In this respect, the 'signature' indicates a kind of phenomenal event which itself precedes and constitutes our usual thinking about discretely separable subjects and objects or events separated in time. For further discussion that is important to my thinking of signatures or apparatuses of capture within a philosophy of difference, see the excellent work of Eric Alliez, *The Signature of the World: What is Deleuze and Guattari's Philosophy?* (London: Continuum, 2005). 'In *practice*, the question is that of a theory of thought capable of diagnosing in our becomings the ontological condition for the real experience of thought' (p. 2). Pushing the same genealogical method back to a Foucault who remained in this respect very close to Deleuze, Giorgio Agamben engages the issues in *Signature of All Things* (Boston: MIT Press, 2009).

5   See Julia Reinhard Lupton, 'Ablative Absolutes: From Paul, to Shakespeare', *Paul and the Philosophers*.

6   See Kiarina Kordela, $*urplus* (New York: SUNY Press, 2008), pp. 27ff. The problem of our dogged attachments to the singularity of factical life, or the passionate attachments which constitute our being within an ontology of 'transcendental contingency', is the key topic of the explorations of Paul in *A Materialism for the Masses*.

7   See, for example, Michel Foucault, *The Courage of Truth: The Government of Self and Others II* (New York: Palgrave Macmillan, 2008), especially the discussions on *parrhēsia*. For links to discussions of immanence as a *topos* in the development of theses on biopolitics, see the lectures in Michel Foucault, *Birth of Biopolitics* (New York: Palgrave Macmillan, 2010).

8   Michel Foucault, *The History of Sexuality*, vol. 3, *The Care of the Self* (trans. Robert Hurley, New York: Random House, 1988), pp. 233ff.

9   Nietzsche's remarks on Christianity as a pop Platonism come from initial statements in Friedrich Nietzsche, *Twilight of the Idols* (New York: Penguin, 1990), p. 11. See also the excellent philosophical discussion in Didier Franck, *Nietzsche and the Shadow of God* (trans. Bettina Bergo, Chicago: Northwestern University Press, 2012). See also the excellent book of Tyler T. Roberts, *Contesting Spirit: Nietzsche, Affirmation, Religion* (Princeton: Princeton University Press, 1998). There is a useful overview to be found in Hans Hübner, *Nietzsche und Das Neue Testament* (Tübingen: Mohr Siebeck, 2000).

10 There is a great deal one could say here, but note the affinities and shared *topoi* of the history of religions research and many of the early developments in theories of crowd psychology, sociology and new materialist ideas on cultural mood. Hermann Gunkel's 1890s analysis of spirit hits upon a decidedly ancient–modern problem of the *materiality* of group consciousness at the same moment that Gustave Le Bon and Gabriel Tarde began to formulate theories of crowd psychology which would in various ways completely scramble notions of individual psychology and autonomy as they were taken up and reworked by figures like Emile Durkheim and Sigmund Freud. Durkheim would begin to discuss both individual suicides and individual religious experiences as regularized expressions of an 'electrical' current within mediated collective life just as Richard Reitzenstein and Franz Cumont would attempt to grasp the history of religions through the language of migrations of moods, climatic shifts in cultural temperature or the flow of an inchoate cultural 'fluid'. In sealing itself off from these movements of thought, British New Testament scholarship effectively sealed itself off from the necessity of *doing cultural theory* (of whatever sort) in relation to biblical interpretation, a move which has fateful implications for the current institutional location of biblical scholarship within the British University.

11 In addition to the note above, we should also mention how early ethnographic discussions of the 'primitive philosophy' of the 'savage mind' functioned as a kind of phenomenological immediacy which cuts across modern distinctions of subject and object, etc., in Lévy-Bruhl (*La Mentalité Primitive*) or Paul Radin (*Primitive Man as Philosopher*), echoing Heidegger's occasional assertion that European phenomenology was a zone of enquiry which had to live as quack psychology or 'occult' phenomena during Europe's commitment to subject–object distinctions. In other words, the history of religions movement studied ancient religiosity as a mode of working through profoundly *modern* intellectual problems.

12 Cf. Foucault, *History of Sexuality*, vol. 3, p. 239. The language of mere surface analogies which must be refused is to be found everywhere in Zahn's work.

13 Ibid., p. 236.

14 Ibid., p. 239.

15 Ibid.

16 Michel Foucault, *Discipline and Punish* (trans. Alan Sheridan, New York: Vintage, 1977), p. 194.

17 For a discussion of the brilliant mode in which Stanislas Breton linked Paul, the later Althusser, Meister Eckhart and Heidegger, see my introduction to Breton, *A Radical Philosophy of Saint Paul.*

18 While there is a great deal that remains to be said on this score, an important contribution to the story of Foucault and Heidegger may be found in Alan Milchman and Alan Rosenberg, eds, *Foucault and Heidegger: Critical Encounters* (Minneapolis, MN: University of Minnesota Press, 2003).

19 See Giorgio Agamben, *What is an Apparatus? And Other Essays* (Stanford: Stanford University Press, 2009).

20 Relevant passages and important issues are engaged in the work of Mika Ojakangas, 'On the Pauline Roots of Biopolitics: Apostle Paul in Company with Foucault and Agamben', *Journal of Cultural and Religious Theory* 11.1 (2010), pp. 92–94.

21 Here we catch a glimpse of the radical shift in paradigm afforded by the simple insight that even Paul's radical polemics in a letter like the one to the Galatians were directed against his competitors within the Jesus movement, and that it is only an idealizing – and perhaps intensely Lutheran – tradition which implies that we should read these as representations as of two religions, two modes of religion and so on. For further reflection on these issues, see my introduction to *Paul and the Philosophers.*

22 While there is *more* than an interest in the displacement of model-and-repetition constitutive of representational thought here in Foucault, we should not miss the way it is nevertheless essential. Later, in his *The Order of Things: An Archaeology of Human Sciences* (New York: Vintage, 1970), Foucault will refuse some of the obvious similarities at work in the Classical episteme and the modern one by pointing to their different mode of relation to the question of representation:

> But this play of correspondences must not be allowed to delude us. We must not imagine that the Classical analysis of discourse has continued without modification through the ages merely by applying itself to a new object; that the force of some historical weight has maintained it in its identity, despite so many adjacent mutations. In fact, the four theoretical segments that outlined the space of general grammar have not been preserved: but they were dissociated, they changed both their function and their level, they modified the entire domain of their validity when, at the end of the eighteenth century, the theory of representation was eclipsed. [. . .] In contrast [to the Classical age], the analysis of man's mode of being as it has developed since the nineteenth century does not reside within a theory of representation [. . .] (p. 367)

23 Foucault, *History of Sexuality*, vol. 3, p. 239.

24 Sloterdijk is for me one of those ingenious thinkers who still repeats Nietzscheanisms against Paulinism without realizing that, read outside the dominant frames of early Christian triumphalist Platonism, Paul is in fact much closer to Sloterdijk's beloved Cynicism (if Stoically inflected). For bubbles, folds and radical passivity, see Peter Sloterdijk, *Bubbles: Spheres I (Microspherology)* (San Francisco: Semiotext(e), 2011).

6

St Gilles between the Divine and the Demonic

Clayton Crockett

In her book *Saints and Postmodernism*, Edith Wyschogrod uses postmodern ideas and insights to illuminate the narratives of saints' lives, and suggests that such a reading can enrich our moral philosophy. In her book, 'the conventions of postmodernism are put into the service of explicating moral dilemmas, and saintly responses are themselves part of the revisioning process'.[1] This reading works against the idea that a life has only one meaning and one goal that is preset or pre-given.

Wyschogrod applies postmodern theoretical insights to a reading of traditional lives of saints. An alternative perspective, taken in this volume, is to view post-structuralist and postmodern philosophers themselves as saints in a way, perhaps because philosophers like Levinas and Derrida express and exemplify philosophical moral virtue. In this essay, I consider Gilles Deleuze as a postmodern saint, based on his work in liberating and redeeming differences. One of the main differences that Deleuze is interested in redeeming is the difference between the divine and the demonic. To be a saint in Deleuzian terms is to be engaged in the work of redemption, but not a redemption of things or beings. Deleuze's saintly work is to redeem differences, processes, flows and becomings, which ultimately means to redeem the intervals or interstices between beings. This between occurs paradigmatically between what could be called the divine and the demonic, God and the Devil, or Christ and Antichrist.

It would be difficult to claim that Deleuze is a saint in any conventional sense. In fact Wyschogrod opposes and critiques his philosophy as being too mystical to be useful for her re-envisioning of moral philosophy. Deleuze strongly opposes any form of conventional religion. His affirmation of a plane of immanence counters the traditional hierarchy of transcendence that makes saints possible and viable in the first place. He denigrates common-sense morality in favour of a philosophical ethics based on Spinoza and Nietzsche. His philosophy attacks the idea of representational identity, and criticizes the notion of a person serving as a model for others to follow. So then, in what way could we consider Deleuze to be a saint?

If a saint is important based on who he or she is, then Deleuze cannot be considered a saint. Only if we think about saintliness as a work can an argument be made. And even here, this is an unorthodox argument, because Deleuze could only be an unorthodox saint. What is the work of a saint? The saint repeats the work of Christ, which is redemption. There are two difficulties here, one of which concerns the notion of repetition, and the other is that of redemption. Repetition usually means repetition of identity, and in this case repetition is tied to representation. Deleuze criticizes philosophy based on a representation of a prior identity, claiming that identity is not pre-given. Repetition is a repetition of difference. So long as redemption involves redeeming any prior identity, redemption is not possible in Deleuzian terms. So Deleuze opposes both of these ideas in their typical form, but his work also suggests transformed understandings of these two concepts.

Insofar as a saint follows and repeats the work of Christ, who serves as a representational model, Deleuze's philosophy cannot be assimilated to sainthood. Deleuze (along with Guattari) claims that Spinoza, one of his philosophical precursors, is the 'Christ' of the philosophers. Why is Spinoza named Christ? Because he showed what 'cannot be thought and yet must be thought, which was thought once, as Christ was incarnated once, in order to show, that one time, the possibility of the impossible'.[2] This possibility of the impossible is a philosophy that demonstrates the plane of immanence as the unthought of every philosophy. A plane of immanence is Deleuze's term for a zone of consistency that inhabits an entire way of thinking and living that is not imposed from above in a hierarchical or transcendent way. In his book *Spinoza: Practical Philosophy*, Deleuze claims that his understanding of Spinoza involves 'no longer the affirmation of a single substance, but rather the laying out of a common plane of immanence on which all bodies, all minds, and all individuals are situated'.[3]

Implicit in this designation of Spinoza as the Christ of the philosophers is an analogy between Christ and Spinoza that can be extended to the notion of a saint, with Deleuze as a follower of Spinoza, whose philosophy serves as a model and unattainable ideal. But the problem then is that Deleuze's philosophy explicitly opposes the representational and analogical modes of thought at work in this comparison. Deleuze's philosophy proceeds based on difference, and specifically in his most important book, a repetition of difference. My argument is that a more interesting but subtle case can be made to consider Deleuze as a saint if we attend to his books *Difference and*

Repetition and *The Logic of Sense*. Here the concept of saint is deformed and dislocated from its traditional religious and its revised moral categories, and transformed into a kind of redemption.

Deleuze provisionally takes the side of the demonic and the Antichrist in order to redeem everything, not as entity but as being/becoming, or what Spinoza calls *natura naturans*. In his philosophy, Spinoza distinguishes between *natura naturans*, or nature naturing, which is a process of becoming, and *natura naturata*, or 'nature natured', which is the determinate nature that results from this process. In *Difference and Repetition*, Deleuze contrasts two forms of repetition. The first idea of repetition is the ordinary view of repetition as a repetition of identity, which he calls 'repetition of the Same', and this repetition is constituted by 'the identity of the concept or representation'.[4] Repetition of the Same is a bare, material repetition that covers up a deeper repetition, a repetition of difference. This second form of repetition, which Deleuze calls a spiritual repetition, is 'grounded in inequality, incommensurability and dissymmetry'.[5]

While the first repetition founded on representation and identity 'is inanimate, the other carries the secret of our deaths and our lives, of our enchantments and our liberations, the demonic and the divine'.[6] To think repetition in terms of the demonic and the divine, Deleuze appeals to a univocal philosophy identified with both Duns Scotus and Spinoza. This idea of univocity is not based on the sameness of being, but a comprehensive vision of being in terms of difference. Deleuze claims:

> It is not a matter of being which is distributed according to the requirements of representation, but of all things being divided up within being in the univocity of simple presence (the One-All). Such a distribution is demonic rather than divine, since it is a peculiarity of demons to operate in the intervals between the gods' field of action [. . .].[7]

Identity is an optical illusion generated by our assumptions about representation; it is actually produced by the deeper interactions of difference and repetition. Repetition is profoundly a repetition of difference, not a repetition of identity. But doesn't there have to be some kind of identity or sameness that is in common to two or more events in order to even be able to call a phenomenon a repetition? The alternative seems to be complete nonsense and anarchy, and a breakdown of repetition.

Repetition is related to time. In *Difference and Repetition*, Deleuze develops a series of three forms of temporal repetition, which occur as three syntheses of time. The first synthesis of time, associated with the present, is habit. The second synthesis is based on memory, or the recollection of the past. Finally, the future occurs based on the eternal recurrence of difference, which passes through a kind of death because only what is different recurs.

Towards the end of the chapter, he raises the crucial question for his entire project: how can difference be related to difference without the mediation of sameness or identity? Taking his cue from Heidegger, Deleuze claims that 'there must be a differenciation of difference, an in-itself which is like a *differenciator*, a *Sich-unterscheidende*, by virtue of which the different is gathered all at once rather than represented on condition of a prior resemblance, identity, analogy or opposition'.[8] How does this form of differenciation work? First, differences must be organized into a series. Second, there must be at least two series that are compared to each other. It is not what they have in common that generates significance, but the difference between the two series. The series of differences forms a diffraction pattern, even though Deleuze does not use this term from physics.[9]

Deleuze says that the second-degree differences play the role of 'differenciator', which means that it is the differences at the level of the series that are overlaid or brought together that emerge as a new creation. Repetition is the force or intensity that brings together the two series in such a way that differences can emerge from the diffraction of series. There do not have to be only two series, but there must be at least two in order for the differenciator to function. Intensity is the key to understanding how difference works by means of difference, not identity. Repetition involves the intensive force that brings together a series of differences to form new differences out of the relation of difference to difference, which is a process of differenciation. In order for difference to work, to function and be productive, there must be intervals, or what Deleuze calls later in *Cinema 2*, interstices between differences that compose a series, and then differences between series, that can be related.

Deleuze focuses on the monstrous or demonic intervals, or more precisely the intervals that exist between the divine and the demonic, to redeem the process of differenciation and repetition as a whole. The divine and the demonic occur along a plane of immanence, a zone of consistency that allows them to be related as differences, and Deleuze's task as a saint is to liberate these intervals or interstices as such rather than the identities that are produced out of them. Although he uses some spiritual language to talk about repetition in *Difference and Repetition*, Deleuze does not often use religious or theological language. One place where he does so is in an appendix to his follow-up book *The Logic of Sense*, in a discussion of the writer Pierre Klossowski. In Klossowski's work, language and body interact in a special way such that 'the act of language [. . .] fabricates a body for the mind' that is a glorious body.[10]

In *The Logic of Sense* more generally, Deleuze contrasts two series, a series of language and a series of bodies. These two series are brought together and the diffraction pattern that emerges is an event. Deleuze associates his discussion of language with the work of Lewis Carroll, and his discussion of body primarily with Antonin Artaud. *The Logic of Sense* 'repeats' *Difference and Repetition* in a way, but more from the perspective of language than from the perspective of things. In taking up Klossowski's thought in his appendix on 'Phantasm and Modern Literature', Deleuze notes Klossowski's 'extraordinary parallelism between body and language', and from this observation he then reflects on the religious language that Klossowski uses in his work.[11] Theology as a special kind of spiritual language cannot be divorced from pornography, which is a writing of bodies in a perverse but important way.

In both cases, theology and pornography, it is a question of the disjunctive syllogism, or that which relates two terms even as it keeps them apart. Deleuze suggests that in Kant's transcendental philosophy, God as the third Idea represents 'the *mastery of the disjunctive syllogism*'.[12] God is thought in exceptional terms, as that which stands outside of and serves as the condition of possibility of such syllogisms, disjunctions and modifications. In Klossowski's work, however, 'it is not God but rather the Antichrist who is the master of the disjunctive syllogism; the "anti-God" determines the *passage* of each thing through all of its possible predicates'.[13] Deleuze prefers Klossowski's emphasis on the Antichrist, following Nietzsche's opposition between Dionysus and the Crucified in *The Antichrist*, because it is the diabolical rather than the divine principle that allows difference to become an 'object [. . .] of pure affirmation' in itself instead of appropriating them for a transcendent theological plan.[14] The conventional order of God as master of the disjunction syllogism understands disjunction in an exclusive and exclusionary sense. The apparent disorder of the Antichrist, however, posits disjunction as an affirmative modification. Deleuze writes that

> The disjunctive opposition accedes to a diabolical principle and use, and simultaneously the disjunction is affirmed for itself without ceasing to be a disjunction; divergence or difference becomes objects of pure affirmation, and 'either-or' becomes the power of affirmation, outside the conceptual conditions of the identity of a God, a world, or a self.[15]

Despite Deleuze's preference for the demonic, he does not embrace the demonic as such as simply the opposite of the divine order; he appeals to the demonic strategically in order to redeem differences and liberate them from the shackles of representation.

Disjunctions are productive rather than exclusive. According to Deleuze, we cannot simply oppose Antichrist to God (or to Christ). Just as the spiritual repetition is hidden below the bare material repetition, the order of the Antichrist that affirms differences lies just underneath or inside the order of God that denies them. Deleuze is concerned not with the demonic, the diabolical or the Antichrist as such, but with liberating differences as intervals or interstices that enable productive and creative repetition, which is a glorious individuating process.

In his late book, *The Fold: Leibniz and the Baroque*, Deleuze expresses a very similar conception of divinity, but he abandons the stated opposition between the order of God and the order of the Antichrist. In his discussion of Leibniz, Deleuze notes that God for Leibniz is the foundation of the best possible world, or rather, the richest compossible world. In an important chapter called 'What is an Event?', Deleuze compares Leibniz to Whitehead. Whereas for Leibniz, the 'bifurcations and divergences of series are genuine borders between incompossible worlds', in modern philosophy these divergences become incompossibilities in a positive sense.[16] God no longer remains outside the world, choosing the best one possible (or compossible), but for Whitehead God 'becomes Process, a process that at once affirms incompossibilities and passes through them'.[17] An incompossible world is one that should not be possible or compossible given an overall plan or axiomatics. But Deleuze is interested in the generation of impossible things or incompossible events, phenomena that occur despite being seemingly inconsistent or incompatible with each other. An event occurs along the border of a divergent series that bifurcates, creating new repetitions and possibilities.

Deleuze admires Leibniz's philosophy, but he views Leibniz's God along lines similar to how he understands Kant in *The Logic of Sense*, as the master of the disjunctive syllogism who remains outside of the play of series. In *The Fold*, instead of Klossowski's order of the Antichrist as an alternative expression of the possibility of liberating differences, Deleuze appeals to Whitehead's process philosophy for a thinking about incompossibility that subjects God to process and becoming. These discussions in *The Logic of Sense* and *The Fold* demonstrate that Deleuze is not simply interested in the divine or demonic per se. He is concerned with the cuts, caesuras or 'demonic intervals' that inhabit the world in an immanent way and compose a glorious body of disjunctions, multiplicities and assemblages.

So Deleuze multiplies oppositions, not to hold onto them, but to put them to work in the process of liberating and affirming differences in their interrelation or repetition. I am suggesting that we view Deleuze's philosophy as a work of saintliness, provided that being saintly is seen as doing this work of liberation, freed from attachment to both the divine and the demonic but able to work between the two to redeem creative becoming. The key problem for Deleuze is how difference relates to difference, and he affirms whatever assists in this process while criticizing whatever ideas constrain or prevent the positive relation of difference to difference.

Recently, with the publication and translation of Alain Badiou's provocative study of St Paul, we have witnessed numerous engagements with Paul and explorations of his significance for contemporary philosophical and religious thinking.[18] Deleuze, however, does not consider Paul a saint in any way, and he closely follows Nietzsche in his hostility towards Paul, as seen in his essay, 'Nietzsche and Saint Paul, Lawrence and John of Patmos'. In this piece Deleuze accuses Paul of 'inventing a new type of priest even more terrible than its predecessors', because Paul relies on the doctrine of immortality to intensify guilt and sin in order to create 'the doctrine of judgment'.[19]

Here Deleuze resorts to the opposition he sets out in the Appendix to *The Logic of Sense* between the order of God (associated with Pauline Christianity) and the order of the Antichrist (associated with Nietzsche).

In this essay, Deleuze opposes Paul to Nietzsche in a way that implies Nietzsche's understanding of Jesus as an idiot in the sense of Dostoyevsky, a simple and innocent being who inadvertently lends himself to the creation of the most terrible persecution machine the world has ever seen. Paul would be the inventor of this machine, and Paul's opposition to the Roman Empire, combined with the image of the Apocalypse, the imminent return of Christ whose return is indefinitely deferred, 'invents a completely new image of power: the system of Judgment'.[20] The Last Judgement is a programme created to enslave the world in its image of vengeful power, to get back at the powers that be for their power, and it is the result of an enormous *ressentiment*.

Nietzsche's interpretation of Christianity is a powerful critique. I would not argue that it is wrong, and certainly Christianity has all of these elements; it is and has been a brutal persecution machine, even if that aspect does not exhaust Christianity. I am suggesting, however, that Deleuze follows Nietzsche too faithfully in his interpretation of 'the black Saint Paul'.[21] Contemporary historical and biblical scholarship has emphasized the radicality of St Paul, and his revolutionary significance that precedes the establishment of a Christian orthodoxy. The line, if there is one, between revolutionary and reactionary does not lie between Jesus and Paul, but falls after them. In addition, as Jacob Taubes suggests, we can better see Nietzsche as a rival to St Paul in his attempt to offer European thought a new system of values, and this viewpoint corrects Deleuze's too-oppositional reading. In his study of the political theology of Paul, Taubes asks:

> Who has determined the values of the Occident, in Nietzsche's own sense, more deeply than Paul? So he must be an important man. Because what did Nietzsche want? The transvaluation of values. Well, so there we have someone who pulled it off! And on this point, Nietzsche is very envious too. So he has to say: this guy pulled it off because the poison of resentment holds sway within him.[22]

Taubes argues that there is an incredible proximity between Nietzsche and Paul, because both were engaged in a similar struggle. Taubes also claims that Nietzsche interprets his experience of the eternal return as a great ecstatic experience in light of Paul's Damascus experience. The eternal return is 'the metaphysical key to understanding everything [. . .] just as the Damascus experience is the metaphysical key for Paul'.[23] Given Deleuze's early work on *Nietzsche and Philosophy* and his consistent affirmation of Nietzsche, I would suggest that Deleuze himself identifies with Nietzsche's project of the transvaluation of values as Taubes expresses it. Deleuze perceives that this transvaluation can only occur on the basis of difference, and on the relation of differences to other differences.

Nietzsche makes a strategic choice for atheism, and in this essay and elsewhere Deleuze follows his lead, because he humanely opposes 'the cruelty of the pang of conscience' and the fact that 'Christianity hypostasizes sacrifice rather than abolishing it, and thus perpetuates it'.[24] We may or may not make the same choice, or we may not know exactly what it means to choose for theism or for atheism, Christ or Antichrist. At the same time, we can read St Paul in a way that avoids a forced choice, and appreciates his profound importance because he generates the sense of what becomes Christianity in terms of the event.

At the same time, we can reread Deleuze beyond his explicit opposition to St Paul, and see how despite his antipathy to Paul (under the spell of Nietzsche), in his overall philosophy Deleuze is engaged in a similar effort to provide meaning and value for the world and for life. Deleuze's thought attends to the sense of the event. And we can define someone as a saint who expresses fidelity to the event, without being caught within the 'either-or' alternative expressed by the opposition of Paul versus Nietzsche, whose contemporary form is expressed as Christianity or nihilism: *tertium non datur*.[25] Even if Badiou and Deleuze differ in important ways in their conception and definition of an event, we can nevertheless envision a convergence here around the notion of an event, and think about the saint as someone dedicated to liberating the event as a repetition of difference. Deleuze offers a subtle, paradoxical, and at its limits even a kind of radical theological thinking in *Difference and Repetition, The Logic of Sense, The Fold* and other books. Deleuze is a saint in a way, but he is a heretical saint, dedicated to liberating or redeeming the differential possibilities in nature and life.

Notes

1   Edith Wyschogrod, *Saints and Postmodernism* (Chicago: University of Chicago Press, 1990), p. xxvii.
2   Gilles Deleuze and Félix Guattari, *What Is Philosophy?* (trans. Hugh Tomlinson and Graham Burchell, New York: Columbia University Press, 1994), p. 60.
3   Gilles Deleuze, *Spinoza: Practical Philosophy* (trans. Robert Hurley, San Francisco: City Lights Books, 1988), p. 199.
4   Gilles Deleuze, *Difference and Repetition* (trans. Paul Patton, New York: Columbia University Press, 1994), p. 24.
5   Ibid.
6   Ibid.
7   Ibid., p. 37. Alain Badiou seizes on this notion of univocity and the concept of the One-All to accuse Deleuze of being a philosopher of the One, but this depends on a distortion of Deleuze's understanding and use of the term univocity. See Alain Badiou, *Deleuze: The Clamor of Being* (trans. Louise Burchill, Minneapolis: University of Minnesota Press, 2000); as well as my

counter-critique *Deleuze Beyond Badiou: Ontology, Multiplicity and Event* (New York: Columbia University Press, 2013).

8 Ibid., p. 117.

9 On the phenomenon of diffraction patterns, see Karen Barad, *Meeting the Universe Halfway: Quantum Physics and the Entanglement of Matter and Meaning* (Durham: Duke University Press, 2007), p. 72.

10 Gilles Deleuze, *The Logic of Sense* (trans. Mark Lester with Charles Stivale, New York: Columbia University Press, 1990), p. 281.

11 Ibid., p. 280.

12 Ibid., p. 295, emphasis in original.

13 Ibid., p. 296.

14 Ibid.

15 Ibid.

16 Gilles Deleuze, *The Fold: Leibniz and the Baroque* (trans. Tom Conley, Minneapolis: University of Minnesota Press, 1993), p. 81.

17 Ibid.

18 See Alain Badiou, *Saint Paul: The Foundation of Universalism* (trans. Ray Brassier, Stanford: Stanford University Press, 2003). See also John D. Caputo and Linda Alcoff, eds, *St. Paul Among the Philosophers* (Bloomington, IN: Indiana University Press, 2009); Creston Davis, John Milbank and Slavoj Žižek, *Paul's New Moment: Continental Philosophy and the Future of Christian Theology* (Grand Rapids, MI: Brazos Press, 2010), and Hent de Vries and Ward Blanton, eds, *Paul and the Philosophers* (New York: Fordham University Press, 2013).

19 Gilles Deleuze, *Essays Critical and Clinical* (trans. Daniel W. Smith and Michael A. Greco, Minneapolis, MN: University of Minnesota Press, 1997), p. 37.

20 Ibid., p. 39.

21 Ibid., p. 37.

22 Jacob Taubes, *The Political Theology of Paul* (trans. Dana Hollander, Stanford: Stanford University Press, 2004), p. 79.

23 Ibid., p. 85.

24 Ibid., p. 87.

25 See the expressions and formulations of Radical Orthodoxy, including John Milbank, *Theology and Social Theory: Beyond Secular Reason* (Oxford: Blackwell, 1990), Catherine Pickstock, *After Writing: On the Liturgical Consummation of Philosophy* (Oxford: Blackwell, 1998) and Conor Cunningham, *Genealogy of Nihilism: Philosophies of Nothing and the Difference of Theology* (London: Routledge, 2002). See also their essays in *Theology and the Political: The New Debate* (ed. Creston Davis, John Milbank and Slavoj Žižek, Durham: Duke University Press, 2005).

7

À Saint Jacques

Robyn Horner

I hadn't even known that you were sick.

It came as quite a shock, then, to hear the news on the BBC in the middle of the night. You had already gone, and I hadn't even known to expect it, in spite of the fact that this is always what I should have been expecting, and the knowledge that it marks everything you had written ('I posthume as I breathe'). . . .[1]

I hadn't even known that you were sick; I hadn't even known you. Yes, of course, I had spoken with you those few times, but I never really knew you.

I always imagined that if you were to stop writing, it might just be possible to get a handle on things, to systematize, codify, comprehend. But still you keep writing, long after you have been placed in the grave. And you have laid traps for me everywhere, so that it seems to me that there is never a final word to be said on anything you might have written. You knew this, surely. It is perhaps the one thing that annoys most those who are almost zealous in their opposition to you, as they go on to claim the final word about you. You resist saying it all – as you write you seem to *un*write.

Even death is not the last word.

That's not such an odd thing for someone who may or may not rightly pass for a theologian to say (and who would know about rightly passing?). Strangely enough, neither might it sound odd coming from the mouths of those who tell us now, definitively, that we must take you for an atheist through and through, and that finitude is the key (of course, I disagree). Finitude or not, there *is* no last word.

I am addressing you, now, as though you were here, as though you could be here. I still have your obituary from the newspaper there to one side, and many of your books, by and large, stay always in this place where I write. You haunt everything that I do, though you are not here. And yet I address you. I address you without address. I have no address by which to address you; you are gone without a forwarding address.

They have asked me to address you as a saint.

'*Il faut parler de toi, mais en parlant à toi. Comme si* [. . .]'.[2] Your friend Jean-Luc comes very close here to what you said yourself when Emmanuel passed away: 'those who make themselves heard in a cemetery, end up addressing *directly, straight on*, the one who, as we say, is no longer, is no longer living, no longer there, who will no longer respond [. . .]'.[3] We address the saints in this way, that is to say directly, straight on.

What's the difference between hagiology and hauntology?

I suspect you might laugh, to be called St Jacques, to be called *saint*. Hélène had already played with this notion. . . .[4] I wonder what you made of it? If someone asked about your being a saint, I think you might laugh in disbelief, and protest your innocence, your *disqualification* – first, of course, because you are not Catholic, or even Christian (we must return to this . . .). And then you would ask, in all seriousness, about what it means to be a *saint*, and we would find ourselves divided and redivided so that we would find that there never was one.

Il n'y a pas de Saint Jacques.

A first division

Il n'y a pas de saint. There is no saint. There is no[-thing] holy.

Are we speaking English or French? If we speak English, we are, in any case, immediately directed to look to Old French for the origins of the word *saint*. Yet when we speak French, we are directed only to the first of many ambiguities, which you had already alluded to in '*Foi et Savoir*' when you asked if we can disassociate a discourse on religion from a discourse on salvation, '*c'est-à-dire sur le sain, le saint, le sacré, le sauf, l'indemne, l'immun* (sacer, sanctus, heilig, holy . . .)'.[5] You had been reading Émile, without a doubt, on the idea of *le sacré*.[6] He observes that there is no single, common word for such a concept in the Indo-European languages; moreover, very often there are two words – to venture here only as far as the Latin: *sacer* as well as the *sanctus* from which we inherit *saint*. This reflects, he suggests, '*une notion à double face: positive "ce qui est chargé de presence divine", et négative "ce qui est interdit au contact des hommes"*'.[7]

Sacer itself divides: what is consecrated to the gods also arouses horror. Linked with *sacrificare*, *sacer* is associated with death. *Sacer* carries with it the difference between the sacred and the profane, and the terrible means by which something becomes sacred. For it is ultimately death that *makes sacred*; it is sacrifice that makes communication with the divine realm possible.[8]

Sacer is contrasted with *Sanctus:* 'properly past participle of *sancīre* to enact, ratify, devote, consecrate (compare SANCTION *n.*)', that which in English we translate as 'holy'.[9] Émile points out the inherent circularity of *sanctus:* the *sanctum* is what is *sanctioned* (as sanctioned). *Sanctum* refers neither to what is consecrated to the gods nor simply what is other than *sacer* (i.e. the profane), but what 'is established, affirmed by a *sanctio* [. . .]'.[10]

There is a division at the origin of the thinking around *saint* that is brought out when we return to the English. 'Sacred' and 'holy' are synonyms in the thesaurus, and in that most sacred of tomes, the *Oxford English Dictionary*, we read 'sacred' for 'holy' and 'holy' for 'sacred'.[11] But there is one difference: whatever else can be called sacred, it is used only '*rarely* of a deity'. God is not sacred, but instead holy. Holy is used, we are told, 'of things: pertaining to God or the Divine Persons; having their origin or sanction from God, or partaking of a Divine quality or character'.[12] The sacred refers to what we dedicate to God; the holy is of God, and as such reflects the purity of the transcendent.

Now, you observe the difference between the sacred and the holy, noting the way in which Emmanuel is at pains to distinguish them.[13] In the *Talmudic Readings*, he warns us of the dangers of taking the sacred for the holy, of thinking the sacred and the holy as one and the same:

> I have always asked myself if holiness, that is, separation or purity [. . .] can dwell in a world that has not been desacralized. I have asked myself – and that is the real question – whether the world is sufficiently desacralized to receive such purity. The sacred is in fact the half light in which the sorcery the Jewish tradition abhors flourishes. The 'other side', the reverse or obverse of the Real, Nothingness condensed to mystery, bubbles of Nothing in things – the 'as if nothing is happening' look of daily objects – the sacred adorns itself with the prestige of prestiges. Revelation refuses these bad secrets [. . .]. These [Talmudic] texts [. . .] may perhaps allow us to distinguish the holy from the sacred.[14]

When he asks whether or not the world has been sufficiently desacralized to receive the purity of holiness, he repudiates what we have declared sacred and presumed holy: 'the reverse or obverse of the Real, Nothingness condensed to mystery, bubbles of Nothing in things – the "as if nothing is happening" look of daily objects [. . .]'. We look in vain, then, for the holy in the objects of the sacred. And yet, you remind us again of the etymological links between 'the sacred, the holy or the saved' as they come to us through the German *heilig*, which means both sacred and holy. In the name of *différance*, I hazard, you resist a complete difference between what you describe as '*a natural sacredness that would be "pagan", even Graeco-Christian, and the holiness* <sainteté> *of (Jewish) law* [. . .]'.[15] You resist a difference between the sacred and the holy.

The holy might be *otherwise*, but even as we name it, it is haunted by the sacred, as the sacred is sacred only because of the profane and by means of sacrifice. The purity of the *saint* retains this impurity; holiness cannot present itself *as such*. You cannot be holy without being sacrificed.

A second division

Êtes-vous saint?

Saint, sainte. Adjectif (latin, *sanctus*, sacré). Larousse advises that this is said of God, but also of someone elected by God and recognized by the Church, or of someone who lives according to God's law and follows an exemplary moral or religious life, or of something having a venerable character that cannot be touched. As for the noun, a saint is 'a canonised Christian whose life is proposed as an example by the Church and to whom a public cult is rendered'. Yet a saint is also 'a man or woman of piety and exemplary life'.[16] The *OED* goes further. Not only is a saint: 'a person of extraordinary holiness of life', but this is used 'sometimes ironically', so that a saint is 'a person making an outward profession of piety'. Further again, in colloquial use, a saint is 'an extremely good or long-suffering person'. Yet further still, the title can be 'applied e.g. to persons who are the objects of posthumous reverence in non-Christian religions. †Also *rarely* to heathen deities, etc'.[17]

We can safely say that you have not been recognized officially by the Church, but if you had lived an exemplary moral or religious life, how would we know? You did not circumcise your sons, apparently, yet you – or someone writing in your name – still kept the white *kippa* in your pocket. . . .[18] Then, too, there is the question of that *tallith*:

> So I no longer wear it, I simply place my lips on it, almost every evening, except when I'm traveling to the ends of the earth, because like an animal it waits for me, well hidden in its hiding place, at home, it never travels. I touch it without knowing what I am doing or asking in so doing, especially not knowing into whose hands I am entrusting myself, to whom I'm rendering thanks. But to know at least two things – which I invoke here for those who are foreign (get this paradox: even more ignorant, more foreign than I) to the culture of this tallith, this culture of shawl and not of veil: *blessing* and *death*.[19]

You may have written of a particular foreignness to Judaism, but that tells us nothing as such; it tells us nothing of you *as such* – but that means nothing, for if we had the *as such* we would have lost that for which we are seeking, desiring (I will not say 'hoping', for that would already be to promise too much).[20] Moreover, we could never take your word as gospel, not because you are lying to us, but because every word must always contain the possibility of perjury.[21]

Apparently, you do not know what you are doing when you kiss the tallith, or into whose hands you entrust yourself when you pray, and your prayer can have no destination either you or we could name.[22] It is written that you quite rightly pass for an atheist.[23] But none of this tells us anything about you, as if there had been one, whom we could have known.

We take as read a certain love for ethics – indeed, ethics appears inescapable in your work, even if it is not Lévinasian through and through.[24] We know that you were detained in Prague because of your solidarity with the Czech philosophers, and that you promoted the cause of Nelson Mandela and others. But did you live an exemplary moral life? I don't know; I didn't know you – it's all spin from this distance.

Who could *testify* on your behalf? Hélène, of course, but I will bet that even she does not know – 'O my friends, there is no friend'.[25] She picks up the threads of your non/identification with *les marranes*. A marrano: 'one of those Jews without knowing it and without knowledge, Jew without having it, without being it, a Jew whose ancestors are gone, cut off, as little Jewish as possible, the disinheritor, guardian of the book he doesn't know how to read [. . .]'.[26] One of those Jews – as Derrida, the writer of *Circumfession,* explains – who says 'baptism' instead of 'circumcision', 'communion' in place of *bar mitzvah*.[27] Yet it is more than that. To quote Hélène again: 'here's one who, if there's such a thing as faith, has got it. He prays and does not know what he says. / To think he was a Marrano all along and didn't know it. A true Marrano. Don't tell a soul. It's a secret'.[28] She goes on to cite *Circumfession*: 'if I am a sort of *Marrano* of French Catholic culture [. . .] I am one of those *Marranos* who no longer say they are Jews even in the secret of their own hearts [. . .]'.[29]

More questions open up here, however. The ellipsis – and here it is my ellipsis, not hers – takes the place of 'and I also have my Christian body, inherited from SA in a more or less twisted line, *condiebar eius sale*'. Let us not pretend that this is anything less than very complicated, even – and especially – if it did refer to you. At the very least, I wonder if the Marrano is unknowingly Jewish, or unknowingly Christian. Is there a cultural French Catholic, secretly Jewish without knowing it, and/or one in his place who, *also* having a Latin, Christian body, is somehow secretly and indelibly marked as Christian, whose salted body expresses itself, as in the case of illness or sin, in spite of whatever one might say or claim to profess?[30] Which heritage does this Marrano, if there is one, deny or secretly confess or not know to confess? How does he know which it is? What would it mean for you to confess?

We have to take account of Hélène's gloss on the buggery scene, where we read:

Derrida doesn't tell us, he writes it [*ne nous le* dit *pas, il* l'écrit]. Writing, however, is not telling [Or, écrire, ce n'est pas dire]. The key of Circumfession is precisely that: what is written is not said [ce qui s'écrite ne se dit pas]. Never in his life would Derrida say such a thing [*ne dirait une chose pareille*], never in his life would he be caught in a 'confession' scene. Never will he be caught in a *Catholic* situation, he is not Catholic, there will never be a confession.[31]

Why push the distinction between writing and telling? Is this the difference between writing and speaking? That would be to reinstate a certain privilege of speech over writing, which would be to claim that speech could be precisely what the analyses in *Of Grammatology* or 'Plato's Pharmacy' suggest it cannot be. Telling – on this account – would simply be speech, once more 'dreaming its full self-presence'.[32] She is right that you will not be caught confessing, but not because you are writing. *Il n'y a pas d'hors-texte* – surely Hélène knows that it is *all* writing, and if she knows that, what does she mean by 'telling'? Could you ever have told us anything? Did you ever tell her? Did you ever tell us? Did you ever tell us *without knowing*? Without knowing – you, or us?

In the film bearing your name, you throw us some tantalizing hints. When Amy asks you how you met Marguerite, you defer to your wife: 'Should we tell [*raconte*] or no?' She concedes: 'Go ahead tell. Tell'. You respond: 'I'm not going to tell [*dire*] you everything. No. I'm just going to tell you [*raconter*] superficial things [*les histoires* – stories, cp. *l'histoire*]'.[33] Telling is not simply about speaking, and evidently we cannot press the distinction between *dire* and *raconter* very far, either: in 'The Law of Genre' you write of an 'inexhaustible writing which recounts without telling, and which speaks without recounting'.[34] Perhaps telling, however, is about personal narration. Returning to the film, a little later in the improvised/staged conversation you add:

> Even when I confide things that are very secret, I don't confide them in the mode of a story. At times, I provide certain signs, facts, dates, but otherwise, I don't write a narrative. And so the question for me is the question of narration, which has always been a serious question for me. I've always said I can't tell a story. I'd love to tell stories, but I don't know how to tell them. And I've always felt that the telling is somehow inadequate to the story I'd want to tell. So I've just given up telling stories. I've just given up.[35]

Perhaps 'telling' would be to implicate yourself in a story, to give continuity to an identity that – by all accounts – is not singular, and so continually unravels itself even as it is knitted together. You want to tell, but you can't ever tell if you can tell.[36]

As for confession, then – speaking about *Circumfession* at Villanova (and I have this before me in writing, although I was in the room when you said it), you maintain that a confession cannot be a report of something, but 'becomes a confession only when I ask for forgiveness and, according to the tradition, when I promise to repent, that is, to improve'. It is not a matter of bringing about knowledge of something but of personal transformation.[37] However, to confess is to confess the other – another one, without any certainty that this is the self.[38] This makes it difficult, surely, to ask for forgiveness, although I heard you do this more than once.[39] In Toronto, you go on to explain of *Circumfession*: 'the text has the structure of a confession. It is a text that turns around a possible-impossible confession, around circumcision, and around confession'. You insist: 'I am not making a confession. I am not signing a confession. I am not speaking in my own name'.[40] You tell us that you are not confessing, and that it is not you confessing – because neither you nor we can know if this hits the mark, if it is personal, if there is a story or a history. What is more, neither we, nor you, can tell if you are telling or lying.

You write without telling us any-*thing*, without confessing; you will never confess, but not because you are writing rather than speaking. You will never confess because it is all writing, and writing structurally forbids us from telling *as such*. Writing is both the condition of possibility *and* impossibility of personal narrative.

Let us return to the question of your sainthood. I cannot know if you ever lived an exemplary moral or religious life. Is there some possibility of irony, then, in using the word 'saint' with reference to you? Here it would not be a question of any purely outward profession of piety, as the *OED* envisages, but precisely the opposite. 'Derrida? Yes, he's a real saint!' This would sit well – don't you think – with some of your critics, both academic and religious. For is it not the case that you sought to undermine the established order, that you pedalled meaninglessness in place of truth, that you made a mockery of both philosophy and religion, that you were – shall we say – simply *pernicious* in this regard? Lest it seem that I am indulging in hyperbole, let me quote from that obituary:

> Derrida was the embodiment of the philosopher-rebel, admired for his explosive critique of the authoritarian values latent in orthodox approaches to literature and philosophy. To his critics, however, his work was frivolous, obscure, bogus and invidiously subversive.[41]

As I toyed with the idea of St Jacques, it seemed to me that this might be what they wanted me to say, what they might have expected me to say. In one sense, it would have been all too easy to make an ironic claim. However, since I don't believe it, I would have had to argue that you are not the *enfant terrible*, while not wishing *thus* to sanctify you, to sanctify you in opposition to such diabolization. I am not, of course, opposed to your sanctification (and let us underscore here the ambivalence in the *OED*'s entry, where 'to sanctify' means 'to set apart as holy *or* sacred'), but it must not come about as if by some kind of teenage infatuation, or worse, by means of idolatry.[42]

This leads me to the further possibility that the *OED* affords, that we should call you a saint as a person who is the object of posthumous reverence in a non-Christian religion (or perhaps, even, as a heathen deity). In either of these cases – and depending on how far we are prepared to push 'religion' – you could so easily become St Jacques, Patron Saint of Deconstruction. Yet there would be something violent in such a characterization, inevitably a caricature. It would be violent, not only because a caricature, but because you expended such effort in repelling the establishment of a centre, in derailing the rise of deconstruction as a method or a movement – just one more metaphysics – even if you did not claim to be outside metaphysics. It would be violent, too (and here I have nothing to go on except those few brief encounters, so I am really risking it here), because to name you a saint under these conditions might be to presume that you saw yourself as the centre of a resistance – even one without a centre. It was said to me that you were arrogant (and a misogynist, too). I'd have to say I saw nothing of that. I do not know you, and I cannot say for sure. You were a superstar, indeed, but when you spoke I was struck by a kind of humility.

Saint? I simply don't know.

A third division

Vous êtes sɛ̃.

1. Jacques Derrida [le] Saint Juif

It was Hélène who led us here – blame her. She speaks of the *Saint Juif* as the *sainjuif*, the *singe juif* (the homophone has been nicely communicated in the translation): a Jewish monkey. Despite the fact that I do not, *cannot* know you, I think you would enjoy this one. It would suit you, twinkle in your eye, to be 'a saintly monkey or a monkey of a saint'.[43] You seem to like to turn things upside down, to run off with valuable things that don't belong to you. Not that I am suggesting that everything is *play*. While it does seem at some moments that we are brought to a crossroads where we must choose either the self-delusion of absolute meaning or the anarchy of a kind of endless free association (the free-wheeling of an endless chain of signifiers), you do point out that it is never a question of choosing.[44] No, for someone who plays, you are deadly serious about it. Neither can we choose, then, between the monkey and the saint.

2. Vous êtes un homme sain

You led us here yourself in the French of 'Foi et Savoir' – '*c'est-à-dire sur le sain, le saint, le sacré, le sauf, l'indemne, l'immun* (sacer, sanctus, heilig, holy . . .)' – but it has been elided by Samuel in the English: '*which is to say, on the holy, the sacred, the safe and sound, the unscathed* <indemne>, the *immune* (sacer, sanctus, heilig, holy . . .).'[45] It appears that *le sain* and *le sauf* have been read together, *sain et sauf* (the idiomatic 'safe and sound'), so that in English we perhaps hear 'safe' more than 'sound'. This is important, of course, in the context of being *saved*, which is to be made safe. But it is also to be made whole. A sound>whole>hol/y man? I don't think so. You worried so much over the cut; I don't think it is an overstatement to say that you obsessed over it: 'circumcision, that's all I've ever talked about [. . .]'.[46] The circle was never to be complete; there has always been something a little unsound about you.

3. Dans le sein de Jacques. Au sein de Jacques

In the embrace/heart/womb/*khōra*, of Jacques. In the *sein/saint de* Jacques. In *Saint Jacques*. '[H]ow is one to think the necessity of that which, while *giving* place to that opposition as to so many others, seems sometimes to be itself no longer subject to the law of the very thing which it *situates*?'[47] Remember that the *khōra* gives nothing: 'this *there is*, which [. . .] *gives* nothing in giving place or in giving to think [. . .]'.[48] What does Jacques Derrida give to think? In truth, you can give no thing, although you haunt my thinking constantly.

I have always been struck by the coldness of the descriptions of *khōra*, when a womb should be warm. *Khōra* cannot be a cold place. A womb nourishes – albeit without thought, without thanks – but it is not a place to stay, and we are always and already expelled from it by the time we can long for its protection.

In the middle of Jacques. In Jacques' *milieu*. Framed by Jacques (yes, 'framed' in both senses). To the *sein/saint de* Jacques. To St Jacques. I salute you, all the while 'unable to think what is happening to [you] or happening to me today, namely, this interruption or a certain non-response in a response that will never come to an end for me as long as I live'.[49] I address you, directly, as I must; I speak to you before speaking of you (frankly, because I can never speak of you, not properly, for all my speech is improper). I have omitted here your further injunction – 'and to speak *for* the other whom one loves and admires' – because I simply do not know how I could speak *on your behalf*.[50]

4. Un homme ceint de questions – c'est une question de votre seing

If the signature is not the question among all these questions, then I don't know what is. Geoffrey explains the problem of the signature so well that I cannot go past it:

> Like every sign, including 'I,' the proper name involves the necessary possibility of functioning in my absence [. . .] and [. . .] one must be able to take this absence to a certain absolute, which we call death. So we shall say that even while I am alive, my name marks my death. It already bears the death of its bearer, it is already the name of the dead person, the anticipated memory of a departure.[51]

I knew that death was coming, that death had already been, but I was *shocked* by it. I am shocked by it, to the point where I do not want to believe it. Your signature is everywhere, but you are nowhere to be found.

5. Vous êtes cinq, du moins

A fourth division

There is no Jacques Derrida, or will the real Jacques Derrida please stand up?

I have always found the Jacques/Jackie thing somewhat comical. (What were they *thinking*? You were to become one of the world's foremost philosophers, and they named you after an American movie star? Even worse, they gave you a diminutive name – a child's name, which would not endure the passage to adulthood.) Jacques is much more serious, much more appropriate for the kind of person who is so quintessentially *French*. Except that you aren't French – not really. I had virtually forgotten this until after September 11, when you had trouble getting into the States for the Villanova conference, and it was seriously un-French (and un-American) to be Algerian. Yet I am not sure that you are really Algerian, either. This is the ultimate in auto-immunity: Algerian-Arab-Jews-being-French-and-not-being-Jewish-without-being-Algerian-or-Arab-yet-without-being-French![52] (That does not even begin to address the comment about your being black.)[53]

In any case, for you to be Jackie brings all sorts of interesting side effects, not least – just as you showed in your text for Emmanuel – that *il* so readily becomes *elle*, which we see traced in Hélène's notes to the side of her copy of *Circumfession*.[54] As she explains: '[. . .] the work of Jacques Derrida commences with a name given to a boy *with a feminine ending*'.[55] The effect is compounded by the fact that your secret name, Elie (the name that is *not inscribed* on your birth certificate), also bears this end.[56] This is a neat way to undermine the tension of the opposition between masculine and feminine, although perhaps they gave you hell at school for it. There is still hell to pay for it now, if it is to be read as a takeover – the man who is such a man that he bears a woman within himself. That's one way to read it. I'm not saying I agree with it.

No, we do not have to go very far to find that you are divided: two given names (one of which was never actually *given*), and two names by which you have called yourself for a long time – not only *Je*, but Jacques – a name without a hint of American movie star about it, a name which fits perfectly and unobtrusively into a French university. And then a fifth name, of course, the family name, *Derrida*, by which you are known both as superstar in and as bringer of terror to the literary and philosophical worlds.[57]

How should we call you? What is your real name? How shall we call *you*?

I know the technical answer to this question (or better, I can draw from the writings signed in your name to make a response): there is no one *you*, in the singular. When I look for you, I will only find another in your place, and then the other of that other – *en abyme*, as John suggests.[58] One (the pronoun itself is ironic) is ultimately present neither to oneself nor to others.[59] Moreover, 'the relation to self [. . .] can only be *différance*, that is to say alterity, or trace'.[60] We can speak of singularity, perhaps, in terms of responsibility, but only as always and already divided: 'The singularity of the "who" is not the individuality of a thing that would be identical to itself, it is not an atom. It is a singularity that dislocates or divides itself in gathering itself together to answer to the other, whose call somehow precedes its own identification with itself, for to this call I can *only* answer, have already answered [. . .]'.[61]

Hélène brings this much closer to home. 'He is as if, like (as if he were) another. True, we are all substitutes, but he is a substitute truly like no-one. [. . .] Such substitutingness haunts him, to be conscious of this as-if-being is to suffer, but it is also the condition of wisdom: an antidote for our presumption'.[62] She brings it home that you are never at home, and yet the house is haunted.

The other Jean-Luc might want to argue that you have been given to yourself, given to yourself and to others in being called and responding in love. Being loved and loving serve to give the self.[63] (All that talk of gift – I don't think you dismissed it out of contempt, although perhaps it seemed to you like so much sleight of hand with the language of giving, a *presti-donatation*.)[64] But I think there is something more than nostalgic in the search for Elie, especially 'trying to find out already whom at bottom Elie would have loved, from whom, "last beloved face" he would have chosen to receive his name [. . .]'.[65] To have known whom Elie would have loved – would that not somehow have been to have reached the touchstone, to have touched Elie? And yet not even Elie knows.

Elie does not know, but *Je*/Jackie/Jacques/Derrida call/s to Elie, nonetheless. There is faith in Elie.[66] If nothing else, there is faith.[67]

Could we call you a saint as a man of faith? Could we have faith in you?

Notes

1   Jacques Derrida, 'Circumfession', *Jacques Derrida* (Chicago: University of Chicago Press, 1993), period 5, p. 26.
2   Jean-Luc Nancy, *Reste, viens*, 2004, Available: www.derrida.ws/index. php?option=com_content&task=view&id=3&Itemid=7, 1 July 2012.

3 Jacques Derrida, *Adieu: To Emmanuel Levinas* (trans. Pascale-Anne Brault and Michael Naas, Stanford: Stanford University Press, 1999), pp. 1–2.

4 Hélène Cixous, *Portrait of Jacques Derrida as a Young Jewish Saint* (trans. Beverley Bie Brahic, New York: Columbia University Press, 2004); Jacques Derrida, 'At This Very Moment in This Work Here I Am', *Psyche: Inventions of the Other*, vol. 1 (ed. Peggy Kamuf and Elizabeth Rottenberg, trans. Ruben Berezdivin and Peggy Kamuf, Stanford: Stanford University Press, 2007).

5 Jacques Derrida, 'Foi et Savoir: Les deux sources de la «religion» aux limites de la simple raison', *La religion* (ed. Jacques Derrida and Gianni Vattimo, Paris: Éditions du Seuil, 1996), p. 10.

6 Émile Benveniste, *Le vocabulaire des institutions indo-européennes*, vol. 2, 2 vols (Paris: Les Éditions de Minuit, 1969).

7 Ibid., p. 179.

8 Ibid., p. 188.

9 'saint, adj. and n'. OED Online. March 2012. Oxford University Press. 3 June 2012 <www.oed.com/view/Entry/169847?rskey=EMEcnP&result=1&isAdvanced=false>. 'sanctus, n'. OED Online. March 2012. Oxford University Press. 3 June 2012 >www.oed.com/view/Entry/170521?redirectedFrom=sanctus>.

10 Benveniste, *Le vocabulaire*, p. 189.

11 In fact, 'we cannot in Old English get behind Christian senses in which *holy* is equated with Latin *sanctus, sacer*'. 'holy, adj. and n'. OED Online. March 2012. Oxford University Press. 3 June 2012 <www.oed.com/view/Entry/87833?rskey=0qocPg&result=1&isAdvanced=false>.

12 'sacred, adj. and n'. OED Online. March 2012. Oxford University Press. 3 June 2012. <www.oed.com/view/Entry/169556?redirectedFrom=sacred>.

13 Jacques Derrida, 'Faith and Knowledge: The Two Sources of "Religion" at the Limits of Reason Alone' (trans. Samuel Weber, *Religion*, ed. Jacques Derrida and Gianni Vattimo, Stanford: Stanford University Press, 1998), p. 15.

14 Emmanuel Lévinas, 'Desacralization and Disenchantment', *Nine Talmudic Readings* (trans. Annette Aronowicz, Bloomington: Indiana University Press, 1990), p. 141.

15 Derrida, 'Faith and Knowledge', pp. 15, 24.

16 'Saint', *Larousse Dictionnaire de français* (ed. Gabino Alonso, Vincent Bauge, Vivien Chantepie, Thomas Charlot and Patrice Dervaux, Paris: Larousse, 2011).

17 'saint, adj. and n'. OED Online.

18 Derrida, 'Circumfession', p. 53.

19 Jacques Derrida, 'A Silkworm of One's Own: Points of View Stitched on the Other Veil', *Veils* (trans. Geoffrey Bennington, ed. Jacques Derrida and Hélène Cixous, Stanford: Stanford University Press, 2001), pp. 44–45.

20 See Robyn Horner, 'On Hope: Critical Rereadings', *Australian EJournal of Theology* 15 (2010), <www.acu.edu.au/about_acu/faculties_schools_institutes/faculties/theology_and_philosophy/schools/theology/ejournal/aejt_15/.>.

21 'This inviolability depends on nothing other than the altogether bare device of being-two-to-speak and it is the possibility of non-truth in which every possible truth is held or is made'. Jacques Derrida, *Given Time. 1. Counterfeit Money* (trans. Peggy Kamuf, Chicago: University of Chicago Press, 1992), p. 153. 'Perjury cannot be eradicated because it is part of a true or truthful promise of telling the truth'. Jacques Derrida, 'Composing "Circumfession"',

Augustine and Postmodernism: Confessions and Circumfession (ed. John D. Caputo and Michael Scanlon, Bloomington: Indiana University Press, 2005), p. 26.

22 Richard Kearney, ed., *Debates in Continental Philosophy: Conversations with Contemporary Thinkers* (New York: Fordham University Press, 2004), p. 12; John D. Caputo, Kevin Hart and Yvonne Sherwood, 'Epoché and Faith: An Interview with Jacques Derrida', *Derrida and Religion: Other Testaments* (ed. Kevin Hart and Yvonne Sherwood, London: Routledge, 2004), p. 31.

23 Derrida, 'Circumfession,' period 30, p. 155.

24 See the criticism of Simon Critchley's reading of Derrida and Lévinas in chapter 3 of Martin Hägglund, *Radical Atheism: Derrida and the Time of Life* (Stanford: Stanford University Press, 2008).

25 Aristotle in Jacques Derrida, *Politics of Friendship* (trans. George Collins, London: Verson, 1997), passim.

26 Cixous, *Portrait of Jacques Derrida*, p. 86.

27 Derrida, 'Circumfession', period 14, p. 72, Cixous, *Portrait of Jacques Derrida*, pp. 80–81; 115ff.

28 Cixous, *Portrait of Jacques Derrida*, p. 86.

29 Ibid., Derrida, 'Circumfession', period 33, p. 170.

30 Cf. Derrida, 'Faith and Knowledge', p. 29; Jean-Luc Nancy, 'Opening', *Dis-Enclosure: The Deconstruction of Christianity* (trans. Bettina Bergo, New York: Fordham University Press, 2008), p. 10.

31 Cixous, *Portrait of Jacques Derrida*, p. 102. The emphasis (here in non-italics) is in the original French. Hélène Cixous, *Portrait de Jacques Derrida en Jeune Saint Juif* (Paris: Galilée, 2001), p. 96.

32 Jacques Derrida, *Of Grammatology* (trans. Gayatri C. Spivak, Baltimore and London: Johns Hopkins University Press, 1974, 1976), p. 39.

33 Kirby Dick and Amy Ziering Kofman, *Derrida: Screenplay and Essays on the Film* (London: Routledge, 2005), pp. 73, 75.

34 Jacques Derrida, 'The Law of Genre', *Critical Inquiry* 7:1 (1980), pp. 55–81, p. 73.

35 Dick and Kofman, *Derrida*, p. 77.

36 'In brief, how not to speak of oneself? But also: how to do it without letting oneself be invented by the other? Or without inventing the other?' Jacques Derrida, 'How to Avoid Speaking: Denials', *Psyche: Inventions of the Other*, vol. 2 (ed. Peggy Kamuf and Elizabeth Rottenberg, trans. Ken Friedan and Elizabeth Rottenberg, Stanford: Stanford University Press, 2008), p. 309n.13.

37 Derrida, 'Composing "Circumfession"', p. 23.

38 Ibid., p. 25.

39 For example: Jacques Derrida in Caputo, Hart and Sherwood, 'Epoché and Faith', p. 29, Jacques Derrida, *On Cosmopolitanism and Forgiveness* (New York: Routledge, 2001).

40 Ibid., p. 29.

41 'Jacques Derrida', *The Telegraph*, 11 October 2004.

42 'sanctify, v'. OED Online. June 2012. Oxford University Press. 17 June 2012. <www.oed.com/view/Entry/170480?redirectedFrom=sanctify>. Emphasis added.

43 Cixous, *Portrait of Jacques Derrida*, p. vii.

44   Jacques Derrida, *Writing and Difference* (trans. Alan Bass, Chicago: University of Chicago Press, 1978), p. 293.
45   Derrida, 'Faith and Knowledge', p. 2.
46   Derrida, 'Circumfession', period 14, p. 70.
47   Jacques Derrida, '*Khōra*', trans. Ian McLeod, *On the Name* (ed. Thomas Dutoit, Stanford: Stanford University Press, 1995), p. 90.
48   Ibid., p. 96.
49   Derrida, *Adieu*, p. 5.
50   Ibid., p. 2.
51   Geoffrey Bennington and Jacques Derrida, *Jacques Derrida* (Chicago: University of Chicago Press, 1993), p. 148.
52   Cixous, *Portrait of Jacques Derrida*, p. 115.
53   Derrida, 'Circumfession', period 11, p. 58.
54   Cixous, *Portrait de Jacques Derrida*, p. 15.
55   Cixous, *Portrait of Jacques Derrida*, p. 12.
56   Ibid., p. 13, Derrida, 'Circumfession', period 17, pp. 86–91.
57   Cf. the discussion in Kevin Hart and Yvonne Sherwood, 'Other Testaments', *Derrida and Religion: Other Testaments* (ed. Kevin Hart and Yvonne Sherwood, New York: Routledge, 2005), pp. 4–6.
58   John Martis, 'The Self Found Elsewhere: Phenomenological Faith Meets Deconstructive Doubt', *Pacifica* 22 (2009).
59   Jacques Derrida, *Speech and Phenomena and Other Essays on Husserl's Theory of Signs* (trans. David B. Allison and Newton Garver, Evanston, IL: Northwestern University Press, 1973), pp. 66ff.
60   See 'Eating Well', trans. Peter Connor and Avital Ronell, in Jacques Derrida, *Points: Interviews, 1974–1994* (trans. Peggy Kamuf, ed. Elisabeth Weber, Stanford: Stanford University Press, 1995), p. 261.
61   Ibid. 'Something of this call of the other must remain nonreappropriable, nonsubjectivable, and in a certain way nonidentifiable, a sheer supposition, so as to remain *other*, a *singular* call to response or responsibility'. Ibid., p. 276.
62   Cixous, *Portrait of Jacques Derrida*, p. 53.
63   Jean-Luc Marion, *The Erotic Phenomenon* (trans. Stephen E. Lewis, Chicago: University of Chicago Press, 2007), pp. 29–40; Jean-Luc Marion, *Au lieu de soi. L'approche de Saint Augustin*, 2 edn (Paris: Presses Universitaires de France, 2008), p. 142.
64   Richard Kearney, Jacques Derrida and Jean-Luc Marion, 'On the Gift: A Discussion between Jacques Derrida and Jean-Luc Marion, Moderated by Richard Kearney', *God, the Gift and Postmodernism* (ed. John D. Caputo and Michael J. Scanlon, Bloomington: Indiana University Press, 1999), p. 58.
65   Derrida, 'Circumfession', period 17, p. 88.
66   Caputo, Hart and Sherwood, 'Epoché and Faith', p. 38.
67   Ibid., p. 45.

8

Divine Dissipation: Criminal Sanctity and the Atheological Abrupt in Georges Bataille[1]

Charlie Blake

I am not a philosopher, but a saint, perhaps a madman [. . .]

GEORGES BATAILLE[2]

And when I saw my devil, there I found him earnest, thorough, deep, somber: it was the spirit of gravity – through him all things fall. Not by wrath does one kill, but by laughing. Up, let us kill the spirit of gravity!

FRIEDRICH NIETZSCHE[3]

Things get too straight, I can't bear it.

IGGY POP[4]

The sanctification of a figure such as Georges Bataille in the French intellectual canon brings in its train a number of questions about whether such sanctity can be sought for specific philosophical thinkers according to general paradigms of definition, or whether it must be drawn from the universe of concepts, percepts and affects generated or expressed by the thinker him or herself. In the case of Bataille, the religious, the sacred, the divine and the saintly are all intertwined with a number of themes which might initially appear to counter any remote notion of sanctity, such as: the obscene, the cadaverous, the rotten, the filthy, the erotically perverted, the sensually violent, the excremental and the delirial, not to mention his campaign for a return to human sacrifice. And yet, within these apparent celebrations of that which might be deemed as negative by implication, at least to those of a more conventionally religious or moral sensibility, lies a powerful vision of a new kind of sanctity appropriate to what he called 'inner experience' in our post-industrial, late capitalist, ecologically vulnerable and spiritually etiolated world. It will be the purpose of this brief essay, therefore, to at least indicate how and why this is the case and to determine (by allusion to his own concern with the use-value of the Marquis de Sade[5]), the use-value of Bataille to debates over postmodern sanctification. To this end, it is with the more spectral aspects of his concern with sacred obscenity and what I have called divine dissipation that we shall begin.

In an essay on Bataille and the simulacrum from 1965, Pierre Klossowski opens by making a characteristically negative affirmation concerning his friend's infamous notion of *atheology*. Here, he asserts that in making the utterance 'atheology' itself, in coining the term and using it positively, Bataille gives away a concern with what Klossowski calls '*divine vacancy*'. This is a vacancy that does not merely imply a site once held and then vacated by, as he puts it, 'the name of god [. . .] guarantor of the personal self', but that is also concomitantly, and by virtue of this abrupt departure, a vacancy as well *of* the self. It is an ontological absence, moreover: 'of the self whose vacancy is experienced in a consciousness that, since it is not in any way this self, is in itself its *vacancy*'.[6] In essence, Klossowski's point is understood here in relation to the general question of Bataille and religion to imply that in the absence of, or – and the distinction may well be an important one – subsequent to the death of God, the self is always and already void, and it is only (paradoxically) through the perpetual act of tearing the mask from the dead or absent or dissipated divinity to reveal the emptiness beneath its interminable veils of ritual, dogma or tradition, that the sovereignty of the human self, in its own paradoxical emptiness and limitation, can begin to substantiate.

At the heart of this process of substantiation there also arises a set of desires that are uniquely human and undeniably material as well as collectively self-annihilative. These are desires that are primarily of the body, that is, which are of the Earth and the senses, but which are also darkly angelic, dissipatedly divine and fundamentally celestial or even Gnostic in their aspiration. These are desires, moreover, to be measured on a spectrum of differentiation by degree rather than kind,[7] and which consist of, but are not limited to the following: the desire to communicate, to create, to destroy, to make art, to make perverse and perverted love, to expel and excrete, and most importantly for the socius, the desire to foment revolutionary excess, to generate metaphysical waste and to encourage sacrificial violence in imitation, through Bataille's twisted analogy, of the absolutely inhuman profligacy of our most immediate star: the sun.

Such desires and their expression and exposure in sovereign acts are in no way serene or contemplative for Bataille, but are necessarily violent and often cognitively indirect and confrontational, both to the socio-ethical sensibility and to the rationality that might claim to encode it. They are violent, that is, in imitation of the sun's non- or supra-rational profligacy, its absolute moral neutrality, and yet indirect in the sense that as human agents we could never begin to approach the explosive violence of the sun itself, and must instead approach the sovereign act of which it is the inhuman or divine source through laughter, obscenity, obscurity and sacrilege. Thus, and in Bataille's frequent use of Nietzschean laughter, as well as his complex relationship with both the materialism of Marx and the dialectic of Hegel – in addition to the apparent immaterialism of the Gnostics which so clearly intrigued him[8] – they are acts of sovereign exposure that are also necessarily parodic, pleromatic and profane.

Indeed, as he puts it obliquely in his early surrealistic meditation on love and the sovereign in 'The Solar Anus', in what appears initially to be little more than an obscure list of disparate phenomena, but what is in context the very figure of holy intoxication and criminal sanctification united in love, and thus true sovereignty for Bataille:

> An abandoned shoe, a rotten tooth, a snub nose, the cook spitting in the soup of his masters are to love what a battle flag is to nationality.
>
> An umbrella, a sexagenarian, a seminarian, the smell of rotten eggs, the hollow eyes of judges are the roots that nourish love.
>
> A dog devouring the stomach of a goose, a drunken vomiting woman, a sobbing accountant, a jar of mustard represents the confusion that serves as the vehicle for love.[9]

Bataille's notion of sovereignty is then, and as should be clear from the abstract cartography of love and the sovereign above, somewhat different to the general understanding of this (often admittedly evasive) term in mainstream political or philosophical thought. As he puts it in his later study of general and restricted economies in *The Accursed Share*: 'What is sovereign in fact is to enjoy the present time without having anything else in view but this present time'.[10]

So sovereignty in this formulation is ultimately a hedonistic indulgence in the moment and, typically for Bataille, it is also obscenity and sin, as well as being their absence. Sovereignty is also, however, and consistently, the basis of communication and collectivity, identity and economy (whether a libidinal, material or spiritual economy), and this is where Klossowski's broadly empathetic observations on Bataille's obscurities and profanities are so potentially fruitful. Klossowski's discussion of Bataille and communication, for example, goes on to press upon the latter's atheological concerns and their implications through his own use of the term *simulacrum* in relation to Bataille and communication. This notion of the simulacrum as a conceptual instrument, derived, of course, from Plato and, subsequent to Klossowski, deployed for related though distinct ends by Jean Baudrillard and Gilles Deleuze,[11] is used here in a sense peculiar to Klossowski, as he contrasts it more generally in his writings to what he calls the *phantasm*.

Here is not the place to go into any detailed account of the distinction between the phantasm and the simulacrum in Klossowski, as it has been dealt with very effectively elsewhere,[12] but, for our present purposes, Jean-François Lyotard's summary in *Libidinal Economy* is useful, as described here in Eleanor Kaufman's economical formulation, as:

> According to Lyotard, the difference between the phantasm and the simulacrum lies in the difference between singularity and generality and between inexchangeability and exchangeability. While the phantasm is singular and inexchangeable, the simulacrum would try to 'count as', to make itself exchangeable with the phantasm. In other words, it would try to introduce an economy of reciprocal exchange where such an economy is constitutionally impossible.[13]

Klossowski's distinction between the simulacrum and the phantasm has implications for Bataille's sanctification and the tension in his work between the medieval scholastic concepts of univocity, equivocity and analogy that I will return to in due course.

At this stage, however, there are several preliminary aspects to what I have called Bataille's 'atheological abrupt' to be considered. The first is that atheology, as Bataille defines it in its most general sense, and following Nietzsche's famous proclamation – is the science of the death of God. However, as a number of commentators have indicated, notably Michel Foucault, there is something rather anomalous here for atheists – of whom Bataille was undoubtedly one – in studying or even deeming remotely important, at least in any philosophical sense, the ontological absence of something that is considered to have never even existed in the first place.[14] In that understanding, Bataille's atheology might be said to bear a passing resemblance to Deleuze's assertion that theology after the death of God is the science of 'non-existing entities',[15] and from there, Deleuze and Félix Guattari's decidedly atheistic observation on theology and religion, that 'whenever there is transcendence, vertical Being, imperial State in the sky or on earth, there is religion; and there is philosophy whenever there is immanence'.[16]

The points made here are consistent throughout Deleuze's writings, and specify that philosophy is ultimately concerned with the realm of the virtual, the actual and the immanent and religion (at least, in its post-Abrahamic manifestations), and most of theology with the realms of the illusory and transcendent. As he and Guattari elaborate in *What Is Philosophy?*, for this reason, the death of God is in no way a problem for the philosopher, but instead, signals an achievement that leads to serenity and conceptual production.[17] The problem that Deleuze and Guattari then pose for religion, and for Christianity in particular, is that if, as they assert and argue, philosophy is centrally concerned with immanence and with the production of the new – in this case with the invention and arrangement of concepts (rather than affects and percepts in the arts, say, or functives in science) – then can religion be said to generate new concepts or their equivalent? Or to be more accurate, can religion produce *proper* concepts rather than mere beliefs, fancies, opinions or revelations? Their response to this question, via Pascal and Kierkegaard, is as follows:

> [. . .] perhaps belief becomes a genuine concept only when it is made into a belief in this world and is connected rather than being projected [. . .] [T]here is always an atheism to be extracted from religion.[18]

In this context, and in several highly significant ways (albeit with equally important caveats and qualifications), Deleuze's transcendence might be related to Bataille's notion of discontinuity. This is a discontinuity experienced by, say, those observing the ritual death through sacrifice of another human being – a spectacle that might evoke a sense of the radical discontinuity between life and death in the witness, among other more visceral reactions, but which also potentially illuminates new forms of continuity in the moment in which the subject embraces this radical discontinuity in death and its inner promise/experience of absolute continuity in non-existence, whether in its corporeal reality as existential absence, as death-as-such, or through *la petite mort*. However, and as with sex itself, as with eroticism, as with Deleuze's radical and Manichean and quite possibly the metaphysical separation of desire and pleasure and his association of sex with equivocity and Cartesian dualism,[19] Bataille's atheology differs from Deleuze's transcendental atheism in some very important details. To begin with, Bataille has no desire for the philosophical serenity acquired through the active atheism that Deleuze and Guattari will later signal. Second – in contrast to Deleuze's general disavowal of the religious and of theology as a useful mode of thought – at least outside its historical relation to philosophy, and as is evident from a continuing obsession with its features and its generation of affect and intensity, Bataille values religion intensely without accepting its premises. Indeed, he seeks to extract from religion a sense and experience of the sacred while denying the existence and thus the authority of any supernatural entity, supreme or otherwise. Third, Bataille opposes the homogenous to the heterogeneous in his work, in a form in which the latter embraces a range of phenomena including the spiritual and the holy, the abject and the abjected, the experience of overwhelming affect or passion, and states of madness, drunkenness, delirium and ecstasy. These phenomena are all in an important sense immanent for Bataille, in that they are not imposed by and certainly not judged by any external or transcendental agency, whether political of divine, but they are not in the Deleuzian sense necessarily aspects of univocal being. Thus again, and unlike Deleuze, Bataille is less concerned with univocity as it is generally understood after Duns Scotus and Spinoza and Nietzsche (at least, Deleuze's Nietzsche),[20] than with that which exceeds or breaches all ontological bonds and boundaries, that which cannot be constrained or contained cognitively or metaphysically by the question of singular, divided or multiple ontologies, that which tears univocity asunder, which sullies analogy, and which circles, accordingly around the themes of chaos, catastrophe and devastation as positive terms of equivocity and equivocality.

In spite of the negative associations conventionally attached to notions of catastrophe, excess and entropy, then, or rather because of them, Bataille's celebration of their negative force is less an issue of theodicy or despair in any traditional sense than one of what might be termed a satanic gravity or melancholy, as well as its paradoxically joyous antipathy. This is a sense of inner tension or inner experience, as he termed it, that might be understood in a manner comparable to that which the poet John Milton described as the state of 'darkness visible', a mood of depression, decay and disorder, of entropy and exhaustion, but it is a visible darkness here breached and pierced by an unbearable light of erotic and ecstatic revelation or by shards of blissful obscenity. Thus where Milton in *Paradise Lost* has Satan travelling 'Upborne with indefatigable wings / Over the vast abrupt'[21] and across the void, the darkness; a place:

> Without Dimension; where length, breadth, and height / And time, and place, are lost; where eldest Night and Chaos, ancestors of nature, hold Eternal anarchy, amidst the noise / Of endless wars, and by confusion stand.[22]

For Bataille, the journey of Milton's fallen angel would have been less an attempt to corrupt the nascently human in its embryonic garden than to elevate the consciousness of inner corruption and debasement, of serpentine despair, salacious guilt, sensuality and sin, and, in a sense that William Blake also perhaps discerned operating, however covertly, in Milton's reluctant diabolism, to its highest and most flagrantly eroticized level or plateau, and then, once achieved, dissolve it into the ocean spray and desert sand of the sacred self of sacrifice and vacancy, of death, community and communication.[23]

Notably, Bataille's devil-phantasm is here far closer in spirit, at least overtly, to that of Nietzsche in *Thus Spake Zarathustra*, than it is to Milton's promethean alter ego. This is a devil that Zarathustra describes as his arch enemy, as the spirit of gravity to be opposed by coruscating laughter, by the laughter of the abyss. Indeed, and similarly to Bataille, this is Nietzsche's own very personal devil, the devil to be overcome by any means necessary, the devil, as he puts it, of: 'compulsion, statute, necessity and consequence and purpose and will and good and evil'.[24]

Bataille's debt to Nietzsche is, of course, well attested, overtly and often by Bataille himself, and perhaps the source of that debt finds its most condensed form as both idea and affect in a passage from *Beyond Good and Evil*, where Nietzsche writes of the history of God, and in a manner that so clearly lies behind Bataille's atheology that it is worth quoting at length:

> There is a great ladder of religious cruelty, and, of its many rungs, three are the most important. People used to make human sacrifices to their god, perhaps even sacrificing those they loved the best – this sort of phenomenon can be found in the sacrifice of the firstborn (a practice shared by all prehistoric religions), as well as in Emperor Tiberius' sacrifice in the Mithras grotto on the Isle of Capri, that most gruesome of all Roman anachronisms. Then, during the moral epoch of humanity, people sacrificed the strongest instincts they had, their 'nature', to their god; the joy of this particular festival shines in the cruel eyes of the ascetic, that enthusiastic piece of 'anti-nature'. Finally: what was left to be sacrificed? In the end, didn't people have to sacrifice all comfort and hope, everything holy or healing, any faith in a hidden harmony or a future filled with justice and bliss? Didn't people have to sacrifice God himself and worship rocks, stupidity, gravity, fate, or nothingness out of sheer cruelty to themselves? To sacrifice God for nothingness – that paradoxical mystery of the final cruelty has been reserved for the race that is now approaching [. . .].[25]

For Bataille, the time for that sacrifice to nothingness had arrived in the early twentieth century after the horrors of a modern, industrial war, after the revelations of Marx, Freud, Nietzsche, Darwin and Durkheim, after the surgical expressionism of the *maudit* tradition of Sade, Baudelaire, Rimbaud, Verlaine, Lautréamont, Dada and Surrealism, and subsequently after Alexander Kojeve's angelicized Hegel – but it is a nothingness or will to nothingness that does not merely deny or invert traditional religion, does not merely deterritorialize it, but reterritorializes its most potent elements for the coming catastrophe. Thus, and fourthly for Bataille, there is a sense in which religion, and especially Catholicism, remains a continuing spool of imagery and affect; a flickering atomism of imagery and affect that he will use as simulacra against the 'concept' or 'notion' beloved of the Western philosophical tradition, and which figures such as Jean Paul Sartre and Jean Hyppolite and existentialism and idealism more generally found either incomprehensible or of limited use.[26] In this sense, Julia Kristeva is surely correct when she notes of Bataille that: 'One might be inclined to attribute Bataille's erotic experience to a Catholicism that was taken on to the limit of its sin-laden logic and would lead to its internal reversal'.[27] And although Kristeva takes Bataille's image of abjection and reframes it, as Benjamin Noys has pointed out, in a broadly Lacanian setting,[28] her comment is well taken and certainly tallies with most readers' experience of reading Bataille. Indeed, and as the delirial philosopher and propagandist Nick Land notes more forcibly in an article published in 1995 on Nietzsche, poetry, deicide and shamanism:

> It can seem at times as if Georges Bataille owes almost everything to Christianity; his understanding of the evil at the heart of erotic love, the hysterical affectivity of his writing, along with its excremental obsession, its epileptoid conception of delight, its malignancy, the perpetual stench of the gutter.[29]

Land's insight, framed in a far more provocative thesis on Bataille than that of Kristeva or even Klossowski is also well taken,[30] for some 50 years before this observation, and while living under the Nazi occupation of France, Bataille published *Inner Experience* (1943), the first volume of a trilogy which also included *Guilty* (1944) and *On Nietzsche* (1944). This was a series that was initially, or perhaps subsequently, intended as part of a four, five or possibly even a six volume collection – the structure was never finally settled – to be titled in parodic homage to St Thomas Aquinas, *Summa Atheologica*. In contrast with the systematic arguments of the Angelic Doctor, however, Bataille's vision in this neo-Menippean melange of essays, fragments, notes, reflections, observations, stutterings, obscenities and aphorisms is certainly not one of an ultimate co-determinism between reason and faith, nor certainly the prioritization of the latter over the former, so much as an attempt to blast both of these tenebrous edifices to fragments and then roll around, drooling, puking and lascivious, in the ruins.

If, however, his intentions often appear deliberately and merely blasphemous, even at times infantile, and hence pornographically or affectively oriented rather than critical in the philosophical sense, and thereby allied to the spirit if not to the letter of the textual surrealism, as we have noted, of Lautréamont and Breton or the iconoclasm of Sade and Baudelaire rather than the tradition of Cartesian illumination and clear and distinct reflection or Thomist dialectic, then these apparent intentions and their consistency in his work also, I would argue, indicate a clarity of conception in Bataille's thought which his very evident delight in transgression, obscenity and perversion, enhances as much as it appears to obscure. Indeed, 'such works', as one of Kierkegaard's pseudonymous authors puts it, 'are mirrors: when an ape looks in, no apostle can look out'.[31]

So, if to talk of 'clarity' in relation to the besmeared mirror of Bataille's reflections on politics, eroticism and religion might, initially at least, appear somewhat counter to his style of poetic excess and derangement, it is important to stress that this sense of clarity depends as much on a way of looking as it does on a way of creating or communicating, as much on an affinity of affect as a coincidence of notions or notionality. As Klossowski observes,

The contempt that Bataille has for the notion itself was revealed most notably in *Discussion sur le péché* with Sartre and Hyppolite in particular. There, where others tried to catch him up by means of 'notions', Bataille eluded them at the moment when he made evident a flagrant contradiction: he speaks and expresses himself in simulacra of notions, inasmuch as an expressed thought always implies the receptivity of the person addressed.[32]

Whereas the phantasm has a form of currency and may act as a conduit of exchange in a libidinal or conceptual economy, the simulacrum has no exchange value as such between minds or bodies, and is therefore not a concept or a notion, although it may take the form of an affect or delirium. A simulacrum has no internal stability and yet it communicates, and what it communicates is the incommunicable itself – as experience, as excess. Indeed, as Klossowski continues: 'The simulacrum is all that we know of an experience; the notion is only its residue calling forth other residues'.[33] Thus in using the undoubtedly problematic analogy of the mirror above, particularly in relation to its tangled philosophical history as an instrument of mimesis, it is important to stress that what we are talking of here – and to continue and intensify this analogy for our own ends – is not the broken mirror of hubris and shattered fortune beloved of so many writers of a realist bent, nor the unbounded and yet ultimately regressive narcissism of the aesthete. Nor is it the sensuous gauze filament that Alice famously traverses in Lewis Carroll's tale of transitions, inversions and impossibilities – an image so central to Deleuze's later discussion of depths and surfaces in his pre-Guattarian explorations of constructive philosophy, literary topology and univocity. Rather, it can be grasped not so much as an image either bent or twisted topologically as pure surface, as in Deleuze or arguably in the work of Bataille's one-time friend and neighbour Jacques Lacan, so much as a nexus of affect scattered holographically and simulacrously as fragments and shards and spectral traces through the gauze of his scopoleptic obsession.

Here, and gathered subsequently in imagination more like a malleable fabric of interwoven text and experience than a screen of speculation, this anomalous 'glass' nonetheless reflects and is a mode of reflection (and refraction) concerned primarily with the spectacle of divine dissipation, with the vagrant materialism of an abandoned and dismembered God and his train of shattered angels, with annihilation and debasement as ends rather than means, and most centrally, with a profoundly atheistic mysticism allied to a delirial erotic intensity and a guiding idea of sacrifice as sacrament. It is a glass of infinite grains of sand or substance, substance or sand, that reflects an absence, a vacuum, or as Klossowski put it, a vacancy of self, a vacancy which *is* self, a vacancy *as* self. This is an absent self in mourning, moreover, for a dismembered, decomposing and cannibalized deity who, in a typically Bataillian hesitation, might or might not have ever existed and, in a manner proleptically reminiscent of the divine inexistence and absolute contingency of Quentin Meillassoux, may or may not exist in the future.[34] The deity as phantasm is thereby replaced by the deity as simulacrum, as absent other, as vacancy, as the nothingness to be nihilated.

At this point, and by way of conclusion, it is worth returning for a moment to Aquinas. There is, in this context, a generally undiscovered or undiscussed Aquinas. This is a saint and theologian whose musings in the *Summa* on the consecration of the host and its possible corruption, as Steven Shakespeare has hinted, would have no doubt appealed to Bataille.[35] Here is an Aquinas who observes that: 'it sometimes happens that before or after the consecration the priest dies or goes mad' or 'sometimes, too, it happens, owing to the priest's want of care, that Christ's blood is spilled, or that he vomits the sacrament received, or that the consecrated hosts are kept so long that they become corrupt, or that they are nibbled by mice, or lost in any manner whatsoever'.[36] Aquinas's problem here, as Shakespeare notes, is one of *kenosis*, the emptying of God into Christ and the possibility of divine substance not only being manifested as something infected by material accident, but in a curious sense, almost defined by it, just as the priest vomiting out a rotten wafer must confront the issue of consecration and defilement and is thereby forced to link desecration with the idea of divine substance itself as a defining element of that substance, and thus confront the possibility of an absolute, a totality, God, in a state of decomposition.

To a degree, Aquinas can find ways to resolve these issues through his doctrine of analogy; although this does imply that some things simply cannot be spoken of (opening up the way to an apophantic theology). In brief, this is an argument – central, of course, to Deleuze's thought and advocacy of the univocal – which attempts to resolve the conflict between the *univocity* of Duns Scotus, in which God and creation are all of one substance, so that words used to describe divine and human qualities have effectively the same denotation but only differ by degree, and *equivocity*, in which, say, 'love' or 'being' in human terms are radically distinct in denotation from these terms used in relation to God. The middle way of analogy allows hesitation between some uses of love or being which are effectively the same if used in relation to the human or divine, and some not at all the same.

The significance of this distinction for Bataille is brought out by Kaufman in her essay on substance and Bataille, Klossowski and Deleuze, where she argues that Deleuze's reading of Klossowski positions the latter as being at times equivocal but does so by silent implication against Klossowski's reading of Bataille as radically equivocal, thus repositioning Klossowski's position as akin to Aquinas' analogy. This allows Deleuze to indicate those elements in Klossowski that he describes as belonging to orthodoxy, which Kaufman glosses as being 'akin to the damned position of the lukewarm, being neither hot nor cold, univocal nor equivocal, but trying to smooth things over by having it both ways'.[37] It also allows him to reclaim Klossowski for his preferred doctrine of univocity, and in a move criticized by John Milbank, who defends analogy for his own broadly orthodox position, to effectively freeze analogy and drain it of the dialectic so that it begins to resemble univocity itself. Thus, in Kaufman's synopsis, Deleuze claims that:

'Univocity signifies that being itself is univocal, while that of which it is said is equivocal; precisely the opposite of analogy' [. . .]. Milbank retorts: 'Of course, precisely not. Analogy speaks analogously of the analogical and so truly does escape dialectic. Whereas, if one says that the equivocal univocally is, then dialectic after all ensues: being is also equivocal, differences are a veil for the same sameness'.[38]

However, rather than view analogy as 'lukewarm' and thus undesirable and thus to be abjected as Deleuze appears to indicate, perhaps in the case of Bataille it might be more accurate to view equivocity in these terms, at least in Shakespeare's resonant formulation:

The God who decomposes, is the God who finds divine stasis and impassibility too lukewarm, too tepid for his taste: a God who renounces himself says to himself: because you are neither hot nor cold, I vomit you out of my mouth.[39]

Here we find analogy dissolving into equivocality through a form of projectile vomiting, not so much in the substance of the abjected host, which remains analogical, but in the act of abjection, in the disgust, in the obscenity as it renders the divine sacrificial by making it both heterogeneous and imminent and thereby sacred.

Accordingly, and finally, in contrast with Deleuze, for Bataille multiplicity is not univocity but a species or several species of equivocity, sometimes rendered as dialectic, but in its more extreme form, in the impossible or multitude, as what might be called polyvocity. In polyvocity there are as many substances as there are grains of sand on an infinite beach or drops of water in the endless sea or stars in the void traversed by Satan in Milton's epic. They are all, however, substances that flicker in their multiplicity in and out of existence against the substrate of absolute nothingness, like elementary particles in the quantum vacuum of space and time. They are agents thereby of absolute annihilation and the annihilation of the absolute.

So it is, in a somewhat savage differentiation from both the subsequent univocity of Deleuze and the resurrected doctrine of analogy associated with the Radical Orthodoxy movement of the theologian John Milbank and others, that Bataille celebrates a form of equivocity and concomitant equivocality via simulacrum and phantasm that has as its base a pure flow of thanatotropic desire, a realization of the death drive as the essence of the sacred and the heart, of what it is to be truly human, and thus, at the same time, to be truly in-human. Bataille's ontological hesitation is between a God who either existed and died or never existed in the first place, but in both forms of absence, it is a God who still needs to be perpetually sacrificed rather than to be sacrificed to, so as to provide again and again a wound in the flesh of being, an opening into the sacred as a pure will to nothingness, to emptiness, to vacancy, to void.

Notes

1 I would like to thank Frida Beckman for her invaluable comments on an earlier draft of this essay and Steven Shakespeare and Patrice Haynes for many illuminating conversations on its themes.

2 Georges Bataille, 'Method of Meditation', n. 6, *The Unfinished System of Knowledge* (ed. Stuart Kendall, trans. Michelle Kendall and Stuart Kendall, Minneapolis, MN: University of Minnesota Press, 2001), p. 218.

3 Friedrich Nietzsche, *Thus Spake Zarathustra* (ed. Adrian del Caro and Roger Pippin, trans. Adrian del Caro, Cambridge: Cambridge University Press, 2006), p. 29.

4 Iggy Pop, 'Some Weird Sin', *Lust For Life* (New York: RCA, 1977).

5 Georges Bataille, 'The Use Value of D.A.F. de Sade', *Visions of Excess: Selected Writings, 1927–1939* (ed. and trans. Alan Stoekl, Minneapolis, MN: University of Minnesota Press, 1985), pp. 91–102.

6 Pierre Klossowski, 'Of the Simulacrum in Georges Bataille's Communication', *On Bataille: Critical Essays* (ed. Leslie Anne Boldt-Irons, Albany, NY: State University of New York Press, 1995), p. 147.

7 In this, while I will argue below for Bataille's equivocality, I am in broad agreement with Denis Hollier that Bataille's dualism is not ontological but perspectival, in the sense that rather '[. . .] than a system of thought in the strict sense, dualism is an attitude of thought: dualism is not a dualist system but a will to dualism, a resistance to system and homogeneity'. Denis Hollier, 'The Dualist Materialism of Georges Bataille', *Yale French Studies 58: On Bataille* (ed. Allan Stoekl, New Haven: Yale University Press, 1990), p. 127.

8 See, for example, Bataille, 'Base Materialism and Gnosticism', *Visions of Excess*, pp. 45–52.

9 See Bataille, 'The Solar Anus', ibid., p. 6.

10 Georges Bataille, *The Accursed Share: Volumes II and III* (trans. Robert Hurley, New York: Zone, 1991), p. 199.

11 Notably, in Gilles Deleuze, 'The Simulacrum and Ancient philosophy', *The Logic of Sense* (ed. Constantin V, Boundas, trans. Mark Lester with Charles Stivale, New York: Columbia University Press, 1990), pp. 245–79; Jean Baudrillard, *Simulacra and Simulation* (trans. Sheila Faria Glaser, Ann Arbor, MI: Michigan University Press, 1994).

12 Eleanor Kaufman, *The Delirium of Praise: Bataille, Blanchot, Deleuze, Foucault, Klossowski* (Baltimore, MD: Johns Hopkins University Press, 2001), pp. 113–18; Daniel Smith, 'Klossowski's Reading of Nietzsche: Impulses, Phantasms, Simulacra, Stereotypes', *Diacritics* 35:1 (2005), pp. 8–21.

13 Kaufman, *Delirium*, p. 116.

14 Michel Foucault, 'A Preface to Transgression', *Bataille: A Critical Reader* (ed. Fred Botting and Scott Wilson, trans. Donald F. Bouchard and Sherry Simon, Oxford: Blackwell, 1998), p. 26.

15 Gilles Deleuze, *Logic of Sense*, p. 281. As such, God or gods could feasibly, in Deleuzian (a)theological terms, be said to subsist as events. See *Logic of Sense*, pp. 4–11.

16 Gilles Deleuze and Felix Guattari, *What Is Philosophy?* (trans. Graham Burchill and Hugh Tomlinson, London: Verso, 1994), p. 43.

17 Ibid., p. 92.

18 Ibid.

19 On Deleuze on Cartesian dualism, equivocity and the degeneracy of orgasm, see Charlie Blake, 'A Preface to Pornotheology: Spinoza, Deleuze and the Sexing of Angels', *Deleuze and Sex* (ed. Frida Beckman, Edinburgh: Edinburgh University Press, 2011), pp. 174–99.

20 On Deleuze and univocity, see Daniel Smith, 'The Doctrine of Univocity: Deleuze's Ontology of Immanence', *Deleuze and Religion* (ed. Mary Bryden, London: Routledge, 2001), pp. 167–83.

21 John Milton, *Paradise Lost* (ed. Stephen Orgel and Jonathan Goldberg, Oxford: Oxford University Press, 2004), p. 41, bk. 2, ln. 409.

22 Ibid., p. 56, bk. 2, ln. 893–97.

23 Georges Bataille, *Inner Experience* (trans. Leslie Anne Boldt, Albany, NY: State University of New York Press, 1988), p. 26.

24 Nietzsche, *Zarathustra*, p. 158.

25 Friedrich Nietzsche, *Beyond Good and Evil: Prelude to a Philosophy of the Future* (ed. Rolf-Peter Horstmann and Judith Norman, trans. Judith Norman, Cambridge: Cambridge University Press, 2002), p. 50.

26 On Sartre and Bataille, see Stuart Kendal, *Georges Bataille* (London: Reaktion, 2007), pp. 170–71.

27 Julia Kristeva, *Tales of Love* (trans. Leon S. Roudiez, New York: Columbia University Press, 1987), p. 365.

28 Benjamin Noys, *Georges Bataille: A Critical Introduction* (London: Pluto, 2000), p. 34.

29 Nick Land, 'Shamanic Nietzsche', *Fanged Noumena: Collected Writings 1987–2007* (Falmouth: Urbanomic, 2011), p. 214.

30 For his more general study of Bataille, see Nick Land, *The Thirst for Annihilation: Georges Bataille and Virulent Nihilism* (London: Routledge, 1992).

31 Søren Kierkegaard, *Stages on Life's Way* (ed. and trans. Howard and Edna Hong, Princeton: Princeton University Press, 1988), p. 8.

32 Klossowski, 'Of the Simulacrum', p. 147.

33 Ibid., p. 148.

34 Quentin Meillassoux, 'Excerpts from *L'Inexistence divine*', trans. Graham Harman, in Graham Harman, *Quentin Meillassoux: Philosophy in the Making* (Edinburgh: Edinburgh University Press, 2011), pp. 175–238.

35 I owe this observation on a rarely visited aspect of Aquinas, and with gratitude, to Steven Shakespeare, both from our conversations and from his 'Into the Vomitarium: Diseased Sacraments', a paper on Aquinas and the band Death Spell Omega, first delivered at the Black Metal Philosophy symposium in Dublin in November 2011, and forthcoming in a collection from Pentium Books.

36 Thomas Aquinas, *Summa Theologica of St. Thomas Aquinas* (2nd rev. edn, 1920, trans. Fathers of the English Dominican Province, www.newadvent.org/summa/), III, Q. 83, A. 6.

37 Eleanor Kaufman, 'Klossowski, Deleuze, and Orthodoxy', *Diacritics* 35:1 (2005), p. 54.

38 Ibid., p. 55.

39 Shakespeare (forthcoming as per n. 33, unpaginated draft).

9

St Lyotard on the Differend/ Difference Love Can Make

Phillip E. Davis

Introduction

Jean-François Lyotard has been celebrated as *the* 'saint' of postmodernity. He achieved this status through the publication of *The Postmodern Condition* – an occasional report on knowledge given to the government of Quebec, in which he addressed the crisis of legitimation within knowledge since the nineteenth century. Lyotard's fame arose from a three-word encapsulation of the postmodern condition appearing in that report: namely, the postmodern condition as 'incredulity towards metanarratives'. He is often spoken of therefore as an expert on postmodernity who proclaimed the end of master narratives, who noted that the postmodern condition deals with difference, etc. However, while he may be lauded as a postmodern 'saint', Lyotard's argument is largely ignored. Little reference is made to Lyotard's phrase mechanics as given in *The Differend*, nor to his insight that the event cannot be presented without losing it. Lyotard offers a withering critique of the Christian narrative as a grand narrative functioning under the rule of love. However, Lyotard also raises the critical consciousness of Christianity *ex negativo* that the Christian narrative can become a master narrative, perhaps opening the way to reconceive Christianity as an open narrative of love. In light of Lyotard's critique of Christianity, we will argue that theology should listen to/read this postmodern 'saint' and that theology can benefit from taking Lyotard's critique seriously. In conversation with Lyotard, Lieven Boeve, for example, offers a model of the 'open narrative' as a way for Christianity to bear witness to otherness while recognizing its own particular boundaries. We will accordingly argue that theology should listen to/read this postmodern 'saint', since he offers us a way to renew Christianity from within. However, in contradistinction to Lyotard, we will argue that the Christian narrative is best understood as an open narrative, which is demonstrated in the life of Jesus of Nazareth – a narrative that intentionally remains open to the otherness of the other.

A postmodern 'saint'

Lyotard is thought of as an authority on postmodernity,[1] whose name is often used in conjunction with other postmodern luminaries as Jacques Derrida and Michel Foucault.[2] Lyotard made important contributions to postmodern thought in such areas as economics and aesthetics. As a young man he was a militant member of the radical leftist group *Socialisme ou barbarie*; however, he later became a post-Marxist philosopher who recognized the totalizing tendencies of Marxism – especially as it was practised in Stalinist Russia – although he pined after its dream of economic justice.[3] Lyotard was a fierce critic of capitalism, arguing that it is the current metanarrative that had succeeded in superseding all other narratives, reducing them (and everything else) to the 'moment of exchange'. His withering critique of capitalism in fact forms the conclusion to his magnum opus, *The Differend*.[4] Lyotard also made an important contribution to the field of aesthetics. He pointed out that a dispute (*différend*) exists between aesthetics (art) and philosophy (commentary upon the artistic work), and he struggled to bear witness to the 'presence' of a sublime figurality expressed in the artistic work. Lyotard's offerings in aesthetics spanned his career, beginning with his second book, *Discours, figure*, published in 1971, and culminating in texts on contemporary artists such as Sam Francis, Karel Appel, Marcel Duchamp, Arakawa, Adami and Buren.[5]

Although Lyotard's oeuvre is wide-ranging, complex and unique, it is largely ignored. Lyotard is often referred to as an authority, but his argument is *not* taken as seriously as is his name. Numerous authors, in scores of academic articles, cite his statement concerning an 'incredulity towards metanarratives', using it as an authoritative pronouncement on postmodernism, before launching into their own arguments.[6] Lyotard, therefore, simply functions as an *auctoritas* within their argumentation. He is reduced to a name – a name for an argument. And as Lyotard points out, a name is simply a rigid designator, a quasi-deictic that holds a place in any sentence. A name is a place-holder, an index within which any meaning can be ascribed. The name 'Lyotard' can be used by anyone as an authority to bolster their case in almost any way they might choose.

While many people know the name for the argument, few people know the argument itself. Lyotard announced in *The Postmodern Condition* the preparation of a work that would more fully demonstrate his differential thinking. This book was published four years later as *The Differend*. Very few people reference *The Differend*, since it is a book that is perhaps too difficult for many to read. Lyotard himself notes that the book is 'too voluminous, too long, and too difficult'.[7] Lyotard describes it as a 'pile of phrases', and so it appears. His philosophical argument is based upon the 'phrase' (or sentence), and it analyses how a presented phrase links to a prior phrase. At the linking of every phrase a *différend* occurs – that is, a dispute between two parties in which there is no common idiom for regulating the conflict and, thus, one party suffers wrong because his or her complaint cannot be signified in the idiom being used. Any attempt to signify the person's complaint in the discourse in play or to regulate the dispute in that idiom neutralizes that person's complaint, translating the differend into a litigation (*litige*) and reducing the complainant to silence.[8] Lyotard calls for justice for the one who is thus silenced. He asks that the reader read – that the reader search for a way to express the, as yet, inexpressible sentence, and, in so doing, to do justice to the silenced victim by bearing witness to the differend. In its complex linguistic analysis and in an attempt to do justice to the silenced victim, *The Differend* makes a perceptively searing critique of the Christian narrative; namely, that the Christian narrative too easily becomes a master narrative that oppresses the other.

Lyotard's argument is not an innocent one. It is an argument that implicates those who *use him* to do otherwise. Lyotard is silenced when his name is made into an empty sign, ready to designate whatever we want it to signify. Justice, however, demands that we listen to this philosopher who speaks his difficult sentences, that we bear witness to the differend, and that we try to link justly onto his philosophical phrases.

A Christian saint?

As *auctoritas*, Lyotard has been recognized as a 'saint' for postmodernity, although as a somewhat neglected saint. His position has been turned into a caricature, but he remains an influential leader in postmodern thought. However, the question should be asked: is he a saint in Christian terms? After all, Lyotard criticized the Christian narrative as oppressive, called the Christian God the 'great Zero',[9] and announced the end of the Christian grand narrative. Perhaps it is time to take Lyotard seriously. So doing, we turn now to his analysis of the Christian grand narrative as a master narrative.

Lyotard most fully describes his philosophy of phrase mechanics in *The Differend*. A phrase (i.e. a sentence) is presented. Each phrase presents a 'universe' within which four instances may be situated: addressor, addressee, sense and referent. These instances are situated within the phrase universe according to the rules governing its phrase regimen. Since phrase regimens are heterogeneous to each other, a phrase cannot be translated from one phrase regimen into another regimen without suffering damage (e.g. a logical phrase cannot be translated into a rhetorical phrase, etc.). However, a link must be made to the prior phrase – for even silence is a phrase. The happening of a phrase opens up an abyss and the expectation that a link will be made. However, the phrase that succeeds in linking with the presented phrase will always betray the event involved in the linking as it closes off the expectation that something is happening. The event will always be lost in its very presentation – you cannot present the event without losing it.

Genres of discourse handle the problem of linking phrases from heterogeneous phrase regimens. These discourse genres link the presented phrase to the prior phrase according to their ends (or rules). Discourse genres compete with each other at the linking of every phrase, and there are many genres of discourse. Cognition links the presented phrase with the goal of acquiring *knowledge* by establishing the referent. This is accomplished by naming, signifying and showing the referent. Obligation is a discourse genre staked on *obedience* to an unknown other, whose calling places the addressee under obligation. Simply hearing the request places the hearer under obligation. And there are many other discourse genres – such as rhetoric, humour and speculation – each of which competes with the other discourse genres over linking with the presented phrase. A dispute, therefore, erupts among the genres of discourse at the presentation of every phrase. This differend must occur since only one discourse genre will succeed in regulating the linkage to the presented phrase, and since discourse genres are heterogeneous to each other. Every linking of a phrase involves one winner and many losers, once the end is determined which will govern the linking of that phrase. Lyotard's analysis of phrase mechanics is extremely deep and thorough; however, what is most germane for our discussion is his handling of one discourse genre in particular: the narrative.

Lyotard says that the narrative genre of discourse links every presented phrase with the goal of coming 'to an end' – for example, the 'moral' in a fable. There are different kinds of narratives. Small narratives forget the differend, presuming that the last word will be a 'good one'. This presumption is true even of narratives relating stories about conflicts and disputes (i.e. differends). When the narrative makes its last turn, all of the previous phrases are organized from back to beginning, and an end is impressed upon all prior phrases. Thus, the diachronic operator (namely, the before/after) 'swallows up' the 'now' of the event. Forgotten is the otherness of the event, which is pushed out beyond the narrative's border. As a result, the narrative closes itself off from that which is other to it. The dispute between heterogeneous phrase regimens and genres of discourse is easily forgotten. However, narratives can also make the claim that they can represent all of reality, and it is precisely this claim that Lyotard so ruthlessly resists, for such an assertion leads inevitably to an oppressive grand narrative.

Grand narratives are stories that presume to be able to reveal the meaning of all 'little stories'. They are told by a third-party narrator who stands outside of, and above, the narrative (i.e. by an universal addressor). Grand narratives make universal claims, and they universalize the instances within phrase universes (e.g. addressee, addressor, sense and referent). For example, rather than speaking about an individual person, the grand narrative makes claims about 'humanity'. At each point of the linking of a phrase, the grand narrative determines the rules of linkage and of the instantiation of instances within the phrase universe, according to a governing rule which links all phrases together in parallel under that rule. What Lyotard found so insidious about the grand narrative is the totalized history or project for humanity conveyed by such stories, which denies the witness to the event present in the presenting of a phrase. In fact, he called this propensity – to force all links between phrases to be made according to a rule – evil.[10] One can easily see what Lyotard feared when one thinks about the Nazi rule of linking all phrases and gestures according to the rule of 'pure Aryan blood', or the Stalinist rule of linking according to the rule of 'the worker's paradise' – ending in Auschwitz and the gulags respectively for those who resisted these grand narratives.

Lyotard criticizes the Christian story as also being a grand narrative. It is the story that 'vanquished the other narratives in Rome' by designating 'what is at stake in the genre itself'. Namely, 'to love what happens as if it were a gift, to love even the *Is it happening?* as the promise of good news'.[11] The Christian grand narrative conquered all other narratives for almost two millennia by putting the love of the event at the heart of its project. Thus, love is the rule governing the Christian grand narrative – a rule that operates under obligation. The command to love is a universal rule extended 'to all heroes, all narrators, and all narrates'. Its circular form extends to all narratives, through a decree voiced by the divine Absolute. Lyotard summarizes that command to all creatures: 'if you are loved, you ought to love; and you shall be loved only if you love'.[12] This rule obligates everyone to link every phrase or gesture according to the rule of love. As a result, the story closes around the idea of love, and an interior and an exterior to the narrative are formed. Those on the inside of the Christian narrative are believers, while those who are on the outside of the narrative are condemned as heretics. Lyotard argues that grand narratives are totalitarian, which necessarily oppress those on the outside, that is, those who resist linking phrases according to the operating meta-rule.

A remarkable example is given of one who is oppressed as an outsider by the Christian grand narrative. Joan of Arc witnesses before the authorities that she is under obligation; namely, that heavenly voices have commanded her to wear men's clothing. But she hears a different command from the church rulers, specifically to put on women's clothing. A conflict erupts within

Joan pointing to the differend between divine and Church commands. She asks, 'Ought I to do this?' The reply is that 'God wants it'. But Joan asks, 'Is this His will?' The answer comes, 'He declared His will at the beginning'.[13] Church officials point to the before/after of the Scripture narrative – what was declared in and through salvation history. However, Joan holds on to the 'now' of obligation and of the obligated one – the event of hearing divine instructions. We see here the conflict between two heterogeneous discourse genres: obligation and narrative. The narrative, however, is the Christian grand narrative, and this is the idiom spoken by the ecclesiastical court. Joan's testimony cannot be heard by the court, since it is spoken from within the discourse of obligation: namely, that 'I feel the obligation for some other action'. Joan relents to the authorized interpreters of God's will and she puts on the dress; however, she later obeys her voices and is found wearing male clothing. The court, therefore, condemns Joan as a recalcitrant heretic, and the one who resists the link demanded by the Church, in faithfulness to her voices and to the obligation under which she stood, is burned to death by the Church as a heretic. A saint is condemned, ironically, under the rule of love, because she could not remain within the borders of the Christian grand narrative. She suspected the authority of that tradition, since she had heard voices. Lyotard says that it is this holding of idiolects in suspicion that triggered the burning of witches, the killing of prophets and resistance to the Reformation.[14]

Lyotard's argument moves swiftly in *The Differend* from the obligation Joan expressed to the engendering of a universal history through love. He argues that during the Enlightenment, the idea of love is released from any concept of revelation, and it births a universal history of progress, leading to the emancipation of humanity. Links are now governed by the idea of loving the other on the way to either a 'republican brotherhood' or towards 'communist solidarity'. These new grand narratives are authorized by the idea of the progression of a universal humanity, rather than in a 'myth of beginnings'. But, these Enlightenment grand narratives are resisted by local narratives, which provide identity for 'national' groups and traditions. 'Peoples do not form into one people, whether it be the people of God or the sovereign people of world citizens'.[15] So the differend continues, this time between 'the Idea of freedom and narratives of legitimation'.[16] And yet, Marxism, which was birthed in this decoupling of the idea of love from revelation, now suffers from the grand narrative that has superseded all the rest, according to Lyotard – namely, capitalism, which reduces the event to the moment of exchange.

In view of his withering criticism of the Christian narrative, the question must be asked: can Lyotard be a saint for Christianity? Perhaps he is a 'saint' of the postmodern condition; in which case, he is a saint who has been misused. But can Lyotard also be a saint in terms of the Christian tradition? Certainly not. Lyotard argued against a God he considered to be a great Zero, that does not exist, and that oppresses people in his nothingness.[17]

Lyotard remained steadfastly, vehemently opposed to Christianity, although he continued to be engaged, at least philosophically, with it throughout his life – never stepping completely away from his Christian past.[18] Since Lyotard proclaimed the end of the Christian master narrative, why on earth would we call him a saint?

Retrieving Lyotard for theology

But one could say that saints are not simply heroes; they are people who both suffer and offer criticism. In this light, we would like to engage Lyotard's criticism of the Christian narrative, but not with the intention of either baptizing Lyotard nor of turning his critical philosophy into a sort of negative theology, as theologians have been tempted to do with certain deconstructive philosophies. After all, an overemphasis upon the otherness of the Other can be devastating for a theological reflection on the Christian God. Certainly theology should heed the cautions expressed in apophatic theology; that is, against an over-determined definition of divinity, leading to a kind of onto-theology. But Kearney rightly reminds us that unfamiliarity can easily slide into monstrosity. God can become so other that one ends up with the 'monster God' – an overly sublime God who is ultimately 'indistinguishable from abjection and evil', since 'vertical excess and abyssal excess easily collapse into one another'.[19] Such a God is 'so unfamiliar and ineffable as to be traumatic – that is, *horrible*'.[20] This is a dead-end that we certainly want to avoid.

However, theologians would do well to listen to Lyotard's criticism of Christianity: namely, that the Christian narrative closes in upon itself too easily, thus becoming an oppressive master narrative. Lyotard claims, rightly in our opinion, that the rule governing the closure of this narrative is the rule of love. Since love stands at the heart of Lyotard's critique of the Christian narrative, it is important to briefly look at his understanding of love. Simply said, for Lyotard, love is openness to the other – or better, the ability to link to whatever phrase or gesture happens.[21] However, he makes a distinction between how love relates to the other, either in terms of *representation* or *presentation*. When the other is related to as a representation, the other is reduced to a *what*, and the eventness of the other is disregarded. A Christian idea (or rule) of love victimizes the other by immediately inscribing the other into a narrative 'as if it were a gift', as a representation that serves as a sign demonstrating that 'we' are loved by God.[22] Lyotard resists precisely this kind of love, that links to the other through representation, arguing, rather, for the love that relates to the other as the other presents himself/herself/itself, that is, through presentation. Yet, even this love is not without its risks.

Lyotard says that lovers are 'committed to presence, deprived of representation'. Lovers do not represent their beloveds to themselves;

rather, everything is concentrated upon the 'this, now, yesterday, you'.[23] Sensible experiences – sight, touch, scent, sound and point of view – are 'absolutely singular' for each of the lovers and are, thus, untranslatable. Each person is an 'incommunicable secret', imprisoned in a body.[24] But these singular experiences can be shared intransitively between lovers, and the attempt to communicate such is evidenced in lover's prattle, as a stumbling around among phrases, attempting to express the inexpressible.[25] For love demands that I share my field of perspective with the other, and this makes love dangerous, since the lover who divulges the hidden secrets of that singular perspective is made vulnerable to betrayal. Once the 'unnameable singularity' has been uncovered and found (whether love itself or writing) it can be delivered up to the police, as George Orwell depicts in his novel *1984*. Winston and Julia both betray each other after their arrest, handing their most intimate fears over to the police.[26]

Love opens us to the danger of captivity, and it is a danger that cannot easily be avoided. After all, life begins as a seizure by others who hold us in the bonds of parental love. Lyotard writes, 'We were born from others, but also to others, given over defenseless to them'.[27] This seizure is illustrated by the word *mainmise*, which originally came from French jurisprudence. *Mainmise* is literally the laying of one's hand upon, or the seizing of, one who had been disloyal to the feudal lord. To exercise a *mancipium* was to gain complete and exclusive control over the person seized by the *manceps*. The arrestee was reduced to the position of a slave, having no right to him or herself. Lyotard says that 'dependency is too weak a word to describe this condition of being seized and held by the hand of the other'.[28] Parents, therefore, exercise a *mancipium* over the child. Each child is given over (like a slave) into the hands of its parents, whose parental love can be disastrous – for the child's psyche can be so dominated by the parents' love that the child would never think to leave the parent's *mainmise*. Rebellion against the parent is never contemplated. Parental love comes too quickly for cognition. It comes as a blow to the child's psyche, prior to all cognition, and the blow is so deep that it continues to dominate the child's life even into adulthood. Love, then, is a seizure that may never be lifted.

This idea of love as slavery informs Lyotard's understanding of the Jewish and Christian faiths. Both of these religions require one to listen to the father's voice. The true *manceps* has spoken and freedom comes from hearing that Voice. For the Jew the Voice is located in the text of the scriptures, which must be continually read, reread and interpreted. But the Voice is made flesh for the Christian; therefore, the Voice voices itself, and the need to constantly read and interpret a text disappears. However, for both Jews and Christians the important thing is not what the Voice says but simply that one hears the Voice, since it is the hearing of the Voice that puts one under obligation.[29] Ironically, one is freed by both hearing and being *bound* by the true *manceps*. Although this is true for both faiths, it is taken to a whole different level by the apostle Paul, who urges the Romans to become 'slaves of God', thus abandoning themselves completely to the father's *mancipium*.[30] The way to freedom comes through *enslavement* to God.[31] And the Voice that speaks places the hearer under immediate obligation. When the Voice is heard, the constitution of an 'I' is interrupted, since the call comes unexpectedly. Who is calling is not known; all that is known is that I am being addressed. As a result, the call is oppressive and the 'I' is dispossessed. The apostle Paul preaches Christ as the Voice that speaks 'only at the price of a dispossession, of a devastating affection'.[32] For to hear that Voice is to be disposed of one's self, placed under obligation (i.e. slavery), and required to listen. The Voice that speaks, which we cannot but hear, commands us to love the Lover. Thus, love as seizure – enslavement.

Lyotard's critique of the Christian narrative can be fruitful for theology, since it raises the critical consciousness of Christianity *ex negativo*; namely, that it can be a master narrative. Thus theologians are led to rethink the role of narratives, and Lyotard perhaps opens the way of re-conceiving Christianity as an open narrative of love. Lyotard's differential thought – his intentional, active awareness of and attempt to bear witness to otherness – is an example of philosophy trying to give expression to the as-of-yet inexpressible phrase. Something asks to be expressed in a sentence in a way that conveys what cannot be said. This is signified by a feeling, a stumbling around, in which the speaker tries to 'find the right words'. It's precisely this moment of struggle that illustrates how one attempts to remain open to the occurrence, to an event that needs to be put into words without *reducing* it to something less than it is.

Survivors of the Holocaust, for example, often wrestle with this problem. Some feel the need to leave a witness of their experiences and sufferings; however, they know that by putting the horror into words, it inevitably reduces the enormity of the evil they endured. No words can express the Holocaust, but somehow it must be phrased – lest we forget and the evil be perpetrated once again on a people. One who remains open to the occurrence works hard not to link too quickly to an event (e.g. a phrase or a gesture). Rather, time is taken to think or read and to rethink or reread in a search for a new way to express what has happened in a way that does justice to the event. In Lyotard's terms, a search is made to link onto the survivor's phrase without victimizing him or her once more by translating the event (i.e. reducing it) into something less than what needs to be said. Theologians are, therefore, reminded to do justice to those who must witness to something that as-of-yet cannot be expressed.

Lyotard's differential thought is an example of a philosophical 'open' discourse that attempts to do just that. He also gives us an example of another 'open' discourse.[33] This leads, of course, to the obvious question: are there yet others? Lyotard also helps theology in terms of content, by thinking love in an 'open' manner, that is, love as an openness to the presentation of the other. Love need not turn the beloved into a cognitive project (i.e. an idea) and, thereby, lose the event presented in the arrival of the other. Rather, lovers babbling at each other in the joy of presented love signify that there is, as of yet, no phrase capable of phrasing what needs to be said. Such a love refuses to close itself off – or distance itself – from the other, in order to represent its beloved as an *idea*. Theology can benefit from a reconsideration of love, especially since, as Lyotard points out, it lies at the heart of our narrative.

In light of Lyotard's assessment, we would argue that the Christian narrative is properly an 'open narrative of love', and that this narrative degrades into a closed grand narrative precisely at the moment that it fails to attend to the otherness of the other. Thus, Lyotard is not simply a negative help for theology. He also helps theology positively by suggesting strategies for resisting the narrative's natural tendency to self-enclose through his praxis of differential thought.[34] Lyotard offers theology a way to renew Christianity from *within* its own narrative: a way to 'bear witness to the differend' at every linking of a phrase, striving to keep the narrative structure open, while respecting alterity, all the while knowing that every linking of a phrase betrays the event presented at the happening of that phrase.

An open narrative of love

Although Lyotard is generally not received by religious scholars, he *is* received by Lieven Boeve, who offers the model of the 'open narrative' in response to Lyotard's claims. This model provides a structure for thinking the Christian narrative in a way that remains intentionally open to difference and otherness as a way of resisting the narrative's tendency to degenerate into a self-enclosed master narrative.[35] An open narrative as such is one that pays particular attention to the other's irreducible otherness and witnesses thereto.[36] It refuses to take the observer's position, realizing, in agreement with Lyotard, that the grand narrative attempts to reveal the truth in all small narratives and phrases by universalizing the instances situated within a phrase (i.e. addressor, addressee, referent and sense). Rather, an open narrative resists the 'objective' situating of the self as observer as a means of extracting the meaning of all gestures, phrases and narratives through a cognitive apparatus. Boeve writes, in the open narrative 'there are no observers any more, only participants'.[37] As participants, Christians are aware of the incontestable plurality of their own narrative. They are keenly aware of the multitude of competing stories in our world today. The Christian narrative is one story among many stories. It is a narrative that is situated in a specific space, community and time. As a story that works itself out in time, the Christian narrative is contingent: things could have happened differently than they did. And, while it is *a* particular narrative, it is *our* own *particular* narrative: a story that cannot help but be challenged to relate repeatedly to plurality (i.e. to different narratives and life-options). As a result, the Christian narrative is a story in which its truth 'is lived and experienced'.[38]

As a result of this situating, the question should be asked if the presence of the event can be taken *positively* within the narrative itself. This is an important question, since the Christian narrative narrates the event of God's gracious activity, and since every linking of a phrase necessarily betrays the event. Boeve argues that this is possible, and he notes that Lyotard's philosophical approach is an example of a discourse striving to remain open to the event, knowing that every linking of a phrase betrays that event, while maintaining that the inexpressible must be expressed somehow.[39] Thus, Lyotard's concept of philosophy is an instantiation of an 'open narrative'. However, Boeve also notes that Lyotard fails to provide many details on how we can advance the narrative dimension of the 'open narrative'.[40] Such details are important for any theology that attempts to resist the self-enclosing tendencies of a narrative, while, at the same time, bearing witness to the gracious actions of God within history.

Boeve rightly points out that the Christian open narrative has a critical and a kerygmatic function. The critique of grace is brought to bear against any attempt to too quickly link onto the event and enclose it within a closed narrative. Grace acts to break open such closed, oppressive narratives. At the same time, the command to recount this tale of love is made in the full knowledge that every (re)telling is an attempt to express the inexpressible within language, which must always fail to some extent. Such a retelling is a witness to an Other that is other to the narrative itself, and the Christian narrative does not have to close into a grand narrative so long as it remains self-reflective. Boeve appeals, in this regard, to Paul Ricoeur's argument that thought which reflects upon its own linguistic character cannot continue as (or form into) a grand narrative, since the reality to which language refers is of an order separate from itself (*le même* vs *l'autre*).[41] This otherness remains anonymous in most narratives; however, in the Christian narrative the heteronomy is given a name: Jesus Christ. Boeve notes that the biblical texts refer to God as its 'archi-referent', and this gives them 'a founded character'. He contends that this makes the Christian narrative a founded open narrative and, as such, a different way of bearing witness to the differend. The Christian open narrative, therefore, bears witness to the Other, to its story and to the grace of God's love, while always remembering that the One to which it witnesses radically transcends any attempt at story-telling.

In contrast with Lyotard's assessment that the Jewish narrative is inherently open while the Christian narrative is too determined, since the Voice has voiced itself, Boeve argues that the Incarnation need not lead to a too determined, closed narrative. Rather, he suggests that the naming of the Voice, as Jesus Christ, provides a new opening within the narrative that forecloses a too-quickly made, hegemonic closing of the same. Such an opening is signified, for example, in the paradox between the word as naming the event and the Word, as was expressed at Chalcedon.[42] The Incarnation interrupts the constant, impatient and automatic linking of events that occurs within a master narrative. Jesus Christ, as the Word made flesh, points to One who exceeds the story itself. In fact this One, who steps into history, refuses to be situated exclusively within that story. His arrival in the Incarnation points to a space outside of the enclosed, master narrative. And his words and deeds made a powerful critique against the victimization of those who are silenced by oppressive, religious stories, as with, for example, the woman who anointed Jesus' feet and left forgiven.[43]

We argue here that the Christian narrative is best understood as an 'open narrative' – a narrative that recognizes its particularity, while witnessing to the grace of God's interrupting love. In place of exclusively trying to define the truth, as the 'truth *content*' of our narrative, we are spurred on to *live in* and *give witness to* the truth that ultimately transcends our particular (Christian) narrative through the interruption of the other.[44] The Christian open narrative is a story of love – a love that refuses to prematurely close itself off from the other, a love involved in the inexpressible hidden in every presentation of the other. The Jesus narrative (i.e. the account of his works and teaching) displays a similar refusal to close itself off from the otherness of the other. Time and again, Jesus' life and ministry are interrupted by encounters with the other (lepers, demoniacs, tax collectors, prostitutes, etc.), moments where human need met divine love. Two examples will have to suffice here: the woman caught in the act of adultery, trapped within a closed, condemning logical narrative of sin and punishment, whose story is radically opened by the liberating love of Christ – 'Neither do I condemn you. Go and sin no more';[45] and the sole Samaritan leper, from among the ten lepers, who returned to thank Jesus for his healing and deliverance from a reproving narrative that saw his diseased skin as 'proof' of his guilt and sin, only to hear himself described as a man of faith: 'Your faith has made you well'.[46] These particular phrases (or words) of Jesus, then, are witnesses *par excellence* to the love of God – a love that makes an appeal to sinners and a love that calls for a fundamental attitude of openness towards God. For God *is love*.[47]

Jesus' words, gestures and teaching illustrate a way of relating to the other as an irreducibly particular person. Such a love makes all the difference, since it respects the other, allowing the other to present himself/herself/itself in its irreducible uniqueness, without making a victim of the latter by ignoring the differend. As Lyotard points out, love as presentation is involved in the here, now and other. But he also warns us that a love that reduces the other to a representation, or a symbol, of some universal truth leads inevitably to terror. This is what Joan of Arc's persecutors forgot. By assuming the addressor position – as authorized interpreters of Scripture – they neglected the fact that they too were addressed (as addressees) by that same narrative, and they burned a saint.[48] When God is too sharply defined in our telling of the narrative, the story closes and God withdraws.[49] But the person who remembers that s/he is addressed by the narrative of God's interrupting love allows the o/Other to interrupt his or her story.

Conclusion

Lyotard may be a 'saint' for postmodern philosophy but Christianity may not consider Lyotard a saint. His critique, however, can be made fruitful for theology by pointing out the Christian narrative's propensity for closing itself off into a master narrative. The Christian grand narrative ignores the uniqueness of whatever happens, or is said, or is done. Instead, the person or event is 'translated' into a gift to be received, without listening for what he/she/it is trying to communicate. In so doing, the Christian grand narrative muzzles the person or event and silences his/her/its witness to whatever is occurring. This is all done in the name of love, as proof that we are loved by God. Such a 'love' can oppress the other and burn a saint at the stake – all for the love of God, neighbour and community. Lyotard also helps theology positively to frame Christianity as an open narrative, and his differential thinking can help Christianity to overcome its tendency to close into a master narrative. He also helps us see the importance of loving the other in a way that remains 'open' to the other and to the difference that this entails. Boeve seriously considers the critique offered by Lyotard and offers the model of the 'open narrative', as a way of resisting the narrative's tendency to self-enclose into a grand narrative. Boeve argues that the presence of the event can be taken positively within the narrative itself, since it bears witness to something of a different order. We argue that Boeve is correct in seeing the Christian narrative as an 'open narrative'. This is demonstrated in the liberating love of Jesus, who set individuals free from the closed narratives within which they were imprisoned. God's love, revealed preeminently in Jesus of Nazareth, allows each of us to present ourselves as we choose to do so. Such a love makes all the difference when it attends to the difference (dispute, differend) at hand in the arrival of the other.

Notes

1 In fact, Derrida wrote of Lyotard that 'the now worldwide thought on the "postmodern" has him to thank, as we know, for its initial elaboration'. See Jacques Derrida, *The Work of Mourning* (Chicago: University of Chicago Press, 2003), p. 215.

2 See for instance James K. A. Smith, *Who's Afraid of Postmodernism?: Taking Derrida, Lyotard, and Foucault to Church* (Grand Rapids, MI: Baker, 2006).

3 After its apparent collapse, Lyotard says that Marxism continues as a 'silent feeling [that] signals the differend' arising against capitalism. See Jean-François Lyotard, *The Differend: Phrases in Dispute* (Minneapolis, MN: University of Minnesota Press, 1988), p. 171, §236.

4 See Ibid., pp. 171–81.

5 Many of these previously unavailable texts are being published now by the University of Leuven Press in a proposed five volume series. See, for instance,

Jean-François Lyotard, *Karel Appel: A Gesture of Colour 5*, 1 (Leuven: Leuven University Press, 2009).

6 This is something that Derrida did not do. His long, in-depth 'discussion' with Lyotard led to an 'all-out friendship'. See Derrida, *Mourning*, p. 214. Derrida also tries to express his love for Lyotard in 'the words I cannot find, beyond words [. . .]'. See Derrida, *Mourning*, p. 215.

7 Lyotard, *Differend*, p. xv.

8 Ibid., p. 13, §22.

9 See Jean-François Lyotard, *Libidinal Economy* (trans. Iain Hamilton Grant, Bloomington, IN: Indiana University Press, 1993), pp. 8–9. Lyotard remained steadfast in his rejection of the existence of the Christian God to the end of his career. In his posthumously published book, Lyotard refers to God as a 'despotic authority' that reduces Augustine to nothing through the latter's devotion to this great Nothing. See Jean-François Lyotard, *The Confession of Augustine* (trans. R. Beardsworth, Stanford: Stanford University Press, 2000), pp. 75 and 77.

10 'By evil, I understand, and one can only understand, the incessant interdiction of possible phrases, a defiance of the occurrence, the contempt for Being'. Lyotard, *Differend*, p. 140, §197.

11 Ibid., p. 159, §232.

12 Ibid., pp. 159–60, §232.

13 Ibid., p. 160, §234.

14 Ibid.

15 Ibid., p. 161, §235.

16 Ibid.

17 In fact, Lyotard describes his project as the destruction of religion. 'So we rebegin the critique of religion, so we rebegin the destruction of piety, we still seek atheism, terribly intelligent [. . .]'. See, Lyotard, *Economy*, p. 5.

18 As a boy Lyotard wanted to become a Dominican monk, or a painter or a historian. But he chose an early marriage rather than 'monastic vows'. See Jean-François Lyotard, *Peregrinations: Law, Form, Event* (New York: Columbia University Press, 1988), p. 1. Graham Ward suggests that the posthumously published *The Confession of Augustine* functions as an 'explict[ly] Catholic coda [. . .] to Lyotard's *oeuvre*'. See Graham Ward, 'The Confession of Augustine', *Biography* 24:4 (2001), p. 943.

19 Richard Kearney, *The God Who May Be: A Hermeneutics of Religion* (Bloomington, IN: Indiana University Press, 2001), p. 33.

20 Ibid., pp. 33–34.

21 Lyotard makes it clear that even the ordinary things of life function as links to the presented phrase. He writes, 'I mean that to be in love with a woman, to will that she gives you the child she desires to give you, to arrange your life in order to make possible a life in common with her and the child – that also is a way of "phrasing"'. See Lyotard, *Peregrinations*, p. 4.

22 The event functions as a referent that signifies God's love within the Christian grand narrative. See Lyotard, *Differend*, p. 160, §233.

23 Jean-François Lyotard, *The Inhuman: Reflections on Time* (trans. Geoffrey Bennington and Rachel Bowlby, Cambridge: Polity Press, 1991), p. 201.

24 Jean-François Lyotard, *The Postmodern Explained: Correspondence 1982–1985* (trans. D. Barry et al., Minneapolis, MN: University of Minnesota Press, 1993), p. 96.

25 Ibid., p. 92.
26 Ibid., pp. 94–95.
27 Jean-François Lyotard and Eberhard Gruber, *The Hyphen: Between Judaism and Christianity* (trans. Pascale-Anne Brault and Michael Naas, Amherst, NY: Humanity Books, 1999), p. 2.
28 Ibid., p. 1.
29 Concerning Abraham, Lyotard says, 'What did he hear in the Voice? Not *what* it said, something he could not understand, but *the fact that* it wanted something of him'. See ibid., p. 17.
30 Romans 6.19ff.
31 Lyotard writes, 'One is emancipated from death only by accepting to be "enslaved to God", for "the advantage you get".' See Lyotard and Gruber, *The Hyphen*, p. 8.
32 Ibid., p. 25.
33 Lyotard gives us another example of an 'open' discourse in Judaism. Jewish thought, according to Lyotard, is an attempt to remain open to the occurrence of what the Voice has said through a constant rereading of the scriptural text. See Jean-François Lyotard, *Heidegger and 'the jews'* (trans. A. Michel and M. S. Roberts, Minneapolis, MN: University of Minnesota Press, 1990). The examples given comprise two specific genres of 'open' discourses: philosophical and theological.
34 Lieven Boeve, 'Naming God in Open Narratives: Theology between Deconstruction and Hermeneutics', *Paul Ricoeur: Poetics and Religion* (ed. J. Verheyden, T. L. Hettema and P. Vandecasteele, Leuven: Peeters, 2011), pp. 81–100, p. 87.
35 Ibid., p. 82.
36 For a detailed description of the model of the open narrative see Lieven Boeve, *Interrupting Tradition: An Essay on Christian Faith in a Postmodern Context* (trans. Brian Doyle, Leuven: Peeters, 2003).
37 Ibid., p. 93.
38 See Boeve, 'Naming God', p. 86.
39 Ibid., p. 92.
40 Ibid., p. 94.
41 Ibid., p. 95.
42 Lieven Boeve, 'Jean-François Lyotard on Differends and Unpresentable Otherness: Can God Escape the Clutches of the Christian Master Narrative?', *Culture, Theory, and Critique* 52:2–3 (2011), pp. 263–84, p. 280.
43 Luke 7.36–50.
44 See Boeve, *Tradition*, p. 99.
45 John 7.53–8.11.
46 Luke 17.11–19. Space does not allow for a more elaborate argument; however, this position is more thoroughly addressed in Lieven Boeve, *Tradition*, and Lieven Boeve, *God Interrupts History: Theology in a Time of Upheaval* (trans. Brian Doyle, London: Continuum, 2007).
47 1 John 4.8.
48 Lyotard, *Differend*, p. 160, §234.
49 Boeve, *Tradition*, p. 175.

10

Paul Ricoeur and the Symbolism of Sainthood: From Imitation to Innovation

Todd S. Mei

Despite the way we might think of saints as belonging to certain historical periods and confronting specific historical obstacles, many of us tend to see their acts as universally meaningful, and therefore, as embodying ideals to be emulated in our daily lives. However this understanding carries with it a significant difficulty: there is a risk of interpreting the actions of saints as providing rules of conduct to be followed, as if their meanings were familiar and the re-enactments of their actions affirmed a way of living ethically or piously. Yet we all know from observing children who mimic human actions that imitation does not equate to understanding; nor does it necessarily instantiate the principle or precept from which the action originated. So given this dilemma, how are we to make sense of the actions of saints? Something akin to rules of action, or perhaps as indicators of something more radical? Does the saint's action itself produce a meaning that outruns its performance?

If the answer to this last question is affirmative, then the action of a saint can be said to predicate an 'emergent meaning', that is, a meaning not yet articulated, let alone actualized.[1] A saint would therefore be less a figure of convention, recapitulating the familiar, and more a figure of innovation, indicating a new possibility of being. In this chapter, I employ Paul Ricoeur's theory of symbol to show how, beyond the historical specificity of the lives of saints, their actions can be understood to offer new ways of understanding the possibility for being. Ricoeur's theory is thus postmodern in the broad sense of attempting to account for ways in which linguistic expression discloses meaning non-reducible to the significations immanent to a system or structure – in this case, the Christian tradition. Symbolic meaning, says Ricoeur, 'shatters not only previous structures of our language, but also the previous structures of what we call reality'.[2]

The first two parts of this chapter will deal with explication and clarification – specifically, the problem of imitative action, as partly outlined above, and how Ricoeur's theory of symbol presents an alternative to this problem. The last two sections are constructive with the aim of providing a way of understanding saints symbolically. Because Ricoeur does not devote a great deal of attention to saints, the path of this constructive response takes a slight detour, drawing first on the symbolic significance of the prophet in the Judaic tradition, and then turning to see how the saint fulfils a similar function in the Christian tradition.[3]

The problem of imitative action

The problem of imitative action lies in what it takes for granted. Consider, for instance, that when it comes to undertaking appropriate (ethical) action in a given context, there is, arguably, a temptation to gravitate towards rules as a way of affirming to ourselves and others that the action to be performed is in some sense right or justified. In such instances, one can be said to be applying and imitating 'a rule of action'. What often motivates this temptation is the seal of authority innate to a system of rules, where, in performing an action in view of a rule, one is 'authorized' according to the system's values. Yet, it is obvious that this temptation involves a risk. Rules of action tend to ignore the unique contexts and circumstances of a situation which may demand an appropriate response above and beyond the rules supplied. Given that no two events are exactly alike, one wonders how adequate the idea and use of rules of action may be.[4]

Yet, even assuming that a rule may be appropriate to a situation, a problem still persists: There is no guarantee that the agent, in simply applying a rule, will understand why it should be applied except in some general sense, and furthermore, why the rule was created in the first instance. In other words, a comprehension (or even apprehension) of the reasons and justifications for the rule is by no means necessary for an agent to apply it. An act of charity, for example, may allow the agent to affirm a virtue relating to kindness and donation, but simply performing the act does not require the agent to understand the nature of charity, the given context in which he or she is being charitable or why charity might be a virtue.

It is true, nonetheless, that when looking at the actions of saints, one tends not to think of them as rules of action, but more as ideals expressing a principle according to which one should live.[5] Ideals do not specify the same type of guidance or prescription as rules. Rather, they tend to express specific ethical and religious values, especially when cast in the language of virtuousness. Within a given tradition, an ideal is something one can readily identify owing to the ethical and religious framework that makes it intelligible as something to be sought. Despite this difference, the problem of imitation remains: To identify a saint's action as something to be emulated is to reduce the action to a familiar meaning. And so by identifying an action with an ideal, one assumes that one has recognized the action's meaningfulness and applicability; that in living one's life, 'to imitate' this action is 'to follow' the saint in what is good.[6]

It is questionable in the first place as to whether the action of a saint should be understood as an ideal to be imitated. Indeed, it seems redundant to say that a figure revered by a tradition should offer or affirm only those meanings already familiar within that tradition. Returning to the virtue of charity in Christianity, one can say that it is familiar to us as an act of giving to those in need or those who are worse off than oneself. However, on this view, the narratives and acts of saints involving charitable acts really say nothing new, and they tend to make the extraordinary lives of saints reducible to meanings that could be expressed less ambiguously in the language of tenets or precepts. Furthermore, this type of reduction can actually cause more harm than good since it assumes it has exhausted the meaning of the action in question. Leo XIII, in his encyclical *Rerum Novarum* (1891), utilizes the familiar meaning of charity in this way, seeing it as a remedy for social injustice that ought to be emulated *en masse*. According to Leo XIII, we should emulate 'the heroism of charity' 'towards the lowly and the oppressed'.[7]

> Charity, as a virtue, pertains to the Church; for virtue it is not, unless it be drawn from the Most Sacred Heart of Jesus Christ; and whosoever turns his back on the Church cannot be near to Christ [. . .]. It cannot, however, be doubted that to attain the purpose we are treating of, not only the Church, but all human agencies, must concur. All who are concerned in the matter should be of one mind and according to their ability act together.[8]

Yet his contemporary, the political economist Henry George, argued that charity of this kind does not resolve social injustice but merely responds to the symptoms of what afflicts a society.[9] So while those 'better-off' might be donating to those in need under the aegis of virtue, the problem creating this need remains unresolved. In the end, the act of charity undermines its ethical intent since it prevents one from actually engaging with the root of the problem – that is, why there is poverty in the first instance.

We can also consider how the actions of saints often preclude simple imitation, and invoke a more reflective response to their meaning. Many saints are, in this respect, understood to be suggesting radical social reform, and as well, often performed acts which, if imitated, might end up contradicting other precepts and practices. In her study of celibate marriage and hagiography, Anne Alwis highlights how one cannot simply take meaning at face value when reading about saints; the saintly act of celibate marriage would be entirely impractical if imitated on a large scale, and by implication, would be contradictory to God's commandment 'to be fruitful and multiply'.[10]

Given these problems, imitation seems hardly a viable way of understanding the actions of saint. But if saints do not offer an ideal to be emulated, what are they offering? Ricoeur would say they are *donating* an unfamiliar meaning through the familiar.[11] In other words, their actions rely on a literal or obvious meaning to donate or indicate an entirely new one; their actions are symbolic and the saints can be described as symbols generating new meanings and new understandings within their tradition.

Ricoeur on symbol

A common way of understanding symbolism is to define it as an instance of double meaning in which a primary meaning 'stands for' a secondary one not readily apparent and which requires deciphering through a formal means of analysis, or at the very least, a familiarity with the cultural and historical context in which a symbol occurs. In this sense, we often refer to things such as national flags and gestures as symbols. A national flag can represent the honour of a nation, even to the extent that sacrilege of the flag is equivalent to an attack upon one's homeland. Gestures are often understood to indicate specific emotions within a given cultural context. The wave of a hand in one culture may represent openness and hospitality while in another it may be a gesture indicating irritation or uneasiness.

However, for Ricoeur, such instances are not symbols but rather signs since they signify another meaning already available to us, or rather that is given to us within an existing and closed system of references.[12] Signs denote a meaning already known by virtue of this system, whereas symbols use familiar meaning to predicate a new one. So signs can be said to deal with symmetrical equivalences of meaning where, in contradistinction, symbols involve an asymmetrical relation in which new meaning is predicated. Because of this double meaning, Ricoeur describes symbols as participating in 'the logic of correspondences' where the familiar meaning is seen as primary and the unfamiliar as secondary.[13] He speaks in general of a 'surplus of meaning' innate to symbolism:

> Symbolic signification [. . .] is so constituted that we can only attain the secondary signification by way of the primary signification, where this primary signification is the sole means of access to the surplus of meaning.[14]

This surplus of meaning is, of course, not simply linguistic. It is not only given by the symbol but also persists as a constituent of reality. In other words, reality and symbol are co-emergent for us; the world is already imbued with symbolism because to us the world is always something more than we encounter. The symbol attests to a primordial sense of meaning immanent to our existence yet not fully comprehended by us. The phenomenon of symbol is most readily apparent in the religious, the psycho-analytic, and the poetic.[15] With respect to the religious, symbolism operates according to the notion of sacrality. So when Ricoeur says '[m]an first reads the sacred *on* the world, *on* some elements or aspects of the world', he does not mean we read the sacred *into* the world.[16] Rather, to read it 'on' the world means apprehending the sacred as corresponding to (i.e. in harmony with) the world. Elsewhere he writes, '[w]ithin the sacred universe there are not living creatures here and there, but life is everywhere *as* a sacrality, which permeates everything'.[17] To see things 'as' sacred involves a correspondence that requires understanding how the two – the world and the sacred – in fact are analogous.

This mode of understanding is, more precisely, an act of interpretation that attempts to bring the world and the sacred together through its reflection on the symbol. Ricoeur encapsulates this reflective aspect when stating that 'symbols give rise to thought'.[18] Thought, here, includes both reflection in a general sense as well as a more engaged critical and philosophical reflection that presents possibilities for a tradition's revision. After all, challenges to religion, rather than destroying it, often provide the occasion for their internal revision. And this process often involves a way of divesting a tradition of literal meanings, or at the very least, guarding against them. Or as Ricoeur comments on the challenge of atheism to the literal readings of moral accusation and otherworldly hope,

> In destroying the shelter offered by religion and liberating men from the taboos imposed by religion, atheism clears the ground for a faith beyond accusation and consolation.[19]

By calling into question the literal meanings a religious tradition has taken for granted, critical challenges do not destroy religious symbolism but allow it to be rethought anew.

The thought evoked by symbols thus provides the reflective foundation upon which a community can see how it can affirm its bond to the sacred. This movement *towards* the sacred is a movement of reflection and understanding which is typically cast in religious categories according to the transition from the profane to the sacred. Ricoeur writes,

> That a stone or a tree may manifest the sacred means that this profane reality becomes something other than itself while still remaining itself. It is transformed into something supernatural – or to avoid using a theological term – we may say that it is transformed into something

superreal (*surréel*), in the sense of being superefficacious while still remaining a part of common reality.[20]

At the same time, because sacred correspondence attempts to indicate how the divine is immanent and visible in the world, the function of understanding symbolic meaning is always more than just reflective; it is also practical. A culture or tradition can be seen to gather around this correspondence in how it has appropriated its symbols historically and existentially. Rites are in fact interpretations of the sacred, that is, they instantiate the intentional relation in terms of practices and narratives which constitute a culture's creative nucleus.[21] Nonetheless, the caveat of symbolic meaning should not be forgotten. Because symbolic meaning lives always within the tension between primary and secondary meanings, the understanding and practices which emerge from a specific interpretation of symbols remain open to revision. The sacred can be lived in many ways, as we will see in the instance of the message of the prophet.

So in the most fundamental sense, one can say the role of symbolic meaning in religion is to indicate the relation between the sacred and the profane and how this relation is to be understood and lived by a people. Mircea Eliade, on whom Ricoeur draws extensively, captures the foundational role of symbol aptly when stating that '[i]f the world is to be lived in, it must be founded' on 'sacred hierophanies' – that is an understanding of how the sacred manifests for us.[22]

The figure of the prophet and the original bond

While Ricoeur devoted a great deal of his hermeneutics to the prophet, he did not however discuss much in the way of saints. So applying his theory of symbol to saints and their actions requires, as I am arguing, a detour into his treatment of the prophet who is, for Ricoeur, a figure of exception and transformation.[23] The prophet is in one sense the typological counterpart to the saint. Both act as exceptional figures within their traditions, and central to their exceptional nature is how each is able to represent the human relation to the sacred and how this relation anticipates a new possibility of being. This new understanding, moreover, is not reducible to the ethical level at which change would involve new codes, laws and rules of action. Rather, it operates at a more fundamental level involving our ontological and religious comportment towards being as such.

Thus, as Ricoeur notes in relation to the prophet, this fundamental comportment is cast specifically in the language of sin, whose meaning is first ontological and religious before it is ethical. This distinction is meant to show how sin reflects a fundamental discordance or non-coincidence in being; it is our manner of being situated in the world (ontologically) and in view of God (religiously). The two go together since the ontological is seen as having its substance and source in the religious. It therefore follows that to misunderstand the relation to the religious is to affirm, in some way, a mode of non-being. Turning to the prophet, we in fact see that prophecy announces the misrelation its people have with the world and God, most often in terms of a failure to remember and honour the bond with God. Ricoeur sees this most prevalently in the prophetic warnings against idolatry which he identifies with a nothingness that is ontological-religious:

> [I]f the idol is Nothing in the eyes of Yahweh, it is real non-being for man. This is why Yahweh is jealous of that which is Nothing for him, but which is a Pseudo-Something for man. [. . .] For all the prophets [of the Hebrew Bible], an idol is more than a 'graven image'; it is a model of nothingness.[24]

The religious dimension to sin is animated by our being situated 'before God', that is, in view of God.[25] This view is not primarily mediated by the language of moral injunction, but, according to Ricoeur, by personal relation: 'Sin is not that transgression of an abstract rule – a value – but the violation of a personal bond'.[26] The 'personal' refers to an appropriate relation towards God, an intimate understanding that precedes the ethical. And it is from this relation that the ethical dimension of practice can be developed.

In other words, if sin is an ontological-religious discordance, the way it calls attention to discordance gives rise to a remedy in action that is discreetly ethical in nature: in view of God, one course of action is unfitting while the other is fitting. And these two poles of evaluation are signified by the possibilities of penalty and pardon. One therefore finds imminent threat and possible redemption at play in the prophets' words. Yahweh says to Ezekiel,

> But the people of Israel are not willing to listen to you because they are not willing to listen to me, for all the Israelites are hardened and obstinate.[27]

Yet the prophetic voice is never entirely motivated by the threat of punishment. The words given to Ezekiel are 'sweet as honey',[28] and the possibility for redemption is anticipated when Yahweh says,

> Go now to your people in exile and speak to them. Say to them, 'This is what the Sovereign Lord says,' whether they listen or fail to listen.[29]

Or it can be more overt, as when Isaiah responds to Yahweh:

> You come to the help of those who gladly do right, who remember your ways. But when we continued to sin against them, you were angry. How then can we be saved?[30]

In both examples, God's address simultaneously highlights in the divine 'saying' a warning of 'judgment or salvation' and restoration through the 'recognition of God'.[31] If understanding is a mode of being, it is, in the religious context, one that affirms a specific manner of being-towards-God that, in the ethical context, is either fit or unfit. If the failure to rectify the discordance is most associable with the negative dimension of sin, then the process of restoration through pardon is what Ricoeur refers to as 'sin as positive'.[32] But is this positive dimension reducible to an episode in history, even if a sacred one, that has passed? Not if we persist with the symbolic nature of the prophet, according to which the literal rendering of historical events is the most familiar, or primary, level of meaning that gives rise to a secondary, properly symbolic one.

While the prophetic announcement and judgement appear in a specific context, its written form allows it to be applicable beyond its original audience. Prophecy, in other words, is not about literal history and the future but about the possibilities of being given the specific orientation of a people towards the world and God. Ricoeur thus comments that 'written prophecy' is 'the fixed basis for its subsequent history of reception'.[33] This process of a continued and varied historical reception is evident in how prophetic works animate transformation. 'Prophecy', Ricoeur observes, '[. . .] consists in deciphering future history by giving it in advance a meaning relative to the ethical life of the people'.[34] The meaning is relative *and* ethical precisely because it is the ontological-religious meaning of sin which is interpreted and remedied in the ethical life, that is, as a specific manner in which a people dwell before God. The ethical emerges in, for example, what Isaiah foretells in setting 'crooked things straight' and 'turning back' and shaming those who 'trust in graven images'.[35] While applicable to the specific narrative context to which Isaiah refers, the images of crooked and straight and the status of graven images can be reinterpreted according to any historical context.

To read the prophet as a symbol is thus to understand him such that irrespective of the historical period, his voice speaks to a community, not as a voice in the past, but as one relevant now. Restoration and condemnation are imminent possibilities of being; Ricoeur notes for those who hear the prophet, his words are 'set within a history that is happening now'[36] and thus '[i]t belongs to the genre of prophecy that it remains an announcement deprived of any narrative of its accomplishment'.[37] The meaning of the prophecy remains to be interpreted and actualized, albeit motivated by the penalty of failing to remember God yet crowned potentially for Ricoeur by the transformation from nothingness to being, that is, 'From Death to Life'.[38]

The figure of the saint and the new

In view of Ricoeur's lack of treatment of the saint, there is a difficulty in identifying what the symbolic nature of the saint involves. My strategy in this regard is to build upon the foregoing discussion of the prophet, in general to say that for the Christian tradition, the saint fulfils the same role of innovation. Nonetheless, I want to do this by showing the unique way in which the saint achieves this transformation, or what is noticeable mostly in terms of how past and present play different roles for each. Transformation for the prophet relies on using the future as a means of retrieving the past, which in turn is a means of reactivating the bond with Yahweh. For the saint, the future is the genuine possibility for being; its referent of meaning is not an original bond but a something 'new'. I will then conclude with some thoughts about how one can read the symbolism of a saint's action in view of the example of charity used earlier.

My reference to the similarity and distinction between the prophet and the saint follows a general typological reading as discussed, for example, by Northrop Frye when he refers to the relation between the prophecy and the gospel.[39] Characteristic of this general reading is the distinction in how prophecy, as we saw earlier, accentuates the ethical dimension of action while the latter, as Frye claims, focuses on a 'spiritual metamorphosis', that is, 'an enlarged vision of the dimensions of human life'.[40] While it would be misleading to say the Christian tradition lacks the feature of ethical judgement and dread, or that Judaism lacks the spiritual dimension, Frye's point intends to emphasize how one tradition overtly utilizes and requires the ethical sphere as the milieu of transformation while the other does not. Or, at the very least, if there is a concern for ethical action in Christianity, as in the Sermon on the Mount, it is not the kind of ethical action reducible to pre-existing or traditional principles. Hence, the notion of transformation in the Christian tradition centres not simply on a remembrance or return to an original bond through practices, but on new life. Ricoeur refers to this as 'the beginning of the new creation in the midst of men on earth'.[41]

But in this typological reading, a problem confronts us. For the prophet, the catalyst of a change in understanding is the stark ethical dimension of judgement that links one back to the ontological and religious bond. The ethical sphere in this sense provides the landscape through which the people of Israel return and recover a more original bond to Yahweh. With the saint and the absence of ethical judgement, on the other hand, one can ask what performs this role of initiating a change in understanding? If the primary, familiar action of a saint presents an analogue of another meaning, how is this unfamiliar analogue made knowable?

If the prophetic announcement relies upon the tension between a people's current mode of being and their original bond to God, it can be understood as retrieval; it moves back towards a founding moment made possible by the future inscribed with a warning. In contrast, for the saint, the future is a possibility for positive transformation that is predicated upon what is 'new'; the future is a new modality of being distinct from the past. In this sense, and despite their difference, both the prophet and the saint provide a means by which their audience can envision new modes of being through making what is unfamiliar meaningful, or what Ricoeur refers to as a 'discordant concordance'.[42] Insofar as we attempt to incorporate an understanding of the prophet and the saint into our personal narratives, their actions and words are discordant in the sense that they 'spring up' as something that requires us to adapt our familiar lives to what is unfamiliar. For the prophet, the unfamiliar can be the promise – 'I will gather them from there and bring them to the place I have chosen as a dwelling for my Name'.[43] However, for the saint the possibility of transformation is 'the new', as when St Paul says, 'Therefore if anyone is in Christ, the new creation has come'.[44] What is this new?

For Ricoeur, it is what is possible. But this possibility is not simply one option among many, but a new understanding of the tradition that entails a new mode of being. Thus, when interpreted in relation to Galatians 6.15 – 'Neither circumcision nor uncircumcision means anything; what counts is the new creation' – the meaning of St Paul's words can suggest a move away from the emphasis on rite and practice towards the Word.[45] Ricoeur notes that because kerygmatic faith relies so much on the Word, it has a reflective core that allows it to transform, adapt and become something new. To recall the example of atheism mentioned earlier in a different light, one can say that in a world characterized by secularism, this reflective core provides a means by which the relation to the sacred can be reinterpreted in view of the processes of disenchantment, that is, a world in which the sacred no longer has a place.[46] The emphasis on the Word obviously aligns well with interpreting and reinterpreting a tradition's texts, but it also highlights the individual's role in this process. The one who reinterprets is the one who must understand anew. So in this sense through reinterpretation, through the Word, the individual 'testifies' to a new possibility of being. Ricoeur thus emphasizes the importance of testimony, that is, an attesting and witnessing 'to that effort and desire to be' that joins the self to the tradition by way of interpreting and reinterpreting its symbols:

> Only testimony that is singular in each instance confers the sanction of reality on ideas, ideals, and ways of being that the symbol depicts to us and which we uncover as our ownmost possibilities.[47]

This suggests that the actions of saints have a trans-historical applicability more overt than appears in the announcements of the prophet. The latter requires a reading through its historical context, even if an episode is to be understood as bearing on the present. Both the prophet and the saint are concerned with the present, but the former does so by way of retrieving the past, the original bond. The latter does so without relying on a retrieval, turning instead towards what is overtly new; the new is what overflows and seizes us. As Ricoeur says, 'the logic' characterized by Christianity is one 'of excess, of superabundance'.[48]

Ironically, this logic of superabundance is instantiated in the frugality of St Francis of Assisi. It is not simply that St Francis advocates frugalness as a means of being virtuous, but, in a modern context, performs something more radical. According to Ricoeur, he 'overturn[s] the underlying hypothesis of the modern world' driven by exclusive possession, fear of scarcity, in short, the economic.[49] Symbolically, the frugality of the saint points towards a 'new' relation that celebrates an ontological and religious abundance contrasting with and potentially transforming our relation to the economic. The frugal appears from the economic perspective as meager and poor. Yet, this frugality is, when viewed in relation to superabundance, a response of passing on to others what is not one's own. Ricoeur captures this metanoia as 'Because it has been given to you, you give in turn'.[50] That is to say, the frugality of St Francis can be read as a reaction to superabundance, as an attempt to turn gift into gift (for another). This action, as I am arguing, does not suggest that one imitate St Francis by becoming frugal. Rather, the action itself is a source of reflection according to which the category of gift can be understood anew.

In the same spirit of emphasizing the radical over the familiar, let us return to the act of charity which, when viewed symbolically, can now be said to bring together in a 'discordant concordance' the realm of everyday action and what charity may mean within the Christian tradition. Donating one's wealth is, I want to argue, reinterpreted in view of the larger context of love (*caritas*) and the various episodes in the Bible relating to love and perhaps money, taxation and gift. The charitable action does more than simply put us face-to-face with the one in need since it inevitably calls upon the notions of ownership and gift, both in the sense of immediate possession and the cosmological sense of creation. It elicits questions of just ownership, as for example examined by Aquinas in his considerations of theft, as well as questions about what constitutes those things we might define as alienable in a world that is not ours. As we saw for the political economist Henry George, charity as donation ignores the conditions of poverty that give rise to relative lack. Instead, charity requires to be seen as extending to a consideration of sources of poverty; that is to say, for George *caritas* in the Christian sense means rethinking how love requires first just social conditions.[51] Or, as St Bonaventure understood, love requires first a 'love of justice'.[52] Such statements, unlike ideals that can be imitated, evoke a need to act, but only through a reflection on the very principles and virtues in a tradition that give to any action its worth.

In closing, we can note that for Ricoeur the reflective core of a tradition constitutes its capability and openness to accommodate new challenges and situations. The creativity that the symbolism of saints affords is, in other words, a new economy of meaning that does not react and retreat to conventions, but refigures itself in dialogue with external challenges. Indeed, if the actions of saints maintain the relation between the existential domain and a new possibility of being indicated by the sacred, their actions never announce a course of action that can secure this relation, but instead draw one, through reflection, to see a situation in view of its possible resolution according to the sacred. Saints are therefore not role models in any sense, but figures whose actions indicate ontological possibilities not just for being in the world, but for gaining it as well.

Notes

1 Paul Ricoeur, *A Ricoeur Reader: Reflection and Imagination* (ed. Mario J. Valdés, New York: Harvester Wheatsheaf, 1991), p. 307, quoting Monroe Beardsley.
2 Ibid., p. 85.
3 Due to the scope of this chapter, I leave untreated how Ricoeur's Protestant affiliation bears upon his interpretation of saints within the Christian tradition.
4 There are, of course, more sophisticated accounts of rule following, particularly in relation to practical judgement. See, for example, Kenneth R. Westphal, 'Norm Acquisition, Rational Judgement and Moral Particularism', *Theory and Research in Education* 19:1 (2012), pp. 3–25.
5 Thomas Head, *Hagiography and the Cult of Saints: The Diocese of Orléans, 800–1200* (Cambridge: Cambridge University Press, 1990), pp. 102, 120. The call to imitate was made most accessible in the vitae of saints which might have been read aloud (p. 102). Cf. 'The living Christians who heard and read these examples [. . .] were supposed to imitate the *virtus* which those stories illustrated' (p. 118).
6 Anne Alwis, *Celibate Marriages in Late Antique and Byzantine Hagiography* (London: Continuum, 2011), p. 13. Alwis quotes from Giles Constable, *Three Studies in Medieval Religious and Social Thought: The Ideal of the Imitation of Christ* (Cambridge: Cambridge University Press, 1995), pp. 143–217. My thanks to Dr Alwis for discussing issues of hagiography with me.
7 Leo XIII (1891), *Rerum Novarum*. Available at www.vatican.va/holy_father/ leo_xiii/encyclicals/documents/hf_l-xii_enc_15051891_rerum- novarum_en.html; last accessed 23 September 2012, §§30 and 24, respectively.
8 Ibid., §§30–31.
9 For more on this, see Henry George, *The Land Question: Viewpoint and Counterviewpoint on the Need for Land Reform* (New York: Robert Schalkenbach, 1982). In short, his criticism of Leo XIII concerns ignoring the real problem of social injustice relating to the cause of poverty, which for George was land speculation and monopoly.
10 Alwis, *Celibate Marriages*, pp. 67–74, 79n. 115.
11 Paul Ricoeur, *The Symbolism of Evil* (trans. Emerson Buchanan, Boston: Beacon Press, 1967), p. 16.
12 Ibid., p. 15.
13 Paul Ricoeur, *Interpretation Theory: Discourse and the Surplus of Meaning* (Fort Worth: Texas Christian University Press, 1976), p. 62.
14 Ibid., p. 55. I do not treat the difference between metaphor and symbol in Ricoeur's philosophy. Both rely on the same transformative power arising from the juxtaposition of a literal or obvious meaning with a non-literal

or unfamiliar one. Ricoeur's work on metaphor is quite comprehensive, as he engages with philosophy, rhetoric, linguistics and literary criticism. For his single work on metaphor, see Paul Ricoeur, *The Rule of Metaphor: Multi-disciplinary Studies of the Creation of Meaning in Language* (trans. R. Czenry, K. McLaughlin and J. Costello, London: Routledge, 1977); or for a concise account, see Ricoeur, *Interpretation Theory*, pp. 45–69, and various essays in Ricoeur, *A Ricoeur Reader*. Suffice it to say here that the difference between the two involves the way symbols are 'pre-verbal' (Ricoeur, *Interpretation Theory*, p. 61), or not created within a discourse, while metaphors are created by authors in an already given linguistic system. The 'pre-verbal' aspect of symbol, however, requires a language in order for us to be able to read the world as sacred. See Paul Ricoeur, *The Conflict of Interpretations* (ed. Don Ihde, Evanston, IL: Northwestern University Press, 1974), p. 13.

15   Ricoeur, *Interpretation Theory*, p. 53. One should consider as well socio-political uses of the symbolic which relate to Ricoeur's work on utopia and imagination. He maintains that because *social praxis* is already symbolic in nature, one can say socio-political conceptions and criticisms relating to the good life rely on symbolic meaning as a way of rethinking our socio-political possibility for being. Paul Ricoeur, *From Text to Action: Essays in Hermeneutics, II* (trans. K. Blamey and J. B. Thompson, Evanston, IL: Northwestern University Press, 2007).

16   Ricoeur, *Symbolism of Evil*, p. 10, emphasis in original.

17   Ricoeur, *Interpretation Theory*, p. 61, my emphasis.

18   Ricoeur, *Symbolism of Evil*, p. 19.

19   Paul Ricoeur and Alasdair MacIntyre, *The Religious Significance of Atheism* (New York: Columbia University Press 1969), p. 60.

20   Paul Ricoeur, *Figuring the Sacred: Religion, Narrative, and Imagination* (ed. Mark Wallace, trans. David Pellauer, Minneapolis, MN: Fortress Press, 2007), pp. 49–50.

21   Ricoeur, *A Ricoeur Reader*, p. 482; cf. Ricoeur, *The Symbolism of Evil*, pp. 16–18.

22   Mircea Eliade, *The Sacred and the Profane: The Nature of Religion* (trans. Willard R. Trask, San Diego: Harcourt Brace, 1959), p. 22.

23   For a study of exception and the ethical canon see Colby Dickinson, 'Examining Canonical Representations: The "Exceptionalism" of Ricoeur's Hermeneutics and the Bid for an Ethical Canon' in *From Ricoeur to Action: The Socio-Political Significance of Ricoeur's Thinking* (ed. T. Mei and D. Lewin, London: Continuum, 2012), pp. 229–45.

24   Ricoeur, *Symbolism of Evil*, p. 76.

25   Ibid., p. 52.

26   Ibid.

27   Ezekiel 3.7.

28   Ezekiel 3.3.

29   Ezekiel 3.11.

30   Isaiah 64.5.

31   Paul Ricoeur and André LaCocque, *Thinking Biblically: Exegetical and Hermeneutical Studies* (Chicago: University of Chicago Press, 1998), p. 166.

32   Ricoeur, *Symbolism of Evil*, p. 81.

33 Ricoeur and LaCocque, *Thinking Biblically*, p. 169.

34 Ricoeur, *Symbolism of Evil*, p. 67.

35 Isaiah 42.16–17.

36 Ricoeur and LaCocque, *Thinking Biblically*, p. 170.

37 Ibid., p. 171.

38 Ibid., p. 176.

39 Northrop Frye, *The Great Code: The Bible and Literature* (San Diego: Harcourt Brace Jovanovich, 1982), pp. 125–35.

40 Ibid., p. 130.

41 Ricoeur, *Symbolism of Evil*, p. 270.

42 Paul Ricoeur, *Oneself as Another* (trans. Kathleen Blamey, Chicago: University of Chicago Press, 1992), p. 142.

43 Nehemiah 1.8.

44 2 Corinthians 5.17.

45 Paul Tillich, *The New Being* (New York: Scribners, 1955), pp. 15–24.

46 Ricoeur, *Figuring the Sacred*, p. 65.

47 Paul Ricoeur, 'Toward a Hermeneutic of the Idea of Revelation', *The Harvard Theological Review* 70:1/2 (1977), pp. 1–37, pp. 32–33; cf. p. 28.

48 Ricoeur, *Figuring the Sacred*, p. 279.

49 Ibid., p. 287.

50 Ibid., p. 300.

51 Todd S. Mei, 'Economy of the Gift: Rethinking the Role of Land Enclosure in Political Economy', *Modern Theology* 25:3 (2009), pp. 441–68; Alexandre J. M. E. Christoyannopoulos and Joseph Milne, 'Love, Justice, and Social Eschatology', *The Heythrop Journal* 48/6 (2007), pp. 972–91.

52 Matthew M. De Benedictus, *The Social Thought of Saint Bonaventure: A Study in Social Philosophy* (Westport, CT: Greenwood Press, 1946), p. 194.

11

Saint versus Hero: Girard's Undoing of Romantic Hagiology

Grant Kaplan

Introduction: Modern loss and postmodern recovery

Modernity was not kind to the entire corpus of the cult of the saints extolled in premodern Christianity. Premodern Christianity held up as examples people of whom modernity would have approved, but also many others whose purported miracles were dubious, whose conversions were questionable, and whose moral convictions sometimes failed the test of Kantian purity. From a modern perspective, the old hagiography was incredible, hokey and troublingly apolitical. Could Jerome or Athanasius really be sound ethical models against the backdrop of their political machinations? What about Augustine? Not to mention more recent figures, like Nicholas of Flue, the patron saint of Switzerland. Brother Claus fought with a sword in one hand and a rosary in the other. At home his wife bore him ten children. Responding to a vision to spend more time in contemplation, Nicholas abandoned his family to take up a life of fasting and prayer, subsisting for nearly two decades on nothing but the Eucharist. What could the example of Brother Claus positively contribute to a modern ethic centred on the universality of ethical norms?

If one takes Kant as paradigmatic of the modern turn, then the contrast between modernity and the theology of the communion of saints comes quickly into focus. Kant identifies properly moral actions with pure intentions, and demands in his categorical imperative that moral acts be universally applicable. If we all behaved like Nicholas of Flue, then who would change the diapers? In his *Religion within the Limits of Mere Reason*, Kant makes his famous reduction of religion to ethical activity. Prayer, fasting and ritual do not belong to *pure* religion, which consists in rational, ethical activity and does not rely on superstition, the supernatural, or even the historical, save for didactic purposes.[1]

Postmodernity, whatever it means, surely entails suspicion about modernity's universalizing reason and totalizing ethical systems. Instead of a cogitating, ethical subject, postmodern ethics begins with an Other. It has evoked such *an*-ethical categories as the face, alterity, liminality and difference to call into question and perhaps overturn modern accounts of goodness and holiness. Especially after the Shoah, postmodern discontent with the modern project has led to the reimagination of moral grammar.

It should not come as a total shock, then, that postmodern thought has reexamined the meaning of holiness and the value of the saints. The motto might be, paraphrasing Heidegger's oft-quoted dictum: *nur ein Heiliger kann uns retten*. Edith Wyschogrod's *Saints and Postmodernism* is the most explicit postmodern attempt to come with fresh eyes to hagiology. Influenced by Levinas, Wyschogrod extols the saint's utter concern for the Other. According to Wyschogrod, the saint's life is 'entirely devoted to the alleviation of sorrow and pain that afflicts other persons without distinction of rank or group'.[2] It is hard to imagine how one might integrate the practice of, say, fasting, into such a demand of whole-hearted devotion. Holiness for Wyschogrod, despite many qualifications, looks suspiciously like Kantian moral purity.[3]

Mimetic anthropology, original sin and the Romantic option

For the past 50 years, the French essayist René Girard has tried to articulate the importance of a subtle, perhaps even banal observation about humanity: our desires, more than being self-generated, are learned from others. We not only want what our neighbour wants, we want to share the same desire as our neighbour. This highlighting of *mimetic* desire is by no means original, but his attempt to trace its repercussions has pervaded Girard's work.[4] From this insight emerges his theories not only about the novel, but also about the scapegoat mechanism and the uniqueness of Christianity.

To illuminate the theological upshot to Girard's anthropology, let us imagine a Girardian account of the human being's 'thrownness'. One enters the world and desires according to the desires of one's culture. Paul Griffiths describes this process:

> A world is learned as the house of language is entered and its taxonomies (this is a dog, that is a sunset, here you fall to your knees, there you

curse, this is disgusting, that is beautiful) spin the child's cognitive and affective web with threads so strong that they seem given rather than made, natural rather than a matter of technique and artifice. Culture thus brings, experientially, the very order of things into being and shapes the individual's desires to harmonize with that order.[5]

In matters of taste this reality might seem ethically neutral: we like the music or art or literature that we like because other people like it; or it operates with one further iteration: we loathe it because others like it. Either way we are locked into the desires of the other. Consequent to this pattern of desire, there exists in every culture a mechanism for keeping this desire in control. The second grader calls a member of a certain colour the name her father uses. The sixth grader learns to tease somebody by calling him 'fairy'. The tenth grader might come to find Thanksgiving bearable for the first time in memory because he had such a good time swapping stories about the awful hairpiece that Grandpa used to wear. Girard calls this the 'scapegoat mechanism'. Seemingly benign instances, says Girard, follow the same pattern as more malicious ones; as a solution to the problem of belonging, mimetic desire and the scapegoat mechanism explain social slights and ostracism, as well as stoning, lynching and genocide.

The scapegoat mechanism not only brings intelligibility to these minor incidents, but also accounts for all the ways that we seek to belong to our family, our peer group, our colleagues, our nation. Christianity unveils this mechanism.[6] Through a Girardian lens the Christian anthropological grammar becomes crystal clear. Original sin is the condition that lets it seem so natural to engage in scapegoating. As Girard puts it: 'The original sin is the bad use of mimesis, and the mimetic [scapegoating] mechanism is the actual consequence of this use at the collective level'.[7] For Girard these processes operate on a subconscious level, meaning that one can continue scapegoating only by thinking that one is really doing something else or something more freely chosen. Such is the nature of sin. One can accept the deleterious consequences of culture's impulses without rooting them in an individual's mimetic desire. This option, which Girard means by Romanticism, forms a foil to a more authentic, 'novelistic' or Christian alternative.

Instead of owning up to one's culpability, Romanticism, especially that of Jean-Jacques Rousseau, doubles down on the individual's inherent goodness and blamelessness. For Romanticism, the individual in nature is pure, and she only becomes sinful through her co-mingling with sinful society.[8] Whence springs the Romantic hero, who abandons society's norms and lives freely, *naturally*, unencumbered and uninfluenced by culture's fallenness. Creativity, imagination and originality become the markers of salvation for the Romantic, naturally blameless hero.

It is important to remember that Romanticism arose as a response to Enlightenment rationalism. As both Frederick Lawrence and Charles Taylor have pointed out, the Romantic reaction to Enlightenment rationalism and contract-theory remains thoroughly modern.[9] The crux of Girard's argument is that the Romantic solution is not a real solution. The English translation of the title of his first work, *Deceit, Desire and the Novel*, obscures how the original title previews this critique: *Mensonge romantique et vérité romanesque*. Girard declares in the opening pages:

> The great novelists reveal the imitative nature of desire. [...] The romantic *vaniteux* does not want to be anyone's disciple. He convinces himself that he is thoroughly *original*. In the nineteenth century spontaneity becomes a universal dogma, succeeding imitation. [...] Romantic revulsion, hatred of society, nostalgia for the desert, just as [sic] gregariousness, usually conceal a morbid concern for the Other.[10]

As much as we may admire the asceticism, the devotion, and the self-sacrifice that saints display, most common to all of the saints is the awareness that they have not achieved their holiness on the basis of personal merit. Precisely at the moment where pride seems most fit to enter, the saint rejects such an impulse because it presumes the autonomy clung to so dearly by the Romantics. There is an analogy in Girard's discussion of Proust and the great 'novelists'. For Girard, 'Recapturing the past is to welcome a truth which most men spend their lives trying to escape, to recognize that one has always copied Others in order to seem original in their eyes and in one's own. Recapturing the past is to destroy a little of one's pride'.[11] The two greatest novelists (by which Girard means anti-Romantics), Proust and Dostoyevsky, show the connection between the loss of autonomy and the loss of pride. Instead of a Romantic conversion, where one identifies the hypocrisy of the bourgeois and declares himself exculpated from these mimetic forces, these novelists accept the mediated nature of desire. Girard expounds,

> Pride can never reach its own mediator; but the experience of *The Past Recaptured* is the death of pride, the birth of humility and thus of truth. When Dostoyevsky praises the *terrible strength of humility* he is speaking of novelistic creation.[12]

Only the novelistic path promises the deeper, more authentic experience of conversion vis-à-vis chimeric Romantic conversion.

Humility and sanctity

Humility, of course, is the most slippery of virtues.[13] Let us compare it to justice, one of the four cardinal virtues. If one had fallen into a practice of grading students unfairly, and then, due to some external factor or to a fraternal attempt at correction, one began to exercise greater justice in the distribution of grades, it would be perfectly legitimate to say of oneself, whether Christian or not, that one was becoming more just. It does not work this way with humility, however, because the very act of declaring an increase in humility would belie said increase.

Perhaps the fragility of humility explains the Church Fathers' exaltation of it as the greatest of Christian virtues.[14] Nowhere does the importance of the virtue of humility play a greater role than in the theologian who made so much out of pride: St Augustine. Deborah Wallace Ruddy highlights Augustine's role in the Western Church's appropriation of the centrality of humility in the path to union with God.[15] Belief in the Incarnation, for Augustine, is inseparable from the translation of pride into humility, as he explains in the *Confessions*: 'Nor yet was I humble enough to grasp the humble Jesus as my God, or did I know what his weakness had to teach'.[16] In light of Christ's kenotic love, Christianity could not conceive of itself without this virtue, whereas the pre-Christian world could not imagine an order in which humility *was* a virtue.

A consideration of humility opens up a fault-line in how one interprets the very order of things. In the spirit of modern individualism it is not difficult to detect a trace of an older Pelagian grammar. Our loud insistence on our autonomous freedom rings hollow in the face of deeper reflection. Girard writes, 'The individualism of our time is really an effort to deny the failure of desire. Those who claim to be governed by the pleasure principle are, as a rule, enslaved to models and rivals who make their lives a constant frustration. But they are too vain to acknowledge their own enslavement'.[17] It would be a mistake, from the standpoint of mimetic theory, to argue that there are the pure, pre-lapsarian people who are free of this vanity, or who overcome it through their own self-transformation, as opposed to those who wallow in pitiful sinfulness. True conversion, for Girard, belongs inextricably to the experience of grace: '[Conversion] is not something of our own doing but the personal intervention of God in our lives. The greatest experience for Christians is the experience of becoming religious under a compulsion that they feel cannot come from themselves but from God alone'.[18]

Girard sees the same emphasis on grace in Proust, who might fall under the category of 'postmodern French saint'.[19] The true mark of the change, like that of the person who has become humble, is the acknowledgement of one's being carried along, much more so than one's being in control. And in recognizing this element of passivity, one also recognizes the forces that had been carrying one along while one had perceived being in control of one's desires. Girard continues: '[Conversion] means choosing Christ or a Christlike individual as a model for our desires. It also means seeing oneself as being in the process of imitating from the beginning. Conversion is the discovery that we have always, without being aware of it, been imitating the wrong kind of models'.[20] Yet this is precisely what Romanticism denies. Girard explains,

> The neoromantic prides himself on his revolt against that [bourgeois] hypocrisy, but on the foundation of his 'unconscious' or his ineffable 'freedom' he erects aspirations very similar to those which the bourgeois had based on 'loyalty to principle'. The individual has not renounced his goal of autonomy and glorious mastery; he has not renounced his pride.[21]

Writers like Proust, says Girard, 'do not consider what we call their genius a natural gift with which they were born. They view it as a belated acquisition, the result of a personal transformation not of their own doing, which resembles a conversion'.[22] This quality pervades the lives of the saints, whose almost nihilistic denial of their own self-worth or extraordinary qualities seems insincere to readers ensconced in a Romantic frame of reference.

Just as humility is a tricky business, so too is pride. Girard recognizes that post- or neo-romanticism attempts to go beyond deep feelings by having no feelings at all. Instead of the romantic hero we have the 'slacker' who seems to want nothing and care for nothing. Yet for Girard this iteration is only the Romantic Hero 2.0: 'Whereas romantic readers used to identify with the hero who felt the strongest desire, today they identify with the hero who feels the least desire'.[23] Girard warns against confusing this apparent loss of desire with that of the desert Fathers, who cultivated the virtue of *apatheia*. The saint does distinguish herself from the less holy by totally ceasing to desire. Girard notes the thread of pride running through the (post)-Romantic psychology: 'As soon as the subject who desires recognizes the role of imitation in his own desire he has to renounce either this desire or his pride. [. . .] The choice is between pride and desire since desire makes slaves of all of us'.[24] To preserve one's pride it is a relatively easy thing to sacrifice desire, or the appearance of it. Pride depends on being locked into the desires of the other. Pride's dominance over the slacker, however, becomes manifest in her attempt to communicate these desires through the maximal appearance of disinterest.

Girard draws out the connection between a post-romantic *askesis* of desire and traditional, religious *apatheia*: 'Nondesire once more becomes the privilege as it was for the wise man of old or the Christian saint'.[25] Yet the current day slacker wants nothing to do with those religious practices; he *tries* not to try, or to give the appearance of trying. Girard traces the difference between the two: 'This nondesire of course has nothing in common with abstinence and sobriety. [. . .] This somnambulist hero lives on "bad faith." He tries to resolve the conflict between pride and desire without ever clearly formulating it'.[26] The difference between the two is separated by only a hair's breadth yet by a chasm's depth. There is no holiness without the renunciation of pride, though lack of certainty and of confidence can accompany true holiness. Girard lays out the consequences of this true conversion in the conclusion to *Deceit, Desire, and The Novel*: 'This time it is not a false but a genuine conversion. The hero triumphs in defeat; he triumphs because he is at the end of his resources: for the first time he has to look his despair and his nothingness in the face. But this look which he has dreaded, which is the defeat of his pride, is his salvation'.[27] Girard's distinction between these two states gives shape to Christian sanctity against the backdrop of a (post)-Romantic outlook.

Being given one's desires and sense of identity does not doom one to non-being or even to sinfulness. As humans we cannot stop being locked into the Other.[28] This situation should not cause despair, however. Girard finds a solution in Paul – 'Be imitators of me, as I imitate Christ' (1 Cor. 11.1) – and in Jesus' sermon on the Mount: 'Be perfect, as your heavenly Father is perfect' (Mt. 5.48). The holy person recognizes sinfulness as a pattern of violent rivalry based in desire caught in the crosshairs. The solution lies not in pretending to be above this reciprocity, but in finding in Christ a model for peaceful, non-violent imitation. Girard explains the Pauline appeal to imitation: '[Paul] imitates Jesus who, in turn, imitates the Father. He is just part of an endless chain of "good imitation," non-rivalrous imitation, that Christians try to create. The "saints" are the links of this chain'.[29] By exchanging rivalrous for pacific imitation the saint subverts those unjust systems bent on protecting patterns of antagonistic reciprocity.

The Holy Spirit as advocate

Besides a more explicit account of humility and of good imitation, mimetic theory makes available a pneumatology that can inform the role that the Holy Spirit plays in the process of sanctification. Just as mimetic theory lends greater precision to the virtue of humility, so too does it make explicit what is meant by the gift of the Holy Spirit. The most important location to trace this process is in the farewell discourse of John's gospel. The Spirit, often called *parakleitos* in John, possesses believers in a way not dissimilar to how we can be possessed by a mimetic frenzy. Girard explains: 'The Spirit takes charge of everything. It would be false, for example, to say the disciples "regained possession of themselves": it is the Spirit of God that possesses them and does not let them go'.[30] The *parakleitos*, for Girard, is the defense attorney: '*Parakleitos*, in Greek, is the exact equivalent of advocate or the Latin *ad-vocatus*. The Paraclete is called on behalf of the prisoner, the victim, to speak in his place and in his name, to act in his defense'.[31] Girard implores, 'We should take with utmost seriousness the idea that the Spirit enlightens the persecutors concerning their acts of persecution'.[32] It is through this Spirit that persecutors become disciples reconciled to God and to their victims.

For traditional theology, the Holy Spirit is God, and whatever is true of the other persons is true of the Spirit, except that it is neither the Son nor the Father. Although much has been made about the prophetic upshot of the renewal in the Spirit, the Spirit teaches us the same thing that the Son does.[33] Girard explains:

> The Spirit is working in history to reveal what Jesus has already revealed, the mechanism of the scapegoat, the genesis of all mythology, the nonexistence of all gods of violence.[34]

The unity of the Son's and the Spirit's mission becomes clear in Girard's exegesis of the Johannine farewell discourse. The relationship of Jesus to the Paraclete roots itself in peaceful complementarity rather than agonistic rivalry: 'He will glorify me, since all he tells you will be taken from what is mine' (Jn 16.15). Both through his words and through his non-violent acceptance of the cross, Jesus reveals the mechanism by which the Accuser creates false community at the expense of a hapless victim. Further, in his peaceful return to the disciples, the risen Jesus uncovers the very structures in our religious psychology that move us from denial, through horrific realization, to true forgiveness.[35] The gift of the Spirit is the gift of the spirit of Christ.

This gift, when received, dissolves any prior notion of reciprocity because one knows its superabundance immediately. Like a song that we hear that truly touches us to the point that we *stop* to listen, this is a process of recognizing that something from outside comes inside to transform us. It is impossible to explain this; one must experience it. When Jesus tells the disciples: 'And you too will be witnesses (*martureite*)' (Jn 16.1) this means that they will witness the innocence of Christ, and thus the innocence of all victims. Jesus also lays out the alternative to authentic witness: the worship of another god inspired not through the defense attorney, but through the accuser. Jesus continues: 'Indeed the hour is coming when anyone who kills you will think he is doing a holy duty for God. They will do these things because they have never known either the Father or myself' (Jn 16.2–3). Girard explains in the penultimate paragraph of *The Scapegoat*: 'When the Paraclete comes, Jesus says, he will bear witness to me, he will reveal the meaning of my innocent death and of every innocent death, from the beginning to the end of the world'.[36] What the Holy Spirit gives is what Christ gives: the grace to cease persecuting others and to opt to side with the victims. On this account the Holy Spirit can only come *after* the Son's mission. Saints are those who become holy through embodying the practices and disciplines that transform destructive imitation into the pacific mimesis advocated by John's gospel and by Paul.

There is a danger in interpreting mimetic theory as a notion that could be learned through intellection. Himself a scholar, Girard has always expressed caution about a merely intellectual conversion. In the final chapter of *Things Hidden* he explains,

> No purely intellectual process and no experience of a purely philosophical nature can secure the individual the slightest victory over mimetic desire

and its victimage delusions. Intellection can achieve only displacement and substitution, though these may give individuals the sense of having achieved such a victory. For there to be even the slightest degree of progress, the victimage delusion must be vanquished on the most intimate level of experience.[37]

Catholic Christians, for instance, remember and honour the saints not because they have cogitated better, but because they manifest concretely the holiness that the Church claims as an object of faith. They undergo this conversion and grow into it over the course of their lives.

Noted Girardian James Alison uses mimetic theory to lend greater precision to Girard's Christocentric pneumatology. Alison notes that in Luke as well as in John, 'the Holy Spirit is the Spirit of the risen Lord, the Spirit that was in Christ'.[38] The Spirit, for Alison, makes available the gratuity given to the disciples by Jesus. Alison argues for the inextricability of the Holy Spirit to Jesus. If we understand the Holy Spirit as a vague, numinous presence of God, we miss the whole point of what the farewell discourse says. Alison explains, 'The Holy Spirit is the Spirit of the crucified and risen Jesus, and any joy, peace, and so on that is genuinely of the Holy Spirit is essentially linked to the presence of the crucified and risen one'.[39] Alison emphasizes how the knowledge promised by the Holy Spirit both in John and in Luke (12.11) is not vague, but instead the particular insight of Christ which he calls the 'intelligence of the victim'. He then charts – normatively – the holiness of the Church to its relationship to Jesus as victim: 'It is holy because this community is founded entirely on the forgiveness of the victim'.[40]

As defense counsellor, the Spirit informs us both of the innocence of other victims, and of our own purported innocence. Both institutions and counter-cultural movements can operate in ways that perpetuate lies, forge a sense of belonging over-against an Other, and vilify outsiders. The holiness of the saints, on the other hand, consists in receiving the Holy Spirit, whose function, Alison explains, is 'pleading for the defense, which corresponds exactly to the forgiveness of sins and the process of creatively producing children of God. [. . . This] means that the forgiveness of sins and the creative staging of the passion in the circumstances of the lives of the disciples of Jesus are the same thing'.[41] One could substitute 'saint' for 'disciple' here.

There is a danger in oversimplifying the equation between holiness and defending the marginalized. If holiness corresponds to embodying the Holy Spirit as defense attorney, then might holy people strive to be defense attorneys? Or social-workers advocating for the poor and the voiceless? Without wanting to diminish the good and perhaps even holy people who work in such fields, Girard would demur. Becoming an 'advocate' in the colloquial sense of the term often results in simply picking a side to be on, and perpetuating the mechanism that produces victims. One could note here the story of the Duke lacrosse team and the allegations of rape that it faced. Too many people assumed falsely that the poor, marginalized, African American woman had to be the victim, at the expense of the white, privileged, males who were the victims, in reality, falsely accused. Gil Bailie addresses this phenomenon in his exegesis of the story of Susannah caught in adultery (Dan. 13), which is not yet an evangelical story because it still ends with a lynching:

> Like so many of us moderns, Daniel felt the spiritual power and emancipatory imperative of the Holy Spirit, and he stepped bravely and boldly into the breach to champion the cause of the victim. But as his ardor for justice swelled and his community enthusiastically rallied to his message, another darker social force came into play. The innocence of Susanna was gradually eclipsed in his mind by the moral perversity of the men who had accused her. Imperceptibly, the man who had been the tool of the Holy Spirit became the tool of the Accuser. The result was that instead of a community, remorseful and racked with moral misgivings, carrying out a legally prescribed punishment on an innocent victim, a wildly unanimous mob killed two morally despicable old men in a fit of righteous indignation.[42]

Being holy does not mean possessing the righteous indignation expressed so powerfully by Bill O'Reilly or Michael Moore. To be animated by the Holy Spirit in a real and concrete way means to cultivate the habits and practices made available through the supernatural gift of divine indwelling.[43] *Lumen Gentium*'s universal call to holiness, for example, means that each of us can creatively live out this indwelling, in whatever station life finds us.

Girardian pneumatology offers a fuller picture of what it might mean to be holy in today's postmodern world. The gift of the Holy Spirit, according to John's farewell discourse, leads us to 'all truth'. We can gather that Girard would interpret this truth existentially. This is certainly how Alison interprets it: 'Leading us into the whole truth means *the active and creative overcoming of the lie which is at the root of human culture*, leaving completely behind the recurring fascination with that mendacious story'.[44] Part of what Alison implies here is the way that Jesus creatively and cleverly dealt with challenges, like the one about the woman caught in adultery. Receiving the same spirit as the one possessed by Jesus means gradually learning how to participate in the overcoming of these lies. Our imitation of Christ does not mean that we grow a beard and speak Aramaic while honing our skills in wood-working. It means the creative living out of a response to the scapegoating into which we are inculturated. Alison expands on this in his most recent book: 'The giving to us of the Holy Spirit, is, then, the giving to us of the whole dynamic, the whole power, by which Jesus was able to occupy this place of annihilation, shame and wrath without being run by it'.[45] Saints figure out how to accept this giving that permits new ways of being and belonging. As a result of learning the goodness of Jesus' occupation of this place of shame, 'we find ourselves being set free from being run by any system of goodness and badness over against others, any system of belonging which blesses by cursing'.[46]

This unity hints at an ecclesial shape, as indeed the holiness of the Church must be homologous to the holiness of the saints. Alison's exegesis of the Lukan Pentecost in Acts 2 details how this shape appears. When the Spirit is given, the community it forms will consist of 'self-giving priests,[47] and the first signs of a gracious new human unity not achieved over against someone, but flowing from the self-giving victim'. This event, according to Alison's interpretation of Luke, is nothing less than an 'anthropological earthquake' whose features include 'a completely new form of unity for humans [. . .] being made available at the instigation of a forgiving human victim who lived as if death were not'.[48] For Alison, mimetic theory makes explicit the implications of the pouring out of the Spirit. A new space for breathing is made available, a new assurance is given that replaces fear with hope. Christ's voluntary self-sacrifice opens up a possibility, given over to us when Christ gives out the Spirit both from the cross and from the resurrection, which was not hitherto available.[49]

This essay began by recalling the postmodern recovery of 'saint' as a *topos* for ethical and philosophical speculation, a *topos* largely ignored in modernity. Beginning with the Romantic foil, the essay showed how mimetic theory offered an alternative account of conversion to that of modern Romanticism. It then outlined how, through the quality of humility and an attentiveness to the work of the Spirit, a mimetic theory of sanctity takes a specific and particular shape. In this precision, it is hoped, these thoughts fill in the blank space left in much theology about holiness, which too rarely and too vaguely tells believers what holiness constitutes.

Perhaps it would be fitting to end on a biographical note. At a meeting in the 1980s, where Girard addressed a group of biblical scholars, they asked him what the most pressing tasks were for contemporary biblical studies. Gil Bailie recalls, 'René was gracious and patient and humble. His answer [. . . was]: "[. . .] We are each called to different tasks, so perhaps we should begin by striving for personal sanctity"'.[50] The collection from which this remark has been retrieved, contains autobiographical reflections by over two dozen students and followers. A large majority of these essays include personal notes about Girard's moral virtue, a point of consolation for a system so insistent on going beyond mere theory. Although Girard devoted little of his writing to the subject of sanctity, it is hoped that the arguments offered here demonstrate that mimetic theory offers a rich terrain for those postmodern thinkers interested in continuing a conversation about what holiness might look like.

Notes

1   For a theological critique of Kantian religion, see Grant Kaplan, *Answering the Enlightenment: The Catholic Recovery of Historical Revelation* (New York: Crossroad/Herder, 2006), pp. 23–36.

2   Edith Wyschogrod, *Saints and Postmodernism* (Chicago: University of Chicago Press, 1990), p. 34.

3   Her work has been criticized severely by Theresa Sanders, 'Seeking a Minor Sun: Saints after the Death of God', *Horizons* 22/2 (1995), esp. pp. 184–89; and David Matthew Matzko, 'Postmodernism, Saints, and Scoundrels', *Modern Theology* 9/1 (January 1993), pp. 19–36.

4   Girard has often mentioned Aristotle's remarks on *mimesis* and its centrality to humanity. Aristotle writes in the *Poetics*: 'The instinct of imitation is implanted in man from childhood, one difference between him and other animals being that he is the most imitative of living creatures, and through imitation learns his earliest lesson; and no less universal is the pleasure felt in things imitated' (*Poetics* IV, 1448b). The translation comes from *Aristotle's Poetics* (trans. S. H. Butcher, New York: Hill and Wang, 1961), p. 15.

5   Paul J. Griffiths, 'Culture's Catechumens and the Church's Task', *Handing on the Faith: The Church's Mission and Challenge* (ed. Robert P. Imbelli, New York: Herder & Herder, 2006), p. 46.

6   For Girard's clearest exposition, see, 'Are the Gospels Mythical?', *First Things* 62 (April 1996), pp. 27–31.

7   René Girard, *Evolution and Conversion: Dialogues on the Origins of Culture* (London: Continuum, 2008), p. 198.

8   See Allen Bloom's summary of Rousseau: 'Only in nature or according to nature is man's happiness to be found, for it is there that a perfect equilibrium exists between his desires and his capacity to satisfy them. The movement from nature to society destroys that equilibrium. New kinds of desires or modifications of old ones emerge, and imagination invents satisfactions or dreams of satisfactions that make desire infinite. Nature makes man whole, society divides him. The trouble with man comes from society, not from his nature. He is not suited for social life, and this is not his fault. His desires are, as it were, plugged into the wrong circuits'. *Love and Friendship* (New York: Simon & Schuster, 1993), pp. 43–44.

9   Charles Taylor, *The Ethics of Authenticity* (Cambridge: Harvard University Press, 1991); Frederick Lawrence sums it up well in 'The Fragility of Consciousness: Lonergan and the Postmodern Concern for the Other', *Theological Studies* 54 (1993), p. 62: 'In contrast to the bourgeois ideal of the autonomous, self-determining individual who realizes him- or herself ideally as a bourgeois entrepreneur, producer, and consumer, Romantic subjectivism idealizes the untrammelled self of the Romantic subject who realizes him- or herself by *Habits of the Heart*'s "expressive individualism"'. This quotation finds an echo in Robert Doran's introduction to a collection of Girard's literary criticism: 'The notion of the individual [in the wake of the French Revolution] was no longer tied to the rise of the bourgeoisie, as it was in the eighteenth century; the true individual was now the *exceptional* being. This anti-bourgeois hyper-individualism reaches its zenith in the Romantic

subject, which counterposes a heroic individuality to the indistinct mass of uncomprehending others. [. . .] The search for individuality reveals itself to be a latter-day theology of the self: the replacement of God by the human subject, which is affirmed as the locus of all meaning and authority (Nietzschean pride)'. 'Editor's Introduction' in René Girard, *Mimesis and Theory: Essays on Literature and Criticism, 1953–2005* (ed. Robert Doran, Stanford: Stanford University Press, 2008), pp. xvi–xvii. Or as Girard himself puts it: 'The [romantic] hero is always he who desires most intensely. This intense desire is the only spontaneous desire'. René Girard, *Deceit, Desire, and the Novel: Self and Other in Literary Structure* (trans. Yvonne Freccero, Baltimore: The Johns Hopkins University Press, 1965), p. 269.

10   Girard, *Deceit*, pp. 14–15.

11   Ibid., p. 38.

12   Ibid., pp. 38–39.

13   For a helpful treatment on humility in Augustine, see Deborah Wallace Ruddy, 'The Humble God', *Logos: A Journal of Catholic Thought and Culture* 7/3 (2004), pp. 87–108.

14   Pierre Adnès, 'Humilité', *Dictionnaire de spiritualité* 7 (1969), p. 1153. Cited in Ruddy, 'The Humble God,' p. 104.

15   It is worth citing Ruddy at length here, albeit in a footnote: 'Augustine understood humility as a distinctly Christian attribute. It was inconceivable to him that humility could be valued apart from a belief in the Incarnation. In reference to the various moral systems of his day, Augustine writes: "Everywhere are to be found excellent precepts concerning morals and discipline, but this humility is not to be found. This way of humility comes from another source; it comes from Christ . . . What else did he teach but this humility? [. . .]" In the *Confessions*, Augustine explains that Christian love begins and builds upon the "foundation of humility which is Christ Jesus." All other Christian virtues are built upon and sustained by this foundational Christian attribute that grows out of God's self-disclosure in Jesus Christ. To know Jesus is to know his humility, for he is the archetype and master of humility (*magister humilitatis*)'. Ruddy, 'The Humble God,' p. 88; for the citations in Augustine, *The Confessions* (trans. Maria Boulding, New York: New City Press, 1997), p. 104.

16   Augustine, *Confessions*, VII, xviiii, p. 24; trans. Boulding, p. 132.

17   Girard, 'Conversion in Literature and Christianity', *Mimesis and Theory*, p. 265.

18   Ibid., p. 266. Gil Bailie makes a similar point in *Violence Unveiled: Humanity at the Crossroads* (New York: Crossroad, 1995), pp. 196–97: 'When, by the grace of God, we are able to walk away from a crowd in the grip of a mimetic contagion, it is not because we are the sturdy individualists we fancy ourselves to be. Rather it is because we [. . .] have been moved by a moral force of even greater power than that which the old system of sacred violence has been able to muster'.

19   As Girard points out, Proust only ever took Christianity seriously during the period of his 'breakthrough', following which he lived like an ascetic or a monk to write *A la recherché du temps perdu* in comparative isolation. Girard qualifies that Proust did not become a Christian, but asserts that his *form* of conversion was in fact Christian: 'Everything in the life and legend of Marcel

Proust fits the conversion pattern. He enters great literature just as, earlier, he might have entered the religious life. There is something quasi-monastic about the partly mythical but nevertheless authentic account of his spending the rest of his life isolated from the world, in his cork-lined bedroom, waking up in the middle of the night to write his novel, just as monks wake up to sing their prayers' (Girard, 'Conversion in Literature and Christianity', p. 270).

20 Girard, *Evolution and Conversion*, p. 223.
21 Girard, *Deceit*, p. 249.
22 Girard, 'Conversion in Literature and Christianity', p. 268.
23 Girard, *Deceit*, p. 272.
24 Ibid.
25 Ibid.
26 Ibid., p. 273.
27 Ibid., p. 294.
28 Hegel outlines this dance between self and other in his *Phenomenology of Spirit*. See not only the well-known master-slave dialectic, but also section 5/b, when Hegel starts to talk about community: 'I perceive it in everyone. They are only self-sufficient beings to the extent that I am. I perceive the free unity with the other in them to such an extent that they *are* through me. The self *is* through another. They are to the extent that I am. I to the extent that they are'. *Phenomenologie des Geistes* [Meiner Verlag ed., 236]; (translation and emphasis mine).
29 Girard, *Evolution and Conversion*, p. 222.
30 René Girard, *I See Satan Fall Like Lightning* (trans. James Williams, Maryknoll, NY: Orbis, 2001; French original, 1999), p. 189.
31 René Girard, *The Scapegoat* (trans. Yvonne Freccero, Baltimore: Johns Hopkins University Press, 1986), p. 207.
32 Girard, *I See Satan*, p. 190.
33 Girard picks up on this point in his exegesis of John 14.16–17, when Jesus talks about the disciples being given 'another Advocate', implying of course that he already is one. Girard notes, 'In John's text Jesus makes himself a Paraclete. [. . .] Christ is the Paraclete, par excellence, in the struggle against the representation of persecution'.
34 Girard, *Scapegoat*, p. 207.
35 For a helpful elucidation of this psychology, see Sebastian Moore, *The Crucified Jesus is No Stranger* (New York: Paulist Press, 1977), esp. Part One, ch. 4: 'The Lamb Slain from the Foundation of the World', pp. 13–17.
36 Girard, *Scapegoat*, p. 212; Girard says essentially the same thing at the beginning of *I See Satan Fall Like Lightning*: '[The Paraclete] reveals the innocence of Jesus to the disciples first and then to all of us', p. 2.
37 René Girard, *Things Hidden Since the Foundation of the World: Research Undertaken in Collaboration with J.-M. Oughourlian and G. Lefort* (Stanford, CA: Stanford University Press, 1987), p. 399. Gil Bailie says the same thing in a different way. It bears quoting him at length: 'Those inspired by the Paraclete awaken from illusion and experience dis-illusionment, contrition, and cultural alienation, as did Peter and Paul. The truth to which the Paraclete will lead humanity is not a truth that can be acquired by a simple intellectual transaction, the way, for instance, knowledge can be acquired in a classroom or in a book. The truth that the Paraclete reveals is a cure for the kind of

forgetfulness that myth makes possible. [. . .] That is why, again according to John's Gospel, the Paraclete draws those it inspires to the Cross, for the Cross is the counter-mythological, meta-religious revelatory image par excellence, the pivot around which a worldwide anthropology revolution is now turning' (*Violence Unveiled*, p. 130).

38 James Alison, *Knowing Jesus* (Springfield, IL: Templegate, 1993), p. 26.

39 Ibid., p. 28.

40 Ibid., p. 85.

41 James Alison, *Raising Abel: The Recovery of the Eschatological Imagination* (New York: Crossroad, 1996), p. 67.

42 Bailie, *Violence Unveiled*, p. 196. In the next paragraph he contrasts these results with those of Jesus and the woman caught in adultery (Jn 8.3–11). This raises the question about liberation theology's hagiology, especially when being holy becomes synonymous with being aligned with the poor. See Leonardo Boff, *Saint Francis: A Model for Human Liberation* (trans. John Diercksmeier, New York: Crossroad, 1982), as well as his 'The Need for Political Saints', in *Cross Currents* 30/4 (1980–81), pp. 369–76; Jon Sobrino, 'Political Holiness: A Profile', *Martyrdom Today* (ed. J. B. Metz and E. Schillebeeckx, New York: Seabury, 1983), pp. 18–23.

43 For an illuminating account of desert monasticism as a set of practices to avoid mimetic escalation and violent reciprocation, see the essay by Brian Robinette, 'Deceit, Desire, and the Desert', *Violence, Transformation and the Sacred* (ed. Margaret Pfeil and Tobias Winright, Maryknoll, NY: Orbis, 2011), pp. 130–43.

44 Alison, *Raising Abel*, p. 68; emphasis Alison's.

45 James Alison, *Broken Hearts and New Creations: Intimations of a Great Reversal* (New York: Continuum, 2010), p. 52.

46 James Alison, *Undergoing God: Dispatches from the Scene of a Break-in* (New York: Continuum, 2006), p. 207.

47 Behind Alison's use of 'priest' is a robust theology of the 'priesthood of all believers'.

48 Alison, *Broken Hearts*, pp. 257–58.

49 On this point see Alison 'The Place of Shame and the Giving of the Spirit', in *Undergoing God*, pp. 199–219, esp. p. 207.

50 Gil Bailie, 'On Paper and in Person', in *For René Girard: Essays in Friendship and Truth* (ed. Sandor Goodhart, Jørgen Jørgensen, Tom Ryba and James G. Williams, East Lansing, MI: Michigan State University Press, 2009), p. 183.

12

Holy Mary, Holy Desire: Luce Irigaray and Saintly Daughters

Phyllis H. Kaminski

Two images frame my approach to the topic of saints, philosophy and theology in the thought of Luce Irigaray. The first comes from a visit to the Pantheon. Originally built to replace the church of St Genevieve, the Pantheon became a mausoleum after the French Revolution. It now serves as a burial place and a public space for liturgical functions honouring the great men and women of France.[1] The rotunda is flanked by the stories of two saintly daughters: Geneviève,[2] who still watches over Paris, and Jeanne d'Arc,[3] burned at the stake as a heretic, now one of France's patrons. The impressive frescoes portray both daughters as courageous women involved in the affairs of this world and at the same time in communion with another one.

The second image is Notre Dame during a Vatican initiative to promote dialogue with unbelievers.[4] I was captivated by the sound and light show at this great monument to Our Lady, which I found on YouTube.[5] The narrators are serious and playful. A sober catechizing voice echoes formulas of faith, and 'visitors' wonder about this monument that speaks to them of the fullness of humanity. Then music and light create an encounter with Notre Dame that is solemnly mystical and whimsically irreverent. Chant segues into French pop rock. Swirling angels and statues of biblical kings dance in their niches, then gently still as sacred music and gold light suggest transcendent presence. These living spaces symbolize the secular/sacred and intellectual/popular culture in which Luce Irigaray lives and from which we seek to renegotiate contemporary holiness.

Although she does not dub any contemporary a saint, nor does she deal with saintliness in any traditional way, as Tina Beattie notes, 'Irigaray puts more intellectual energy into thinking about Catholicism than many Catholics'.[6] I have chosen to focus on Luce Irigaray because her paradigmatic theory of difference and her approach to the divine provide fertile terrain as we explore 'French thought' and (re)formulations of 'saintliness'. Irigaray maintains that 'the spiritual task most adapted to our age' is '[t]o pursue human becoming to its divine fulfillment'.[7] In asserting my agreement with that spiritual task, I am aware of her multivalent uses of the word divine.[8] I respect the multiple genres of her corpus, her critique of Western philosophical-theological affirmations, her construction of bodied transcendence, and her connection of divine and human desire. While I have reservations about all that Irigaray means when she speaks of 'becoming divine', in ways that are imaginatively constructive, her ideas open possibilities for speaking difference in women's and men's experience that can be transformative of our thinking about both God and saints.

I look to daughters because, as Irigaray points out, until the position of the daughter changes, the position of women in the world will not change.[9] I turn particularly to Irigaray's reading of the Marian symbol because, while it needs to be understood within the whole of her project, particularly her work on feminine subjectivity and Greco-Roman mother–daughter genealogies,[10] it offers a personal and social approach to holiness that is incarnational and committed to building a world which truly recognizes difference. In short, Irigaray's 'Holy Mary' reconceives traditional theological affirmations and affirms the spiritual task of pursuing human becoming to its divine fulfilment.

To that end, I sketch three interrelated aspects of Irigaray's *oeuvre*: fidelity to Incarnation; the cultivation of an interiority proper to women; and transformed relations between the sexes. Within Christianity, reverence for the body, silence nourished by disciplined desire, and a praxis of faith that labours for justice have long been proposed as ideals. Irigaray appropriates and deconstructs these traditional ideals and corresponding religious practices to suggest how sexual difference matters in considerations of the holy. In fact, her understanding of sexual difference troubles all traditional categories based on a unitary sex neutral subject or on gender complementarity.[11] The difference between the sexes is a question of sexual relations and also of the way religious traditions and cultures organize not just intimate relations but all areas of life (familial, civic, ecclesial) in terms of gender, genealogy, racial, ethnic and every other difference. To include all these differences, Irigaray has begun speaking about *sexuate* difference and the cultivation of identities that include the different sexes without reverting to the domination of one by the other.

Moreover, Irigaray's focus on symbolic process resonates with the Catholic intellectual tradition. Her creative imagination, though at times irreverent, is keenly aware of the power of symbol and attentive to the energy of desire. In addition, the ongoing development of her thought, especially on difference, points to transformative spiritualities for both women and men that involve a radical rethinking of human–divine relations. In her own assessment of how her philosophy has progressed, Irigaray states:

> [T]he first part of my work amounts to a criticism of Western tradition as constructed by a single subjectivity, a masculine subjectivity, who has elaborated a logic and a world according to his own necessities. In the second part, I try to indicate mediations which permit a feminine subjectivity to emerge from the unique and so-called neutral Western culture, and to affirm herself as autonomous and capable of a cultivation and culture of her own. The third part of my work is devoted to defining and rendering practicable the ways through which masculine subjectivity and feminine subjectivity could coexist, enter into relation without submitting or subjecting the one to the other, and construct a world shareable by the two with respect for their own worlds.[12]

From my perspective, all of these are relevant to a consideration of the interaction of contemporary French thought and historical notions of saintliness.

Thinking through difference: Daughter and woman

Irigaray shares in the postmodern conviction that the era of history into which we are entering requires radical transformation. She insists, however, that this new era, which she calls 'the era of the *couple*: of the spirit and the bride', requires as a condition of its possibility that 'woman [. . .] be longed for, loved, valued as a daughter'.[13] In ways that move beyond current polarizations, Irigaray invites us to think and speak differently about the place and role of *woman*. She does this by engaging daughters (and others) in a process of consciousness raising that leads to inner transformation and committed action.

Although she works primarily with Anglo-European White culture, her approach to difference sheds light on present and future possibilities for daughters of all colours and cultures. On one level, Irigaray intends the term 'daughter' to designate individual bodied persons in all their concreteness. Yet her understanding is never simply biological. I claim that 'daughterness' is a structural concept, one that brings self-awareness and self-understanding always in relation to the existing order and its expressions of desire. Changing that order involves a spiritual becoming wherein adult daughters realize autonomy and relatedness with (m)others like themselves, and, recognized as desiring subjects in their own right, women no longer serve as objects of exchange among men.

While Irigaray maintains that it is a grace to be born a daughter,[14] she is keenly aware that the effects of original sin have fallen most heavily on daughters. The daughter lives 'in a world where she has become invisible and blind to herself, her mother, other women and even men, who perhaps want her that way'.[15] As Irigaray looks to the divine fulfilment of human beings, she holds firmly to an incarnational principle that 'the other' represents an opportunity to *become* through love. Embodied love is inseparable from desire and, especially for daughters, sharing love must include themselves as desiring subjects. Thus the place of the daughter throughout her individual life cycle is a touchstone to the kind of transformed relations (both interpersonal and social) that feminists, contextual theologians and spiritual authors envision and hope to enflesh.

Holy Mary: Daughter, woman and mother[16]

For Catholic Christians, Mary is a familiar symbol, one central to the community's construction of women's identity, their dignity and their vocation. Read within the body of her works, Irigaray's re-presentation of Mary connects with all that she says about 'the other, woman' and about speaking of and from a position of difference. As she does with the Western philosophical canon, Irigaray reads the Christian story of Mary otherwise. Her reading reframes cultural expressions of the incarnate word of God in history. If, as Irigaray maintains, the sacrificed body of the woman upholds the symbolic order, Christianity presents its daughters with a paradigmatic model. Mary, unique virgin and mother, assented totally to God's plan that she 'conceive him in whom "the fullness of deity" would dwell "bodily"'.[17] The mariological tradition, with its focus on Mary's uniqueness, conceals and reveals the sacrifice of women. It is not surprising then that Irigaray often turns to Mary in order to seek a different 'grammar'[18] for the story of redemption.

The gospels contain very little about the woman who birthed Jesus. Fortunately art, popular devotion, and apocryphal texts have represented Mary in ways that freely represent her humanity and her saintliness.[19] In Christian imagination, Mary often exceeds patriarchal limits. Irigaray explores this excess and finds *something-more*[20] for feminine subjectivity. With references scattered throughout her works and in a recent essay on the mystery of Mary,[21] she reimagines women's relation to divine immanence and transcendence, to their own bodies, and to other women and men.

Fidelity to Incarnation

Irigaray grounds her efforts to discover and cultivate new paradigms for human becoming in the Incarnation because of its emphasis on the radicality of love in human and divine becoming and because of its social consequences. Theoretically, the mystery respects every body as potentially divine: 'Each man and each woman are virtually gods'. Yet this message, especially as it concerns women, 'is most often veiled, obscured, covered over'.[22] In Christian history and in Irigaray's corpus, Mary serves as the multivalent representation of the Incarnation and its doctrinal expressions. She creates, as it were, a way to bridge what is revealed and concealed in the mystery of the Word becoming flesh.

Irigaray linked the Annunciation and the Crucifixion as early as her work *Marine Lover*. She argued there for redemption in the body of Mary. Mary's *fiat* had a double meaning. Her 'yes' made possible the Incarnation. However, Mary's 'yes' was equally a 'no' – 'a no to her own life'.[23] The one woman revered for her full participation in the Incarnation, death and resurrection of the Son of God did so only by her own crucifixion, a crucifixion concealed, hidden in male-dominant symbolic discourse. Instead, from Mary's *fiat*, Irigaray constructs a theology of Incarnation where Jesus and Mary mirror God's love in human and divine becoming.[24] She discovers in Mary's body a yes to life, 'the fruit of a new covenant between word and nature, between logos and cosmos'.[25] As Kelly Oliver points out, 'Mary represents the in-between [. . .] through whom we might imagine another economy of exchange that does not require sacrifice, a divine that does not require a dead god'.[26] This virgin daughter opens tangibly to life-sharing transcendence. The Annunciation, as first instance of a living word made flesh in the body of a woman, heralds the possibility of a non-patriarchal order – the advent of a loving, non-violent divinity.

In an Irigarayan theological anthropology, Mary represents woman as and for herself. She finds union with transcendence not by denying her body but within it. In her womb, God is Other, but an other who becomes her flesh, her blood. When Mary brings forth her child, she births a living God. Irigaray, in effect, asserts of Mary at the Annunciation what Rosemary Ruether said of Jesus on Calvary: this incarnational mystery proclaims a *kenosis* of the patriarchal God.[27] Such an assertion involves more than a different reading of the theological symbol. It requires a female imaginary, and this means not only exposing the unsymbolized, repressed underside of Western thought; it also involves a social process of creating something that does not yet exist.

To read the mystery of Incarnation in this direction, Irigaray draws on her familiarity with longstanding Catholic devotion and her experience of a wooden sculpture of Anne and Mary.[28] The Annunciation remains a central redemptive symbol, and Irigaray discovers within it a dialogic process rooted in the Anne-Mary genealogy. She suggests that Mary daughter of Anne, reveals 'the path of her incarnation as a woman: the path of the relationship inside herself between body and words'.[29]

In order to explain this 'path of incarnation', I turn to Irigaray's interpretation of the doctrine of the Immaculate Conception. Catholic

dogma affirms Mary 'conceived without sin' in terms of her relationship to
Jesus the Christ:

> The most Blessed Virgin Mary was, from the first moment of her
> conception, by a singular grace and privilege of almighty God and by
> virtue of the merits of Jesus Christ, Savior of the human race, preserved
> immune from all stain of original sin.[30]

Irigaray reads Mary's sinless conception in terms of her relationship to
her mother. Anne, a woman faithful to herself, deeply desired a child and,
through grace, conceived a daughter. Seeing herself acting within the spirit
of Roman Christianity, Irigaray develops the theme of grace concealed and
revealed, to bring out the female flesh hidden in dogmatic discourse.

Anne's grace remained hidden, but her daughter, the blessed fruit of her
womb, was born fully graced. Mary, daughter of Anne, learned her graced
origins from her mother. In her *credo au feminin*, Irigaray writes extensively
of Mary, a girl-child whose breath (*esprit*) has not been stifled. Anne raised
Mary with integrity, to be a woman of faith and freedom, generous, open
and responsive to the winds of the Spirit.[31] Mary, faithful to her Incarnation
as a daughter desired, grew to be an adolescent who was free, loving, and
capable of intersubjectivity. The portrait of Mary in *Souffle* plays out the
possibility voiced in 'Divine Women' 'that God might be made flesh as a
woman, through the mother and the daughter and in their relationships'.[32]

Mary's body thus becomes a site of radical transformation as the first
instance of the incarnate God in human flesh. Although we may assume that
Irigaray is not a devoted reader of the universal *Catechism of the Catholic
Church*, in surprising ways, she echoes its affirmation that Mary 'was [. . .]
the most capable of welcoming the inexpressible gift of the Almighty'.[33] For
Irigaray, as for the *Catechism*, Mary's virginity is key to that capacity but
Irigaray's virginal symbol deconstructs current doctrinal formulations.

Virginal integrity and an interiority
of her own

Adding yet another layer to her designation of the new era of history (the
era of the spirit and the bride, the era of the couple), Irigaray wonders
whether we are now in 'the era of virginity'.[34] Newness applies because
Irigaray envisions a world in which the virginal body is not at the service
of a phallic economy. If patriarchy rests on the sacrifice of the mother, it
has also sacrificed the body of the virgin daughter.[35] Mary and Anne offer
Irigaray a way to foreground the maternal genealogy hidden in incarnational
theology. She further imagines through Mary the daughter how virginal
integrity can empower women to stand in their difference socially, physically,
psychologically and linguistically.

Irigaray's longstanding yoga practice colours her reading of artistic representations of the Annunciation. Mary's hands crossed over her breast represent one of the *chakras*, an energetic centre 'situated at the crossroads of various physiological and spiritual functions'.[36] In this centre, virginity refers to 'the opening of a transcendental space' in relation to self and to others.[37] Mary's closed lips do not negate her sexuality but preserve an intimacy with her own body.[38] Mary expresses something new and positive about women's responses to the divine. This daughter is no longer bound by fusion or adherence to another, or by instinct or submission to nature. She knows her own desires and expresses freely her autonomy-in-relation.

Mary thus embodies a challenge Irigaray sees for women who would live in fidelity to Incarnation according to their gender. Mary discovers her word, is faithful to it, and integrating her word with her body, makes of that body a living and spiritual flesh.[39] Positive understandings of both female *jouissance* and desire offer daughters a way to reconceive the meaning of their personal integrity and female embodiment in a dynamic relation with God, with others and the world.

Yet, such a transformation of consciousness cannot happen without personal and corporate effort. At every stage of life, daughters need a practical strategy to think through dominant religious messages about virginity and one's submission to the Word of God. Irigaray suggests a practice that is challenging but widely accessible: the cultivation of silence.[40] Silence that is 'the condition for a possible respect for myself and for the other within our respective limits'[41] takes most seriously the present order. It assumes that the already existing world is not complete.

Silence that is chosen creates a space, a gap that can open a spiritual path. The path is not based on the dichotomous understandings of body/soul, body/word, sex/spirit or nature/culture. The fulness of silent presence to one's self and attentiveness to the often forgotten surrounding air awaken an awareness of the dynamic web of relationships in which we all exist. Such a practice of silence can foster freedom and resistance. Irigaray encourages Christian women to learn from Mary's quiet integrity and the free relational word she embodied. This daughter started out on a path of the 'not-yet-coded', and prepared the world for 'the revelation of a truth that has yet to manifest itself'.[42] For Irigaray, that truth concerns what it means for women to incarnate the divine.

Intersubjective desire in graced words and flesh

Mary's bodied transcendence helps Irigaray illustrate what it means to assert that 'sexed belonging' becomes a 'dimension of consciousness and not just a natural given'.[43] In the framework of Irigarayan sexuate difference, Mary inaugurates an interpersonal communion between the genders that is 'not reducible to need, nor to instinct, nor to natural fecundity'.[44] Although by no means automatic, learning from Mary's fidelity to Incarnation can anchor contemporary Christian women in identities that are gender specific but not fixed. They, in turn, can become more capable of working for just relations that respect difference(s).[45]

How does Irigaray show Mary embodying relational identity without falling into the trap of hierarchical dualities? She remains with the Annunciation and focuses on the dialogue and the waiting. The mystery of Incarnation occurs in 'words and listening shared voluntarily', *before* it occurs in the body of the Virgin Mary, 'in the place where word and flesh fecundate one another intentionally'.[46] God does not touch Mary's body without asking her if that is what she wishes. Moreover, Mary's body is not simply natural. In dialogue with her mother, she has embodied and expressed the graced word she already is. Therefore, her readiness for relation with the divine other does not imply a death to self in submission to the word addressed to her. There is mutual desire in the multileveled dialogue mediated by the angel. In Irigaray's language, the conception of a divine child 'is preceded by the transition from an almost undifferentiated corporeal matter, and from a separation between the genders, to an alliance in the word between man and woman'.[47] Mary thus stands as one who can help women and men refound relations 'on the basis of an interiority without power. [. . .] Flesh itself becomes spiritual while remaining flesh; affect becomes spirit while remaining love'.[48]

Touch, breath, and silence coalesce as Irigaray draws on Christian, Hindu and Buddhist ideas to interpret this central redemptive moment. In ways that play with our conceptual boundaries, Irigaray imagines the Annunciation more as a question from God than as an announcement by the angel. The conception of the divine child does not take place without Mary's freedom and desire, without God's patient listening. Their free sharing of silence, breath and speech reveals an engendering that is corporeal and spiritual at the same time. The Lord knows his own desire, interiorizes it and shares it in word and flesh. Mary knows her own desire. She has known loving intimacy with her mother. As a young woman, she wants fruitful relations with another. Mary speaks from her own interiority and remains faithful to herself. Her 'yes' inaugurates an exchange with the other gender that is freely desired, not one of necessity. This historic conception, Irigaray suggests in *I Love to You*, symbolizes new possibilities for relations between the sexes. Mary and her divine child form an alliance that could incarnate the finality of History or at least lead the way to a new era.[49]

Imagining Mary and the Lord as a couple is perhaps the most troublesome aspect of Irigaray's scenario. By her own admission, Jesus and Mary do not make the kind of male–female couple she describes elsewhere in *I Love to You*. Nonetheless, as Mary Aquin O'Neill suggests, if women are to see their humanity permeated with the divine, we must look at both Jesus and Mary: 'To have an image of what it looks like to be "human to the utmost" [. . .] we must imagine them both'.[50] I suggest with O'Neill that women and men must examine the gender implications of all theological affirmations.

There is fecundity in Irigaray's paradigmatic couple and the daughter's role in its various manifestations (the placental couple, the mother–daughter couple and the heterosexual couple).[51] While the first and third of these receive close scrutiny in Catholic theology, the absence of the second deprives the tradition of a fundamental resource. Focusing on Mary as daughter, woman and mother sheds light on present dilemmas and offers a new way of thinking through difference. Mary can engender in herself another like her mother. She can also engender difference *in* herself and in another by bringing a boy-child into the world. The great challenge for theology comes in thinking through incarnational formulations of difference, human and divine, as well as sexuate difference in any paradigmatic coupling. While Irigaray's Marian model remains incomplete and elliptical, it contributes to what Hannah Bacon calls a 'generous' orthodoxy, one which does not simply repeat ancient formulas but remains an emerging incomplete process always receptive to the voice of the other.[52]

Saintliness and difference: For future negotiations

How does Irigaray's Mary contribute to a postmodern sensibility in relation to 'saintliness'? Irigaray never mentions saintliness as such, but her commitment to sexuate difference within human development to its divine fulfilment has much to offer theologies of God, theological anthropology, spirituality and ethics. In terms of the limited focus of this essay, she offers substantive matter to feminist theologies, Christology, and mariology. Through Mary, we glimpse the revelatory capacity of maternal genealogy and of virginal integrity. Both give symbolic expression to a different way of being in relation to the divine. Mary, daughter of Anne, symbolizes the graced mystery of daughterness hidden in Christianity. 'Capable of welcoming the word of the other without altering it',[53] this holy daughter inaugurates the mystery of Incarnation, giving flesh to the Living Word of God. She invites all daughters to their primary spiritual task, 'assuming, affirming, and expanding [their] identity as adult women in its difference(s)'.[54]

The incarnational dialectic between bodies and words continues. In an increasingly violent technological world, the task of connecting natural, civil and religious coexistence is particularly urgent. Irigaray's love of wisdom, as a philosopher and spiritual seeker, points not only daughters but also sons in the direction of a new economy of relations, an intersubjective world that recognizes difference in non-hierarchal ways and that values the cultivation of energy for the being and becoming of all. Dialogue across linguistic, ethnic, religious and cultural borders has not made Luce Irigaray less 'militant for the impossible'.[55] Those of us who work with her thought and reckon with its fluid use of words – its multiple genres, its self-questioning and its questioning of us as readers – know the risks of speaking (as) women. But speak we must.

To return to my opening images, Luce Irigaray stands between the Pantheon and Notre Dame, in dialogue with the Greeks, her fellow philosophers and with Christian theologians and mystics, challenging her culture to think and move towards a life-giving future. She exposes the gendered cultural assumptions that have shaped our understanding of divinity, humanity and their function in any construction of 'the saint'. As a feminist theologian, I especially appreciate her dialogic and dialectical approach to one's fidelity to Incarnation. She does not merely critique the *Logos* of Western philosophy and patriarchal Christianity. Her living words displace its univocal meaning by inscribing the irreducibility of difference in the incarnational process of becoming human (with all the messy concreteness that human becoming entails). Does Luce Irigaray provide new understandings of what a saint could be said to be in today's world? Does she stand as an eschatologically liminal figure whose life and work anticipate divine fulfilment for those daughters (and sons) still considered the least among us? To those queries, I respond with a full-bodied 'yes'.

Notes

1   www.pantheonparis.com. The dedication on the façade reads 'aux Grands Hommes, la Patrie reconnaissante'. Accessed 29 May 2011.
2   www.newadvent.org/cathen/06413f.htm. Accessed 29 May 2011.
3   www.jeannedarc.info. Accessed 29 May 2011.
4   See http://chiesa.espresso.repubblica.it/articolo/1347285?eng=y. Accessed 29 May 2011.
5   www.youtube.com/watch?v=Gb1TAzEM-4U&feature=related, http://www.youtube.com/watch?v=jIkxaDe4DIU. Accessed 29 May 2011.
6   Tina Beattie, 'Carnal Love and Spiritual Imagination: Can Luce Irigaray and John Paul II Come Together?', *Sex These Days* (ed. Jon Davies and Gerard Loughlin, Sheffield: Sheffield Academic Press, 1999), p. 161. See also Tina Beattie, *New Catholic Feminism: Theology and Theory* (London: Routledge, 2006) for her analysis of Catholic neo-orthodoxy and particularly her treatment of Hans Urs von Balthasar and Luce Irigaray.
7   Luce Irigaray, ed., *Key Writings* (New York: Continuum, 2004), p. 186.
8   See Morny Joy, *Divine Love: Luce Irigaray, Women, Gender, and Religion* (New York: Manchester University Press/Palgrave, 2006); Gillian Howie and J'annine Jobling, eds, *Women and the Divine: Touching Transcendence* (New York: Palgrave Macmillan, 2009), especially Luce Irigaray, 'Toward a Divine in the Feminine', pp. 12–25; and C. W. Maggie Kim, Susan M. St. Ville and Susan M. Simonaitis, eds, *Transfigurations: Theology and the French Feminists* (Minneapolis, MN: Fortress Press, 1993), especially Elizabeth Grosz, 'Irigaray and the Divine', pp. 199–214.

9   Luce Irigaray, *Thinking the Difference: For a Peaceful Revolution* (trans. Karin Montin, New York: Routledge, 1994), p. 112.

10 See Gail Schwab, 'Mothers, Sisters, and Daughters: Luce Irigaray and the Female Genealogical Line in the Stories of the Greeks', *Rewriting Difference: Luce Irigaray and 'the Greeks'* (ed. Elena Tzelepis and Athena Athanasiou, New York: SUNY Press, 2010), pp. 79–92. For a thorough treatment of Mary and Irigaray, see Tina Beattie, *God's Mother, Eve's Advocate: A Gynocentric Refiguration of Marian Symbolism in Engagement with Luce Irigaray* (Bristol: Centre for Comparative Studies in Religion and Gender, University of Bristol, 1999).

11 Irigaray's understanding of sexual difference includes the difference inscribed in the anatomy of each sex. However, sexual difference does not refer to a simple binary opposition. It connotes a relationship to sex inscribed above all in the human psyche, in cultural representations, in social/material structures and in religious symbols. The dominant symbolic order sustains representations of 'man' (the normative inclusive human) by keeping 'woman' (particularly female bodied reality) the hidden, unrepresentable Other. Seeking equality within this order, which Irigaray calls 'the economy of the same', women contribute to its maintenance and their effacement. She seeks to create an 'economy of difference', a space in which women claim their difference as subjects in language and in culture, and live as bodied selves in their own right. Penelope Deutscher argues convincingly that, because this space does not yet exist, Irigaray's politics of the impossible challenges us both to imagine the possibility of such a world and to keep asking why at present it remains impossible. See Penelope Deutscher, *A Politics of Impossible Difference: The Later Work of Luce Irigaray* (Ithaca, NY: Cornell University Press, 2002).

12 Luce Irigaray, ed., *Conversations* (New York: Continuum, 2008), p. 124.

13 Luce Irigaray, *Ethics of Sexual Difference* (trans. Carolyn Burke and Gillian C. Gill, New York: Cornell University Press, 1993), p. 148.

14 Luce Irigaray, *Le Souffle des Femmes: Luce Irigaray présente des crédos au féminin* (Paris: Action Catholique Générale Féminine, 1996), pp. 200–02.

15 Irigaray, *Thinking*, p. 112.

16 Significant portions of this section first appeared in Phyllis H. Kaminski, 'The Daughter's Dilemma: Luce Irigaray, Incarnation, and Embodied Spirituality', *Theoforum* 33:1 (January 2002), pp. 77–92. The different direction of the argument here reflects my ongoing work with Irigaray.

17 Catholic Church, *Catechism of the Catholic Church* (Mahway, NJ: Paulist Press, 1994), §484.

18 Luce Irigaray, *This Sex Which is Not One* (trans. Catherine Porter, Ithaca, NY: Cornell University Press, 1985), p.143.

19 See Judith Dupré, *Full of Grace: Encountering MARY in Faith, Art, and Life* (New York: Random House, 2010); Sally Cunneen, *In Search of Mary: The Woman and the Symbol* (New York: Ballantine Books, 1996); Rosemary Luling Haughton, 'Hail Mary: The Wisdom of a Subversive Devotion', *U.S. Catholic* 66:5 (May 2001), pp. 34–38.

20 Luce Irigaray and Slyvère Lotringer, eds, *Why Different?: A Culture of Two Subjects* (trans. Camille Collins, New York: Semiotext(e), 2000), p. 33.

21 Luce Irigaray, *Il Mistero di Maria* (Milano: Paoline Editoriale Libri, 2010).

22 Luce Irigaray, 'Egales à qui?', *Critique* 43:480 (May 1987), p. 425; 'Equal to Whom?', trans. Robert L. Mazzola, *Différences* 1:2 (1989), p. 64.

23 Luce Irigaray, *Marine Lover of Friedrich Nietzsche* (trans. Gillian C. Gill, New York: Columbia University Press, 1991), pp. 166–67. See also Kelly Oliver, *Womanizing Nietzsche: Philosophy's Relation to the 'Feminine'* (New York: Routledge, 1995), p. 124.

24 Irigaray, *Souffle*, p. 185.

25 Irigaray, *Marine Lover*, pp. 181, 190.

26 Oliver, *Womanizing Nietzsche*, p. 191. Oliver shows how Irigaray draws on both Freud and Lacan to set up the mother–child relation as the prototype and condition of possibility for all subsequent relations.

27 Rosemary Radford Ruether, *Sexism and God-talk: Toward a Feminist Theology* (Boston: Beacon Press, 1983), p. 137.

28 Luce Irigaray, *Je, tu, nous: Toward a Culture of Difference* (trans. Alison Martin, New York: Routledge, 1993), pp. 25–26; also Irigaray and Lotringer, *Why Different?*, p. 32.

29 Irigaray and Lotringer, *Why Different?*, p. 34.

30 Pius IX, Ineffabilis Deus, 1854: DS 2803. Cited in *Catechism of the Catholic Church*, §491.

31 Luce Irigaray, *I Love to You: Sketch of a Possible Felicity in History* (trans. Alison Martin, New York: Routledge, 1995), p. 140; also Irigaray, *Souffle*, p. 205.

32 Luce Irigaray, 'Divine Women', *Sexes and Genealogies* (trans. Gillian C. Gill, New York: Cornell University Press, 1993), p. 71; Irigaray, *Souffle*, pp. 186–89.

33 *Catechism of the Catholic Church*, §722.

34 Irigaray, *Souffle*, p. 208.

35 Irigaray, *Thinking*, p. 112.

36 Irigaray, *I Love to You*, p. 137; also Irigaray, *Souffle*, p. 205.

37 Irigaray and Lotringer, *Why Different?*, p. 159.

38 Irigaray, *Il Mistero*, pp. 27–28.

39 Irigaray, *Souffle*, p. 187.

40 'The silence that accompanies her lips touching one another is [. . .] not necessarily negative, but can represent a privileged place of self-affection for a woman. [. . .] Joining our lips, just as joining our hands, is a way of gathering with ourselves, of reuniting the two parts of ourselves for self-affecting'. Irigaray, 'Toward a Divine', p. 18.

41 Irigaray, *I Love to You*, p. 117.

42 Ibid.; Irigaray, *Il Mistero*, p. 58.

43 Irigaray and Lotringer, *Why Different?*, p. 99.

44 Ibid., p. 163.

45 Charting a course primarily through sexual difference does not ensure that one engages with other differences such as race and class in any productive way. For more on the limitations and possibilities within Irigaray's work in this regard, see Ellen T. Armour, *Deconstruction, Feminist Theology, and the Problem of Difference: Subverting the Race/Gender Divide* (Chicago: University of Chicago Press, 1999), p. 181.

46 Irigaray, *I Love to You*, pp. 123–24.

47 Ibid., p. 141. In *Marine Lover*, Irigaray spoke of 'the Word's faithfulness to the flesh' rather than 'submission of the flesh to the Word' (p. 169).

48 Irigaray, *I Love to You*, p. 148.

49 Ibid., p. 141. In this new era, there would be different criteria for civil organization and systems of economic exchange. Irigaray imagines motherhood as a component but not a priority of female identity. Mary figures in her model of the right to virginity without maternity, a right which is not cash-convertible by the family, the state or religious bodies. A woman would have a legal right to choose to become a mother without Church or state exercising, either directly or through institutions, financial or ideological power over her. See Irigaray, *Je, tu, nous*, pp. 86–88; Irigaray, *Thinking the Difference*, pp. 59–63.

50 Mary Aquin O'Neill, R. S. M., 'Female Embodiment and the Incarnation', in Francis Eigo, ed., *Themes in Feminist Theology for the New Millenium (I)* (Villanova, PA: Villanova University Press, 2002), p. 55.

51 See Debra Bergoffen, 'Irigaray's Couples', *Returning to Irigaray: Feminist Philosophy, Politics, and the Question of Unity* (ed. Maria C. Cimitile and Elaine P. Miller, Albany, NY: State University of New York Press, 2007), pp. 151–72.

52 Hannah Bacon, 'A Very Particular Body: Assessing the Doctrine of Incarnation for Affirming the Sacramentality of Female Embodiment', *Women and the Divine*, p. 228, and n. 1, p. 249.

53 Irigaray, *Souffle*, p. 188; Irigaray, 'Redemption of Women', *Key Writings*, p. 152.

54 Irigaray, *Souffle*, p. 189.

55 Irigaray, *I Love to You*, p. 10.

13

A (W)holy Human Subject?: Saintliness and Antiphilosophy in the Work of Alain Badiou

Meghan Helsel[1]

Introduction

Despite its complexity, its use of mathemes and reliance on Cantorian set theory, the argument of Alain Badiou's *Being and Event* does not begin with a deduction, or even an axiom, but with in his words, a 'wager'. In order to begin his argument, Badiou wagers that his argument is in fact possible; he wagers that 'that *ontology is a situation*'[2] (his emphasis), or, in other words, that a philosophical reflection on being is in fact available to philosophy. And Badiou *must* wager: in the same sentence Badiou writes that he 'maintains' the language of wager is the only possible response to what he refers to as the 'Great Temptation', the temptation to 'reduce ontology to paradox'.[3] He goes on to say that 'philosophical "ontologies", historically, have not resisted' this temptation.[4] In the 400 pages of *Being and Event*, using the resources of set-theory, poetry and Lacanian analysis, Badiou will resist this 'Great Temptation' admirably, perhaps too admirably, not only arguing explicitly that ontology is available to philosophy, but also claiming that ontology is the only true material for philosophy.

However, according to Badiou, the most dangerous part of the Great Temptation is less the desire to admit that ontology is paradoxical than the desire to point beyond philosophy. Systems of thought belonging to the Great Temptation are 'characterized by an ethics of mystical ascent', and as such deny philosophy and seek instead for 'the absolute singularity of saintliness'.[5] Not enough philosophical grit is left in this singularity to produce an ontology 'fully transmissible within knowledge',[6] and instead such thought maintains that 'being cannot be signified within a structured multiple, and that only an experience situated beyond all structure will afford us an access to the veiling of being's presence'.[7] In *Being and Event* Badiou calls these systems of thought characterized by the 'Great Temptation' 'Ontologies of Presence', but they are in fact closely related to what in the rest of his oeuvre he calls 'antiphilosophy'. A sort of fundamentalist ontology of presence, antiphilosophy denounces and condemns philosophy,[8] and invites others to escape the false reign of philosophical truth and take refuge in ineffability. However, this identification brings to light an irony in Badiou's tactic: the technique whereby a smart wager is offered as a way to escape a badly lived paradox is a signature move of antiphilosophy. In other words, Badiou couches his declaration of opposition to ontologies of presence in a rhetorical move lifted from the annals of the 'Great Temptation' itself, and his magnum opus begins with a triumphant declaration of faith using terms borrowed from his tempters.

Plundering the resources of one's opponents in order to articulate why one must take up arms against them testifies to, at the very least, a profound ambivalence towards antiphilosophical 'Ontologies of Presence'. In this essay, I would like to argue that the first step towards explaining the ambivalent intimacy, and enmity, of Badiou's engagement with antiphilosophy is to attend to the figure of 'saintliness' in Badiou's critique of antiphilosophy. This saintliness, we shall see, is in reference to an unacceptably risky subjectivity, a singularity that does not instantiate a truth but vanishes into pure act. Yet this singularity is in close relationship to what Badiou himself calls the 'problem of "double origins" of the process of fidelity',[9] or what we might describe as the causally problematic genesis of the Badiouian subject in relation to the event. Because of the central place of the subject in Badiou's philosophy, connections between an antiphilosophical singularity and the faithful subject to a truth procedure lie at the core of Badiou's thought, at the intersection of his master concepts: truth, the subject and the event. These master concepts have intricate articulations, and paying attention to the relation between antiphilosophical singularity and the great temptation will sharpen the joints of the formation, bringing to light the primary importance for these master concepts of what Badiou calls the 'Two', over and above what he calls 'Oneness' and 'void'. Furthermore, attending to the importance of the Two in the domain of love, the subject, and the event, will allow us to see antiphilosophy as occupying a complementary subject position to Badiou's thought, and thus will allow us to surmise that the intensity of his engagement with antiphilosophy is due to the fact that Badiou's philosophy is in a kind of arranged marriage with antiphilosophy. For the survival of *his* thought he must reject antiphilosophy as different, for the survival of his *thought*, he must incorporate antiphilosophy into his universalism.

Badiou: An overview

Badiou's philosophy turns along two axes: his theory of the subject, and his theory of philosophical endeavour. In turn, the thought of both of these axes is governed by a drive (an infinite drive, some might say) to experience, proclaim and defend truth. In terms of the subject, Badiou's goal is to 'refound the connection between truth and the subject'[10] and to defend a conception of truth as random, personal and universal. In terms of philosophy, he desires to find a conceptual system and a form of reasoning that would provide a framework in which truths could be expressed and understood. His philosophy will be platonic and will be charged with interpreting the language that is proper to being, in order to produce a receiving framework for the truths coming out of being. For Badiou, the language is mathematics, and the receiving framework is philosophy. All of Badiou's formal treatises (as opposed to his interventions) simultaneously construct and are constructed from a frame of formally derived thought. For *Being and Event*, the branch of mathematics used is set-theory, and the philosophy it engenders is an ontological commentary, delimiting the acceptable space and form for truths.

Badiou founds his ontology with the claim that the 'One' of being is not, and that therefore being is properly considered as void. What presents itself to us is in fact not being at all, (since being is void) but instead are elements drawn from the void and ordered, counted as One. This Badiou calls 'Oneness', which unlike the 'One', is. These 'ones' of presentation are always groups of elements, sets or multiples, counted as One. Everything, then, even Oneness, is contingent and multiple in its being. Furthermore, the count is always unstable, since all multiples drawn from the void must continue to include the void as part of them. Because of this instability, Badiou posits that every multiple is in fact counted twice – that there are two levels of presentation: the count, and the count of the count, or the state, which verifies the first count by creating a new set, not by counting the multiples of the first set, but by counting the pieces or 'parts' of the multiples. The state 're-presents' the original situation. But because there are always more pieces of the multiples than the multiples themselves, the state is always larger, 'excessive' to the situation which gave rise to it: representation is larger than presentation. The presentation of the multiple lacks a name, and constructing a stable name through naming the parts creates a gap between the representation of the multiple and its presentation. As such, the constitutive elements and/or procedures of being are fundamentally dislocated, and always overlap incompletely. Indeed, this dislocation and overlapping is a mark of the void, the furtive being behind all presentation.[11] All of the productivity of Badiou's theory lies in the tension inherent in this incomplete overlapping. The overlapping allows for the sustainability that exists in being, and the incompleteness allows for the new, the infinite, and ultimately, truth.

Badiou's theory of the subject can only be understood in the context of Badiou's ontology. The subject is at once the agent, the means and the effect of the coming into being of the new, infinite, truth: he is the effect within humanity of the productive powers of dislocation. The subject is twice on the margins of presentation: first, he comes into being with two things drawn from the edge of the void: the singular name of the event, along with the event itself, and second, his identity and being is always and only the local status of what Badiou calls a 'finite indexing procedure', which instantiates its own categorization of multiples apart from the first count of presentation of and re-presentation's count of the parts. In this way the subject creates a 'Oneness' that does not fit easily into presentation and that directly rivals the state: the subject is an alternative count of presentation.

The relationship between the event and the name holds the key to the bizarre being of the subject, and explains how this transgressive alternative count becomes possible. The event activates unpresented pieces of the situation in such a way that it needs a name to be counted, to become fully a part of the situation. But this name, to do justice to the event, can only be provided by what Badiou, referencing Nietzsche, calls an 'illegal will'.[12] This illegal will is, or belongs to, the subject, and produces the name in the form of what Badiou calls an intervention.

> The intervention touches the void, and is thereby subtracted from the law of the count-as-one which rules the situation, precisely because its inaugural axiom is not tied to the one, but to the two. As one, the element of the site which indexes the event does not exist, being unpresented. What induces its existence is the decision by which it occurs as two, as itself absent and as supernumerary name.[13]

Because it is named in this unique way, the event has the form of the Two, and thus is 'a presented yet incoherent multiple'[14]: it is named, but it avoids the 'One' of presentation, because its existence is validated only through its effects. And fidelity to the event, which discerns the effects of the event, also exists in the form of the Two – through its count, it *divides* the One of the situation into things that are affected by the event and things that are not. Because this fidelity is an active engagement with the world and a test of it, Badiou also calls it a 'truth procedure'. (Badiou, however, also specifies four 'generic procedures' that encompass all fidelities: these procedures are 'artistic, scientific, political and amorous'.[15]) But something must, again, 'do' this fidelity, in the same way that something must name the event – and this 'operator of connection' is again the illegal will – or in this case the illegal will materialized in the form of the subject. Therefore, 'subjectification takes place in the form of a Two' but it 'subsumes' this Two through the proper name.[16] The name of the event, which is in turn named by the subject, both proclaims the Two and stitches it together in the Oneness of presentation. But this Oneness of presentation, like the name, only comes through splitting the situation. In other words, a subject does not just split the situation through decision, but also creates a line of presentation following the event through a process Badiou calls 'forcing'. Essentially the creation of a language of the event, this 'forcing', decides on the effects of the event, even as the event and its fidelity remain under the Two and are incompletely presented. Thus, within the simultaneous structure and dislocation of being, the subject's will and action guarantee the being of the event and the availability to knowledge of its consequences. '[A] subject is at the intersection, via its language, of knowledge and truth.'[17] Antiphilosophy threatens Badiou because it offers a theory of the subject congruent to his own but articulated within a very different philosophical vocabulary and played for very different philosophical stakes. Despite the emphasis on ontology and the formal structures of math in Badiou's system of thought, the subject guarantees all knowledge. And if Badiou gets the subject ever so slightly wrong, his philosophy, by its own admission, cannot guarantee its own knowledge.

Antiphilosophy: An introduction

In an essay entitled 'L'anti-philosophie: Lacan et Platon', Badiou defines antiphilosophy as an 'apparatus of duplicity',[18] a discourse that claims double status: it separates from philosophy in order to condition it, desiring to join the generic procedures of love, politics, science and art.[19] At the same time it joins philosophical discourse in elaborating theories of the subject, being, truth and ethics. '"Anti-philosophy" refers to the ambiguity of these two relationships, one of distance, the other of crossing'.[20] In L'Antiphilosophie de Wittgenstein, Badiou describes antiphilosophy not as duplicitous, but as self-destructive, not in terms of its relation to philosophy, but in terms of its philosophical auto-vasectomy, which it operates through a set of philosophical or rhetorical moves. The first is a 'linguistic, logical, and genealogical critique of the sentences of philosophy. A destitution of the category of truth'.[21] The second is defining philosophy as '[. . .] an act, for which the telling of stories about truth is rainment, propaganda, and lie'.[22] And the third is '[. . .] the call made against the philosophical act, for another act, radically new [. . .] this unheard-of act would destroy the philosophical act, while at the same time clarifying its noxiousness'.[23] The final effect of these three moves is the emptying out of the category of truth and investment of meaning in the antiphilosophical act, denying the capacity of structures of language, and of the philosophical argumentation that relies on them to respond to or communicate the most important aspects of reality: 'The antiphilosophical act consists of letting what there is show itself, given that "what there is" is precisely that which not a single true proposition can say'.[24] In the face of the furtive character and enormity of the antiphilosophical act, truth becomes either bald 'empirical verification' (Wittgenstein)[25] or only a potential result of the act itself (Nietzsche).[26] In either case, meaning is elsewhere than in truth, beyond the world and in purified language (Wittgenstein),[27] or beyond the world and in the speaking subject (Nietzsche).[28] Ultimately, Badiou argues, this antiphilosophical act vanishes, leaving nothing but its 'madness' (Nietzsche)[29] or its 'negative preparation' (Wittgenstein).[30]

Badiou argues that the separation of truth and meaning is at once the great gift and the great risk of antiphilosophy. In separating the two, the antiphilosopher prepares the true site of philosophical modernity: the philosophical defense and elucidation of truth without recourse to meaning. However, the cut between truth and meaning, once made, contains the temptation to choose the wrong side, as the antiphilosophers end up doing ('[. . .] [T]he antiphilosophical act is *without truth*').[31] Because the writings of antiphilosophers make an argument only as a means to proclaim an act, ultimately the only means to judge the act, the only guide to the effectiveness and authenticity of their antiphilosophy is their own life, their life as an 'existential singularity'.[32] The sense of antiphilosophy as written artefact is found in the act of the antiphilosopher. 'The antiphilosopher therefore necessarily speaks in his own name, and must show this "own" as actual proof of his saying'.[33] Because of this, antiphilosophy is intensely autobiographical in content and confessional in nature: confession '[. . .] is itself a sign of the power of the act'.[34] Furthermore, the writing of antiphilosophy is itself the antiphilosophical act, but with a twist: the showing of the 'own' as proof of the saying has the paradoxical effect of making the writer vanish.[35] Nietzsche becomes the in-human operation 'Nietzsche'[36] and must contain the world, including the past and future,[37] and the Wittgensteinian subject is conceived not in terms of substance, but as 'what belongs to the world, not as one of its elements, but as its boundary'.[38]

Badiou substitutes for the clarifying, radical powers of the act the persistence of a determined, creative subject. This subject names the event while it is still indiscernible, in the realms of art (poetry) and math, but also in politics and love. Truth, not meaning, is subjective, or rather, truth and subjectivity are the same thing. '[. . .] [T]ruth is a process, and not an illumination'[39] and because of this, for truth to last, the subject must last, and last even as the identity and reality of the event constantly is being put into question. In traversing these points, the subject must rely on 'a belief (that) occurs in the form of knowledge'.[40] The subject must know, even as he proclaims in the hesitant future anterior, that his declaration is truth. But the only guarantee of this truth is the subject's existence. And so, '[i]n this sense, the subject is confidence in itself'.[41] As such, truth can both *be*, and be sustained over time. Antiphilosophers, Badiou argues, not only deny the being and sustainability of truth, but destroy the subject that makes such being possible.

Saintliness and antiphilosophy

Badiou uses 'saintly' to describe antiphilosophy and antiphilosophers as reliably as any homerian epithet. To take the most obvious case, his book on Paul of Tarsus is titled *Saint Paul*. Though he does not refer to Paul as 'Saint Paul' within the text, he does affirm in passing that '[. . .] Paul *is* a saint'[42] in the same breezy way he describes him as an '[. . .] antiphilosopher of genius [. . .]'.[43] The link between antiphilosophy and saintliness is also tightly drawn in the case of thinkers not already canonized by the Catholic Church. The original title of Badiou's essay, republished in 2009 as 'L'antiphilosophie de Wittgenstein', was 'Silence, solipsisme, sainteté: L'antiphilosophie de Wittgenstein' ('Silence, Solipsism, Saintliness: The Antiphilosophy of Wittgenstein'). Wittgenstein, of course, is known to have a long and fraught relationship with Catholicism, but in 'Casser en deux l'histoire du monde?' ('Breaking in Two the History of the World?') Badiou also connects Nietzsche, not known for his appreciation of Christianity, to saintliness. Nietzsche is a 'prince of contemporary antiphilosophy' in part because 'there is something princely in his way of governing, by a sort of interior saintliness, the radical peril of his act'.[44]

For Badiou, '[t]he religion of the antiphilosophers is a material that, holding back from philosophy, they seize upon to name the singularity of their act'.[45] Religion is not the source of antiphilosophy, but is rather a proxy for the essential innovation of antiphilosophy, the singularity of the act. Furthermore, both the religiousness and the singularity of the antiphilosophical act flow from the fact that (for Nietzsche, Wittgenstein and Paul) the antiphilosophical act takes the form of a decision for life. For Wittgenstein, '[t]he archi-aesthetical act is that which decides God against death'.[46] The 'archi-political act of Nietzsche must itself decide life against God'.[47] And Paul '[brings] about through the event an unqualified affirmation of life against the reign of death and the negative'.[48] To a certain way of thinking, antiphilosophers produce or actualize religion by life and thought: they re-vivify religion and turn it into God: 'The act is that through which the word "God" acquires meaning'.[49] But the meaningfulness of God is internal to the categories produced by the necessities of the antiphilosophical fight against philosophy; 'God', for the antiphilosophers, is less transcendent than tactical.

However, the unicity of God does help illustrate the specific singularity of the antiphilosophical act: the antiphilosophical act is singular because it represents a kind of complete achievement of the subject, such that the fullness of the subject comes to its rightful place, coincident with the fullness of the world. Like God, the subject must uniquely contain and border all things. According to Badiou, in the thought of Wittgenstein this coincidence is a given, the work of antiphilosophy is only to realize it. 'The uniqueness of the subject is coextensive to that of the world: "I am my own world" [T.5.63], and it is only "existing", structured, through the world'.[50] For Nietzsche this coincidence must be created: in the subject's arduously claimed rupture of the world lie the new subject and the new world, which by fact of their goodness coincide. Badiou describes the 'madness' (folie) of Nietzsche as '[. . .] he is in some fashion, on both sides of it, that he is the name not only of what proclaims the event, not only the name of the rupture, but ultimately the name of the world itself'.[51] For Nietzsche, God is doctrine, morality, the frozen, dead truth, and so it is the name for the dead world that the singularity of the antiphilosophical act breaks into. But this first dead world is as equally included in the antiphilosophical act as the new live one: '[. . .] ultimately there must be the disinterested fiction of the creation in entirety, not only of the new world, but also of the old one'.[52] To produce this kind of 'God' the antiphilosophical act must be singular. Because it produces 'God' it must be saintly. If self, world and God are all achieved in the act then it is true that the act testifies to the most radical singularity possible, a kind of armed solipsism.

One can understand why Badiou, devoted to infinity as well as persistence, would object to the tragic nature of antiphilosophical subjectivity. For Badiou, the subject is not destroyed by his fidelity, but created by it. And one can also understand why this self-sacrifice would be called saintly: even today, martyrs do not need posthumous miracles to be beatified. But the explosive character of the revolutionary act is not the only or even the most profound reason for the saintliness of antiphilosophy. Antiphilosophers are singular, not only in the sense of being extraordinary, or inassimilable, but in the much more ordinary sense of being set apart, of being single, of being alone.

> As part of the claim to exist at the height of their antiphilosophical act, Nietzsche and Wittgenstein are, one and the other, completely pledged to solitude, and each one wants to show this solitude. But they carry this out in opposite directions. The first exhibits the saintliness of an unfathomable affirmation. The second, the saintliness of the one who renounces the unspeakable and vile authority of death in favor of 'the mystical element'.[53]

This quotation equates saintliness with 'shown solitude'. And again, this intuitively fits with the figure of the saint: saints, as a rule, are celibate creatures. In many ways this shown solitude encapsulates antiphilosophy – the necessity of auto-biography, the act that cannot be shared – antiphilosophical singularity is indeed a kind achieved solitude, displayed as fulness. However, Badiou is not referring to this, at least, not primarily. Solitude, for him, means to be 'seul', that is, single, not in a relationship. To put it simply, antiphilosophers hate women.

> Have we ever seen more appalling people, in their explicit statements about women, than Pascal (did he ever notice anyone other than his sister?) Rousseau (the Sophie of Emile!) Kierkegaard (the neurosis of marriage!) Nietzsche (let's not even mention it!) or Wittgenstein (on this particular point the half-openness of a half-homosexuality).[54]

This may seem a small, unsurprising point; in general, philosophers speak of women even less than they speak of love. But Badiou's complaints about women-hating antiphilosophers[55] are not about philosophy's ordinary misogyny. They are about the (in)ability to fall in love. The examples speak less to misogyny than to failed or abortive relationships. Wittgenstein's homosexuality is suspicious because Badiou sees it as a failure to commit: 'the half-openness of a half-homosexuality'. Antiphilosophy, while claiming to join one of the four generic procedures, seems to cut itself off from the most important one: love. And since, for Badiou, love is the only generic procedure in which a majority of people can hope to attain subjectivity, to be unable to fall in love is grave indeed.

Love and the event

For Badiou, love is necessarily romantic love. More specifically, it is an implicitly sexed life-long partnership flowing from romantic love: the model is traditional marriage. Love is '[. . .] first of all, a lasting construction. Let's say that love is a stubborn adventure'.[56] And this construction is immanent, the making of a world, 'a creative existence' out of the 'absolute difference that exists between two individuals'.[57] The coming-into-existence of a love has the form and order of a truth procedure as described in *Being and Event*. There is first the event (in this case, the encounter) then the naming of the event (the declaration of love in what Badiou calls the 'Scène des Deux' (the Scene of the Two)) and then the fidelity to the event, taking the form of the traversal of 'points', challenges that threaten, and then reaffirm, the validity and even existence of the encounter. Love is both a declaration of faith in happenstance, in the effects of a purely random encounter, and an almost-godly creative endeavour, a chance to fix the intensity of the encounter in the humdrum of daily life, a chance to 'inscribe this eternity in time'.[58] This endeavour, this faithfulness to the encounter gives rise to a shared subjectivity. In love, '[s]he and I are incorporated into this single Subject, the subject of love'.[59] This subject is a fully fledged Badiouian subject, worthy of a place in *Being and Event*: 'I claim that love is indeed what I call in my own philosophical jargon a "truth procedure", which is to say, an experience in which a certain kind of truth is constructed. This truth is the truth about the

Two. The truth of difference as such'.[60] This truth of 'difference as such' is a little bit different than most other truth: it speaks of the faithful subject as constantly divided from itself. In other words, the unique subject of love is the Two of love as it exists in constant negotiation, a constant effort to live one's own life from the perspective of the other person: '[Love] is a life that is constructed, no longer from the one's point of view, but from the point of view of the Two'.[61] Only love is a subjectivity built around the breaking of the subject: the faithfulness particular to it is simultaneously an un-making and a making of the subject.

The constantly negotiated and reworked subject of love means that love also has a distinctive relation to the event. 'The declaration [of Love] solidifies into a name that the encounter has for being the void of disjunction. The Two that lovingly operates is rightly the name of the disjunctive in its disjunction'.[62] In his stipulation that the Two of love names the disjuntive as such, Badiou claims that love is but a process that has the same being as the event. And, as we have seen before, the event has for being both the void and the site it comes from: 'The undecidability of the event's belonging to the situation can be interpreted as a double function. On the one hand, the event would evoke the void; on the other hand, it would interpose itself between the void and itself'.[63] In the situation, the first moment of its presentation, the event splits itself. But in the moment of decision, of the event's naming, the event is also split: the decision stabilizes the event through pairing it with its site. 'Every event is thus given, on the statist surface of the decision, as an excrescence whose structure is a Two without concept'.[64] But the coincidence between the form of love and the form of the event means that love is the concept of the Two. The being of the event, as Two, is Love, or to reverse the equation, one could say that Love is the rarest of all things, an event that persists over time.

The nature of love as a continual event would explain the extravagant claims that Badiou makes for love: if the fidelity that constitutes truth instantiates universality, Badiou claims that love, in turn, guarantees the universality of truth. 'The main thing is that love, as I said, is the guarantor of the universal, since it alone sheds light on disjunction as the single law of a situation'.[65] The fact that the 'Two' of love and the repeated Twos of the event are congruent is not happenstance – love, in fact, is the only way in which a human can understand that the splitting of a situation can in effect guarantee its infinite perdurance. 'One, Two, infinity, such is the numericity of the procedure in love'.[66] Just as the infinity of being only enters presentation through the gap opened up by the event's split and doubling at the edge of presentation, so can the infinity of truth only come from the gap in the subject, a gap that is completely actualized in the single subject that is the subject to love, composed of two human lives.

From the perspective of Badiou's philosophical account of love, disgust at the perpetually single antiphilosophers becomes both more comprehensible and more puzzling. Comprehensible, because to be without access to love effectively implies all the other criticisms that Badiou makes of the antiphilosophers: no universality, no truth and no engagement with infinity – no persistence through time. But puzzling too. After all, the main criticism of antiphilosophers was the violent nature of their act, the tragedy implied by the split in the self. In the same way that love installs the subject by making him live through not-him and thereby creating the world, the act was supposed to cut the world in two, to end it and re-constitute it. In Badiou's analysis, the splitting was objectionable because it was the splitting of the world, which would imply the end of the world, the annihilation of the subject. However, in love we see that not every splitting of the subject leads to an annihilation of world. In some cases, it can legitimately lead to creation. Why is Badiou so sure that the split proper to the antiphilosophical act will in fact do this? Perhaps it is for the very simple reason that in the subject of Love, there are two people from the beginning – it is only when they come together that they are split. But this is not a valid response. As we have seen, the advent of the standard (single) subject in the process of subjectification also 'takes the form of the Two'.[67]

> Subjectivization, the singular configuration of a rule, subsumes the Two that is under a proper name's absence of signification. [...] What the proper name designates here is that the subject, as local situated configuration, is neither the intervention nor the operator of fidelity, but the advent of their Two, that is, the incorporation of the event into the situation in the mode of the generic procedure.[68]

Though the subject may be a 'singular configuration of a rule' it is only singular because of the Two that exists to be subsumed, the subject is the 'advent of their Two'. One could argue that the antiphilosopher's split, instead of being annihilation of the subject, could equally be seen as an affirmation of the fundamental nature of the subject: as a process whereby a Two becomes singularly public, presented in excess of the state. Antiphilosophy would thus be re-habilitated in a Badiouian manner, using Badiou's vocabulary.

Badiou himself does not take this path. One might also surmise that the antiphilosopher's subjectivity is objectionable because of its supposed directionality: the achieved one of the antiphilosopher's singular subjectivity tends towards the void of the Two, as opposed to what Badiou seems to describe as the fundamentally unifying function of love. But here again, there is a problem. For Badiou, void is the creative element, not the world; the void is the name of being; only the shocking appearance of the void (the One that is not) is able to produce infinity. 'The Two rears up through the invasion of the one, an invasion which leads at once, without mediation, to infinity.'[69] One could well argue that the void left in the aftermath of an antiphilosophical act invites infinity all the more firmly into the world.

So what is wrong with antiphilosophy? We return to Badiou's final criticism of antiphilosophers: they cannot fall in love. Furthermore, they cannot fall in love because they cannot approach women. Antiphilosophers split, but they do not fall in love: they are objectionable because their effraction is un-sexed: in their lack of approach to women they are simultaneously too masculine and too androgynous (because they have no access to the difference of sex at all). But then, what is wrong with masculine androgyny?

Two subject positions and universal humanity

In the introduction to Badiou's most systematic text on love, an essay entitled 'Qu'est-ce l'amour?' ('What is Love?'), Badiou makes this startling claim: 'First of all, I will show that the significant link between "woman" and "love" involves all of humanity, even going so far as to legitimize its concept'.[70] He goes on to argue that the identity of the female sex (which he clarifies, is only identified within the Two of love, and does not have relation with the biological sexuation of the person carrying this subject position), its relation to the function of castration, and its experience of humanity, guarantees humanity as a site that can welcome truth.[71] In this way, femininity is not only produced by love, but guarantees love.

To recapitulate, love is the process whereby the truth of multiplicity, that is, of the void, manifests itself as truth within being. 'Love fractures the One according to the Two. And it is this point from which it is thinkable that, even though worked-over by disjunction, the situation is really such that there were something of the One, and that it's this One-multiple that all truth makes sure of.'[72] But in this universality, love presents a problem: it creates a single truth that must be equally available to two distinct subject positions. Badiou claims that these subject positions are named 'man' and 'woman'. The nature of these positions is dependent on their different visions of humanity; each one experiences, within the universal support to truth that is humanity, a different relationship between the generic procedures of politics, science, love and art. Badiou, in the course of his argument, has determined that love has four functions – four necessary dispositions for the fidelity. They are: wandering, immobility, imperative and narration. The distribution of these necessities into the 'Two' of love 'axiomatically' produces definitions of the sexes: '[. . .] because "man" will be axiomatically defined as the position in love that couples necessity and immobility, while woman is that which couples wandering and narration'.[73]

Love is a generic procedure, and each individual love is a single truth procedure, of a single subject, carried out by two humans, who receive their gendered identities through the process of love. This means that their knowledge, their carrying out, the forcings and the faithfulness to the event of love will never coincide.

> The two will operate as though disconnected. There will have been only one love-truth of the situation, but the (truth) procedure of this

uniqueness develops in the disjunction that it makes into truth. The two sexes don't not know each other, they know each other veridically in a disjunctive fashion.[74]

The one truth of love is incommunicable between the two halves of the subject. Yet it is shared between the halves; the couple produces one love.

The truth of love can only be communicated through 'Humanity'. 'Humanity is that which supports the infinite singularity of truths that inscribe themselves in these types (the generic procedures). Humanity is the historial body of truths.'[75] Humanity for Badiou is less biological, or animalian, and more ontological. That is to say that all ontological existence that participates in the production of truth can be said to be, in some sense, human. The human function testifies to truth, at the same time that truth testifies to humanity. It is a 'historial' body that allows for a narration, tells a story (*histoire*) about truth. (Badiou writes Humanity as H(x), x being a subject/truth procedure.) At the level of humanity, the disjunction between the genders expresses itself in the different kind of stories that each tells about truth: each gender speaks differently. 'The feminine statement targets being as such. Such is, in love, her destination, which is ontological. The masculine statement targets the change of number, the painful split of the One by the postulation of the Two. It is essentially logical.'[76] Badiou later goes on to say that:

> These schemas shed light on the fact that the feminine representation of humanity would be at once conditional and tied together, which allows for a more complete perception, and when necessary a more sudden right to inhumanity. Whereas the masculine representation is at once symbolic and separating, which can make for a good amount of indifference, but also a larger capacity to conclude.[77]

Already, we begin to see the importance of femininity for humanity. Feminine discourse is ontological: humanity is the ontological support for a truth procedure. Feminine representation is 'conditional and tied together' and love is what makes a single truth procedure out of the repeated disjunction of the event and fidelity to it. The stories that women tell are uniquely suited to the humanity function, so much so that Badiou is led to posit (axiomatically, once again) that '[. . .] a woman is the (male or female) one for whom the subtraction of love *devalorizes* H(x) in its other types of science, politics, and art. Conversely, the existence of love deploys H(x) in all of its types, and first of all in the most connected, or crossed'.[78] Love makes women come alive, experience humanity, and, lack of love makes them doubt the existence of truth. Whereas for men, love is a truth like the others, and any kind of truth will do for humanity. In other words, since love, which makes truth out of disjunction, is the guarantee of universality, the feminine need for love to justify humanity testifies ontologically to the universality of humanity. 'The feminine position demands for H(x) a guarantee of universality. It only ties the components of H together under this condition.'[79] Women bring universality together with the ontology that supports truth, which means, according to Badiou's analysis, that his philosophy is feminine, and that he is a woman.

By way of conclusion: Badiou, the Two and antiphilosophy

Badiou's argument about the sexes, resting as it does, at almost every step, on axiomatic definitions, is not very strong, or about as strong as Lacan's argument about the inaccessibility of the 'Two' that Badiou demolishes in 'Sujet et Infini'. But the implications of it are interesting because they clarify several movements within Badiou's thought, not least of which is his ambivalent relationship with antiphilosophy. If Badiou is, at the level of his philosophy, a woman, his indignation at the antiphilosophers' distain for women becomes immediately comprehensible. For Badiou, lack of openness to women would mean a fundamental distrust of infinity. But this distrust of infinity refers, in the context of love, to a too-great desire for wholeness, for completeness. The problem with the antiphilosophers is finally not the structure of the act, or their lack of fidelity, but it is their inability to break in relation to another, to cease from being their proper world. As Tracey McNulty writes, summarizing Badiou's account of love, 'In this sense, love does not so much interrupt or question the subject's integrity as complete a subject whose closedness is its lack'.[80] The saintly antiphilosopher would be he who, in his desire to contain all things, cannot be completed.

But I would like to point out that the kind of femininity that Badiou claims for his philosophy is, in another way, also a masculinity. Feminine thinking is constructed through love, which, at the level of fidelity, if not of sexed bodies, is always heterosexual. To 'think feminine' is also to think primarily heterosexually. And this means, paradoxically, that femininity opens up a masculinity for Badiou, one that he primarily accesses through the oft-commented-upon virile mood of his philosophy, the force of belief and the force of will that is required by his subject. And so, to criticize the antiphilosophers for a lack of openness towards the feminine is also to criticize them for not being masculine enough: to not will or believe enough. But at the same time, the turn that Badiou's philosophy operates, from logic to ontology to truth to humanity, or from masculinity to femininity to heterosexuality to universality, constructs antiphilosophy as its opposite: whether Badiou takes the position of male or female, Badiou needs antiphilosophy as its own hetero-sexed philosophical partner. Without a partner, however hidden or opaque, Badiou would foreclose himself from the most accessible access point to the Two given to humans. To have his fidelity, the philosopher needs the saint.

Notes

1 I would like to thank Colby Dickinson for his patience during the editorial process, and Chris Hackett for letting me know about this project.

2 Alain Badiou, *Being and Event* (trans. Oliver Feltham, London: Continuum, 2009), p. 27.

3 Ibid., p. 26.

4 Ibid., p. 27.

5 Ibid.

6 Ibid.

7 Ibid., p. 26.

8 Alain Badiou, *L'Antiphilosophie de Wittgenstein* (Caen: Nous, 2009), p. 21. If a French version of a source is cited, the translations are my own.

9 Badiou, *Being and Event*, p. 393.

10 Alain Badiou, *Saint Paul: The Foundation of Universalism* (trans. Ray Brassier, Stanford: Stanford University Press, 2003), p. 7.

11 '[. . .] the void is the latent errancy of the being of presentation'. Badiou, *Being and Event*, p. 76.

12 Badiou, *Being and Event*, p. 209.

13 Ibid., p. 205.

14 Ibid., p. 208.

15 Ibid., p. 510.

16 Ibid., p. 393.

17 Ibid., p. 406.

18 Alain Badiou, 'L'antiphilosophie: Lacan et Platon', *Conditions* (Paris: Seuil, 1992), pp. 306–26, p. 325.

19 In the essay the list of domains is the following: politics, poetry, love and science. Badiou does not state explicitly that he is speaking of generic procedures (ibid., p. 325).

20 Badiou, 'L'antiphilosophie', p. 325.

21 Badiou, *Antiphilosophie*, p. 17.

22 Ibid.

23 Ibid.

24 Ibid., p. 21.

25 Ibid., pp. 43–44.

26 Alain Badiou, *Casser en deux l'histoire du monde?* (Paris: le Perroquet, 1992), p. 14. Accessed via Scribd : www.scribd.com/doc/41941206/Casser-en-Deux-l-Histoire-Du-Monde

27 Badiou, *Antiphilosophie*, pp. 44, 100.

28 Badiou, *Casser en deux*, pp. 16, 18–19.

29 Ibid., p. 7.

30 Badiou, *Antiphilosophie*, p. 89.

31 Ibid., p. 55.

32 Ibid., p. 28.

33 Ibid., see also Alain Badiou, *Casser en deux* p. 7.

34 Ibid., p. 87.

35 Ibid., p. 89.

36 Badiou, *Casser en deux*, p. 8.

37 Ibid., p. 15.
38 Badiou, *Antiphilosophie*, p. 78. See also Bruno Bosteels, 'Radical Antiphilosophy', *Filozofski vestnik* 2 (2008), pp. 155–87. http://filozofskivestnikonline.com/index.php/journal/article/view/54. Bosteel's account of antiphilosophy emphasizes the centrality of the act to this strain of thinking. He argues that 'antiphilosophy teaches us that the real danger, including for Badiou's own philosophy, is . . . the radicalism of the pure event as absolute beginning or the treatment of the event as some kind of archievent, that is to say, in the end, the conflation of the event with the act'. Bosteels, 'Radical Antiphilosophy', p. 177. This essay was heavily influenced by an early reading of Bosteel's text. Though our arguments differ in focus, our texts do complement each other.
39 Badiou, *Saint Paul*, p. 15.
40 Badiou, *Being and Event*, p. 397.
41 Ibid., p. 387.
42 Badiou, *Saint Paul*, p. 39. Emphasis Badiou.
43 Ibid., p. 108.
44 Badiou, *Casser en deux*, p. 24. Bosteels also notes the connection of antiphilosophy and saintliness. Bosteels, 'Radical Antiphilosophy', p. 175.
45 Badiou, *Antiphilosophie*, p. 25.
46 Ibid., p. 30.
47 Badiou, *Antiphilosophie*, p. 31.
48 Badiou, *Saint Paul*, p. 72.
49 Badiou, *Antiphilosophie*, p. 83.
50 Ibid., p. 80.
51 Badiou, *Casser en deux*, p.15
52 Ibid., p. 16.
53 Badiou, *Antiphilosophie*, p. 31.
54 Ibid., p. 35. Cited in Bosteels, 'Radical Antiphilosophy', p. 166.
55 See also Bosteels, 'Radical Antiphilosophy', pp. 165–67.
56 Alain Badiou and Nicolas Truong, *Eloge de l'amour* (Paris: Flammarion, 2009), p. 41.
57 Ibid., p. 65.
58 Ibid., p. 53.
59 Ibid., p. 29.
60 Ibid., p. 47.
61 Ibid., pp. 38–39.
62 Badiou, 'L'antiphilosophie', p. 263.
63 Badiou, *Being and Event*, p. 182.
64 Ibid., p. 209.
65 'Badiou, 'Qu'est-ce l'amour', *Conditions* (Paris: Seuil, 1992), pp. 253–73, p. 272.
66 Ibid., p. 264.
67 Badiou, *Being and Event*, p. 393.
68 Ibid., p. 393.
69 Badiou, 'L'antiphilosophie', p. 304.
70 Badiou, 'Qu'est-ce l'amour', p. 254.
71 See also the discussion of sexual differentiation in Alain Badiou, 'Sujet et infini', *Conditions* (Paris: Seuil, 1992), pp. 287–306.
72 Ibid., p. 264.

73 Ibid., pp. 267–68.
74 Ibid., p. 269.
75 Ibid., p. 259.
76 Ibid., p. 269. Cited in Tracy McNulty, 'Feminine Love and the Pauline Universal', *Alain Badiou: Philosophy and its Conditions* (ed. Gabriel Riera, Albany, NY: State University of New York Press, 2005), pp. 185–212, p. 190.
77 Ibid., p. 272.
78 Ibid., p. 271.
79 Ibid., p. 273.
80 Tracy McNulty, 'Feminine Love', p. 197.

14

La Nouvelle Philosophie . . .: On the Philosophical Significance of Sanctity in Jean-Yves Lacoste's *Experience and the Absolute*

W. Chris Hackett

Your silence is an ecstasy of sound/and your nocturnals blaze upon the day.

GEOFFREY HILL, *'Pavana Dolorosa'*

What does the saint have to do with philosophy?

In answer to our guiding question we shall turn to the best of contemporary guides, Jean-Yves Lacoste, and to his *Experience and the Absolute* (1994) in particular, a book which proffers a significant conceptual role to the fundamental theme of the Mystical Doctor, St John of the Cross (the 'dark night'), and even poses the figures of the saint and the 'holy fool' as the (philosophical) 'subject' par excellence.

It is perhaps a well-kept secret that Hans Urs von Balthasar considered that the way to overcome the modern invention of the bifurcation of 'spirituality' and 'theology', and even, more broadly, of 'sanctity' and critical reflection on human being in the world in general, was, in the first place, through a 'phenomenology' of the saints.[1] Yet if Balthasar considered the saint the ideal theologian (and the theologian, in many respects, the ideal philosopher)[2], it is perhaps not stretching words too far to suggest that Lacoste considers the saint the ideal philosopher, inasmuch, at least, as the saint is the human subject stretched to its most radical limits and thereby *discloses* to us something – indeed, *proposes* it as the essential thing – about our humanity that otherwise remains hidden. We shall have to see for ourselves . . . But surely it is here, with the saint in particular, that we have well reached what Lacoste calls the 'frontier zone' between philosophy and theology, a frontier in which phenomenology, as the method that recognizes no a priori limits in the object(s) of its investigation, is well-suited indeed.[3]

To make a first approach towards understanding the philosophical significance of the theological category of sanctity – and a first approach is certainly all we can accomplish here – I will examine the key image of the mystical theology of St John of the Cross, the 'dark night', and its use in Lacoste's *Experience and the Absolute*. The path of the following investigation is therefore straightforward: (1) an approach to the place of the dark night in the thought of John of the Cross will lead to (2) a brief, commentary-style reflection on Lacoste's text, seeking a general appreciation of his philosophical use of the Sanjuanist image. A concluding remark will take the perspective that Lacoste seems to lend us: the figure of the saint, whose 'liturgical' being-before-God in the 'dark night' of faith discloses a freedom that is nothing if not a 'sign of contradiction' to both an atheist world-horizon and a pagan, sacralized earth, represents – better, enacts or incarnates – the identification of the darkness of faith with the excess of light coming from beyond the strictures of world and earth. If for St John of the Cross the 'dark night' is the paradoxical presence of a blinding divine light, then for Lacoste it represents a path that stretches philosophical reflection to its limits, and beyond them.

St John of the Cross and the Dark Night

In the *Dark Night* John tersely defines his theme: 'This dark night is an inflow of God into the soul' (DN II.v.1).[4] It seems that the pain of the Dark Night is a result of the very presence of God, present in a manner totally invisible to the soul. He calls therefore the presence of divine wisdom to the soul 'night and darkness' as well as 'affliction and torment'. He gives two reasons for this wounding invisibility of the divine presence: 'First, because of the height of the divine wisdom which exceeds the capacity of the soul. Second, because of the soul's baseness and impurity; and on this account it is painful, afflictive, and also dark for the soul' (DN II.v.2). This absent-presence of God purifies the soul, in a process of separating it from both sensual and intellectual attachments that come between the soul and God. The objective and subjective dimensions of the darkness interpenetrate one another here, and, further, the latter takes its ultimate meaning from the former.[5]

However, it is also true to say that the night's 'general meaning' is, as Karl Wojtyla says, that it 'signifies the privation of the pleasure of any appetite or desire'.[6] Thus for John there are different nights for different appetites; the basic division being, of course, between the sensual and intellectual nights, according to the two basic dimensions of the composite human being. Yet the Night is, from this perspective, whether sensual or intellectual, located finally at the site of desire that traverses both dimensions, particularly the 'faculty's' own emptiness, and the soul's as well insofar as desire presides over the whole soul as its principle of movement. So, for John, the presence of the divine teacher in the Dark Night teaches the soul that it must, to quote Kierkegaard from the *Postscript*, learn to 'relate to the Absolute absolutely', that is, to strive for a relation to God that ever strives to correspond to his absoluteness, and therefore to let go of all of the will's disordered relations, its prizing of finite objects at the expense of its true end – living as if God were merely a 'thing' in competition with other things, which is precisely what sin elects to believe. So St John says: 'The necessity to pass through this dark night [. . .] to attain divine union with God arises from the fact that all of a person's *attachments to creatures* are pure darkness in God's sight. Clothed in these affections, people are incapable of the enlightenment and dominant fullness of God's pure simple light; first they must reject them' (*Ascent*, I.4.1, emphasis added). This is the case because, insofar as creatures are already in themselves 'darkness' compared to God, considered in themselves, they bear no likeness to God, since, John says epigrammatically, 'two contraries cannot coexist in the same subject' (*Ascent*, I.4.2). Again, it is the mystery of human freedom that makes the creature a 'contrary' to God, which, *in* God, it is not. Such a fallen perspective is an illusion of the human will. The 'competition' lies at the level of human affections.

Given this broad meaning of Dark Night as located in the creature, still the central point is that this blindness and purgation is caused by *God's* 'inflow' in the soul. Thus it is right to interpret the Dark Night as a lack in the creature, but only insofar as God is 'secretly' present to it. The desire truly to 'awaken' to the real presence of God in the soul, to truly taste, touch and see God as he truly is, is the fuel of the 'burning' passion of the Dark Night; the impossibility of ever finally reaching a settled end in the pursuit is its agony. The unity of these poles *in the encounter* with the living God, finally, is ecstasy:

> And if I rejoice, Lord,
> in the hope of seeing you,
> yet seeing I can lose you [*en ver que puedo perderte*]
> doubles my sorrow.
> Living in fear
> and hoping as I hope,
> I die because I do not die.[7]

Yet still, paradoxically, the end, spiritual union with God, is achieved, beyond sensing, as 'an understanding without understanding' [*de un entender no entendiendo*],[8] a 'loving communion' and 'intimate communication', a resolution of bliss as the soul receives itself in its loss of self in God.

Therefore the soul, until the end of its dark journey when it is thoroughly purified and united solely with God, must continually choose *between* the infinite and finite affections: it must, in other words, refuse to rest in any facile vision of a god who stands over against the things of the world. Thus, most importantly, and this perspective is often lost in interpretations of St John – and it cannot be emphasized enough – at the end of the Dark Night, when the soul achieves its union with God and is purified of all attachments in the world, it is truly 'awakened' and receives them back in a wholly new manner. Here the soul can freely 'relate to relative things relatively',[9] according to their proper mode, and enjoy the fulness of created things as they really are: totally transparent to the divine life. Here loving God and the creature are finally one and the same. The soul encounters an absolute reversal of intentionality as it 'knows these things better in God's being than in themselves'. In his last work, *The Living Flame of Love*, John utters these profound words: 'And here lies the remarkable delight of this awakening: The soul knows creatures through God and not God through creatures' (LF, IV.5). After the negation of everything, love remains – and in love nothing is lost.

So, it must never be lost to us that the Dark Night, though a preparation for the highest mystical union, is already a hidden participation in it, insofar as it is a result of God's hidden presence – under the sign of the cross, as we have already seen, and as necessary for the union as the cross is to Resurrection. For John, only perseverance through the slow torment of the Dark Night, to the point of a death to the attachments of the senses and of the intellect, can achieve the desired end of the soul, its resurrection to all things in God. One cannot rest in an abstract and as it were 'metaphysical' recognition of the non-competition of God and creatures; rather, such a 'vision' must be lived; we must be wounded by it and finally awoken to it. This thesis of St John is fueled by the same convictions, for example, as Augustine's conjectures about the resurrected body at the end of *Civitate Dei* (XXII.29), in which he speculates how, in the *eschaton*, the body and the whole world of things will no longer be an impediment to the vision of God, but rather paradoxically one with it.

The thematic of the night in *Experience and the Absolute*

Let us now turn to an examination of the role of St John's theme in *Experience and the Absolute*. The text is divided into two parts. There are two key paragraphs specifically on 'the night' (§§30 and 55) and one appears in each of the major parts of the book. In what follows I will offer, in a loosely commentary style, a description of the salient elements of the text, pausing for a deeper look at these two paragraphs and the role of their thematic in the text as a whole.

The first part, 'Man and His Place' (Chs 1–5), presents a phenomenology of man from the vantage of topology, in terms of 'place'. That is, for Lacoste, the question of the meaning of human being must be approached from the vantage of place, since to exist as human is to be somewhere, to be 'embodied' (§1). Now the first horizon of human *topos* is 'the world': we, as human beings, fundamentally 'inhere' in the world; we exist in the basic modality of 'being-in' (§2). Yet our inherence in the world is a dynamic paradox, for Lacoste: if a particular place is where human being is found, the world is our place. Thus the world seems to define us; it is our radical limit; it recedes in its appearance as the horizon of our place; the world precedes us and is greater than us; it is a power to which we are ultimately passive, but which is also the condition for the possibility of our opening up in place (§3). We are therefore at the same time not-at-home in the world: by opening to us, it threatens to open us in a radical manner (§4). Yet the world is not the only possibility of our human 'being-there'. Besides the world, there is also the earth, which, through its intimate play of the 'four-fold' dimension, earth and sky, mortals and gods, safely covers us and allows us the experience of being-at-home (§§5–6).

This rehearsal of Heideggerian themes is developed by Lacoste by allowing the essential Heideggerian options to exist side by side, in a sort of dialectic: the atheistic and pagan become two aspects of place, two fundamental possibilities or primary modes of human inherence. Lacoste notes from this vantage that corporeality, embodiment, is actually prior to world and earth: Because corporeality exists across world and earth, these become only two topological options, even if they are necessary for *Dasein* (§7). Yet it is also true that the tension of this dialectic points beyond itself to something else, another way of being human, of figuring place: the liturgical, a relation to the Absolute, above the four-fold of the earth, and beyond the closed-off world of sheer being-there (§§8, 12). The liturgical thus discloses itself as having everything to do with place, but it is concerned with the essential *excess* of place.

Essentially, liturgical dwelling refigures human inherence from being-there to being-toward (God) (§15). With this new possibility open, Lacoste offers a fascinating analysis of three possible modes of the liturgical's transgression of place: exclusion (the mystic's transcendence of the world's horizons), reclusion (the eremitic radical minimalization of place) and *dépaysement* (state of perpetual pilgrimage) (§§9–11). Each of these three liturgical modes sets aside the world and earth and thereby changes the way we relate to our embodiment. In other words, the world and earth are 'bracketed' and the liturgical subject finds itself dwelling on the very edge of worldly and earthly experience (§17). These liturgical transgressions call into question the definitiveness of all world-earth topologies by an act of *free decision* (a liturgical 'reduction') to dwell otherwise, an alternative possibility that enacts an overdetermination and symbolic subversion, not of place and corporeality per se, but rather of atheistic and pagan modes of immanence that, implicitly or explicitly deny the freedom of human being to elect its mode of being there, even to the transgression of place in the liturgical.

The essential point for us is that liturgy is figured *eschatologically*: this means it is paradoxically a historical work that exceeds history by bracketing world and earth and playing with place prior to their determinations; it does so primarily in a symbolical way and opens up to the possibility that the world and God are jointly given (p. 34). Because inherence – embodiment – is essentially an act of opening in the world that does not exhaust the possibilities of the human (signified by our perpetual 'restlessness' in the world), the act of opening to God, 'exposition', unfolds as a real possibility (§16). In other words, the worldly opening of inherence is a closure to the 'beyond being': our restlessness with this fact reveals that it does not tell us all that we (possibly) are. The exposition of liturgy is, in contrast to the dialectic of world and earth, essentially a 'non-experience' (§§19–22). The 'parousiac presence'[10] of God is only anticipated, expected, desired: a capacity for experience that is normally, and indeed normatively it seems, unfulfilled. Because of this, liturgical knowledge is not dominated by experience at all; it is rather fundamentally intellectual, *contra* Schleiermacher. Rather, it is a place of 'boredom', where 'nothing happens' (cf. p. 148). So, Lacoste says, liturgy is '*entr'acte*': it breaks open from within history but, paradoxically, history continues alongside it (cf. §§23, 31). As such, the liturgical 'I', in hope, is the 'eschatological I' (or 'soul', cf. §25), shaped by its expectation for the future that exceeds the 'absolute future' of being-toward-death and thereby refigures temporality as much as spatiality through the power of symbols. Here we can see most clearly Lacoste's basic *philosophical transposition* of biblical eschatology, for which, in the death and resurrection of Jesus Christ, the 'new age' or the 'last days' have already arrived, even though the 'present age' or 'history' itself continues 'as if' nothing fundamentally novel happened, as if, the *apocalypse* of resurrection of Jesus had no bearing on the processes intrinsic to history (dominated by the horizon of death, precisely as Heidegger said).

Further, the liturgical subject, though existing at the world's margins, is still responsible in the world (§§25–30): This is why liturgical conscience is 'unhappy': the tension between the world and the Absolute, in which the world 'comes between' the soul and God, is not even partly assuaged by the hope for a final reconciliation, but rather makes the liturgical conscience all the more anxious.[11] This is partly why the liturgical alone rigorously grounds the 'ethical meaning of facticity' – contra Levinas, whose ethical phenomenology is, according to Lacoste, too constricted: He takes a 'regional experience' and makes it the whole; he fails to see the rest of existence outside of moral obligation and therefore skews human being-in-the-world

(§28). It is tempting to offer the formulation here that the liturgical, with its basic eschatological categories, not ethics, is the real 'first philosophy' – or should we say 'last philosophy?'[12] For Lacoste, only liturgy *possibly* transcends regional experience, since it is precisely the distinctions of world/ earth/kingdom that fill the world with *Mitsein*, where Hegel's master and slave are potentially, and even sometimes actually reconciled as they 'pray together' in the church, which is open to all, without discrimination. So the work of liturgy and the labour of ethics are ultimately two poles of one (eschatological) structure, which Lacoste calls the 'Kingdom' (§37). Here liturgy's *divertissement* increases ethical anxiety and contributes a greater concern for the world; ethics, on the other hand, is a 'step back', that precedes the violence of history and anticipates the Kingdom (§29). Liturgy alone, then, by allowing the light of eternity to shine on every moment of existence, awakens one to the real importance of being-in-the-world and thereby invigorates one to ethical action. It is the transgression of the Kingdom into the present order of the world through the symbolic and unfulfilled mode of liturgy, that makes ethics all the more pressing.

Thus, Lacoste, for better or worse, has profoundly 'linked the destiny of liturgy to that of ethics' as the new, as it were, *duplex ordo* of the Kingdom. Yet how specifically do these two poles relate? Since liturgy cannot replace or totally enfold within its horizon the continual demand of ethics that comes with living in the world, liturgy must find time *entr'acte*. Since already we have seen that liturgy transgresses *topos*, and is both non-experience and non-event, Lacoste places it primarily under the sign of the vigil, the night of patient waiting, which is the 'kairos' of the liturgy and is juxtaposed with the daytime experience of ethics. Liturgy is unnecessary, rooted in a free decision, whereas ethics is absolutely unavoidable and never finished ('tragically infinite') insofar as we exist inescapably with others in the world where the justice of the Kingdom is only anticipated at best. It is paradoxically the radical superfluity of the liturgical which grounds the necessity of the ethical.

Faith in the night: With and without works

Hence §30, 'The Nocturnal Site of Liturgy', is primarily concerned with, as we have already mentioned, the coordination of 'the work of ethics and liturgical inoperativity' (p. 145). It seems that Lacoste wants to say that the liturgical dimension is forged in the night as it makes a place for being before God that the various authorities over our being-in-the-world have no hold. The 'night' therefore stands for the secret of human freedom. The vigil is the place where it is most dramatically realized. Liturgy, even as it is the 'highest work: *opus Dei*' (p. 78), is essentially 'useless' in the world. Specifically, liturgy resists modernity's 'equation of Being and doing [*de l'être et du faire*]' by refusing, that is, 'to enter into any logic of production in the name of a logic bound up with more urgent stakes'. The 'logic' of this resistance is described in this, the first paragraph on the thematic of the night.

With its essential distance safeguarded, Lacoste moves to the affirmative aspects of liturgy's praxis. The nocturnal character of liturgy signifies most importantly the distance of the praying person from history, the marginalization of place and in this way the rejection of the claim to supremacy of the world and earthly modes of inhering. Yet, even so, the one who prays anticipates the fulfilment of that very history itself. Human beings are still 'earthly' and even 'worldly': they are finite. The liturgical transgression or 'bracketing' of place does not undo the essentiality of place (and corporeity) to human being in the same way that Husserlian 'bracketing' does not undo or negate our thetic or natural attitude (but rather observes it) – and in the same way, further, that the final fulfilment of liturgical experience in the *dénouement* of the eschaton itself does not negate place and corporeity either (for there is, indeed, at the heart of eschatological hope itself a resurrection of the dead). We know what our true work in the world is only when we achieve the distance from which we can actually see it. The vigil, therefore, ultimately signifies in this respect 'the surplus of meaning we give to our humanity' (p. 79).

What the characterization of 'existence as vigil' prepares for is an understanding of the relation of liturgy and the world in relation to what Lacoste calls the 'originary' (§§33–37). The eschatological hope for the total completion of the work of ethics (justice) and the anticipation of the return of God (the unification of worldly and liturgical existence) are thus irreparably tied together since justice to and for the human other is only possible when the other is not a distraction from God (or vice versa . . .), that is, when the world, paradoxically, no longer comes between the soul and God. Ethics wishes and works for the Kingdom but can never fulfil it; liturgy is the 'conversion' that exposes this fact by admitting both the radical nature of evil that affects our every action and, by virtue of its possibility as a 'new beginning', is a request for and hope in forgiveness of the 'moral I' which always fails to fulfil its basic obligation. What this new beginning of liturgy points to is that the world and earth are 'initial diversions' themselves; it flips the whole presupposition of the originality of the atheistic world or pagan earth on its head; liturgy, precisely in its radical superfluity, 'subverts' the claim of ethics as fundamental, and calls into question the self-conception of the day of work as the most originary, and rather beckons human freedom to accept the possibility that liturgical existence, life lived, as Calvin said, *coram Deo*, is most fundamental to human being. Only the Kingdom is our true home; the fundamental 'restlessness' discovered in liturgy, finds its home there and 'subordinates our commerce with world and earth to our relation with the Absolute'. This restlessness proposes itself as the paradoxical mode of the manifestation of that very presence of the Kingdom. Liturgical *ipseity* precedes ethical subjectivity even as it waits in the dark for the fulfilment of that which we cannot achieve in the day, that which we must nevertheless ceaselessly strive to realize. Not only is it true that 'the circle that unites liturgical reason and ethical reason is the fundamental rhythm of existence, which, transgressing its native conditions, desires the accomplishment of the human beyond what can be derived from our facticity' (p. 76), but also, most importantly, '[l]iturgy, understood in its broadest sense, is the most human mode in which we can exist in the world or on the earth [. . .] beyond the historial play between world and earth, man has for his true *dwelling place* the *relation* he seals with God or that God seals with him' (p. 98). With these words, and with the basic lineaments of *the philosophical transposition of eschatology completed in the symbol of the night*, the first part of Lacoste's *disputatio* is brought to a close. And here we are prepared for the further elucidation of the eschatological that will now come.

A kingdom of fools

The second part of the book is an analysis of 'Fundamental Experience' (Chs 6–9), which further explores the paradoxes of the relation between liturgical non-experience and the experiences of world and earth (*Erlebnis*). Fundamental experience traverses across a path from the central determination of the night to its most radical (and therefore determinative) expression in the extravagance of the fool who dances along the edge of the world under the sign of the cross. To get to that point one must first acknowledge that since the excess of human capacity for experience beyond world and earth makes possible the description of liturgy as the possible heart of a fundamental understanding of the nature of humanity (the high note on which the first half of the text ended), the liturgical first brings both the immediacy of 'life' and facticity into question (§§39–40). Liturgy resides at a fundamental distance from the 'self-giving immediacy' of things, insofar as it is born of faith and governed by knowledge, which comes after the fact of existence and points out, in its excess, the veiling over of the Absolute that such an immediacy enacts. The strangeness of liturgy to the facticity of being-in-the-world, its nighttime contestation, even its 'contradiction' of it, reveals that liturgy is not a regional experience, since, in Lacoste's terms, liturgy proposes nothing less than an existence composed of what is absolutely essential to it (§40) – or, in other words, as we have seen, it makes a *claim*, or rather a *call* to human freedom out of the midst of its 'restlessness' to recognize it even in the poverty of its non-parousiac presence as its most native, that is 'most human' possibility.[13]

Yet the contingency of knowledge and existence is basic to factical existence, and the historical manifestation of the Absolute 'redistributes' the field of possibility by a direct reversal of inquiry: here we ourselves are put into question (§§41–42). This does not annul the modes of being in world and earth, but rather brings the whole dialectical structure of existence into question. Thus openness to eschatology becomes definitive of liturgical existence, the possibility of the fulfilment to our fragmentary, vacillating existence (§43). A first approach to how eschatology refigures the liturgical subject is the topic of a long excursion into Hegel's thought (§§44–52).

I can only bring forth a single essential point here. Hegel, according to Lacoste, teaches the liturgical subject, who dwells in both history and the new order of the Kingdom, to begin to answer the question of how the future shapes the present, by conceiving it primarily as a fixed perspective, or even by investing the whole of her present at every moment of its occurrence. Hegel's unity of the cross and Resurrection, what we ought to no doubt call an 'over-realized eschatology' (precisely in its collapse of eschatology into philosophy), though flawed, demonstrates, nevertheless, a crucially important eschatological notion. Hegel's problem, Lacoste says, is not, in the first place, that he brought into radical proximity the Resurrection and the cross, but that his eschatology is over-realized, without an interval between them (i.e. cross and Resurrection) as (relatively) discrete events, as they are for the liturgical I, though for which, to be sure, they are nevertheless reconciled in the *eschaton* – and thus manifest in the present if only symbolically and therefore by way of anticipation. Even so, Hegel, by contrast to Schleiermacher, rightly understands eschatology, in the present, as fundamentally related to knowledge, not experience: 'the Absolute is not something [man] feels, but someone he knows' (p. 132). For Lacoste, it is the proper relation between cross and Resurrection that helps us rightly configure the division of eschatology into the familiar categories of already/ not yet. Since history continues on after Good Friday, reconciled existence comes (invisibly) side-by-side with the world. Thus liturgical existence is shaped by its 'fragile' place between two worlds, as the 'next to last', or 'preeschatological' existence (Bonhoeffer's *die vorletzten Dinge*).[14]

Eschatology, or the 'Dazzling Darkness' of philosophy

Now we have rapidly reached the second great section on the thematic of the night. With the introduction of the 'next to last', the thematic of the night immediately takes on new and deeper significance (§55). As the sign of the next-to-last, inhabiting the interval between cross and Resurrection, night is a place of non-vision and non-feeling, experienced as a division 'which separates us both from the "earth" and the *eschaton* and returns us to knowledge (to faith) alone' (p. 146).[15] The night therefore has a secretive dimension, similar to the Sanjuanist sense of an encounter in the deepest recesses of the soul, in which God's hidden presence leads us away from the 'dubious charms' of the earth's (pagan) religious experiences (where god is invariably an element of a greater whole). 'The night thus radicalizes or schematizes the conditions under which man now faces a God who has been made manifest' since man can only now fall back on faith. Like St John of the Cross, Lacoste interprets the night of non-experience as primarily pedagogical: 'Radical inexperience, "aridity", the "desert" [. . .] the liturgical night neither proves the absence of God nor denies his proximity: on the contrary, it teaches us to think them better' (pp. 147–48). For Lacoste, the liturgical I must be stripped of its false equations of God with relative experiences through the purgations of the night, of which, for Lacoste (following Heidegger), *boredom* is a principle mood and even one of nocturnal experience's principle 'secrets' (p. 148) since it is of the essence of the night to learn 'to open oneself up to God' (p. 151), an often wearying task.[16]

One can now see that the liturgical 'reverses' the intentionality of the human gaze, which always falls short of its divine 'object'. When man faces God, then, he realizes that God's intention precedes him and subordinates him as well as his projects to God's own. Such 'subjection' is simply part of creaturely existence. In the terms of experience, this reversal within liturgical existence can be understood as making us 'objects' and God 'subject' (p. 151). In other words, consciousness is 'disoriented', and the I is 'decentred'. Lacoste calls this ego, decentred before God, the 'soul', which should be understood primarily as oriented in the most radical passivity to God, recognizing its essential creature-hood. It should be emphasized here again that this radical passivity before God is the result of a *free decision* of the subject to dwell liturgically, characterized by a willingness to become purely open to God (§§57–58), to abandon oneself to God, to bury oneself in him in the hope that the radical self-exposition of the liturgical will (eschatologically) call forth a God who is love, or better, is a response to *this* God's prior call. The view espoused here significantly resonates with the notion of St John of the Cross in the *Living Flame* (as we have seen above) of the final reversal of knowledge achieved in the *eschaton*, when creaturely being no longer stands between God and the soul, where God becomes the means towards the soul's eschatological relation to the creaturely world and therefore the fulfilment of all justice. The mystery of such freedom in the self-abandonment of love (and its eschatological return in the gift of all things shared with God) is the reason why it is wrong to consider such a decentring and 'objectifying' of the (liturgical) ego by God an 'ontotheological return'.[17]

Now the reversal of intentionality 'experienced' by the man before God is only meaningful as an anticipation of this final eschatological reversal. In the meantime, the achievement of this passivity helps the liturgical subject discover the sheer giftedness of Being, namely that 'Being and non-Being *actually passes through our present*, and that we cannot face God *without admitting that he continues his benevolent giving*' (p. 160). Thus before God, the liturgical subject discovers that his 'ground is not within himself' and 'abnegates' himself totally to God (§59). This act of 'will-to-powerlessness', in which the liturgical I 'lets be' the absolute priority of the Other's will, and, in contrast to the will-to-power which merely affirms the self's own existence, paradoxically wills all the more because it wills the will of God who promises more than the 'immanent reality of "life"' (§§59–60). Only the possibility, of course, of the final apocalyptic fulfilment of such a promise in the Parousia, lends its meaning to the present. Yet such is the radicality and fragility of the liturgical decision.

Yet abnegation already exceeds mere being by receding before God. The logic of this paradox unfolds in kenotic existence, the definitive form of liturgy, exemplified by the fool. Because the fool lives under a promise that is totally unrealized, he lives in a state of deficiency, yet the fool knows that 'giving praise is more worthy of man than his highest exercise of reason' (p. 186), since mere human wisdom cannot grasp the highest form of existence which exceeds it. More fundamentally the fool never ceases to remind us:

> The *eschaton* does not come to be realized simply because we wish to attenuate our participation in the play of the world as much as possible. The fool's extravagation shows him to be a minimal rather than a transfigured man. If his experience is not to be disqualified, if one must admit that it in fact houses the greatest proximity there is between (mortal) men and God, it must then be said that it is beyond all measure: this is not to say that it is measured (and found wanting) against a limitless presence in the world, or measured against the entirely realized *eschaton*, but that it rejects all measures. (p. 188)

The fool realizes the eschatological '*distentio animi*', as it were, all the way even to the point of a violent fissure within itself, dwelling 'on earth' as if it were already 'in heaven'. One would be tempted here to note the bizarre phenomenon of saints and mystics known as bi-location . . . At any rate clearly Lacoste's 'holy fool' accords with Balthasar's Sanjuanist figuration of the mystic as the theological subject par excellence:

> When one's beloved is none other than God, the ego's experience of losing the ground under its feet as a result of genuine love is none other than the beatific shudder of self surrender which every believer is basically disposed to experience and which the mystic actually experiences already here on earth.

Balthasar describes the paradoxical content of this experience, like Lacoste, by using Sanjuanist/Theresian imagery that gestures towards its essential decentring and refiguration of the ego. He continues: 'This is the experience of leaving one's own house in a dark night, and of the arrow that burns like lightning through the very heart and bores deep into the centre of the ego, there to implant the Thou'.[18] Clearly the symbol of the fool stands to critique the (Hegelian) temptation to rationalize the primarily intellectual character of the non-experience of the night. Yet the dark night itself, like Theresa's burning arrow, is the arrival of an *absolute* alterity irreducible to any ontotheological competitive scheme (or the 'postmodern' critiques thereof).

The players in the night: Saints and fools

The final three paragraphs of the text (§§71–73) briefly elaborate the paradoxical form of this conclusion. The essence of the fool's experience is *kenotic*, shaped by the 'blinding reality of the passion' (p. 189). The fool, in his radical humiliation, literally performs a *sequela Christi* to the radical limits of human being and is therefore said to be one who 'symbolically dwells in Good Friday', in the world, precisely by incarnating the life of the resurrection and of the eschaton ahead of the end. He can thus only appear as a 'sign of contradiction', or 'foolishness' (to use biblical language) in the present.[19] In the fool therefore one sees the 'humiliated humanity of God himself' for, reciprocally, one sees the destiny of the fool only in light of the destiny 'of the Crucified in whom and by whom God restores peace between man and himself' (pp. 190–91). The election of this destiny, is for the Christ-like fool, 'absolute'; it stands over-against the world with a poor superfluity and a wild liberality. Lacoste's ability to draw this connection is rooted in his Sanjuanist theology of the night, which, as we have seen, ties together – *through* the 'split' that occurs in participation in the cross which only then truly makes present the Resurrection in a hidden way – the mind purged of all phenomena and the 'dazzling darkness' of God's secret presence.

This connection between the liturgical exposition and non-experience allows for a final critique, then, of religious experience: true 'theological anthropology' is an *anthropologia crucis* insofar as it is Christ, 'the minimal man par excellence', who tells us – precisely in the form of a dead body hanging limply on the cross – what it means (at least for now) to be before God. Insofar as '*homo liturgicus*' *lives* (paradoxically!) in the dark of death, in the next to last, *between* death and resurrection, this is definitively the case. Yet still, it is joy after all for Lacoste that has *the last word*, for the promise of the event of Resurrection allows us to read our dark vigil in its light, and await, with the patience of the fool, the unimaginable fulfilment of everything human – the possibility par excellence and the meaning, then, of our very human being.

*

But, in light of all this, to return to our question: what does the saint have to do with philosophy? We can say, at least for Jean-Yves Lacoste: if more than nothing than just about everything. But this everything is only manifest as a mere possibility, and all the more so if it is the absolute possibility. Man is free to choose his way of dwelling, in the world, on the earth, liturgically before God: he dwells in freedom. It is the saint and the holy fool who dwell beyond the limits of the world, on the edge of the earth, in a mode of being that manifests heaven only by contradicting, to borrow a word from

St Paul, the 'powers' that order the world as much as the earth. Paradoxically it is this dwelling that proposes itself to human being as *the* way and not a work (*Wege – nicht Werke*): and even as the fullness of the meaning of human being, if only in the mode for now of anticipation and promise. The final meaning of human being can, for now, only be answered in the dark. Yet this darkness is itself an answer. For now at least it is in the mode of darkness that the light of resurrection shines, and even proposes itself as 'the light of the world' as much as a renewal of 'the face of the earth'. And if the darkness hides a secret presence, and is even the very form of its presence, as in St John's Dark Night, then philosophy as much as theology already share the ever-shifting borders of the same wild frontier, at least insofar as they are concerned, if only finally, with the same thing, the meaning and truth of human existence, or, less presumptuously, human experience.

And what if God, the living God, is the matter, in the end? Then it is the saint, in his *corpus*, that speaks the greater human word (*logos*). Here we give flesh to thought. Embodied thought – is such not the *end* of philosophy? The kenotic life burns in the darkness as a 'living sacrifice'. It is in this way or path of the self as a kenotic wager or absolute sacrifice, in which the impenetrable opacity of the flesh and the luminous brightness of the word become one, that the saint can be understood to 'offer himself' – and as such – the philosopher par excellence. We have here, with the saint, a (Pauline) critique of reason, certainly, but also the proposal of its radical rediscovery in the region of mystery (*mysterion*) and history governed by Christian eschatology, and thus in the realm of a 'new thinking'.

Notes

1 See his remarks, for example, concerning the task of a 'supernatural phenomenology' in the introduction to the monograph on St Thérèse in *Two Sisters in the Spirit: Thérèse of Lisieux and Elizabeth of the Trinity* (trans. Donald Nichols et al., San Francisco: Ignatius Press, 1992), pp. 26, 39.

2 Balthasar famously considered the Christian to be the 'guardian of metaphysics in our age'. See the conclusion to *The Glory of the Lord*, vol. 5: *The Realm of Metaphysics in the Modern Age* (trans. Brian McNeil and John Kenneth Riches, San Francisco: Ignatius Press, 1991). Cf. also his remarks in his all-important essay (especially, I suggest, for understanding Lacoste), 'Theology and Sanctity', in the collection *Explorations in Theology*, vol. 1 (trans. A. V. Littledale and Alexander Dru, San Francisco: Ignatius Press, 1989), p. 195.

3 For these remarks, see the introduction to Lacoste's *La phénoménalité de Dieu: neuf études* (Paris: Cerf, 2008).

4 Quotations of St John of the Cross are taken from the Carmelite edition of his complete works, *The Collected Works of St. John of the Cross* (trans. Kieran Kavanaugh, OCD and Otilio Rodgriguez, OCD, Washington, DC: ICS, 1991). These quotations will be cited in text.

5   Key texts in the background of the following brief discussion of Sanjuanist
    mysticism are Henri-Charles Puech, 'La ténèbre mystique chez le Pseudo-Denys
    l'Aréopagite et dans la tradition patristique', *Études carmélitaines* 23:2 (1938),
    pp. 33–53; Edith Stein, *The Science of the Cross* (Washington, DC: ICS, 2003);
    Karol Wojtyla, *Doctrina de Fide apud S. Joannem a Cruce* (Rome, 1949) [*Faith
    According to St John of the Cross* (trans. Jordan Aumann OP, San Francisco:
    Ignatius, 1981)]; Louis Bouyer, *The Christian Mystery: From Pagan Myth to
    Christian Mysticism* (trans. Illtyd Trethowan, Edinburgh: T&T Clark, 1989).

6   Wojtyla, *Faith*, p. 97. See *The Ascent of Mount Carmel*, I, 3, 1, for this general
    definition in St John.

7   Stanza 6 of 'Stanzas of the soul that suffers with longing to see God'.
    See *Collected Works*, p. 56.

8   From Stanza 4 of 'Stanzas concerning an ecstasy experienced in high
    contemplation', ibid., p. 53. This syntax of 'modus sine modo' is critical in the
    Christian mystical tradition: it runs from Augustine to Bernard of Clairvaux to
    John of the Cross.

9   Kierkegaard again, from the *Postscript*.

10 For this notion in Lacoste, see 'Liturgy and Coaffection', p. 102, as well as
    Présence et parousie (Ad Solem, 2006).

11 Cp. Hegel in the *Phenomenology of Spirit*: 'That [this division of
    consciousness] is in fact no distinction is something of which this
    consciousness is unaware; on the contrary, the making of the distinction
    appears to it as a contingent act having no essential connection with what
    is brought about by that act; and the unity which links the two together,
    viz. the said act and the End, falls asunder for this consciousness'. See *The
    Phenomenology of Spirit* (trans. A. V. Miller, Oxford: Oxford University Press,
    1977), p. 158.

12 If I may offer here my dissertation, strongly indebted to Lacoste, as an
    extended reflection primarily on this theme: *Philosophy from Oracles:
    Meditations on Last Philosophy*, The University of Virginia, 2011.

13 'Only the kingdom can be a homeland for us, and we do not live in the
    Kingdom, even if its order is not simply transcendent to that of the world and
    death. We can attempt to make the dimensions of our lives conform to those
    of liturgy, or at least will that they do so. This possibility should not deflect
    our attention from the fragility of eschatological anticipation, nor from the
    ambiguity in which our facticity is enshrouded. It is nevertheless the desire
    presiding over this anticipation [. . .] which most accurately signifies the
    meaning of our humanity' (§37, p. 98).

14 Lacoste gets the basic conceptuality of the 'next to last' from Bonhoeffer
    (cf. pp. 2–3). For Bonhoeffer, *die vorletzten Dinge* stems from a concern with a
    life of action in the present order of things in which society is secular and God
    is hidden and therefore not experienced. In his *Ethics*, he returns from a purely
    eschatological concern, as in, for example, The *Cost of Discipleship*, to a
    concern with the mode of human life *after* the Cross and *before* the *Parousia*.
    For Bonhoeffer, following Barth, the reality of things has been definitively
    transformed in the event of reconciliation of the Cross. The 'next to last' is
    the mode of life that lives wholly for that hidden reality, inasmuch as one
    anticipates the completion in the *Parousia*. This view expands Bonhoeffer's
    early conception of the 'orders of preservation'. See Dietrich Bonhoeffer

Ethics; Dietrich Bonhoeffer Works, vol. 4 (Minneapolis, MN: Fortress Press, 2005), pp. 146–70. Bonhoeffer's notion of 'secret discipline', a later development of his theology of the 'next to last' (in *Letters and Papers from Prison*), seems to correspond well with Lacoste's idea of 'the vigil' and the thematic of the night as well as his 'split' eschatology more generally.

15   Cp. Jüngel's comments in his *God as the Mystery of the World*: 'But, given the conditions of the world, God's coming to the world cannot be seen. If this were to be made visible, then, as one option, the end of the world would have to be postulated. For God's divine way of appearing would surpass the world's possibilities, which are divided into space and time and thus within time into the various tenses of time, and consequently cannot facilitate the appearance of the eternal God in an eternal or divine way. If such an appearance were thinkable, then it would only be as an appearance which abolished the world' (p. 378).

16   For Heidegger on this essential 'attunement' (*Stimmung*) see §29 of *Being and Time*.

17   For a reading of Lacoste's liturgical subject that raises the spectre of metaphysical ontotheology precisely on this point, and which I do not imagine fully or adequately to engage here (though nevertheless regarding which I would at least like to raise an objection), see the essays by Joeri Schrijvers (*the* authority on all things Lacoste), 'Jean-Yves Lacoste: A Phenomenology of Liturgy', *Heythrop Journal* 46 (2005), pp. 314–33. 'Phenomenology, Liturgy and Metaphysics. The Thought of Jean-Yves Lacoste', *God in France* (ed. Peter Jonkers and Ruud Welten, Leuven: Peeters, 2005), pp. 207–25, 'Ontotheological Turnings? Marion, Lacoste, and Levinas on the Decentring of Modern Subjectivity', *Modern Theology* 22:2 (April 2006). Schrijvers' recent works, *Ontotheological Turnings? The Decentering of Modern Subject in Recent French Phenomenology* (Albany, NY: SUNY Press, 2011), and *An Introduction to Jean-Yves Lacoste* (London: Ashgate, 2012), are profound and definitive statements of this position.

18   Hans Urs von Balthasar, *The Glory of the Lord: Vol 1: Seeing the Form*, p. 193.

19   Cf. Luke 2.34 and 1 Corinthians 1, respectively.

15

The Night of Living Flesh and Sainthood in Michel Henry

Joseph Rivera

Introduction

The popularity of Michel Henry continues apace in France and shows no signs of waning, and the reception of his work in English-speaking scholarship is steadily advancing among philosophers and theologians. Henry first rose to prominence in the mid-1960s as a creative phenomenologist, and subsequently, garnered attention as a critic of modernity, labelling its culture of fabrication, mass industry and consumption, conquest through technology and unreflective late political liberalism a form of Barbarism. Deeply read in the history of philosophy, the author of several novels and a connoisseur of fine art (he devoted a text to Kandinsky), it was not until the mid-1990s that Henry made a decisive theological turn if only as a natural continuation in what was already a theologically informed trajectory aimed at upsetting the nihilistic ideology of Enlightenment rationalism that pervades contemporary Western culture.

To bring to light some of the core ideas associated with Henry's theological turn we introduce his remarkable, if sometimes baffling and always radical, philosophical analysis of the Incarnation. In attending to the unique manner of givenness by which it is made manifest, we intend to show that the gift of the Incarnation, for Henry, can evoke a spirituality of the sort enjoyed by the saint. The Incarnation for Henry is not only the event whereby Christ assumes flesh. It is also the strange but necessary event (if the nihilistic spirit of modernity is to be avoided) whereby Christ takes on flesh inside me, giving my flesh to me. And there, in that same concrete manifestation, the

Incarnation draws me into the very life of God so that I become in my essence illumined before divine glory. Understood as a movement accomplished deep inside me, the Incarnation elicits the saint to put into play self-mastery and ascetic skilfulness to figure the way down into the nocturnal site of Incarnation, a primitive site of utter passivity untouched by perceptual acts through which the mind constitutes objects before its gaze. God cannot be grasped by a higher cognitive act that conceptualizes God as an object for thought. This descent into passivity is a descent into my flesh that discloses the purity of love, the delight of the heart, as it is sustained by the invisible radiance of God.

The spiritual life of the saint therefore celebrates the mystical body of Christ, the 'Word made flesh', as the concrete site for communion with God. But the mystical body of Christ extends beyond my relation to God. In Christ I also commune with the wider body of saints. What would an experience with the other fully governed by the Incarnation be like? Henry's prioritization of the Incarnation means that Christian spirituality is refined within the complex network of the invisible lineaments of the mystical body of Christ, wherein my body relates to your body in an intimate and ineffable communion. I am in you and you are in me, a theological conception of flesh that highlights a pure and simple unity; the virtue of such a living unity is that it opens up a common genealogy between saints. There is, in other words, a decisive caesura situated between my natural genealogy and my divine condition as a Son of God born from the absolute life of God.[1]

Living as a saint amounts to admitting a simple, but difficult, truth: I am not one but two bodies. For Henry, the awareness of the two-sided nature of the body is manifest as, on the one hand, an invisible subjective 'feel' that grips me inwardly, and, on the other, a visible objective texture that fixes me as a three-dimensional silhouette with a particular depth and volume in the exterior world. My exterior body holds within itself a living flesh, an invisible inner content that endlessly receives its life through God's invisible but concrete self-donation in Christ. In consequence of this donation, my flesh is comprised entirely of Christ, a divine substance that is nocturnal in nature, appearing in a sphere with no exteriority, no outside and no world involved. The spirituality of the saint brings this truth to life precisely because the saint can, from that invisible reservoir, draw out vital subjective resources that invoke God's presence, bringing it to the surface (or just below the surface). Without denying the saint's bodily existence in the world, Henry is emphatic that saintliness, holiness and purity are to make themselves felt in a subjective manifestation sharply juxtaposed with the visible body on display in the world. The saint is a living soul the world cannot accept and whose ascetic practices offer a spiritual profit immeasurable by the standard of the world. The 'world has hated them, for they are not of the world any more than I am of the world'.[2] The saint is the very negation of the world if the world represents the horizon where only bodies limited to their inert spatial polarity can appear. Henry's conception of flesh, as we shall see below, is generally consistent with, and lends impetus to, the spiritual rigour evident in, for example, Maximus the Confessor's call to endure the privative experience of charity attested to by the early Christian communities. We must become perpetually in union with divine grace that springs forth 'from within' after mindful and purposeful detachment from the world.[3] Our purpose, in what follows, is merely to lay out the logic of the structure of this double body Henry advances, to elucidate the course of the saintly life that may naturally flow from it and to call attention to the intrinsic spiritual orientation of the Incarnation.

The sanctity of all flesh

In a recent interview Henry contends that his work on the Incarnation is equivalent to a conceptual archaeology that leads back to the origin of flesh itself. Once excavated, flesh flashes forth at its base as a pure incandescent matter (*matière incandescente*).[4] Because it is an inner and thus invisible 'matter' manifest within the exterior body, flesh belongs to the process by which the soul feels itself feeling as it crushes against itself in an utterly passive self-embrace. As a living pathos submerged within itself, the secret of flesh is that, as an inner disposition, it bears within it the very presence of God. In its essential receptivity, the union with God is accomplished through the communication to the soul of the mystical body, the love exchanged between the Son and Father and, ultimately, the bond of their reciprocity that is the Holy Spirit. To communicate to me the same love the Father communicates to the Son, Christ raises me up, as a Son of Light, in an eternal movement into the life of the Trinity to share in the absolute motion of divine glory – what Henry phrases (awkwardly) as the 'interior reciprocity between Father and Son enjoyed in their common bond, the Spirit'.[5] Understood in this manner, the luminosity of flesh emanates an invisible luminosity because it is maintained in and through divine life, the 'Light of Truth incarnated in Christ',[6] whose interior illumination shines brightly and intensely with the invisibility of a white light incapable of appearing as mediated by the ordinary 'outside' horizon of the visible world. Without distance from its divine source, and thus in perfect union with the bare essence of God, living flesh is not a discrete object but a nocturnal affectivity that proliferates in, even swells with, the life of Christ. My flesh forms an inviolable union with God's infinite glory and thus contains 'not merely traces of life but absolute life'.[7] Such an archaeology appeals to a theological vision about the unity between the revelation of my flesh and the self-revelation of God in the 'Word made flesh'.

Dedicating most of his work to unveiling this common substance with great imaginative force and philosophical depth, Henry perhaps puts forward the 'saint' as an exemplar of such a living communion of flesh. The life of the saint can be depicted, after Henry, as a life of trial that sets into operation a lived experience whereupon the Word of Life is heard in the affective centre of my life: namely, my 'heart'. Constitutive of the heart's pulse, Christ is never separate from the soul's affective seat. I come into myself as this particular self while remaining in submission to Christ in my inner depth. What Christ feels is also what I feel. I am 'predestined to receive the fruit of the Word'[8] in my heart, wherein Christ speaks and through which my self-identity crystallizes – my heart is my essence. Mute in the world, and resident in my heart, the Word of God evades the noetic synthesis of language, its structural play between signs in which I apprehend that the sign 'table' (for example) points to that object in the corner of the room.

Henry's work intends to isolate what is brought to light by a pre-critical (or post-critical) mystical reading of the gospel of John, one that speaks to the radical disjunction between Christ and the world. This style of reading scripture is to shift the focus from the critical study of the kingdom of God in the world and its variegated incarnations in human history to the meditative enjoyment of the truth that I am in mystical union with Christ outside of the world. There is for Henry 'that of the world, in which everything is seen from the outside, and that of life, in which everything is lived from the inside [. . .] such that the latter is never separated from God's self-revelation'.[9] Henry's exaltation of mystical flesh is motivated by the absolute Johannine juxtaposition between, on the one hand, the *world* where Christ was continually displaced as a resident alien and where 'he came to that which was his own but his own did not receive him',[10] and, on the other, the *acosmic Christ* where the presence of God always reigns and where Christ dwells outside the world, for 'before Abraham was, I am'.[11] Henry is adamant that latter point encapsulates the 'essential kernel of Christianity'.[12] Ordered by a 'logic of the invisible', flesh appears in abstention from the world. For the sheep parable of John 10, for Henry, states explicitly that Christ constitutes a triumphal arch under which each of us must pass not only to enter into relation with Christ but with each other: for is Christ not the good Shepherd that joins us together in an invisible communion of saints?[13]

Such a secret cannot come into full view, however. The mystical union we share in Christ cannot be revealed as a relation made possible by the subject's correlation with objects or the body's relation to the complex manifold of sense impressions. As lived entirely within the sphere of self-affection, my unity with you on the basis of Christ resists the display of the world. The invisible nature of such a unity means, moreover, that it cannot assume a unity consisting of a plurality of objective displays or a multiplicity of empirical horizons brought together as a mosaic available to see in the world. All flesh is unified in an invisible and organic singularity within the

Son of God: 'for the Word is that place from which all are born and in which all are identical with each other'.[14]

One should receive the impression that Henry's Christology suggests that while it may not be obvious from my body's exterior display in the world, the inner possibility of all my bodily acts or manifestations in the world is based upon an interior flesh endlessly given to me by the life of Christ, hence, 'there is a single and selfsame life [.] . . and it has the same meaning for God, for Christ and for man'.[15] Henry's 'phenomenology of sainthood' maintains that all flesh is saintly in that it enjoys immediate union with the living power of Christ, and this unity is nocturnal, invisible and pure: 'In the depths of its night, our flesh is God'.[16]

To clarify such a mystical, and yet philosophically rigorous, vision of the Incarnation, we begin with the phenomenological framework with which Henry begins: namely, Husserl's phenomenology of the body (*Leibkörper*).[17] Given the peculiar structure of the Incarnation and the phenomenological character of the *Leibkörper* advanced by Henry, an obvious step must be taken to ensure my union with the Incarnation: the implementation of a radical disparity between interior flesh (*Leib*) and exterior body (*Körper*). By splitting the body into discrete segments, Henry accomplishes the decisive shift from the world to Christ. This move enables Henry to clarify the style of givenness by which the 'Word made flesh' appears. But to shed light on Henry's approach to the Incarnation, it may be helpful to note how classic theological reflection on the Incarnation can be fruitfully modified first from a Husserlian perspective. For Husserl, appearing is always an appearing *of* something *to* someone, a dual structure that enacts the ongoing harmonization between the genitive and dative poles of manifestation.[18] Fitted to this order of display and inscribed within the kenotic movement from inside and outside, one must say the Incarnation unmistakably denotes a phenomenological appearing *of* Christ's flesh *to* human flesh. Not considering himself equal to God, Christ took the form of a servant and emptied himself in humility. Becoming one of us, moving from inside God to the 'outside' of the world, Christ was 'made in human likeness [. . .] and found in appearance as a man'.[19] Descending into the world-horizon and disrupting the fabric of history from within by dying on a cross and rising from the dead, the incarnate Christ was manifest as a humble servant cast into the world to redeem it and to draw it towards its eschatological telos. Christ is beheld, in this ancient hymn captured in Philippians 2.5–11, as a visible historical body, as a divine manifestation most evident in Christ's humble visibility. The Incarnation is traditionally understood here as divine revelation of God to something that is distinct from God (a distance between God and creation), a distance traversed by God in Christ's hypostatic union. Such a traditional view of the Incarnation finds no place in Henry's thinking. As will become instructive for us momentarily, Christ's Incarnation (taking flesh) and our Incarnation (taking flesh) are one and the same self-revelation in Henry's peculiar scheme.

We return to Henry's juxtaposition between world and Christ. Henry invokes the principle of the 'duplicity of appearing' as the principle that foregrounds not just the radical distinction between the world and Christ but also the radical distinction internal to the body itself. Given its programmatic status, the principle of duplicity orders the manifestation of all phenomena according to an absolute duality: either an invisible appearance of pure auto-affection (i.e. interiority with the genitive and dative situated in an original unity and thus with no fracture or distance) or a visible display of hetero-affection (i.e. exteriority, distance between genitive and dative). This duplicity structures the fundamental contrast between subjective flesh (*Leib)* and objective body (*Körper).* It is not insignificant to note that in order to bring to light the nature of flesh (*Leib)* Henry looks to language used in the prologue to the gospel of John, which ascribes to Christ a 'taking-flesh', not a 'taking-body'. For the gospel of John, 'does not say that the Word had taken a body [.] . .'. Rather, 'it says that the Word was made flesh and thus it is a question of *flesh* and not *body'*.[20] Henry continues, 'for it is not a question thus of "form", of "aspect", or of "guise", but of reality. In itself, in its essence and reality it is the Word, and as the Word, it is that of the Word made flesh'.[21] Turning attention away from the objective, historical body of Jesus of Nazareth whose presence unfolded in first-century Palestine, Henry maintains that the Incarnation is acosmic – invisible and without relation to the world. Understood in these terms, the visible body (*Körper)* of Jesus of Nazareth does not bear any necessary resemblance to the 'Word made flesh'. The Incarnation, for Henry, assumes a manner of givenness with a unique style of verification all its own and thus consists of a revelation that affirms itself with an apodictic certainty – a revelation whereby what appears and the appearance are co-original and thus identical, a style of appearing Henry names auto-affection.

The materiality of auto-affection is immediate and self-confirming. Given as a formidable power, auto-affection makes itself felt inside itself, generating a living substance that continuously affects itself by crushing itself against itself so that 'life [flesh] plunges into itself, crushes against itself, experiences itself, enjoys itself, constantly producing its own essence [. . .]'.[22] The world is that primal 'outside' which throws living flesh outside itself. Opened up as a horizon by the streaming movement of temporality, the world is positively foreign to the invisible union of living flesh with the 'Word made flesh'. The unity is a secret unity because its phenomenological structure is conceived under the form of a living *present* set over against the flowing temporal ecstasies of *future* and *past.* As such, the living present belongs to the form of self-presence in possession of a stable and self-secure unity. Christ assumes flesh just in the manner of the living present – by way of an acosmic or non-temporal Incarnation that presupposes no gap, no exteriority, no hetero-affection, no temporality and thus no world: 'Neither the mode of life's giving as self-giving and as self-revelation nor the pure phenomenological substance of which this self-revelation is made, belongs to the world in any shape or form'.[23] Henry does not deny that Christ, as a historical personage, assumed a physical, objective body disclosed within time and space. But, the luminous display of the world under which the visible body appears is simply bracketed as a subsidiary and unnecessary aspect of the Incarnation.

The Incarnation is not only lived within the Trinity but, too, within my life, the depth or reservoir of affectivity inside me. In the pathos-soaked embrace of my auto-affection, I am given to myself by Christ's incarnate auto-affection. Christ's living flesh replicates itself inside my flesh, carrying along my own feeling of myself as it continually arrives inside me as a primal impression. Christ's Incarnation, in short, makes possible my own coming into flesh as one who feels this body that I have as my own body. But my flesh is not my own. My flesh is given to me by the 'Word made flesh'. Henry writes:

> I am not myself, and cannot be, except by way of Life's original ipseity. The pathetic flesh of this ipseity, in which Life is joined to itself, is what joins me to myself such that I may be, and can be, this me that I am. Therefore, I cannot join me to myself except through Christ, since he has joined eternal Life to itself, creating in it the first Self. The relation to self that makes any me a me is what makes that me possible; in philosophical language, it is its transcendental condition [. . .]. Christ is the transcendental condition of these transcendental me's.[24]

Does this 'transcendental Christology', not pose an obvious theological problem? Does not feeling Christ's flesh within my own flesh introduce an element of hetero-affection within the impenetrable sphere of auto-affection? Inserting Christ as the source and ongoing possibility of my own auto-affection, according to Henry, is *not* introducing an element of hetero-affection. This is because Christ's flesh and my own flesh share the same living essence. They are structurally manifest together, co-given in one absolute, nocturnal auto-affection. To feel myself in radical immediacy without reference to anything outside the ego is therefore *not* to exclude divine flesh.

What theological conclusions may we draw from such a radical analysis of the Incarnation?[25] Might this phenomenology of Incarnation cast the dark cloud of heresy over Henry, invoking the spectre of Docetism whose teachings ascribe to Christ's earthly body the status of illusion set over against a pure interior core? It seems difficult to deny that Henry's duplicitous body gravitates towards the grievous imbalance of this and other early church Christological heresies. Henry's preoccupation with the essence of Christ's flesh at the expense of its appearing as a body to other bodies in the visible display of the world is symptomatic of the kind of absolute dualism upon which Docetism(s) trades.

Henry's phenomenology of flesh, moreover, prompts the issue of how my flesh and body interrelate, broaching a familiar problem that runs from

Plato to Descartes: the soul versus body distinction.[26] While such Western philosophical debate is important in Henry's work and reflects a topic for another time, our point in this section has been to highlight that the interior, subjective body (*Leib*) Husserl analysed is singled out and thematized from a theological point of view. The *Leib* so understood by Henry is pristine, holy and in ongoing living relation with 'Word made flesh' insofar as the objective body on visible display de-realizes flesh and empties it of its meaning because the body can achieve nothing more than the deplorable rank of simple thing visible for all to see among other things.[27] If I inhabit a duplicitous body, how do I proceed from my exterior *Körper* to my interior *Leib*? Is there a practical convention or spiritual practice I can perform thereby enabling the revelation of divine life to grip my flesh anew? While Henry speaks little of the life of the saint or the praxis of sainthood, he nevertheless marshals theological resources that foster reflection on an ascetic spirituality, a mystical mood that takes flight from the world, once and for all. We nominate the performative dimension of Henry's mystical spirituality as the 'saintly reduction'.

Transcendental reduction as saintly reduction

We have already acknowledged that the principal thematic motif of Henry's theological turn is one of interiority, that is, that my inner flesh is subsumed within Christ and thereby born of a divine act carried out in every instant entirely *apart* from the temporal streaming and spatial sequencing of the visible *Körper* in the world. By amplifying its capacity to bracket the world, Henry impresses upon Husserl's well-known doctrine of the 'reduction' a theological imprint.[28] Whereas the conceptual apparatus of Husserl's phenomenological reduction is typically understood as an abstract philosophical principle that enables the philosopher to meditate on how objects are constituted by a conscious ego, Henry attends, in contrast, to how the reduction permits not just the philosopher but the Christian certain spiritual stimulus that may induce concrete union with God and the body of saints.

Husserl characterizes the reduction as a reflective exercise that brackets or parenthesizes the world, a reduction that effects a return to an original essence. The transcendental reduction, as it became known, intends to find out exactly how the ego is like a residue, like a pure substance that remains after the abstraction. Husserl strives to dispel, through steady and continuous application of the reduction, the ego from its naïve attachment to the world. For the unreflective person a certain attitude is natural – that the surrounding world stands over me and is finally there as nothing more than an open and transparent horizon given without further ado. But the world is never simply there, laid bare and exhausted as a unchangeable blank space, and thus, as a monotonous display of sameness. Construed in this way, Husserl's reduction does not function to disqualify the world's appearing, for the world always impinges on the ego, giving itself to the ego as an object of attention and reflection. When the philosopher meditates by putting into play the transcendental reduction, the world is not annihilated but becomes 'in a quite peculiar sense, a *phenomenon*'.[29] Husserl therefore states quite clearly that the proper province of the phenomenological reduction is the constituting power of consciousness – that the world is constituted by consciousness.[30]

An important, but often neglected, aspect about Husserl's theory of the phenomenological reduction is that he insists that it must be maintained, habitually, as an ongoing attitude about my relation to the world. In *Ideas I,* Husserl likens the process of enacting the phenomenological reduction to a conversion, an existential renewal or, more pessimistically, to a struggle or difficult trial to free oneself from dogmatic notions about the nature of the world.[31] It is naïve to live in the natural attitude, so once I undergo the conversion to the transcendental attitude, I must remain under its tutelage. Husserl is consequently concerned with how the transcendental condition for the possibility of the world is, after all, an accomplishment of the ego's own constituting consciousness. The world is always constituted inside me, as distinct from me, but inside me nonetheless.

Henry welcomes Husserl's strategy to employ the transcendental reduction as a means to unveil the interior sphere of human life.[32] Henry agrees with Husserl about the basic nature of phenomenology as a transcendental practice, 'insofar as it takes into consideration the givenness in which every experience is rooted. The reduction returns us to this original domain and, as Husserl notes, is transcendental'.[33] Yet Henry is critical of Husserl about the degree to which the Husserlian reduction can purify the ego of all 'outsideness'. While Husserl may have sought to bracket the exterior world in order to come back to it with the transcendental attitude, Henry thinks that only a saintly reduction which reduces the self to its absolute subjective purity given to it by Christ entirely apart from the world is worthy of the name 'transcendental'.

How does the saint access such a primitive site, the original source of life and the unity of all saints in Christ? The saintly reduction appears for Henry to be the only course of action, a Godward movement towards the living present inside the saint that, of necessity, requires a simultaneous movement away from the world-horizon. As the saint actively draws on its inner, nocturnal reservoir from whence its ascetic skills are refined, the saintly reduction utterly brackets the world. This accomplishment takes the saint back to that pure residue left over after the disqualification of the world: the interior living flesh (pure *Leib*) as it is continuously born with all flesh within Christ's Incarnation. The communion of saints in Christ is necessarily an inward communion, where all souls become the invisible operations and action of God. Fleeing from the world and the outward appearances of my body, I bracket everything outside of me once and for all. Depicted as a journey without return, the movement of the spiritual life of the saint is one governed by a descent inward into the subjective feel of flesh as it is lived in unity with the 'Word made flesh'.

While the course of action is clear, Henry typically avoids systematic consideration of examples that may lead one to accomplish its intended goal. Perhaps one may find a general 'way of being' can be adduced in Henry's line of inquiry. Henry discusses at length, for example, a Christian style of ethics shaped by the great paradoxes of the beatitudes.[34] To 'move' in love towards the other, Henry insists that the saint must practise acts of mercy that are not motivated by self-interest or economic gain. The poverty of the saint is cashed out in great spiritual riches and blessing. To be first is to be last. I love the other by forgetting myself. To be truly active in the world I am to reject the world by remaining poor in spirit and meek in manner. To find myself as I really am, as a living 'me', I am to remove myself from all egocentrism and place myself in the rank of last. This arch-humility orients me away from myself, which in turn, provokes a 'staggering-into-myself' as an immediate coming into Christ, as an abrupt reduction of my ego: 'not as I will, but as you will'.[35]

Another example of the saintly reduction can be observed in Henry's discussion of the 'I-Can' (Husserl). The 'I-Can' is discharged as a primal sense of possession or power through which I know myself to be in charge of my own body, its movements and destiny. Henry articulates a reduction that eliminates the autonomy of such a self-subsisting egoism. To have an 'I-Can' is to have sense of singularity, of self-presence, to know directly and without explicit thematization I am the one who acts. But for Henry, the saint transfigures the 'I-Can' by remaking it into a passive receptacle of God's grace. My 'I-Can' in reality emerges in and through Christ, whose flesh is manifest in me, empowering all that I do, my very bodily acts. The saint must dispel the illusion that the 'I-Can' is an autonomous power that draws from its own resources. I am a living creature in possession of myself, for Henry, only because I am first possessed by God.[36] To remain mindful that I am 'not my own', argues Henry, I must flee from acts of evil, malice, greed, violence and inhabit a passive, even pacific, life of peace, joy, wisdom and love that is interested in, because it is vulnerable to, the flesh of other saints in the mystical body of Christ. The particular shape of this course of action is marked by non-reciprocal sacrifice, a gift given without expectation of return.[37] To love those who do not love me is to abandon the conviction that the law of symmetry and reciprocity must be maintained in my relationships with others. By the same token, this is to abandon rivalry, competition, violence, power, prestige and autonomy. To understand my primal 'I-Can' properly, I must abandon the 'world' and its laws. I must love those who hate me and embrace the truth of such a paradox that is foolishness to the world.[38]

Rolf Kühn helpfully describes Henry's unique proposal of a saintly reduction as a rupture from the world, a 'leap' (*saut*), or an all-at-once movement that proceeds from the visible display of the world-horizon to the field of invisible display inside my elemental self-present flesh.[39] Henry designs the saintly reduction as a radical 'leap of faith', a Pascalian wager[40] that leads one into the very depth of life by way of a radical and ascetic bracketing of the world. It must be emphasized that the application of the saintly reduction does not perpetuate the Husserlian idea of a disinterested onlooker or spectator, as if the saint could rise above his life and observe it without prejudice. The saintly reduction, as Henry conceives it, is thus the work of a pure receptivity both motivated and set into operation by the desire of Christ himself, as the 'Word made flesh' appears in its acosmic sphere. The 'leap' into life circulates within itself, proving that my desire for life is already within me as it is given to me, forming me in my pure transcendental essence as this interior 'me'. I leap into life, therefore, by way of a radical detachment from the field of visible display, by way of rejection of the world, as a counter-movement aroused by and brought to fruition according to Christ's internal rhythm. By virtue of the nocturnal purity of flesh yielded by the saintly reduction, I experience the deep pathos of 'myself' within divine life's generative self-donation in the transcendental life of Christ. There is no question that Christian mystical spirituality informs Henry's practical phenomenology – perhaps this is why there are studies comparing Henry to both Meister Eckhart[41] and St John of the Cross.[42]

Henry's theological turn highlights, in conclusion, a Christic flesh that fills the dark chamber of my living flesh inside me. As the essence of my singularity, my flesh co-appears with Christ within the concrete mystical body (where all flesh lives) that cannot be indexed or seen in any empirical, intentional or worldly sense. Certainly there is more than a mild Docetism at work in Henry's appropriation of the Incarnation as well as Manichean themes at play in his saintly reduction. The radical dualism that splits the body in half is no mere substance dualism, but rather, is correlative with a Gnostic dualism that prompts a flight from the body. A sympathetic reading of Henry, similar to the rendition we provided above, ought to understand that perhaps, more than anything else, what is won by Henry's theological turn is a theory of the self, of the soul, fully realized inside God. The death of God theology so popular in the 1960s and the secular mood that has settled in our contemporary age consists, so observes Henry, in an absolute negation of selfhood. For Henry, without God, there is no self, no ipseity and thus no 'me'. The prophetic nature of Henry's work is evident in his critical stance towards contemporary secular culture and its unreflective assumption that the body can be fully explained by the exterior body, brain synapses and motor movements. Henry thus writes, 'the negation of God is identically the negation of man'.[43] Or more directly, and without reserve in its polemics, Henry writes, '"The death of God", a dramatic leitmotif of modern thought attributed to some audacious philosophical breakthrough and parroted by our contemporaries, is just the declaration of intent of the modern mind and its flat positivism. But because this death of God destroys the interior possibility of man, since no man is possible who is not first a living Self and a "me", it strikes at the very heart of man himself'.[44] Only by way of the radical reduction, mystical detachment from the world, can the life of the saint find itself renewed in the life of the Spirit where the invisible communion between saints is joined together in the common love that is the Spirit of us all.

Notes

1   Michel Henry, *Paroles du Christ* (Paris: Seuil, 2002), p. 58.
2   John 17.14.
3   See for example, Maximus the Confessor, *The Ascetic Life and Four Centuries of Charity* (trans. Polycarp Sherwood, Westminster, MD: Newman Press, 1955).
4   Michel Henry, *Incarnation: une philosophie de la chair* (Paris: Seuil, 2000), pp. 39, 47.
5   Henry writes, 'They are in the other, the Father in the Son, the Son in the Father according to an interior reciprocity (where the one is experiencing, living and loving the other) that is an interiority of love, that is their common Love, their Spirit'. Henry, *Paroles du Christ*, p. 108.
6   Ibid., p. 125.
7   Michel Henry, *Entretiens* (Paris: Sulliver, 2007), p. 122.
8   Henry, *Paroles du Christ*, p. 118.
9   Michel Henry, *I am the Truth: Toward a Philosophy of Christianity* (trans. Susan Emanuel, Stanford, CA: Stanford University Press, 2002), p. 175.
10   John 1.11.
11   John 8.58.
12   Henry, *I am the Truth*, p. 62.
13   Henry meditates at length on this parable in ibid., chapter 7, 'Mans as "Son within the Son"'.
14   Henry, *Incarnation*, pp. 353–54.
15   Henry, *I am the Truth*, p. 101.
16   Henry, *Incarnation*, p. 373.
17   Edmund Husserl, *Ideas Pertaining to Pure Phenomenology and a Phenomenological Philosophy, Second Book* (trans. R. Rojcewicz and A. Schuwer, Dordrecht: Kluwer Academic, 1989), §§ 35–42.
18   This genitive and dative duality is what Husserl refers to when he writes, 'the meaning word "phenomenon" is twofold because of the essential correlation between *appearing* and *that which appears*'. Edmund Husserl, *The Idea of Phenomenology* (trans. Lee Hardy, Dordrecht: Kluwer Academic, 1999), p. 69.
19   Philippians 2.7–8.
20   Henry, *Incarnation*, p. 26.
21   Ibid., p. 27.
22   Henry, *I am the Truth*, p. 55.
23   Ibid., p. 97.

24 Ibid., p. 115.
25 The best critical reading of Henry's theory of flesh is Emmanuel Falque's essay, 'Y a-t-il une chair sans corps?' in *Phénoménologie et christianisme chez Michel Henry: Les derniers écrits de Michel Henry en débat* (ed. Philippe Capelle, Paris: Cerf, 2004), pp. 95–133.
26 It is necessary to affirm that both *Leib* and *Körper* are components of the body in Henry, for it is only with the friction between them that Henry is forced to conclude that they relate by way of paradox. If there were no body (or if it were absorbed within the flesh), then there would be no need to describe the relation of flesh and body as a paradox. See Henry, *Incarnation*, pp. 282–83.
27 Henry writes, 'The derealisation of the flesh happens in and by the appearing of the world'. See ibid., p. 219.
28 See, for instance, 'La question de la vie et de la culture dans la perspective d'une phénoménologie radicale' in *Phénoménologie de la vie, tome IV* (Paris: Presses universitaires de France, 2004), pp. 11–29.
29 Husserl, *Crisis*, p. 152.
30 For more on the reduction, see especially, Husserl, *Cartesian Meditations: An Introduction to Phenomenology* (trans. Dorion Cairns, The Hague: Martinus Nijhoff, 1977), §15.
31 See note in Husserl, *Ideas I*, §62.
32 Michel Henry, *Material Phenomenology* (trans. Scott Davidson, New York: Fordham University Press, 2008), p. 16.
33 Ibid.
34 See Henry's chapter on ethics in *I am the Truth*, ch. 10, 'The Christian Ethic'. Also see Henry, *Paroles du Christ*, p. 55.
35 Henry, *I am the Truth*, p. 211; Matthew 26.39.
36 See Henry, *Incarnation*, §§26, 30, 34–35.
37 Henry, *Paroles du Christ*, p. 46.
38 Ibid., p. 72.
39 Rolf Kühn, 'La contre-reduction comme "saut" dans la Vie absolue', in *Retrouver la vie oubliee: critiques et perspectives de la philosophie de Michel Henry* (ed. Jean-Michel Longneaux, Namur, Belgium: Presses universitaires de Namur, 2000), pp. 67–80.
40 Henry, *Paroles du Christ*, p. 72.
41 For Henry's discussion of Eckhart, see Michel Henry, *Essence of Manifestation* (trans. Girard Etzkorn, The Hague: Martinus Nijhoff, 1973), §§39–40. For those unfamiliar with Eckhart, it is both his theory of the birth of God in the soul and his theory of detachment or *Abgeschiedenheit* (i.e. detaching from the desires of the world) that Henry takes up. For more on Henry's adoption of Eckhartian themes, see Nathalie Depraz, 'Seeking a Phenomenological Metaphysics: Henry's Reference to Meister Eckhart', trans. George B. Sadler, *Continental Philosophy Review* 32:3 (1999), pp. 303–24.
42 For more on the 'night' of auto-affection in relation to the dark night of the soul, see Ruud Welten, 'The Night in John of the Cross and Michel Henry', *Studies in Spirituality* 13 (2003), pp. 213–33.
43 Henry, *I am the Truth*, p. 263.
44 Ibid., p. 265.

16

The Unknown Saint: Reflections on Jean-Luc Marion's Understanding of Holiness

Petra Elaine Turner

Saint, Saint, Saint est le Seigneur, le Dieu des armées.
La terre est remplie de sa gloire.[1]

What does it mean to be a saint? What does it mean to embrace and be embraced by the holy? For holiness and its attendant notions of saintliness and sainthood rest at the edges of expressibility, and therefore pose difficulties for anyone seeking a satisfactory response to the question posed above. In a recent essay on the subject, entitled 'The Invisibility of the Saint', Jean-Luc Marion opens his inquiry into saintliness with a threefold invocation of *le saint*, calling to mind the Sanctus as recited in the Roman Catholic mass: 'The saint. What sort of saint? No one has ever seen a saint. For the saint remains invisible, not by chance, but by principle and by right'.[2] This purposeful liturgical reference draws together the two elements of the present discussion. In French, these are bound up in the single word *saint,* which one can translate as both 'holy' and 'saint'. The saint is one who participates in holiness and is infused with it, and yet it is also holiness which sets God apart from human beings.

As the quintessential trait of God as God reveals Godself to human beings, holiness is the mark of that otherness which surrounds the human encounter with God, and 'generally defines the setting apart that distinguishes what belongs to divinity in opposition to what remains in the world'.[3] It presents God as one who rests outside the modes of human experience, and, even when the individual is confronted with the self-revealing God, establishes a space which human categories cannot penetrate. This remains true even when the individual is herself subsumed into that holiness and participates in it. *La sainteté*, or saintliness, is therefore a phenomenon which resists categorization and eschews positive recognition. In the individual's interaction with and practice of holiness, therefore, its ungraspability and perceptual invisibility govern the way in which she receives holiness and shapes the way in which she performs it. As such, the ungraspability of holiness is one of the primary elements in the present discussion, and to help elucidate it we will turn to Marion's other work.

Although Marion's understanding of holiness forms the central subject of this present essay, in theological circles, Jean-Luc Marion is best known for his theory of the saturated phenomenon. In this theory, the phenomenon is marked by an excess of intuition – where the term *intuition* refers to the self-presencing of the phenomenon – that overwhelms its perceiver, inscribing in her a stance of astonishment and a realization of her inability to fully grasp the phenomenon in its entirety. In her relation to the phenomenon, the perceiver is thereby displaced, and her conscious awareness of the phenomenon – her *intentionality* – no longer governs the way in which the phenomenon appears, but is rather subject to what the phenomenon gives of itself to perception. She is placed in the position of being overawed by that which gives itself to her.

One might readily and rightly liken this stance to one of adoration or genuflection. Indeed, although the notion of saturated phenomenality has since broadened to include all phenomena, the origins of the practice remain tethered to the original aim of including those religious phenomena that lie at the edges of expressibility. This religious harmonic points towards a space for holiness that lies at the heart of Marion's thought. Like the burning bush before Moses, Marion's phenomenology illustrates a world where phenomena present themselves authentically and inviolably. In this, he positions the individual in an open and welcoming stance that makes space for the luminous excess of intuitions that impact her in all their astonishing otherness. It is this stance that allows for a phenomenality of holiness.

Granted, not all saturated phenomena present holiness to the individual. Marion's expansion of the theory to non-religious phenomena widened the receiver's gaze with respect to all phenomena. But in the case of holiness, Marion's phenomenology finds its true home. In his analysis of *la sainteté*, he relies upon both his theory of saturated phenomenality and also his earlier work in *The Idol and Distance* and *God without Being*, although he does not explicitly refer to them. In keeping with his work on the saturated phenomenon, Marion emphasizes the excessive phenomenological surplus of holiness, the way in which it remains inexpressible and unbearable in this excess, and yet is received and responded to despite the gap which marks it as distinct from the human experience it inhabits. Because of this quality, the advent of holiness in the individual's experience primarily elicits the individual's recognition of her own limited capacity to receive and express the excessive phenomenality of that which is before her.

But it is not simply that the capacity of the individual is perceptually limited; it is morally limited as well. For Marion, *la sainteté* draws forth not only the recognition that the individual cannot express the holiness of God, but also the awareness that God's holiness exposes the individual's sinfulness. As such, Marion's understanding of the reception of holiness binds into a unified phenomenological movement the inexpressibility and moral disparity which is intrinsic to the relation between God and human beings. Consequently, the saint, in Marion's view, is she who recognizes a more profound sense of her own limitations before the face of the holy, and a more intense awe in the presence of this ungraspable excess. The holiness of the saint, in other words, remains hidden, even from herself, in a profoundly self-abnegating ignorance.

This essay attempts to elucidate that interplay of recognition and ignorance which for Marion constitutes both saintliness and also the recognition of *la sainteté*. Because he develops several themes which rely heavily upon his phenomenology of givenness and its appended theory of the saturated phenomenon, this essay will flesh out Marion's description of holiness with a more overt recourse to this theory. In so doing, the following pages will shed light on an intriguing understanding of holiness, which brings a deeply Catholic understanding of the relation between God and the individual into fruitful contact with phenomenological motifs.

An undefinable holiness

A carefully crafted definition is the initial step in many academic analyses of an attribute. A definition, however brief and ultimately incomplete, provides a starting point for the examination of the thing in question. But for Marion, the tendency to define holiness involves itself in a certain measure of contradiction. In order to call someone a saint, he states: 'One must first know what this word *holiness* actually means, have direct experience of it oneself, and, finally, be able to assign the quality thus signified to someone [. . .] be able to probe the other's heart'.[4] But the difficulty is that one tends to define attributes by one's own personal or perceptual experience of that attribute. Strictly defining holiness in oneself or another rests upon this foundational experience and thus undermines what holiness truly is, unduly limiting it: 'Indeed, when a group or a faction declares someone a saint, their definition is restricted to what this group or that faction (and thus their respective ideologies) imagine as holiness'.[5] This factional definition, however, overlooks a central aspect of holiness. Because 'the alterity of holiness' derives from 'God's alterity'[6] and is imposed upon the individual with this alterity intact, holiness itself cannot be comprehended by the individual. However vast the experience of holiness by any individual or group may be, it always remains a limited and incomplete experience. Any definition of it masks the ungraspable breadth of the phenomenon. In other words, through this definition the individual sets up an idol.

If an *idol*,[7] as noted in Marion's earlier work *God without Being*, 'presents itself to man's gaze in order that representation, and hence knowledge, can seize hold of it', then 'the gaze makes the idol, not the idol the gaze – which means that the idol with its visibility fills the intention of the gaze, which wants nothing other than to see'.[8] The perceiver who gazes upon a phenomenon in this manner has an intrinsic element of seizure embedded in her act of perception. In essence, the idol in Marion's earlier work serves as a mirror of human intentionality[9] directed towards the phenomenon. The *intuition*, or self-presencing, of that which gives itself to her perception conforms to her intentionality of it, rather than the reverse. It is this mode of perception that Marion wishes to avoid.

In *The Idol and Distance* and *God without Being*, Marion uses the term *idol* to denominate a mode of perceiving God that renders God comprehensible, and in this to differentiate that mode from another mode of perceiving God, which he terms the *icon*. The icon, in contrast to the idol, does not limit itself to the fulfilment of the individual's intentionality, nor does it stop at the perception of the visible, but rather engenders or impels vision. In the individual's relation to the icon, 'the visible is deepened infinitely in order to accompany, as one might say, each point of the invisible by a point of light'.[10] Rather than being a mirror of human intentionality as is the idol, the icon, as John McQuarrie has noted, 'is transparent toward God and indeed comes from God'.[11] It is the phenomenal and noetic space where what is perceived is only a fraction of what is given, and the excess of this givenness renders the icon conceptually ungraspable. Through this move, Marion emphasizes God's ungraspability, and forces a recognition of the inadequacy of comprehensive concepts of God.

Marion employs a similar distinction in his understanding of holiness. The human desire for comprehensibility coupled with an uncomfortability with impenetrable mystery join to promote a tendency towards stable definitions of things. Because holiness is the mark of God's qualitative difference from human beings, however, such a desire to impose a definition, to make holiness what the individual expects it to be, profoundly flattens out the experience of holiness. This is true for the reception and recognition of holiness in an external phenomenon or person and also the awareness of holiness in oneself. In the case of the recognition of holiness, a stable, non-provisional definition automatically excludes those phenomena which do not conform to one's personal perception or experience of holiness. This flattened understanding of that which is other and outside of human experience renders holiness familiar, where for Marion holiness should certainly be intimate to the individual, but always strange and astonishing.

The dangers of comprehensibility become particularly evident, however, when a positive definition becomes part of the claim to personal holiness. As Marion notes, 'someone who lays claim to sanctity disproves it in him or herself' because to affirm holiness in oneself is to 'fall into the massive trap of pride in one's own satisfaction and self-affirmation [. . .] but above all' such an affirmation disproves it 'because holiness is unaware of itself'.[12] If one's definition of holiness matches what an individual perceives of it, as well as what she finds within herself, and she uses this definition as her sole rubric, she is setting forth her understanding of holiness as an idol. In this, moreover, she is establishing herself as the image of that conceptual idol, a move which ultimately becomes philosophically and morally untenable: 'idolized sanctity immediately presupposes that those who assert and define it claim to know what holiness means, hence they claim to experience it and consequently to incarnate it themselves'.[13] For Marion, the truly holy individual *must* therefore have no sense of her own holiness, for to have a sense of her own sanctity would be to misapprehend the intrinsically ungraspable phenomenality of holiness, and in this misunderstanding, to embody attributes that run counter to her assertion. Consequently, when one experiences *la sainteté*, one always experiences it as something outside of and foreign to oneself, and perceives and receives it as a conceptual lack, as a space where the profane cannot enter.

Because it pertains to Marion's understanding of holiness, it is important at this time to distinguish between a lack within an individual's concepts, and the intuitive lack in the thing perceived. The gap in an individual's perception of a phenomenon which conveys holiness is a space that structures itself as a lack experienced not as an emptiness but rather as an excess. It is not that the phenomenon itself is holding its intuition back or that the phenomenon is actually 'poor' in intuition, but rather that the intuition is so great that it exceeds the human ability to conceptualize it. This distinction serves as a foundational tenet in Marion's theory of saturated phenomenality, and serves as part of the bedrock upon which his understanding of *la sainteté* rests.

The saturated phenomenon

The theory of the saturated phenomenon, which itself is part of the larger phenomenology of givenness, is an extension and inversion of several key concepts found in Edmund Husserl's phenomenology, most notably the Husserlian principle of principles which demands a 'return to the "things themselves"'.[14] Taken from the pages of *Ideen I* (1913), this principle is one of the founding pillars of Husserl's phenomenology, and constitutes part of what Husserl considered his 'breakthrough' into phenomenology.[15] By itself, this principle refers first to the given – to that which gives itself to perception – and hence to the intuition of the given, which is that which renders the given present to the perceiver. As Marion describes Husserl's position, 'what is intuited is at the same time given: thus signification is verified if intuition fills the directed intention'.[16] In other words, in the individual's relation to the thing perceived, the emphasis rests upon the individual's intentional consciousness of what is perceived. In this relation, Husserl shackles the individual's reception of intuition to her intentional consciousness of it – such that the intuition of the thing itself can, at its utmost limit, only completely fill this individual's intentional consciousness of it. It cannot exceed that person's intentionality, and this complete fulfilment is the ideal, and not the norm, of the phenomenological relationship.

While Husserl's tenet of the phenomenon's self-givenness inspired Marion to construct his own brand of phenomenology, he believes Husserl takes a wrong turn when he subordinates the reception of intuition to the limitations of human intentionality, a move which among other things shifts the emphasis from the inadequacy of perception to the inadequacy of intuition. Such a stance does not allow for the possibility of an excess of intuition which the individual's intentional consciousness cannot comprehend, and thus imposes the individual's intentionality upon the phenomenon, which unduly limits it. In Marion's view, Husserl's emphasis upon the constituting function of the perceiver constrains what the given – that gives itself to the perceiver – is able to give of itself, preventing it from making 'itself visible'.[17] As such, 'the revolutionary breakthrough of the principle of givenness is bound to consciousness rather than the inverse'.[18] The Husserlian structure of intentionality predetermines the limits of intuition, and thus defines intuition as being *for* the perceiver. This rather idolatrous stance allows that perceiver to have priority over the phenomenon itself.

Rather than maintaining with Husserl that the perceptual presence of a phenomenon is only receivable to the degree it fulfils its perceiver's intentional consciousness of it, for Marion the intuitions of these saturated phenomena exceed and precede the perceiver's constituting intentionality. This understanding shares affinities with his earlier understanding of the icon with respect to human conceptions of God. The intuition of that which gives itself is thus not strictly limited to the confines of human receivability, but is lodged firmly in the right of the given to give itself to consciousness without restriction: 'in other words, givenness precedes intuition and abolishes its Kantian limits, because the fact of being given to consciousness (in whatever manner) testifies to the right of phenomena to be received as such, that is to say, as they give themselves'.[19]

In his description of those phenomena which offer excessive intuitions which overfill the intentional consciousness, Marion emphasizes that these saturated phenomena retain a poly-vocal sense, having manifold meanings which are not assimilable to any single concept or group of concepts. In other words, the intentional aim directed towards the given phenomenon cannot bring into phenomenality the whole of that which is given, because it cannot foresee all that is given:

> Intuition gives (itself) in exceeding what the concept (signification, intentionality, aim and so on) can foresee of it and show [. . .]. They are saturated phenomena in that constitution encounters there an intuitive givenness that cannot be granted a univocal sense in return. It must be allowed, then, to overflow with many meanings, or an infinity of meanings, each equally legitimate and rigorous, without managing either to unify them or to organize them.[20]

This poly-vocal sense, which is a marker of the phenomenon's otherness and inassimilability, ensures the individual's openness and subjection to the given. Because Marion recognizes that these polysemic giftings occur in different ways, he presents these saturated phenomena under four names, each of which emphasizes a mode of appearing: the event, which 'saturates the category of quantity'; the idol, which 'subvert[s] the category of quality carried to the maximum';[21] the flesh, which undoes the category of relation; and the icon, which is freed from the category of modality.[22]

To these four, Marion adds the saturated phenomenon of r/Revelation, which includes within it the other four and as such represents the preeminent saturated phenomenon and the outermost limits of saturation – 'the saturation of saturation',[23] as it were: 'The phenomenon of revelation not only falls into the category of saturation (paradox in general), but it concentrates the four types of saturated phenomena and [. . .] by confounding them in it, it saturates phenomenality to the second degree'.[24] This last mode makes space for the possibility of divine revelation in the phenomenological realm.[25]

Because Marion insists that phenomenological saturation is normative rather than a nigh unattainable ideal, this understanding of Revelation situates it as the exemplar of this normativity: 'From the common-law phenomena, there followed, through a variation of intuitive possibility, the saturated phenomenon or paradox; likewise, from the latter, there follows, as an ultimate variation on saturation, the *paradoxōtaton*, the paradox to the second degree and par excellence, which encompasses all types of paradox'.[26] As the limit case of saturation, Revelation demonstrates the profundity of its self-gift to the receiver, and in this, the receiver's more apparent incapacity to receive this self-gift in its entirety, and the necessary recognition of the provisionality of her response to it.

The introduction of Revelation into the present discussion returns us to holiness proper, and to the incapacity of perception that is intrinsic to it. As the phenomenal event of God's self-manifestation in the world, Revelation is marked in its advent by holiness. Indeed, although in *Being Given* Marion leaves unspoken the structure of holiness that is embedded within this understanding of Revelation, his essay on saintliness presents God's self-revelation, God's manifestation in the world, as the content which the presence of holiness signals: '[God] reveals himself inasmuch as no one – no one other than Him – can enter into the vicinity of his holiness, which separates him from any other [*tout autre*] as the Wholly Other [*Tout Autre*]'.[27] Like an invisible threshold, holiness comes to its receiver as that which distinguishes Revelation from strictly this-worldly phenomena. Indeed, one could say that holiness serves as the impact of that incomprehensibility upon the receiver. And yet it is not merely an outline drawn around Revelation. Rather, every aspect of God's Revelation is, dare I say it, *saturated* with holiness. Phenomenologically speaking, holiness designates Revelation's otherness in every respect, and it is this very otherness that renders holiness itself indefinable.

Because the two are intertwined, Revelation's epistemic and phenomenological excess imparts the same to holiness. In one's encounter with holiness, just as in the encounter with Revelation, holiness presents itself to its receiver as a phenomenological space marked by a sense of the weight of its saturation, but which human beings do not have the capacity to encompass. In 'The Invisibility of the Saint', Marion uses the story of the burning bush to illustrate this point:

> 'God called to him out of the bush, "Moses, Moses!" And he said, "Here I am." Then he said, "Do not come near; put off your shoes from your feet, for the place on which you are standing is holy ground." [. . .] And Moses hid his face, for he was afraid to look at God' (Exod. 3:4–6). God's alterity imposes itself as absolute precisely as the alterity of holiness. And the alterity of holiness is manifested precisely as it remains invisible [. . .] it cannot become an object for the intentionality of a gaze [. . .]. Holiness marks the realm of God's very phenomenality – the invisible visibility.[28]

Several aspects of holiness are demonstrated here: the summons attached to holiness, holiness' perceptual invisibility and Moses' response to it. The fact that God must tell Moses that the place is holy indicates that there is no explicit outward sign of holiness, despite Moses' summons towards it. Once he hears God's command, however, Moses responds by hiding his face, because he fears to gaze upon God. For Marion, this invisibility and refusal to gaze makes manifest holiness' resistance to becoming an intentional object. But this very pairing demonstrates a certain visibility that holiness engenders. This is not a visibility of holiness itself, but is rather a visibility present only in the reception of holiness and the response to it. As such, although holiness cannot be adequately defined or perceived within the confines of a traditional phenomenological approach, Marion locates the manifestation of holiness in the alteration of the receiver who encounters it. It is thus that although holiness remains and must remain invisible, its 'visibility' occurs in the response of the one who receives it and who participates in it. For this reason, we now turn to the recognition of holiness.

Recognizing holiness

Recognition

Speaking about the recognition of holiness is a tricky business when we are discussing Marion's understanding of the phenomenon, particularly since his primary aim for the bulk of 'The Invisibility of the Saint' is to emphasize holiness' invisibility to perception and resistance to definition. As such, talking about the recognition of holiness seems to be antithetical to his project. However, while an individual might not be able to adequately express or comprehensively define holiness, she nonetheless experiences the impact of the phenomenon upon her. This impact is so profound that the manifestation of holiness, although perceptually invisible, inscribes itself in the individual's response to it, and in her alteration because of it. It is this inscription that enjoins a recognition of the phenomenon.

The previous section of this essay discussed the conceptual ungraspability of *la sainteté*, and this constitutes one portion of this impact. This noetic incapacity is analogous to the epistemological weight an individual feels when she experiences the breadth of what she does not know about a given subject, but which she knows is nonetheless present *in* that subject. However, the conceptual excess that an individual receives (and yet cannot grasp) in her encounter with that which manifests holiness marks only one aspect of the excessive lack that she experiences. The other element of lack is the moral or ethical disparity which writes itself upon the individual. These twin elements shape her response to *la sainteté*.

The recognition of holiness thus emerges as a heightened awareness of the opposite in oneself. As Marion notes, 'The law of holiness makes sin obvious, demonstrating through counterproof the non-holiness, the profanation, of the people'.[29] This acknowledgment of an individual's sinfulness alongside her noetic incapacity marks holiness as inassimilably distinct from the individual herself. Like Moses, the individual fears to gaze upon God 'for man cannot see [God] and live'.[30] This fear is grounded upon the realization that she is not like God, and that she as such cannot comprehend God fully; she cannot, in essence, gaze upon the face of the Holy One. Her sinfulness or tendencies towards it mark her as part of the profane against which the holy crashes. As such, she receives, as it were, only the 'back' of God's holiness, a holiness manifested only insofar as it remains covered and therefore invisible. The individual in effect experiences holiness only inasmuch as she recognizes the uncrossable gap between her and it. In this way, the very quality of her experience of the holy, wherein she receives a phenomenon that manifests holiness but does not offer it to perception, mimics the way in which her reception of the holy itself presents a noetic and moral veil between her and the face of God.

For Marion, this distinction of *la sainteté* from its receiver bears some phenomenological similarities to death, in that 'undergoing the limit experience of death [. . .] means *not* having experienced it, *not* knowing *anything* about it, precisely due to having been able to return from it'.[31] Those who have reached this limit without crossing it know with a greater depth of clarity that they have not experienced it. In the same way, the individual who encounters holiness knows that she is not holy, for the very impact of it upon her impresses her with this sense. Holiness, however, differs from death in that while a close encounter with death offers one merely a not-knowing about the phenomenon, the encounter with holiness imparts a counter-knowledge about the self. Placed in a more phenomenological register, this counter-knowledge compels a recognition of one's basic inclination to impose one's own perceptions upon phenomena, and to therefore move from that stance to one of openness before the phenomenon at hand.

Reconfigurations

At this point, it is worthwhile to note that with regard to the reconfiguration of the individual's stance, this essay treads along the edges of Marion's thought in suggesting that the encounter with holiness can alter an individual's fundamental stance towards the phenomenon. This suggestion diverges from Marion's phenomenology of givenness as he originally set it forth, in that his theory maintains the individual's openness to – and expanded reception of – saturated intuitions as embedded in her very structure, rather than as something the individual chooses to engage in with respect to the phenomenon. However, his description of the individual's reception of holiness, and the acknowledgment of her insufficiency in the face of it, seem to indicate a fundamental shift in the individual's stance, wherein the individual acknowledges her sinfulness – or in phenomenological terms, her tendency towards governing the appearing of the phenomenon – when confronted with the holy. Grounding this claim, however, requires a brief excursion into Marion's construction of the individual.

Because Marion's phenomenology shifts the priority from the individual to that which gives itself to the individual, and thereby frees the intuitions of the given from a governing intentionality, it also restructures the individual, casting the perceiving individual as primarily a receiver, or as Marion has variously denominated her: *l'adonné* – the gifted one, *l'interloqué* – the interrogated one.[32] These terms indicate that the individual is opened out to the given; she is gifted with the intuition of the given, she is questioned by that self-givenness, and in this shift and re-naming, the priority of the individual over the phenomenon vanishes. Under such auspices, *l'adonné* has no control over the constitution of phenomena. Rather, her intentionality serves 'to open a world' for the phenomena thrust upon her.[33] By shifting the weight upon the phenomenon in this way, Marion explicitly unravels the Husserlian relationship between perceiver and perceived; that which is perceived has priority over she who perceives, and thus the given remains unconfined in its self-givenness.

Although this description of *l'adonné* seems to offer a wondrous hospitality towards that which gives itself, Marion's phenomenology has undergone criticism on just this point from several different scholars because this stance is not a choice on the part of the individual, but rather her basic state, and can give the impression of being a restrictive understanding of the person. Among these critics is Shane MacKinlay, who in his book *Interpreting Excess* notes that Marion's construction of *l'adonné* in this fashion renders her too purely passive,[34] since she cannot 'decide not to respond or even refuse it [. . .] the responsal is nothing like an optional act'.[35] It is true that Marion emphasizes the passivity of *l'adonné* and her displacement from the role of governing subject, an emphasis made primarily to protect the right of the given to give itself to perception. Any intentionality that can limit the appearing of the phenomenon is thus too strong. In emphasizing this, however, Marion sees the relationship between *l'adonné* and that which gives itself as one in which the impact of the latter intimately affects the constitution of the former, and he wants to preserve that dynamic from being vitiated by a resurgence of intentionality.

In this dynamic, the impact of the given alters *l'adonné*, such that, as the given becomes phenomenalized through her, she also becomes phenomenalized through that same event. In a certain sense, therefore, the individual only becomes present after the given has impacted her:

> The receiver does not precede what it forms by means of a prism – it results from it [. . .] before the not yet phenomenalized given gives itself, no filter awaits it. Only the impact of what gives itself brings about the arising, with one and the same shock, of the flash with which its first visibility bursts and the very screen on which it crashes [. . .]. It is itself received in the exact instant when it receives what gives itself.[36]

Here, Marion poetically describes the way in which that which becomes phenomenal affects and alters the individual in ways which are unforeseen and cannot be governed. To attempt to govern the impact of the given presupposes that the individual knows all the ways in which a phenomenon affects her, and as such constitutes a false governance. Consequently, a completely open stance – and a recognition of this stance in the phenomenology concerning it – is the only authentic option available to Marion. The alteration of *l'adonné* that occurs is therefore dependent upon her inability to resist or refuse the intuitions bestowed upon her by the given, and to remain open to them. The difficulty is that human beings are rarely that straightforward in their relationships to phenomena, and thus, as MacKinlay notes, Marion's phenomenology presents us less with a description of how human beings typically view phenomena, and more with 'a *description* of the way we should *endeavor* to encounter phenomena'.[37]

When Marion describes *la sainteté* in his essay, however, he begins by pointing out the misapprehensions of those who seek to define holiness and thereby unknowingly render their definition idolatrous. Implied in this negative description is Marion's preference for the alternative stance which he sets forth both in the example of Moses and also in his insistence upon the recognition of sinfulness that occurs in the encounter with holiness. In this stance, those who encounter holiness can simply receive it and in that reception acknowledge their limitations, and consequently the provisionality of their concepts as well as the alterity of that which they are receiving. This possibility is enfleshed through recourse to Marion's earlier distinction between the conceptual idol and icon.

That these alternatives are present in this essay indicates the possibility of a difference in modes of reception. This possibility lessens the criticisms levelled against Marion's construction of *l'adonné* because it allows both for an individual's refusal to receive phenomena, and also casts Marion's phenomenology as the way we should endeavour to receive phenomena.

If we return to the example of Moses and the burning bush, we see Moses summoned into a posture of reverence through God's words. This change in stance, from curiosity to adoration, occurs in the context of Moses' encounter with a manifestation of the holy, and thus one might reasonably argue that this alteration is merely this alteration which occurs when *l'adonné* is confronted by the phenomenalized given. To an extent, this is true, but in the alteration that occurs because of the impact of the given, the individual's fundamental stance does not change. Because the encounter with holiness involves a realization of one's moral and conceptual inadequacy, however, the individual's fundamental perspective and governing intentionality of necessity undergo revision. This revision indicates that the individual is, in her relation to phenomena, far more complex than Marion's previous work detailed, and within these complexities, still allows for the impact of the given to profoundly remake the one receiving.

This alteration reveals the space where the individual's recognition of holiness constitutes her participation in it. Because holiness is only visible through the change it effects in the individual, and through her subsequent response to that which has altered her, her acknowledgment of holiness without making claim upon it brings her into the practice of it. The altered stance that holiness effects in *l'adonné* shifts her into a posture of kenotic self-abnegation, as if the individual were bowed before the holy in an attitude of genuflected adoration. Her recognition of holiness, then, can only occur once the phenomenon has already enfolded her into itself, once she herself has begun the progress into that which remains other, and in so doing stepped into the phenomenological invisibility that surrounds holiness. It is at this point that we turn, finally, to the practice of holiness in the saint herself.

The unknown saint

As we have seen, the recognition of holiness enjoins a participation in it, for to recognize the holy is already to be caught up in it, even as the individual retains a clarified sense of her insurmountable distinction from it. Yet this does not mean that the individual who thus embarks is suddenly sainted, but rather that she has entered into the holiness that has confronted her. That being said, the fundamental shift in perspective that enables and constitutes this entrance does make space for subsequent and progressive revisions to this perspective as holiness continues to impact the individual. It is through this progression that one becomes a saint.

In this holy dance of encounter and change, two movements occur which progress inversely: clarity of perception and worldly visibility. As noted above, the impact of holiness inscribes itself upon and renders itself visible through the alteration and response of the individual. This inscription, however, also grants an increasing clarity to the individual in question. As she continues to be caught up in and changed by the holiness of God, she is able to bear more of the holiness which confronts her: 'manifestation can only be fulfilled to the extent that the eyes can bear it'.[38] This is not to say that she can bear the fullness of holiness as it presents itself to her. This is never the case, for 'the impossibility for humans [. . .] to bear the visible will increase according to the extent of the manifestation of the holiness (more radical and hence dazzling)'.[39] As the extremity of holiness expands, the individual's own receptivity to it diminishes, and her sense of distinction from it becomes more profound. In this way, the foundational elements which rendered possible her reception of holiness – her acknowledgment of her sinfulness and limitedness which convey her differentiation from the holy – expand as she continues to undergo this transformation by and into holiness.

As the individual's reception of (and sense of differentiation from) holiness increases, however, her visibility in relation to the world decreases. According to Marion, because holiness marks the alterity of God as utterly distinct from human beings and the surrounding world, holiness remains invisible with respect to commonly perceivable phenomena: 'holiness cannot give itself to be seen to what is not (yet) holy'.[40] The things in the world that do not participate in holiness cannot perceive it. For this reason, holiness must bestow itself upon the individual in order for her to receive it. This very need for holiness to bestow itself, however, creates the conditions for the individual herself to cross into the invisibility which marks out holiness' phenomenality.

In Marion's view, Christ exemplifies this same invisibility: 'This manifestation of holiness, even and above all in the flesh of the Word, literally respects [holiness'] fundamental characteristic – its invisibility from the world's point of view, its invisibility as an object available to intentionality'.[41] As is clear from this passage, Marion construes invisibility as primarily phenomenological in nature and therefore he also construes the term *world* along the same lines. Within this phenomenological framework, however, he also unites *world* with its overtly theological meaning. Within Marion's essay, it does not therefore merely refer to a physical and material realm, but also to a perspective which seeks to grasp more than it should. In the context of Marion's thought, therefore, the world represents a sort of phenomenological *libido dominandi* which stands in contradistinction to the holy. As such, the holy remains invisible within the context of the world and to those bound to a worldly perspective. This occurs not only because holiness is phenomenologically imperceptible, but also because the worldly perspective stands in opposition to holiness. For this reason, it is appropriate that the most profound example of holiness should, within the sphere of the world, be the most hidden from view: 'This contradiction culminates in Christ's silence and disfigurement at the time of his Passion, where the maximum of holiness is swallowed up by the maximum of invisibility, of death.'[42] Because of its distinction from this world, Christ is thus able to offer 'the paschal glory' of this moment only insofar as those who encounter it 'can "bear" it'.[43]

Marion's emphasis on the invisibility of Christ's holiness serves to situate the difference between the holy and the profane, and in this, to present the invisibility of the holy not only as something which characterizes holiness per se, but also something in which those who receive God's holiness also participate. To be sure, as the individual abandons her governing intentionality and adopts the stance which arises from the impact of the holy, she begins to partake of the invisibility which characterizes the manifestation of holiness. She in effect begins to become invisible to the world's point of view. But she also receives invisibility. Because she receives holiness only insofar as she is able to bear it, that which she cannot bear remains invisible to her, experienced as a phenomenological excess which itself promotes and sustains the individual's sense of her own finitude before the infinite. This latter sense, which forms the foundation of her humble stance before the given, perpetuates the mode of her relation to holiness. It is thus a necessary part of that relation, even when the person is a saint.

If the practice of holiness is a journey wherein the individual, in a stance of humble access that has been enjoined by the advent of holiness, is continually confronted and changed by that holiness, then the saint is simply the one for whom this progress has drawn her fully into the invisibility spoken above. For Marion, the saint is therefore one whose perspective is utterly governed by the manifestation of the holy, who has completely abandoned the perspective of the world for the continual progress into the infinitude of *la sainteté*. Although Marion's phenomenology of givenness seems to emphasize a certain stasis on the part of the receiver, his work on holiness draws from itinerarian themes, implying the possibility of ascent and movement. In 'The Invisibility of the Saint', he implies this when he references Pascal's three orders or states of mind, which are hierarchically ordered – the order of the flesh, the order of knowledge and the order of the heart, 'where only charity rules its activities [*commerce*] and its holiness'.[44] Each of these states presents a particularized view of the world, and while the one who enacts a given view 'sees the orders that are inferior to it, but remains invisible to them',[45] that same person cannot see the perspective of that order or orders which resides above her own. They remain invisible to her. In the same way, the perspective of holiness into which the individual has been drawn remains invisible to the perspective of the world, even though the one who resides within the perspective of holiness perceives the world's view with greater clarity.

The saint, however, would not be able to remain a saint if she affirmed her saintliness in contradistinction to these other views. As Marion notes at the beginning of his essay, 'no one can say "I am a saint" without total deception [. . .] because holiness is unaware of itself'.[46] She is, in effect, invisible to herself. This mode of self-ignorance derives from the perspective enjoined by the individual's encounter with holiness itself, and to undo it would be to slip back into the profane, into the fold of the world. Encircled by the endless and unencompassable surfeit of intuition that characterizes holiness, the saint embraces that which is unknown to her and yet luminous, just as she is herself embraced by the holiness which draws her into its 'invisible visibility'.[47] In this way, the phenomenality of holiness makes itself manifest in the saint, even as this manifestation remains hidden from the world, not because it is withheld, but rather because it cannot be received by the world.

Conclusion

In her book *A Genealogy of Jean-Luc Marion's Philosophy of Religion: Apparent Darkness*, Tamsin Jones argues that the tensions in Marion's phenomenology between his insistence upon the universality of his method, and his equal insistence on freeing phenomena of the constraints imposed upon them create unnecessary difficulties.[48] If, however, Marion were instead to speak 'of a practice of clearing away obstacles to the appearance of the phenomena *as much as is humanly possible*, a discipline of cultivating patience, a sense of expectancy, and the capacity for reception', Jones suggests that Marion's thought might then be construed, in the spirit of Pierre Hadot, as a 'humble method'. [49] Formulating Marion's phenomenology as 'a discipline or spiritual exercise [. . .] gives one room to consider how habits, bodily practices, and contemplative disciplines, might shape our capacity to receive what is given. Marion has thus far given scant attention to the practical application of this theory'.[50] Marion's phenomenology of the saint offers the beginning of this shift in emphasis.

In his discussion of holiness, Marion seeks to account for both the invisibility of the holy from the perspective of the world, and also the altered perspective which the entrance into and embeddedness in the holy effects in the individual. In this, he utilizes his phenomenology of givenness as a foundation, but in his discussion of *la sainteté* he employs it as a discipline, a way of being in relation to the phenomenon at hand, and with consequences for the way in which the individual perceives and is perceived by the world. This development of his thought strengthens the themes of his phenomenology at the very point where they had received criticism. It is as if, through its extension into more overtly theological discourse, the phenomenology of givenness finds its truest home.

More importantly, however, Marion's phenomenology of the saint presents us with the outline of a spiritual discipline, wherein the individual who is confronted by the holy gives way to it, offers it hospitality, and is in turn embraced by it and altered by it. He is, in effect, describing the framework of a love relationship between the holy and the saint. As Marion noted of Pascal's hierarchy, the order of the heart is governed only by charity, and as in any truly loving relationship, the individual, in progressing towards her beloved, does not count the cost or minutely mark her progress. Her eyes are filled with the other, not with herself. As such, the saint's own vision of holiness thus presents both a widening of the gaze and also a directedness of that gaze towards that other. As this other remains 'invisible to that which does not itself belong to holiness',[51] so the one who participates in holiness takes up in herself that same quality, reflecting in herself and in her own particularity, the marks of the one to whom she belongs.

Notes

1 French translation of the *Sanctus* in the Mass. *Missel Romain* (ed. G. Droguet and R. Ardant, Limoges), p. 98. In English, 'Holy, Holy, Holy is the Lord, the God of Hosts, the whole earth is full of his glory'.

2 Jean-Luc Marion, 'The Invisibility of the Saint', *Saints: Faith without Borders* (ed. Françoise Meltzer and Jaś Elsner, trans. Christina M. Gschwandtner, Chicago: University of Chicago Press, 2011), p. 355. As the translator, Christina Gschwandtner, notes, Marion's opening words play on the manifold meanings of the French term *saint*, particularly its dual usage as both a noun for a holy individual, and as an adjective which we would translate as *holy*. This plurality of meanings occurs throughout Marion's essay. Gschwandtner writes: '*Sainteté* can mean "sanctity," "saintliness," "sainthood," "godliness," or "holiness." Marion is assuming all these connotations, and they should be kept in mind whenever the term *saint* or *holy* appears in English' (p. 355). This present essay will also take up this plenitude of connotations.

3 Ibid., p. 359.

4 Ibid., p. 355.

5 Ibid., p. 356.

6 Ibid., p. 360.

7 It is important to note here that Marion's usage of the term idol alters over time. I am here using the term 'idol' as he originally established it in *L'idol et la distance* (1977) and *Dieu sans l'être: Hors-texte* (1982). This usage,

I would argue, underlies the whole of his project, whereas his subsequent usage of the term 'idol' as a nominative description of a type of saturated phenomenon is a secondary usage that relies upon the earlier, and more distinctively theological, differentiation between idol and icon. The same can also be said of his use of the term 'icon', which undergoes a similar progression.

8   Jean-Luc Marion, *God Without Being* (trans. Thomas A. Carlson, Chicago: Chicago University Press, 1995), pp. 9–10, 10–11.

9   As noted in the Introduction, intentional consciousness, or *intentionality*, refers to the individual's conscious perception of the thing. The concept is based upon the premise, originally found in medieval thought, that the individual's consciousness is always already consciousness of something, and never stands purely on its own.

10   Marion, *God without Being*, p. 20.

11   John McQuarrie, 'God without Being', *The Journal of Religion* (1993), p. 100.

12   Marion, 'Invisibility', p. 356.

13   Ibid.

14   Edmund Husserl, *Ideas Pertaining to a Pure Phenomenology and to a Phenomenological Philosophy, First Book* (trans. F. Kersten, Boston: Kluwer, 1983), I.35.

15   J. N. Mohanty, 'The Development of Husserl's Thought', *The Cambridge Companion to Husserl* (ed. Barry Smith and David Woodruff Smith, Cambridge: Cambridge University Press, 1995), p. 55.

16   Jean-Luc Marion, *The Visible and the Revealed* (trans. Christina M. Gschwandtner et al., New York: Fordham University Press, 2008), p. 4.

17   Jean-Luc Marion, *Being Given* (trans. Jeffrey L. Kosky, Stanford: Stanford University Press, 2002), p. 8.

18   Tamsin Jones, *A Genealogy of Marion's Philosophy of Religion: Apparent Darkness* (Bloomington: Indiana University Press, 2011), p. 85.

19   Marion, *Visible*, pp. 4–5.

20   Jean-Luc Marion, *In Excess: Studies of Saturated Phenomena* (trans. Robyn Horner and Vincent Berraud, New York: Fordham University Press, 2002), p. 112.

21   Marion, *Being Given*, pp. 228–29. Note that this description of the idol, while related to his understanding of the term in his earlier works, does not bear a negative connotation, but merely describes one variety of excess, which is perhaps best represented by the surfeit of visibility that is found in a painting.

22   Ibid., p. 232.

23   Ibid., p. 235.

24   Ibid.

25   I must note here that, like many of Marion's terms, the term *revelation* undergoes development over time. In *Being Given*, Marion distinguishes between lower case *revelation*, which designates a possibility of revelation, which Marion suggests is as far as one can go philosophically, while the capitalized term *Revelation* indicates the actuality of divine revelation, and is more properly theological. As Marion's thought progressed over time, the term *revelation* broadened to refer to the act of the phenomenon revealing itself to the receiver, regardless of whether that phenomenon possessed religious valences or not. In consequence, the capitalized term *Revelation* slowly took over the meanings of the fourth category. In the context of the present

paragraph, I am using the term *revelation* as Marion used it in *Being Given*, with a nod to the eventual conversion of the term to a more purely actual sense of Revelation.

26 Ibid.
27 Marion, 'Invisibility', p. 360.
28 Ibid.
29 Ibid., p. 361.
30 Ibid., p. 360. This passage references Exodus 33.20.
31 Ibid., p. 358.
32 The French terms for the receiver are masculine in gender. In this essay, however, the primary pronoun used for the generic individual is feminine. This joint usage is intentional.
33 Marion, *Being Given*, p. 258.
34 Shane MacKinlay, *Interpreting Excess: Jean-Luc Marion, Saturated Phenomena, and Hermeneutics* (New York: Fordham University Press, 2010), p. 33.
35 Marion, *Being Given*, p. 288. MacKinlay also refers to this passage. See *Interpreting Excess*, p. 32.
36 Ibid., p. 265.
37 McKinlay, *Interpreting Excess*, p. 98.
38 Marion, 'Invisibility', p. 361.
39 Ibid.
40 Ibid.
41 Ibid.
42 Ibid.
43 Ibid.
44 Ibid., pp. 361–62.
45 Ibid., p. 362.
46 Ibid., p. 356.
47 Ibid., p. 360.
48 Jones, *Genealogy*, p. 135.
49 Ibid.
50 Ibid.
51 Marion, 'Invisibility', p. 362.

17

Laruelle and the Messiah Before the Saints

Anthony Paul Smith

The recent realist and materialist turns in Continental philosophy are, of course, not entirely new. François Laruelle has been developing a theory in the name of matter (against materialism) and the Real (against realism) for the last 30 years. For the last years of his teaching career, before his mandatory retirement (French academics must retire at the age of 65), he was Professor of Contemporary Philosophy at the University of Paris X, but he himself eschews the title of philosopher, calling himself a 'non-philosopher' to the bemusement and chagrin of his contemporaries. This title is a performance of what to the philosophers' eyes can only appear to be a fool. And this foolishness becomes a further stumbling block to his contemporaries and potential philosophical readers when that foolishness takes on a particularly holy character. François Laruelle, holy fool to philosophers who proclaims peace to them and a Last Good News to all humanity. But also heretic to the theologians, the one who proclaims to them the Future Christ above the Saints.

This use of theological language can be found throughout Laruelle's corpus, but Laruelle's engagement with theological material has been a blind spot in the early reception of his work. In part this owes to the plastic nature of non-philosophy, its pragmatic impulse. For non-philosophy is first and foremost about making theory, practising theory in an increasingly pluralistic manner. So the themes that Laruelle has written on throughout the years are incredibly vast, from what we could term philosophy proper (a number of important texts on Heidegger, Nietzsche, Derrida, Deleuze and some lesser knows figures like Ravaisson and Simondon) to ethics, psychoanalysis,

writing, violence, epistemology and quantum mechanics. The fact that
Laruelle's work on Derrida remained untranslated at the height of interest in
Derrida's philosophy has less to do with the quality of that work and more to
do with the vagaries of translation and intellectual trends.[1] And so Laruelle
became known in the English-language world mostly for his valorization of
science and his heretical reading of Kant as deployed by Ray Brassier in the
development of his own philosophical work. The enthusiasm for Brassier's
work among a new generation of philosophical readers led to a confusion
of Brassier's excellent reading and use of Laruelle with the sum total of
Laruelle's own work. But François Laruelle's theory of science is intractable
from his theory of the messiah or what he terms the Future Christ. In essence
what both theories focus on is the pragmatic identity of the human person,
or what he calls 'Man-in-person'. All sorts of misunderstandings could
arise depending on what the readers' backgrounds are, but this is not an
essence that is given transcendentally; rather the essence is equal to the
immanence of the person. This is not an identity that is relational, for all
identities will have some aspect that will remain foreclosed to relationality.
Nor is this to assume what the human is, but rather just to begin to ask the
question. In the scope of investigating what might be required for an answer
Laruelle works through various human materials like science and religion.

Laruelle's understanding of messianity can be placed within the history of a
Nietzschean separation of Christ from St Paul, or Christ from the development
of Christianity, though only as a preliminary but not sufficient attempt
to orient the reader. Still, within Laruelle's consideration of Christianity
there is always a kind of Protestant impulse that declares the primacy of
the messianic act of Christ over any attempts to 'read' this messianic act
as a declaration developed by tradition. Non-philosophy develops, then,
a messianity sans-religion (the reference is not properly to Derrida, but rather
to the sans-culottes), that is messianity without religio, without 'binding' to
a tradition. This puts him at odds with a certain philosophical understanding
of saintliness, namely that developed by Alain Badiou. In his recent 2011
work Anti-Badiou, Laruelle reflects on the question that is often posed
regarding his work: whether it is not an expression of a certain kind of
religion, namely Christianity. He responds, 'this Christianity, as we elaborate
in Future Christ: A Lesson in Heresy, would not be like the Christianity
of that other great purifier, St. Paul'.[2] As Laruelle reads Badiou, it is the
figure of St Paul, as the one who took the radicality of Christ and began
the process of codifying or purifying it into a tradition, after whom Badiou
models his own practice of purifying philosophy. The implication is that if
philosophy will look to saints and to saintliness, modelling themselves on
the codification and purification of an always-perverse proliferation present
in the messianic act, then non-philosophy will never look to saints but rather
to the Future Christ and to messianity. If saints are always proclaimed by
their tradition and thus there forms a kind of dialectic between the actions

of the saints as a sign of what that tradition ought to be and the authority of the tradition to decide upon who is a saint, then a messiah is always proclaimed outside of any tradition; a messiah is a stumbling block and foolishness, and can only be reinscribed into a tradition through a violence to the body of that messiah.

In this essay I will further trace and develop Laruelle's understanding of the messiah, but rather than focusing on the question of religious traditions (which I develop elsewhere), I will instead focus on the way this theory, derived from religious materials, is woven together with material from the sciences. This ultimately reveals Laruelle's underlying idea that philosophy was made for humanity, not humanity for philosophy and extends this to include the declaration that science and religion were made for humanity, not humanity for science and religion. Material science and religion are in a unilateral relation to the question of salvation or what Laruelle instead calls 'assistance to humans': theory and practice unified for the sake of humanity. Thus religion, just as philosophy from this perspective, is fully compatible with a kind of science, as something that can be known and used. As he stated in a recent interview, 'Philosophy is now going to have that status of an instrument, or of a supple means, as its disposition. It can be manipulated by non-philosophy. We must avoid fixing non-philosophy on inert objects, so on Christ, Art, etc. It's not because of Christ that I am a non-philosopher. But being a non-philosopher, Christ becomes very interesting. [. . .] I have had the tendency to say that everything must pass by science. Take theology for example: it is a science of Christ'.[3] And what does that science reveal? Not a purity, but instead a good *métissage*; a lack of purity; a mixing. The word is closely related to mestizo, more familiar to English speakers, or even 'mixed race'. Laruelle is here abstracting the concept to the philosophical level, valorizing it over purity, and saying that this is what the messiah is. Not purity, but what from the perspective of purity is seen as perversion.

Christ and the World

This strange appellation 'Future Christ' used by Laruelle may bring up many questions for readers. It certainly would not seem to touch on the heart of a reconfiguring of philosophical practice under a different axiom of relation to science. Yet, this is exactly the claim I am making; that Laruelle's non-Christology, first traced through *Future Christ: A Lesson in Heresy*, originally published in 2002 in France, and taken up again under a theory of 'messianity' in the 2010 work *Philosophie non-standard: Générique, Quantique, Philo-fiction*, goes to the heart of his understanding of science. For both science and religion require a subject, and messianity is the modality of the subject common to both. To make sense of this we will have to trace the relationship of the man-in-person to the modalities of subjectivity. I will explain and define these terms below, but for now we can translate them into more easily recognizable terms if we think of them as the relationships between two relatively autonomous things that are, in this case, the human and science or religion. For underlying the non-philosophical practice is the axiom of relative autonomy for all things, a kind of equality at the level of causality and effect, since both the human and science or religion are relative to or caused by the Real. This notion of relative autonomy allows the non-philosopher a kind of flat ontology, so popular these days, without ascribing any form of sufficiency to this ontology. So, no, the world is not just a human construct and yes, the inhuman elements of science and religion (tannins in wine or the history of the Eucharist) do have their own actual powers, but to confuse this flat ontology with a being itself (as all ontologies tend towards) is an act of auto-inclusion or co-determination of the Real it describes. These technical terms take on a more poetic name in the work of Laruelle: that of the World. And so, in order to move to the theory of the subject present in non-philosophy we first have to trace the structure of the World that the subject is not.

Non-philosophy has been practised with reference to Gnosticism since at least Laruelle's 1981 book *Le Principe de minorité*, where we first see his twin interests in religion and science emerge, but in *Future Christ* Laruelle makes this nascent connection between non-philosophy and gnosis explicit. There he writes, 'Gnosis, above all Mandaean Gnosis, along with Christianity, is one of the greatest thinking about Life, and it wants to radically distinguish itself from the thought of Being without always reaching precisely there for the reasons of philosophy'.[4] Gnosis, as a largely forgotten and murdered religious and philosophical practice, is to be valued for its irreductive form of thinking: a thinking that aimed, though ultimately failing according to Laruelle, to think the radical identity of things, separate and withdrawn from any kind of totalizing sufficiency. In other words, the popular image of the Gnostics (who Laruelle entreats us to remember no longer exist because they were – despite Christians theologians' constant fears that Gnostics are all around us! – *all* murdered and turned into victims) as anti-body covers over the truth of their true object of critique. For what we take to be the Gnostics' hatred of the material is actually hatred of the World; of this-World; of the notion that Life (what Laruelle rethinks under the more radically immanent category of the 'lived') radically had to submit or enclose itself within the identity of the World and therein lose itself.

The World is such an important concept for non-philosophy, albeit in a negative mode, that it is considered to be both an element of the vocabulary of non-philosophy and its syntax. In Laruelle's '*Glossary Raisonné*' to *Future Christ* he gives us this definition of World as vocabulary, 'Other name for philosophy under its two forms. Philosophy is world-shaped, the World is thought-world'.[5] In the form of syntax, 'world' is deployed by Laruelle to further 'world-shape' other forms of material taken by philosophy as something it can dominate; 'A composition by addition of the suffix "-world" to the term in question (God-world, Christ-world, etc.) indicates a sense of sufficiency'.[6] And of course, sufficiency is the 'pretension of philosophy to co-determine the Real or Man who is foreclosed for it'.[7] The resistance to this sufficiency is not some childish act of rebellion against philosophical adults who know better; rather the struggle, rebellion or revolt against the World arises out of the fact of its failure: 'The divine creation – the World – is a failure, this knowledge is one thing gnosis acquired'.[8]

So the messiah, the future Christ, is not of this World and there is a radical separation of man-in-person and the World: this is the central gnostic impulse of non-philosophy. But non-philosophy moves past the traditional and disappeared practice of gnosis insofar as it does not aim for a total destruction of this world. The World, as an image of sufficiency, remains material, and indeed Laruelle says:

> If it is necessary to start again completely differently from that failed knowledge that is philosophy, we do not simply reject it on religious grounds like the ancient gnosis rejected the World as evil and illusion. *It is our only material*, and the science that the Moderns have acquired meanwhile gives us a means of knowing, that is to say of modelling, that complex object, failed knowledge, and a means of making use of it on the basis of Man-in-person who is not modern or ancient. We are the new Gnostics who think that there is a salvation even from evil. Philosophy, form of the World, is our prison but the prison has the form of a hallucination and a transcendental illusion, not the form of flesh – it is itself knowable.[9]

So Laruelle's struggle against the World is always a struggle, not only against the bad demiurge, but against the bad theoretician, 'the Philosopher or the Theologian, who have created a failed knowledge'.[10] And thus salvation is always a matter of saving gnosis, of a theoretical practice that allows human beings to craft something completely different from the failure of divine creation, the World.

The theory of the Future Christ

Now who is this 'we' who suspend their faith and refuse to give into faith? It is certainly not planetary or worldly philosophers, those who do not wonder what to make of the World-in-person. It is the 'we' of the Future Christ, the Christ-subject who we are without having by hope or obedience identified in ourselves as such, identifying that we are already in every way as Man-in-Man, subjects merged with their non-Christian performance. The theory of the Future Christ is the immanent practice of its theory; our only faith is practical and additionally a pragmatic of the old Christianity.[11]

At the basis of Laruelle's description of the Future Christ (or Christ-subject; the two terms are equivalent) is the idea that the radical immanence of Man-in-Man is cloned as a subject with different materials which give that subject its particular, intentional modality as differentiated from its presentation as a transcendental illusion or Christ-world. One of the aspects of non-philosophy that is often maligned but misunderstood is Laruelle's distaste for so-called examples, the idea being that words like 'Christ-world', 'Man-in-Man', 'Christ-subject', or the like are just jargon for already understood ideas to which these jargonistic terms can be reduced. But Man-in-Man and the Christ-subject are not representations; they are theoretical practices. To understand them, one has to *understand them*. Reducing things to other things is not the full practice of thought, but practicing thought is more closely related to religious practices or scientific practices than philosophers often realize. For example, the practice of a religious faith is never simply a matter of assenting to some belief = X, but that belief = X is always inscribed in a number of religious practices like prayer, confession, reading, writing, giving alms to the poor and so on. With regard to the theoretical practice of non-Christianity, it is a matter of bringing assistance to the World, to saving the World, even though one's identity is radically separate from the World, by way of knowing or modelling the World theoretically. As Laruelle himself puts it regarding his theory of non-Christianity and the Christ-subject, '*thinking it is already to practice it*'.[12]

That said, and without reducing these ideas to some already predetermined meaning, what exactly do they model? They model precisely what elements are at work in what can be done with religion, specifically Christianity. What can be done with Christianity? Well, quite simply, it can be turned into a material that will be universally of use to humanity in dispelling the transcendental illusion that human beings are something other than what they are. In a less twisted manner, we can say that Christianity can be used, when one no longer assents to a series of orthodox proclamations claiming to be a Christian but instead take themselves as a Christ-subject, to assist in showing that human beings are not reducible to something else – that human beings have a radical identity prior to the subsumption of any transcendental term. Man-in-Man names that aspect of one's humanity that is always foreclosed, or unable to be understood relationally, to the World. The Christ-subject (Future Christ) names the way that this Man-in-Man is cloned as a subject using religious material. And the Christ-world is a kind of figure of the Antichrist, always already caught up in the identity of Christ given by the various churches, where Christ is taken as transcendent and sufficient. Laruelle summarizes his entire theory of the Future Christ in one of my favourite lines from that work, which captures how non-philosophy is able to mutate and make use of religion as well as the immanent reason for the theory of the Future Christ in general. There he writes,

With the cloning of every man as *subject*, humans, despite or because of their in-sufficiency, take up existing under the form of an *organon*, precisely the Future Christ, the authentic relationship to the World and to history in totality rather than in the manner of their phenomena. The old Christ had been conceived in transcendence and the World (in sin?), he was without doubt an organon but still on the model of mediation or instrument (for a reaction or rebirth). Christianity cannot overcome its failing of identity and faith by a profusion of churches and orders, of dogmas and authorities, saints and priests, actions and ritual operations. The Future Christ rather signifies that each man is a Christ-organon, that is to say, of course, the Messiah, but simple and unique once each time. This is minimal Christianity. We the Without-religion, the Without-church, the heretics of the future, we are, each-and-everyone, a Christ or Messiah. [...] By its practice, this is only a half-programme, only unilateral, of a constitution of the Christ-subject giving aid to the World and against it.[13]

Generic messianity

As I mentioned in the Introduction, Laruelle's interest in material outside philosophy has always had a dual nature in that it was never 'just science' or 'just religion', but the two somehow always arise together in his thinking. So it is unsurprising that Laruelle develops his theory of the Christ-subject, moving from the Future Christ to a generic messianity in his 2010 work *Philosophie non-standard*. Here Laruelle aims to 'achieve' non-philosophy by bringing together philosophy material with the material of quantum physics, banging them together in a virtual particle collider, and it is the figure of Christ that comes to speak to the subject that science requires if science is going to be put to the work of assistance spoken about in *Future Christ* and discussed above. There he writes:

> It is of course strange to speak of messianity as concerning the human cause of the science of philosophy, even though the notion of 'determination-in-the-last-instance' should have set down the path of this completely apparent paradox. [...] Here Christ is the simple historico-concrete model of genericity under the form of the superposition of the One and the Multiple, a mediation which 'saves', as generic, human subjects.[14]

And, yes, it is indeed strange to speak of messianity in this way! Messianity translates the French neologism *messianité*, and indicates an activity, rather than the usual messianism, which would refer to a constellation of ideas. Of course Laruelle is not saying that these ideas are not active, but he is directing our attention by focusing on the active element here. This is not the place to examine the concept of determination-the-last-instance in detail, but what Laruelle is indicating by creating a kind of equivalence between messianity as the human cause of science is that messianity is the real cause of science. That science, whether it is the science of physics or the science of Christ (theology), arises out of a certain messianic act. But what does Laruelle think this act consists in? Simply, it is a kind of embodiment, not of a worldly identity, but a generic identity between the irreducibility of one's individual identity and the individual multiplicity of humankind.

This is what the 'superposition of the One and the Multiple' refers to. Superposition is an incredibly interesting phenomenon, one that the scientist and phenomenologist Peter Steeves thinks can help unify biological and cosmological theories in line with the work of Lee Smolin, in a way that is not altogether different from Laruelle's own advocacy of a proliferation of unified theories.[15] When two wave-particles are in superposition with one another they can be expressed by mathematical idempotence $(1+1=1)$, referring to the fact that when these two waves are superposed with one another they do not produce a synthesis but instead their individual identities remain while a new third identity is produced that nevertheless remains those two waves. When two particles are in superposition, when one particle spins the other particle also spins in an opposite and equal way, meaning that the spin is always balanced between the two. This is what Laruelle calls the generic identity expressed by the historical Christ. There is some relationship, a kind of media-without-mediation which is to say without synthesis, between the One and Multiple that is developed in this non-philosophical unified theory of philosophy and quantum mechanics.

In Laruelle's recent work, the generic functions as a matrix within which thought develops; a generic matrix provides certain determinations for thought (the matrix itself is determined not by a meta-matrix, but by its in-One character). Laruelle's formulation of this generic, which characterizes this matrix, is derived from philosophical materials. The importance of the generic for non-philosophy has only recently come to the forefront and comes, to my mind, to replace the idea of 'minimal' that is more operative in *Future Christ*. Laruelle tells us in *Introduction aux sciences génériques* and *Philosophie non-standard* that he derives the generic from the line Feuerbach – Marx – Badiou. What's important in each of these philosophical constructions is the connection between humanity and science, a connection or more accurately 'idempotence' that is thought more radically (that is more immanental) in Laruelle. The importance of the generic in Feuerbach is largely lost to us in the Anglophone world since *Gattungswesen* is usually translated in English as 'species-being'. However, the French translation captures this as *être générique*, literally 'generic being'. Now this formulation of the generic is taken up by Marx and it is Marx, Laruelle claims, who truly initiates the generic science-thought that thinks scientifically from the universality of the human. He takes this up in his thinking of Christ, writing,

> The messianic force of thought is not a metaphorisation of Christ, rather it is the generic secularization [*laïcisation*], and less still does it

give a Christian interpretation of science in general. Though it is through a certain reference to the mediation of Christ as unity of God and man consonant with the unity of the Undivided and the Divided that the generic is called messianic according to this material or this symptom that integrally belongs to philosophy, and so an immanent messianity as superposition is affirmed of Man-in-person. But the messianic is not simply religious, it is a complex cause, also partly scientific, and more profoundly constituted as *en-semblage*, a generic alliance or unilateral complimentarity.[16]

So this generic element of messianity is central to our understanding of what Laruelle aims to do through his mutual complication of religious and scientific material within a relationship of unilateral complimentarity, referring to the fact that all of this is ultimately always for the service of assistance to the World, but more importantly to the human beings that all of us are.

Conclusion

What I have aimed to do in this very short essay is to reveal the intimate connection between Laruelle's use of religious and scientific materials in his construction of the positive project of non-philosophy. Due to space I have had to elide the explanation of a number of important questions, though thankfully secondary engagements with Laruelle's work are growing.[17] And this is ultimately in line with Laruelle's pluralistic and fractal practice, with fractal expressing here, at the level of an organic phenomenon modelled by mathematics, the great proliferation of ideas and theories produced by non-philosophy. One idea always spawns another, all unified (though not forming a unity) in their always unilateral relationship with the Real-One.

Ultimately, non-philosophy is concerned with liberation. This is not a possible liberation, but a kind of virtual liberation that is always present within the radical immanence of the human. When one is able to actualize this, one is not merely a sign of possibility (what we may call saintliness from a non-philosophical perspective), which Laruelle suggests is too easily reinscribed within the World, but is 'in flesh and blood' or Man-in-person: the future itself. Laruelle often refers to the future under an adjectival form as 'the futural' and he defines it in this way: 'The futural is an excess which, as generic, contains [a number of attributes] but pushed through a certain indetermination within immanence, it is discontinuous and continuous, unilateral, predictable within the limits of certain givens as conditions of the least reference, but ultimately unpredictable'.[18] By using this adjectival form, 'the futural', Laruelle disempowers certain philosophical systems that confuse the future with a kind of substance or power that gets separated in idealist philosophical forms from human pragmatics. One is futural, but one is not the future, and so when a human being is a messiah, as any human being can be, they express this characteristic of being 'ultimately unpredictable'. In this way the difference between the Messiah and the Saints is brought to the fore. For saintliness, as Laruelle understands it through the Nietzschean opposition of St Paul and Jesus Christ, points to the past, creating a hierarchy projected into that past which undergirds the authoritarian claims of the Christian Church to be the only true site of salvation, the only true mediator between salvation and human beings. This goes too for the secular and subtractive version of this authoritarian claim, like we find in Badiou.

Consider again Badiou's theory of events which produces subjects. The subject is formed in relation to its response to a particular truth-event in some field (though only four are really allowed: love, art, science or politics). That response is predictable, while the event is not. Under Laruelle's theory of radical immanence the subject is always a kind of superposed clone with a body that is itself something like Badiou's truth-event. Meaning, where Badiou posits a split between event and subject ultimately turned into an inconsistent unity by some transcendent and determined action (fidelity or infidelity), Laruelle rejects that split and instead says that the One-Real of the body is unilaterally related to the truth and to the subject produced. In other words, to turn away from the difficulty of this language, the existence of the messiah, which any person may be, is the truth. Within science and religion we see that the practices do not form some saintliness, but rather are expressive of a wild liberty that has no equivalent of exchange. Take traditional theological proclamations about the Being of God being in God's action; of God's freedom being in God's necessity, and apply them instead to human beings. This is the messiah of non-philosophy which needs no mediators, but is herself salvation: 'Human beings have a problem that only they can solve: what to do with the World? Salvation or rebellion? Exploitation or therapeutic? Consumption or consummation?'[19]

Notes

1   This is true even though Leonard Lawlor, himself firmly within the mainstream of Continental philosophy, credited Laruelle's *Philosophies of Difference* as an inspiration for a part of his reading of Derrida. See Leonard Lawlor, *Derrida and Husserl: The Basic Problem of Phenomenology* (Bloomington: Indiana University Press, 2002), p. 262n. 4.

2   François Laruelle, *Anti-Badiou. Sur l'introduction du maoïsme dans la philosophie* (Paris: Kimé, 2011), p. 50.

3   François Laruelle, 'Non-Philosophy, Weapon of Last Defence: An Interview with François Laruelle', *Laruelle and Non-Philosophy* (ed. John Mullarkey and Anthony Paul Smith, Edinburgh: Edinburgh University Press, 2012), pp. 241, 250.

4   François Laruelle, *Future Christ: A Lesson in Heresy* (trans. Anthony Paul Smith, London: Continuum, 2010), pp. 38–39.

5   Laruelle, *Future Christ*, p. xxviii.
6   Ibid.
7   Ibid.
8   Ibid., p. 39.
9   Ibid., p. 41. Emphasis mine.
10 Ibid.
11 Ibid., p. 115.
12 Ibid., p. 116.
13 Ibid., p. 117.
14 François Laruelle, *Philosophie non-standard. Générique, quantique, philo-fiction* (Paris: Kimé, 2010), p. 440.
15 See H. Peter Steeves, 'Mars Attacked! Interplanetary Environmental Ethics and the Science of Life', *The Things Themselves: Phenomenology and the Return to the Everyday* (Albany: SUNY Press, 2006), pp. 127–45 and Lee Smolin, *The Life of the Cosmos* (Oxford: Oxford University Press, 1997).
16 Laruelle, *Philosophie non-standard*, p. 440. I've had to leave *en-semblage* untranslated and give my condolences to the translator who takes on the task of translating this very important, but very difficult book. In French *en-semblage* is a neologism derived mostly from *ensemble* which means both 'together' and 'set' in the mathematical sense, and so the reference is playing in part on Badiou. But *semblage* is also a reference to the Lacanian 'semblance' and the separation of the word into two word plays, as Laruelle always does, on the syntax of *en* or 'in'. The sense carried here points to the meaning of messianity being constituted within a wider set, having an identity, but one that is never essentialist or determined by a single discourse.
17 The standard references are John Mullarkey, *Post-Continental Philosophy: An Outline* (London and New York: Continuum, 2006) and Ray Brassier, *Nihil Unbound: Enlightnement and Extinction* (Basingstoke: Palgrave, 2009). There is also a new collection of essays that promises, I hope, to be very useful, see *Laruelle and Non-Philosophy* (ed. John Mullarkey and Anthony Paul Smith, Edinburgh: Edinburgh University Press, 2012).
18 Laruelle, *Philosophie non-standard*, p. 450.
19 Laruelle, *Future Christ*, p. 113.

INDEX